The Complete Idiot's Reference Card

Karma for the Twenty-First Century

Using the Tarot's Major Arcana cards, this reading shows us the karmic potentials and pitfalls for humankind as we enter the new millennium:

➤ The **World R** shows that we will be uneasy about the many changes to come, and may also represent a lack of vision or a refusal to learn from the lessons of the past when facing the challenges of the future.

➤ **Strength** indicates our compassion and need to develop trust and self-confidence.

➤ **The Lovers** reminds us that we must choose the right partners and appropriate relationships.

➤ **The Hierophant R** shows that traditional ways of looking at things may be overturned or go through dramatic changes. After all, it's a new millennium!

STRENGTH.

THE LOVERS.

alpha books

Your Hand Is Your Map to the Road Ahead

The palms of each generation reflect the spirit and potential of the time. Use the knowledge your palm holds to help you make a personal transition to the 21st century. Your thumb and fingers, and the lines and mounts of your palm, create a microcosm that represents the macrocosm of your self.

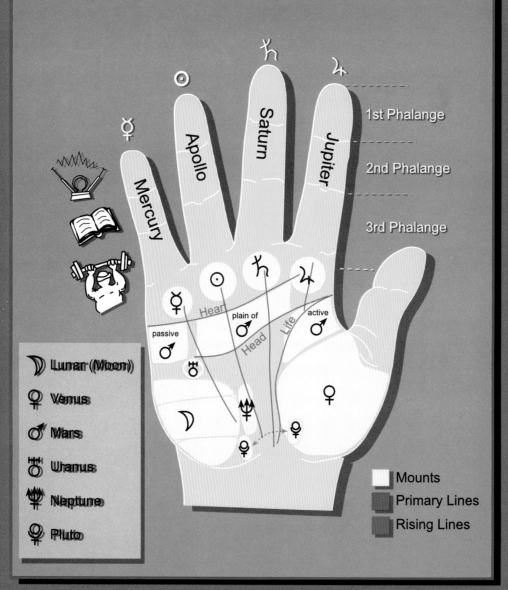

Palmistry illustration by Kathleen Edwards.

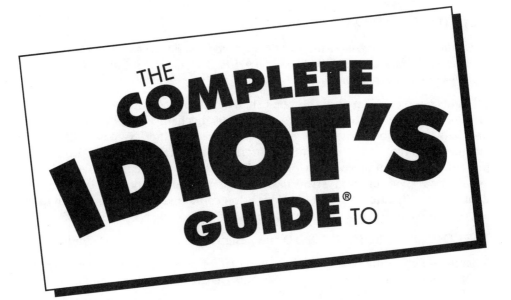

THE COMPLETE IDIOT'S GUIDE® TO

New Millennium Predictions

by the New Age Collective and Lisa Lenard

alpha
books

A Division of Macmillan General Reference
A Pearson Education Macmillan Company
1633 Broadway, New York, NY 10019-6785

Alpha Development Team

Publisher
Kathy Nebenhaus

Editorial Director
Gary M. Krebs

Managing Editor
Bob Shuman

Marketing Brand Manager
Felice Primeau

Acquisitions Editors
Jessica Faust
Michelle Reed

Development Editors
Phil Kitchel
Amy Zavatto

Assistant Editor
Georgette Blau

Production Team

Book Producer
Lee Ann Chearney/Amaranth

Development Editor
Matthew X. Kiernan

Production Editor
Michael Thomas

Copy Editor
Lynn Northrup

Cover Designer
Mike Freeland

Illustrator
Jody P. Schaeffer

Designer
Scott Cook and Amy Adams of DesignLab

Indexer
Brad Herriman

Layout/Proofreading
Melissa Auciello-Brogan, Terri Sheehan, Julie Trippetti

Contents at a Glance

Part 1: The Bridge to the 21st Century   **1**

1 New Age Meets the New Millennium   3
An introduction to the New Age Collective.

2 Humankind Through the Millennia   15
What's the big deal about the millennium, anyway?

3 New Millennium Oracle   27
Some numbers to back it all up.

Part 2: Meet the Dawn: Astrology   **37**

4 An Astro Primer   39
An introduction to astrology.

5 Heaven on Earth   57
Houses and planets.

6 Astrological Cycles for the 21st Century   69
Symbolic invitations to shift consciousness.

7 How Planetary Cycles in the New Millennium Affect *Your* Birth Chart   87
You and the new millennium astrologically.

8 Predictions, Visions, Challenges, and Weavings   117
Synthesis of key cycles.

Part 3: Two's Company: Numerology   **129**

9 Numerology and the Language of Numbers   131
An introduction to numerology.

10 New Millennium Numbers at a Glance   143
Looking at the numbers behind the new millennium.

11 Your Personal Numbers for the New Millennium   157
All about your personal year.

Part 4: Picture This: The Tarot   **169**

12 What's in the Cards?   171
An introduction to the Tarot's Major Arcana.

13 Tarot's Minor Arcana: Wands and Cups   191
An introduction to Wands (your enterprise) and Cups (your emotion).

14 Tarot's Minor Arcana: Swords and Pentacles   209
An introduction to Swords (your action) and Pentacles (your money).

15 Questions, Questions, Questions 231
We ask the cards about money, family values, society, politics–and the Pope.

16 More Questions, Questions, Questions 255
We ask the cards about medicine, health, the environment, space travel, and the arts.

17 What the Tarot Says About *You* in the New Millennium 275
Your horoscope, your destiny, your wish, and your decisions.

Part 5: Know It All: Psychic Intuition **291**

18 Intuitive Tools for the New Millennium 293
An introduction to intuition.

19 Mind/Body Medicine and Beyond: Using the Power of the Mind and Spirit to Heal 303
Tapping into your own healing power.

20 Psychic Awareness for the New Millennium's Global Community 315
Consciousness tools for the 21st century.

21 Psychic Prophecies and Predictions for the New Millennium 327
Tapping into global intuition for the new millennium.

Part 6: In Your Hands: Palmistry **339**

22 A Hand-y Map to the Future 341
An introduction to palmistry.

23 The Imprint of Each Generation 367
A look at the hands of the 20th century.

24 A Hand in the New Millennium 385
A look at the hands of the future.

Part 7: Living in the New Millennium **397**

25 Science and Medicine 399
Everyday living in the new millennium.

26 Economics and Finances 411
Money in the new millennium.

27 Are We Ready for the New Millennium? 423
The New Age Collective looks to the cards.

Appendix A: Glossary 438
Appendix B: Y2K Hotline and Web Sites: Be Prepared! 443
Appendix C: Further Reading About the New Millennium 446
Index 449

Contents

Part 1: The Bridge to the 21st Century   1

1 New Age Meets the New Millennium   3

How This Book Came About 3
Why Intuitive Arts Are Important to the New Millennium 4
   Hieronymus Bosch's Millennium: The Third Day of Creation 5
   July 20, 1969 5
   From Galileo to Einstein to Sagan 6
An Introduction to the New Age Collective 7
   Astrologer Sheila Belanger 8
   Palmist Robin Gile 9
   Numerologist Kay Lagerquist 10
   Psychic Intuitive Lynn A. Robinson 11
   Tarot Reader Arlene Tognetti 11
   Writer Lisa Lenard 12
The Future Enters into Us 12

2 Humankind Through the Millennia   15

Our 20th-Century Fascination with the Future 15
   1984, Brave New World, 2001: A Space Odyssey 16
   From Cubism to Andy Warhol to… ? 17
Just When Does the New Millennium Begin? 19
   A Brief History of the Calendar 19
   My, Oh, Maya! 22
   Set Your Clocks! 22
Passages: Millennial, That Is 22
The Last Thousand Years: From Morse Code to Satellites 24
The Next Thousand Years: From Y2K to… ? 24

3 New Millennium Oracle   27

What's a Book on the New Millennium
  Without Statistics? 27
Stats About the American Lifestyle 28
   At Our Leisure 28
   An Aging America 29
   Cultural Diversity 30
Stats About Countries and Cultures All Over the World 30
   An Aging World, Too 30
   Stats About World Population and People 31
Stats About the Earth 33
Stats About the Universe 34
Our Great Human Adventure 34

Part 2: Meet the Dawn: Astrology   37

4 An Astro Primer   39

Astrology Basics 39
   An Intuitive Art of the Spirit 40
   Are You in Synch? 41
   Planets Live in Signs and Houses 41

Signs and Wonders 43
   Energies: A Little Give and Take 44
   Qualities: Initiators, Stabilizers, and Adapters 44
   Elements: Smooth Operators 46
More About Sun Signs 47
   Your Universal Signature in Time and Space 47
   Events Have Astrological Signatures, Too 48
   The Astrological Mandala: What Does a Chart Look Like? 49
Circling the Zodiac: From Aries to Pisces 50
   ♈ *Aries, the Ram: March 21 to April 20* 50
   ♉ *Taurus, the Bull: April 20 to May 21* 51
   ♊ *Gemini, the Twins: May 21 to June 22* 51
   ♋ *Cancer, the Crab: June 22 to July 23* 52
   ♌ *Leo, the Lion: July 23 to August 22* 52
   ♍ *Virgo, the Virgin: August 22 to September 22* 52
   ♎ *Libra, the Scales: September 22 to October 23* 53
   ♏ *Scorpio, the Scorpion: October 23 to November 22* 53
   ♐ *Sagittarius, the Archer: November 22 to December 22* 54
   ♑ *Capricorn, the Sea-Goat: December 22 to January 21* 54
   ♒ *Aquarius, the Water Bearer: January 21 to February 19* ... 54
   ♓ *Pisces, the Fishes: February 19-March 21* 55
Little Fish in a Big Universe 55

5 Heaven on Earth   **57**

The Soul Has Many Mansions: The 12 Houses 57
An Earth's-Eye View of the Solar System 59
   The Sun, the Moon, the Nodes, and the Planets 59
   What's a Retrograde? 61
When Planets Are in Aspect to Each Other 62
   Paired Planetary Cycles Are Symbolic
    Maps of the Times 63
Planets That Are Symbolic Change Agents
for the 21st Century 64
   The Social Planets: Jupiter and Saturn 65
   Wild Card Ambassadors: Chiron and the Centaurs, the Comets ... 65
   Transpersonal Planets: Uranus, Neptune, and Pluto 67
   Karmic Portals: The Nodes 68

6 Astrological Cycles for the 21st Century   **69**

Gateways of Initiation for Each Paired Planetary Cycle 70
   A Quick Trip Through the Moon's Phases 70
   Other Planetary Pair Cycles 70
Hard Aspects: Symbolic Invitations to Shift Consciousness ... 71
   Conjunction: The Seed Gate ♂ 72
   First Quarter Square: The Action Gate □ 73
   Opposition: The Harvest Gate ☍ 73
   Third Quarter Square: The Reflection Gate □ 73
Cycles to Look Forward To 74
   Jupiter-Saturn: Social Change and Manifestation 75
   Saturn Cycles: Laying a Foundation and Building on It ... 76
   Chiron Cycles: Paradigm Shifts into Greater Healing 78
   Uranus Cycles: Liberation into Authenticity 79
   Neptune Cycles: Dissolving Illusions, Embracing the Spirit ... 80
   Pluto Cycles: Detoxing from the Old, Empowering into the New ... 81

Birth Charts for Two Centuries 81
    The Cosmic Job Description for 1,000 Years 81
    January 1, 1900 81
    January 1, 2000 83

7 How Planetary Cycles in the New Millennium Affect *Your* Birth Chart   87

Have You Had Your Birth Chart Done? 87
    How to Get Your Chart Done 88
    Basic Birth Chart Interpretations You Can Make Yourself 89
    A Closer Look at Hillary Rodham Clinton's Birth Chart 91
    Interpreting Events in Your Own Chart 91
    Synthesizing Your Own Chart with the Bigger Picture 92
    House Definitions 93
Important Astrological Events as Transits to Your Birth Chart 94
    Neptune-Pluto Conjunction of 1892 94
    Uranus-Pluto Conjunction of 1965–1966 96
    Uranus-Neptune Conjunction of 1993 97
    New Moon Solar Eclipse of August, 1999 98
    Chiron-Pluto Conjunction of December 30, 1999 100
    New Moon of May 2000 100
The Saturn-Jupiter Challenges and Opportunities for Each Sun Sign
  in the 21st Century 102
    2000 to 2020: Aries ♈ to Pisces ♓ 103
    2020 to 2040: Aries ♈ to Pisces ♓ 104
    2040 to 2060: Aries ♈ to Pisces ♓ 106
    2060 to 2080: Aries ♈ to Pisces ♓ 107
    2080 to 2100: Aries ♈ to Pisces ♓ 109
The Evolutionary Tasks of Four Generations 111
    Parent Born January 1, 1940 111
    Child Born April 1, 1970 113
    Grandchild Born July 4, 2000 114
    Great-Grandchild Born October 31, 2030 115

8 Predictions, Visions, Challenges, and Weavings   117

Are You Ready to Change?: 21st-Century Cosmic
  Growth Assignments 117
    The Age of Aquarius: What Is It and When Does It Start? 118
    Healing the Split Between Body and Mind 119
    Planetary Dances in the 21st Century 120
    Saturn Can Dance!: Saturn Cycles in the 21st Century 120
Transpersonal Invitations to Evolve: The Cycles of Uranus, Neptune,
  and Pluto 121
    Liberation from Illusions 121
    The Hippie Legacy: The Continuing Cycle of the
    Uranus-Pluto Seed Gate of 1966 122
    The Civilization of Information: The Continuing Cycle
    of the Neptune-Pluto Seed Gate of 1892 123
When God Was a Woman 123
    The Return of the Goddess 124
    The Primacy of Mother Earth: Cycles in Taurus 125
    The Yin Experience at Mid-Century 125
Take Up the Challenge: Be a Conscious Weaver with the Gods 127

Part 3: Two's Company: Numerology   129

9   Numerology and the Language of Numbers   131

Numerology Is the Language of Numbers 132
  Numbers Are Symbols of Vibration and Energy 132
  Energy of Numbers 132
  We're Picking Up Good Vibrations 134
  Raising Our Vibration from the 1 to the 2 135
  What It Means to Raise Our Vibration 135
Changing Channels: Moving from the 1 to the 2.......................135
  Millennium Numbers: Millennium 1000 136
  Millennium 2000 137
  Millennium 3000 138
Legacy of the 1: Where We've Been 139
  Positive Expression of Number 1 139
  Negative Expression of Number 1 139
Leaping to the Number 2: Where We're Going 140
  Negative Expression of Number 2 140
  Positive Expression of the Number 2 141

10   New Millenium Numbers at a Glance   143

Living with the 2..143
  Getting Connected 144
  Blending, Merging, and Getting Balanced: Ø Opposition 144
The New Millennium Model 145
  Finding a "Tribe" 145
  Return to the Feminine: The Age of Gaia 145
  New Paradigms for the New Millennium 146
  Relationships: The New Dynamic 147
  Slower Rhythm: Kairos Time 148
  Interdependence: We Are Family 149
Year 2000: The Big One 150
  2000 Has 3 Zeroes 150
  The 2 in 2000 150
  The Math Behind "Y2K" 150
The First Millennium Cycle, by the Numbers 152
  Numerological Cycles 153
  The First Nine Years of the New Millennium: 1999–2007 153
The Birthday and Life Path of the New Millennium 155

11   Your Personal Numbers for the New Millennium   157

Basic Meanings of Numbers 1–9 157
  Let's Get Personal 158
  The Message of the Personal Year 159
  Figuring Your Personal Year Number 159
  Figuring the Calendar Year 160
  Months by the Numbers 160
  One Example of a Personal Year 161
Figuring *Your* Personal Year Numbers from 2000 to 2009 161
Personal Year Themes 162
  1 Personal Year: Beginnings and Knowing the Self 163
  2 Personal Year: Relate and Cooperate 163
  3 Personal Year: Express Yourself 163

4 Personal Year: Hard Work *163*
5 Personal Year: Change *163*
6 Personal Year: Responsibility and Home *164*
7 Personal Year: Rest and Rejuvenate *164*
8 Personal Year: Achievement *164*
9 Personal Year: Endings *164*
Personal Year Vibes Under the 2 .... *164*
The Balance Number: Your Ability to Deal with Difficult or
  Threatening Situations 165
    Balance Number Interpretations *165*
    One Woman's Balance Number *167*
The Numbers and Your New Millennium 167

Part 4: Picture This: The Tarot 169

12 What's in the Cards? 171

A Picture's Worth a Thousand Words 171
  Take Some Time to Get to Know the Cards *173*
  Seeing Is Believing *173*
  Upright and Reversed Tarot Cards *176*
Tarot's Major Arcana 177
  Your Karma and Destiny Challenges *177*
  Keys 0 Through 21: From the Fool to the World *178*

13 Tarot's Minor Arcana: Wands and Cups 191

Tarot's Minor Arcana 191
  Your Everyday Choices and Challenges *192*
  Wands: Your Enterprise *193*
  Cups: Your Emotion *201*

14 Tarot's Minor Arcana: Swords and Pentacles 209

You and Me Against the World 209
  Swords: Your Action *210*
  Pentacles: Your Money *217*
Interpreting Tarot Spreads and Doing Readings 225
  When You're Reading Someone's (or Your Own!) Y2K Cards *225*
  A Karma Spread for the 21st Century *226*

15 Questions, Questions, Questions 231

Everybody's Curious About the New Millennium 231
  Keep a Tarot Journal of Your Questions and Answers *232*
  Remember, Fate Is What You Make It *233*
Ask Away!: Questions About Money 234
  How Strong Will the Global Economy Be in 2000–2005? *234*
  How Will the U.S. Stock Market Do from February 1999 Through 2001? ... *239*
  Will Social Security Still Be Around When You Need It? *242*
  How Will Attitudes Toward Money and Finance Evolve? *243*
Ask Away!: Questions About Society and Politics 243
  Will the Battle of the Sexes Continue in the 21st Century? *243*
  It Takes a Village: Family Values *246*
  Will There Be a Woman President? *248*
  Will We Have a Pope or Not in 2000–2005? *251*
Cultivating Patience and an Open Mind 252

16 More Questions, Questions, Questions 255

We Know There's More You Want to Find Out 255
Ask Away!: Questions About Technology 256
Will the Y2K Crisis Be Our 21st-Century Titanic? 256
How Will We Use Nuclear Technology? 257
Some Cards for Corporate America 260
Ask Away!: Questions About Medicine and Health 262
Will There Be Cures for Cancer? For AIDS? 262
How Will We Heal, Body, Mind, and Soul? 265
Ask Away!: Questions About Our Earth 267
What Will Happen to the Environment? 267
Will We Travel to Other Planets by the 24th Century? 269
What Happens to Art, Music, and Literature? 270
Anything Goes?! 273

17 What the Tarot Says About *You* in the New Millennium 275

A Fool's Journey to the Future 275
What Kind of Year Will 2000 Be for YOU? 276
What You Want to Know (And Why?) 277
Your Year 2000 in a Horoscope Spread 277
A Sample Horoscope Spread: What the Cards Mean 280
What's Your Destiny? 283
What's Your Wish? 284
What Decisions Do You Need to Make? 287
Spinning the Wheel of Fortune 289

Part 5: Know It All: Psychic Intuition 291

18 Intuitive Tools for the New Millennium 293

What Is Intuition? 293
The New Millennium Is a Time of Change 294
Tools for the New Century 294
Why Is Listening to Intuition Important? 295
Are You Intuitive? A Quiz 295
Building Your Intuitive Power 296
Practice Your Intuition 296
Feeling the "Vibes" 297
Take the Steps: Developing Your Own Intuition 297
Using Your Head 298
"If Only": An Intuitive Exercise 299
You Can Do What You Want! 299
Your New Millennium Doesn't Have to Be a Game of Chance 300
1. Listen to What You Tell Yourself About Your Life 300
2. Practice Positive Statements and Envision Success 300
3. Pay Attention to What Excites You 301
4. Ask Your Intuition Questions and Then Listen for the Answer 301
5. Pray and Meditate 301
6. Take Action 301
7. Be Aware of Life's Natural Ebbs and Flows 302

19 Mind/Body Medicine and Beyond: Using the Power of the Mind and Spirit to Heal   **303**

Thinking About Healing 303
   21st-Century Medicine 305
   Prayer as a Healing Force 305
Tapping into Your Own Healing Power 307
   Miracles of the Mind 307
   A Prescription for the New Millennium 308
When Your Life Is Out of Balance 308
   Learning to Listen to Your Body 309
   Why We Get Sick 310
   When Getting Sick Has a Payoff 310
   Using Imagery to Explore Your Symptoms 311
   Your Inner Physician: An Exercise 311
A Healthy Balance for the 21st Century 313

20 Psychic Awareness for the New Millennium's Global Community   **315**

Consciousness Tools for the 21st Century 315
   We Don't All Think Alike... and That's Good! 316
   Meditation Techniques Tap Psychic Intuition 316
   Intuitive Insight Exercise 317
Getting Along in the New Millennium 319
   Economic, Social, and Personal Challenges 319
   Our Human Intuition Could Be Our Salvation 320
Recognizing Our Shared Humanity 321
   Connecting Spiritual Traditions 321
   The Power of Our Minds to Create the World 322
Star Trek Isn't Just Science Fiction 324
   Envisioning a World Community 324
   Reaching for the Stars in the New Millennium 325
We Are the World: Embracing Hope and Optimism 325

21 Psychic Prophecies and Predictions for the New Millennium   **327**

Is the Y2K the End of the World? 327
Prophecies and Predictions 328
   What Exactly Did Nostradamus Predict? 329
   Edgar Cayce and the New Millennium 330
   Contemporary Voices: The Predictions of Robert
     Ghost Wolf 331
Ancient Voices: Hopi and Mayan Predictions 332
   Emergence to the Fifth World: Hopi Prophecies 332
   The Mayan Calendar: Does It Pinpoint the End of the World? 333
Earth Changes: Our Magnetic Shifts 334
Is the New Millennium a Renaissance of Intuition? 335
How Psychic Intuition Helps Us Make the
   Millennium Shift 335
   Crossing the Border 335
   No Looking Back 336
A Thousand Years from Now 337

Part 6: In Your Hands: Palmistry   339

22 A Hand-y Map to the Future   341

What Is Palmistry? 341
    The Hand as a Map 342
The Strength of the Thumb 343
A Tour of the Fingers 346
    The Mercury Finger: The Communicator 350
    The Apollo Finger: The Creator 352
    The Saturn Finger: The Lawmaker 352
    The Jupiter Finger: The Leader 353
Getting a Line on the Future 354
    The Heart Line: The Story of Love 354
    The Head Line: It's All in Your Head 355
    The Life Line: Quality of Life 357
    Rising Lines: Highlighting Your Strong Points 357
    Special Lines: Is Your Career in Your Hands? 358
Your Mounts: Where the Action Is 358
    The Mount of Mercury: Healer, Teacher,
    Cameraperson, Spy 362
    The Mount of Apollo: Where Your Talents Lie 362
    The Mount of Saturn: Dad, Grandpa—
    and Your Boss, Too 362
    The Mount of Jupiter: Spirituality, Strength—
    and Your Pets 363
    The Mounts of Mars: Anger and Passivity in the Hand 364
    The Mount of Venus: How Much Love You've
    Got to Give 364
    The Lunar Mount: The Ability to Receive, Your Mother,
    and Your Creativity 365
    Latecomers: The Mounts of Uranus, Neptune,
    and Pluto 365
Putting It All Together 366

23 The Imprint of Each Generation   367

Every Generation's Hands Are Unique 368
    From Leonardo to the Borg 368
    Finding a Generation's Future in Its Hands 369
Born 1921–1940: Conservative Pragmatism 370
    A Depression and a World War Leave Their Marks 371
    "Think of the Poor Starving Children in China..." 371
Born 1941–1960: You Say You Want a Revolution? 372
    What's Uranus Got to Do with It? 373
    Struck by the Sun: Apollonian Talents and Risk-Taking 374
The Quantum Leap: What's All This About a Mid-Life Crisis? 374
    Too Much Moon: From Moods to Indulgences 375
    We Are Survivors 375
Born 1961–1980: The Conservative Backlash 375
    Life Without a Strong Moon 376
    Defining One's Own World 376
    "I Vant to Be Alone!" 377
    "I'll Never Have Kids!" 377
    Politicians Aren't Special 378

Born 1981–2000: Cheerful Pragmatists 378
  What's Eccentricity, Anyway? *378*
  The Multi-Talented Synthesist *379*
  Staying Close to Home *379*
  No Mid-Life Crisis for Us, Thanks *380*
  Bad Tempers Wane *380*
  Celebrating Diversity *380*
Life, Health, and the Pursuit of Happiness 381
  Finding a Generation's Longevity in Its Hands *381*
  Finding a Generation's Health in Its Hands *381*
  Finding What Matters to a Generation in Its Hands *382*
  How Many Hands Does It Take to Make a Generation? *382*

24 A Hand in the New Millennium   385

What We Can Learn About Tomorrow from
  the Hands of Today 385
  Not Lost in Space *386*
  Life on Earth *386*
Animal Rights 387
  A World of Vegetarians? *387*
  Mushrooms: The Meat of Tomorrow *388*
  Animals Are People, Too *388*
  What's in It for the Animals? *389*
Race Is Less of Issue 389
  Jupiter Is an Idealist *389*
  Uranus Is the Innovator *389*
When Nerds Rule the World 391
  Pocket-Protector Spirituality *391*
  Gods and Monsters *391*
From Tattoos to Six-Million-Dollar Bodies 392
  From Adornment to Enhancement *392*
  Mr. Data, I Presume? *392*
Spiritual Breakthroughs 393
  Children of a Greater "God" *393*
  In Order to Create a More Practical Union... ....*393*
A Lack of Cataclysm 394
  Asteroids, AIDS, and Accidental Bombs *395*
  The Survivor Instinct *396*

Part 7: Living in the New Millennium   397

25 Science and Medicine   399

A World Without Borders 399
  The Internet Century: A Wired World *400*
  The Information Collective: Our Thoughts Are One? *400*
Smart Stuff 401
  Smart Medicines *401*
  Smart Clothing *402*
  Bill Gates' Smart House *403*
Human-Engineered Evolution 403
  Attack of the 300-Pound Tomato?: Feeding the Earth *404*
  Cloning: Copies vs. Originals *404*
  The Human Life Span: The 120-Year-Old Teenager *405*
Back to the Future: Will Mr. Fusion Be a Reality? 406

Fusion and Fission 406
Nuclear-Powered Space Travel 407
Will the Earth Survive Global Warming? 407
Earth as a Living System: James Lovelock and
Gaia Theory 408
Planetary Collapse or Global Salvation? 408

26 Economics and Finances   411

Mr. Greenspan, Are We at the Dawn of
the New Economy? 412
Tech World 412
Taking Stock 413
What About Social Security? 414
Keeping Current 415
Euros vs. Dollars vs. Yen (and Don't Forget
the Renminbi...) 417
When Credit Is King: The Cashless Society 417
One Earth, One Economy 418
Is a Global Economy in Our Future? 418
Why Diversity Is a Good Thing 418
The Star Trek Generation 419
Will Humankind Outgrow the Need for Money? 419
One Universe, One Economy? 420
What We Value 420

27 Are We Ready for the New Millennium?   423

What the Cards Have to Say: Are We Ready? 423
An Interview with the Experts 426
Astrological Insights 426
Doing the Numbers 428
Using Psychic Intuition 431
Lending a Hand 433
How About It: Are You Ready? 434
Your Tarot Spread 434
Other Insights 436
Humanity's Future on Spaceship Earth 436

A Glossary   438

B Y2K Hotline and Web Sites: Be Prepared!   443

Y2K Hotlines 443
Web Sites to Access 444

C Further Reading About the New Millennium   446

New Millennium, General 446
Astrology 446
Numerology 447
Palmistry 447
Psychic Intuition 447
The Tarot 447

Index   449

Foreword

The Complete Idiot's Guide to New Millennium Predictions offers readers some fascinating insights that promise to facilitate our transition, personal and collective, into the new millennium. Yet why would I, a credentialed parapsychologist with a doctoral degree from the University of California, Berkeley recommend *The Complete Idiot's Guide to New Millennium Predictions?* After all, parapsychology is a science. The scientific study of extrasensory perception has, since 1969, been approved by the American Association for the Advancement of Science. Why would a legitimate scientist encourage readers to explore the esoteric intuitive arts?

The ironic truth is that even the most outrageous of the esoteric arts has something to offer us—and perhaps the more outrageous, the more depth there is. The great trap of the "old millennium" mind is in supposing that we now understand the universe sufficiently to be able to discard certain old and worn-out patterns of thought, or certain new and untested modes of being. So, the subjects of this book—astrology, palmistry, numerology, tarot and psychic intuition—are no longer taught in the universities as they were in previous ages.

One of my faculty advisors at Berkeley, Professor Diane Shaver Clemens, was a specialist in the history of technology, as well as the history of U.S.–Soviet diplomatic relations. It was an act of courage for her to support a graduate student working on an individual, interdisciplinary degree in parapsychology. But it was only after I received my diploma that Diane opened up to me about some of the factors in her own personal history that motivated her to lend the weight of her academic reputation to my studies. It turned out that, while she was a professor at M.I.T.—a bastion of western materialism—she met privately with a group of professors who were determined to personally investigate various "taboo" subjects.

One professor chose astrology. Another dowsing. Another looked into acupuncture. Another professor decided to inquire into the obscure healing art of "radionics." Yet another looked into reading tea leaves. Another tarot cards. Another numerology. One professor chose to study the Chinese I Ching oracle. Diane chose to investigate palmistry. At each of their very private meetings, these esteemed academics reported to each other that their explorations were yielding uncannily surprising, positive results. No area was exempt.

How are we to explain this? My best answer is that the esoteric arts all succeed through the activation of the intuitive mind—that part of us that links our individual identity to the life of the cosmos. Is it any surprise that these arts seem so irrational, since the infinity itself transcends the comprehension of the rational mind?

The Complete Idiot's Guide to New Millennium Predictions can serve as a bridge connecting us to the larger life of the cosmos. The key to its proper use and enjoyment is to understand that, however small and insignificant we may be, we are always situated at the center of our own universe—for space always extends out from us equally in all directions no matter where we are. When we remain grounded in our own center of being, we can look out upon the whole universe with greater clarity.

Jeffrey Mishlove, Ph.D.

Jeffrey Mishlove, Ph.D., is host of the national, weekly public television series *Thinking Allowed*, as well as the daily Wisdom Radio series *Virtual U*. He also serves as President of the Intuition Network, a nonprofit organization dedicated to helping create a world in which all people are encouraged to cultivate their intuition. He is author of *The Roots of Consciousness* and *PSI Development Systems*. He is a licensed psychotherapist and received a unique doctoral degree in Parapsychology in 1980 from the University of California, Berkeley. Access Dr. Mishlove's Web site at www.mishlove.com.

Introduction

Whether you're looking to find the future of the world or your own future in the new millennium, you need look no further than this book. As you'll discover, the more we use the intuitive arts to explore our past and present, the better equipped we are to understand and forge the possibilities of our future.

In these pages, you'll be learning about:

➤ Astrology

➤ Numerology

➤ Palmistry

➤ Psychic intuition

➤ The Tarot

Each of these disciplines offers unique insight into both the self and the larger world, and, after you've been introduced to each one, we'll give you some thoughts about what that particular discipline foretells for the new millennium.

How to Use This Book

Five separate intuitive arts—and five different New Age experts—collaborated on this book, and so we've divided the book into sections that introduce each intuitive art and then allow the individual expert to make his or her predictions for the new millennium.

This book is divided into seven parts:

Part 1, "The Bridge to the 21st Century," introduces you to the New Age Collective, takes a brief look at the calendar, and then takes a quick trip through some of the statistics for the 20th century—and for the future.

Part 2, "Meet the Dawn: Astrology," introduces astrologer Sheila Belanger, who gives you an astrological primer and then helps you explore the astrological and planetary cycles for the new millennium.

Part 3, "Two's Company: Numerology," introduces numerologist Kay Lagerquist, who discusses the language of numbers, and then takes a look at both the numbers for the new millennium—and some numbers of your own.

Part 4, "Picture This: The Tarot," introduces Tarot reader Arlene Tognetti, who spends some time helping you get to know the cards, and then does some Tarot spreads to see what the cards have to say about the new millennium.

Part 5, "Know It All: Psychic Intuition," introduces intuitive psychic Lynn Robinson, who explains just what intuition is, and then explores the mind/body connection, and psychic tools you can use in the 21st century—and beyond.

Part 6, "In Your Hands: Palmistry," introduces palmist Robin Gile, who gives you a hand-y map for reading your palm, and then explores generational differences in both the 20th and 21st centuries.

Part 7, "Living in the New Millennium," takes a look at what scientific and economic forecasters predict for the future, and then gathers all the members of the New Age Collective together for their thoughts about a Tarot reading to see if we're ready for the new millennium.

Extras

In addition to exploring our future through the intuitive arts of astrology, numerology, palmistry, psychic intuition, and the Tarot, we've provided additional information to help you understand the future. Here's what you'll find in these boxes:

Out of Time

Here we'll warn you against making mistakes when it comes to planning your future.

Ask Spaceship Earth

In these boxes you'll find helpful tips to guide you through the new millennium.

Speaking Y2K

Here's where you'll find definitions to help you understand just what all this New Age lingo's about.

Time Capsule

Need additional information? Curious about the background? These longer informative sidebars give you facts and data you may not have known.

Acknowledgments

As the late Jerry Garcia sang, "What a long, strange trip's it's been." Amaranth and the New Age Collective have collaborated on any number of books with writer Lisa Lenard, but never have we encountered so many speed bumps, road blocks, and detour signs along the way. A millennial wake-up call? We're not sure—but we are delighted to have the book completed before the millennium begins!

Two thousand thanks to the members of the New Age Collective: Sheila Belanger, Robin Gile, Kay Lagerquist, Lynn A. Robinson, and Arlene Tognetti. Two thousand more to Lee Ann Chearney at Amaranth for the larger vision that made this book possible, to publisher Kathy Nebenhaus, editorial director Gary Krebs, managing editor Bob Shuman, assistant editor Georgette Blau, development editor Matthew X. Kiernan, copy editor Lynn Northrup, production editor Mike Thomas, and the rest of the Alpha/Macmillan editorial gang for their usual insightful comments—and for knowing the difference between "its" and "it's." Infinite thanks from Lisa to Bob and the dogs for the usual support and back-up music.

Sheila Belanger would like to honor all the students, colleagues, and teachers of astrology from whom she has received insightful wisdom and enthusiastic support. She thanks the New Age Collective; the book's amazing key writer, Lisa Lenard; the book's producer, Amaranth; and the production staff for their deep commitment to this book. Finally, she honors the wondrous and mysterious planets, stars, and universe in which we live, whose beauty has inspired stargazers for countless centuries.

Robin Gile wishes to thank his community of intuitive and psychic associates, both local and national, living and passed. The warmth and variety of support as well as other energies generated by these exceptional people have helped him to be a professional in a field that is unique and challenging. He is blessed to do work he believes in and loves while helping people daily. Thanks also to writer Lisa Lenard.

Kay Lagerquist would like to recognize her numerology students for their insights in investigating the mystery numbers; to thank Lisa Lenard for encouragement and for "mothering" this book and its writers; to Lee Ann for her vision; and to all those ladies of the California Institute of Numerical Research who spent 25 years studying and clarifying every aspect of numerology as we know it today. She would also like to honor Dr. Juno Jordan, the "grandmother of numerology," who brought this wonderful subject into the last century.

Lynn Robinson would like to thank her husband Gary for all his encouragement, support, and amazing copyediting skills. You are the best! Thanks also to her virtual assistant, Shane Brodock, who is an organizational and marketing genius; to writer Lisa Lenard; and to her stepson Cliff: May you continue to trust your intuition to guide you into the new millennium.

Arlene Tognetti would like to thank Lisa Lenard for a wonderful job of keeping us to task and adding her great sense of humor and creative talents to this book. We all hope that the public will enjoy this book's attempt to help them with the challenges and changes ahead for all of us. "May we live in interesting times" is truly what we have in the 21st century. The metaphysical tools that are presented in this book will help us to keep our center and enlighten us to what we can do to keep our focus. I would like to thank the Advanced Tarot Class for their help and insights in our Tarot chapters: Bob Bridge, Karen McClure, Cindy Louie, Lori Johnson, Stefanie Zabirsky, Chris Reinche, Brad Reppen, and Deby Smith.

Trademarks

All terms mentioned in this book that are known to be or are suspected of being trademarks or service marks have been appropriately capitalized. Alpha Books and Macmillan General Reference cannot attest to the accuracy of this information. Use of a term in this book should not be regarded as affecting the validity of any trademark or service mark.

Part 1

The Bridge to the 21st Century

What happens when New Age sciences meet the new millennium? The New Age Collective believes that their synergy can help us learn about the future, where "no one has gone before." Before we do, however, we'll explore just what a millennium is, and take a look at some millennial statistics as well.

Chapter 1

New Age Meets the New Millennium

> ### In This Chapter
>
> ➤ Why a book about the new millennium?
>
> ➤ Intuitive arts and the new millennium
>
> ➤ Introducing the New Age Collective
>
> ➤ Looking to the future

This is *not* just another book about the new millennium. Nor is it a book about Y2K, which, by the time you read this, may well have come and gone without a whimper. Rather, this book is a complete look at the new millennium, incorporating both New Age and scientific disciplines.

The New Age Collective is a compendium of experts: astrologer Sheila Belanger, palmist Robin Gile, numerologist Kay Lagerquist, intuitive consultant Lynn A. Robinson, M.Ed., and Tarot reader Arlene Tognetti. Together with writer Lisa Lenard, this group will give you an informed look at the new millennium, a look at the future based on the past and present, and the not-so-ancient intuitive arts of the New Age.

How This Book Came About

More and more people are interested in the *intuitive arts* of the *New Age*, and even "rational" scientists are taking a second look at what these ancient arts have to tell us.

Speaking Y2K

The **intuitive arts** include astrology, numerology, palmistry, psychic and intuitive abilities, and the Tarot. Because they can't be "proven" in the strict sense demanded by "rational" science, there are those who feel these disciplines aren't legitimate. **New Age** is a collective term for practitioners and followers of the intuitive arts. Its derivation comes from the concept of the "new age" of Aquarius, which, based on the precession of the equinoxes, will be occurring at about the same time as the new millennium.

We felt that it would be both interesting and exciting to take a positive look at our transition from "old" millennium to new millennium, using the lens of the intuitive arts as our basis. But rather than stop with just these intuitive disciplines, we're including what more traditional scientists—from physicists to biologists to economists—predict for the new millennium as well.

Why Intuitive Arts Are Important to the New Millennium

Until the 17th century, New Age intuitive arts were a part of everyday life. With the advent of "modern" science, however, they began to lose their credence, as "rational" scientists scoffed at what they called "superstition" and "myth."

Today, people are recognizing the importance of these practitioners of the intuitive arts to human spirituality. Mythologist Joseph Campbell (1904–1987) pointed out that without our stories to guide us, we've become a civilization that's adrift—a collective ship without an anchor. And psychoanalysis pioneer Carl Jung (1875–1961) used our collective unconscious as the basis for his research into the human psyche. We'll be coming back to the ideas of both of these pioneers throughout this book.

New Age intuitive arts provide important keys to everything from human spirituality to why we do the things we do. To state just a few examples, the intuitive arts can help you:

➤ Explore who you are through your astrological chart.

➤ Study the macrocosm of your self through the microcosm of your palm.

➤ Take a closer look at your possibilities through a closer look at your numerological profile.

➤ Explore your dreams and archetypes via the Tarot.

➤ Get in closer touch with your inner self via your psychic intuition.

In short, the New Age intuitive arts can help you learn more about yourself, and hence, your world.

Hieronymus Bosch's Millennium: The Third Day of Creation

From millennium to millennium, our views of the earth and its place in the universe have evolved as we have. When Hieronymus Bosch painted the triptych *The Garden of Earthly Delights* around 1500 (it now hangs in the Prado museum in Madrid, Spain), most believed that the earth was the center of the universe.

When the outer panels of Bosch's triptych are closed, they show a representation of the earth, which was believed to be the center of the universe. In Bosch's depiction, this globe is in turn enclosed by a larger hollow globe that represents the sphere of fixed stars, which is itself enclosed by a ring that shows the signs of the zodiac relative to the orbit of the Sun.

When the panels are opened, they reveal a triptych depicting the Creation, Earth, and Hell.

Eden, the Creation, for example, is a place of peace and perfection, while Hell is a place of evil and sin. The centerpiece of the triptych, however, is Earth itself, and here, Bosch depicts flawed Earth with its temptations and pleasures.

Shortly after Bosch painted this triptych in 1514, Pope Leo X asked some astronomers to examine why the seasons kept drifting from the months. One of the astronomers who tackled the problem, Copernicus, noticed that the main problem wasn't the calendar itself, but something else entirely: The earth wasn't at the center of the solar system; the Sun was. With this discovery, the view Bosch depicts made way for the modern one we accept today.

> **Ask Spaceship Earth**
>
> As you study Bosch's painting, keep in mind that the sphere represents a perfect form, as well as the infinite and eternal perfection of God and the cosmos.

July 20, 1969

Now let's cut to July 20, 1969. If you were alive then, you were probably glued to your TV set, watching Neil Armstrong take the first step on the Moon. By 1969, we knew that our solar system was just one of many, and that our galaxy was just one of many as well.

"That's one small step for a man, one giant leap for mankind," Armstrong said as he took his first steps on the earth's original satellite. In these days of instant communication via e-mail, with thousands of man-made satellites now orbiting the earth, it's hard to remember what a truly amazing technological feat those first steps were. The computer that powered that mission to the Moon had less power than your average home Pentium III PC system does today!

July 20, 1969: Astronaut Buzz Aldrin approaches the left leg of the Eagle lunar module. Humankind walks on the Moon. Photographer: Neil Armstrong. Courtesy: NASA.

From Galileo to Einstein to Sagan

Everyone wonders about the unexplainable, even the great minds of their day. Three such men—Galileo, Einstein, and Sagan—refused to accept the limits of rational science as their own.

Galileo (1564–1642) may be revered today, but in his own time, he was tried and convicted as a heretic for daring to suggest that the earth moved around the Sun. *"E pur si muove!"* ("But it does move!") he said, after recanting his theory to save himself from the *auto-de-fé*.

Three hundred years later, Albert Einstein (1879–1955) was fascinated by the unexplainable. "The most beautiful thing we can experience is the mysterious," he said in *What I Believe* in 1930. "It is the source of all true art and science."

Then, in 1972, astronomer-author Carl Sagan (1934–1996) designed a plaque that was sent into space aboard the Pioneer 10 and 11 satellites. Sagan's plaque, shown below, depicted a man, a woman, and a representation of Earth's galaxy.

Sagan was among many scientists who believe that intelligent life has certainly evolved on other planets in addition to Earth. We'll be discussing this possibility in more depth in Chapter 26, when we take a scientific look at the future.

From these 20th-century futurists, we're now going to move to some 21st-century ones. That's because it's time to meet the New Age Collective.

Out of Time

Apollo 11 was the mission during which Neil Armstrong became the first man to walk on the Moon. Two missions later, Apollo 13 became a near disaster—and a sobering reminder of how little humans really knew about their own technologies.

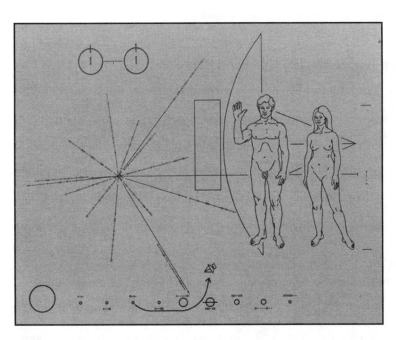

Carl Sagan and colleague Frank Drake hoped these images would point intelligent extraterrestrial species to our planet. The future will tell... Artwork for the plaque was prepared by Linda Salzman Sagan. Courtesy: NASA.

An Introduction to the New Age Collective

This book is the collaborative effort of five experts in their respective fields, a writer, and a production team. Three of the experts are based in the Pacific Northwest, one is in Massachusetts, and the fifth, like the writer, lives in New Mexico. The production team is scattered from New York to Maryland to Indiana. As you can see, this truly is a country-wide production!

Time Capsule

Each of the experts we'll be profiling has spent years, if not a lifetime, learning his or her particular art. Palmist Robin Gile and Tarot reader Arlene Tognetti, for example, were born into metaphysical families. Numerologist Kay Lagerquist and psychic intuitive Lynn Robinson became fascinated with their respective disciplines in their 20s. And astrologer Sheila Belanger found astrology to be a natural outgrowth of her counseling career.

Astrologer Sheila Belanger

Sheila Belanger began studying astrology in her early 20s. She is an inspiring and compassionate educator, astrologer, and writer. She holds a master's degree in transpersonal psychology. A counseling astrologer since 1984, Sheila has pioneered the exploration of astrology, ceremony, and shamanism. Sheila is a lively and spirited presenter at national and international astrology conferences.

Sheila offers a diverse selection of lectures, workshops, and retreats, including advanced classes and in-depth mentoring for professional astrologers; a popular series of quarterly lectures for the layperson on current astrological cycles; and longer, reflective retreat experiences in nature that weave together astrology and shamanism. She teaches both in the Pacific Northwest and around the country.

Through her business, SB Consulting, Sheila produces a quarterly newsletter on astrological cycles; a series of audio tapes on astrology topics for the professional as well as the layperson; and a Web site on navigating the current key planetary cycles.

"I'm participating in this book because as a collective of writers and design team members, we are offering a model for the collaborative and mutually supportive ideals of the '2' vibration of the new millennium.

"Astrology is relevant to the new millennium because it is a science of the spirit and enables individuals to track the larger perspective of collective and personal evolution. Knowledge is power and self-knowledge is the greatest spiritual gift we can give ourselves."

Palmist Robin Gile

Robin Gile, co-author of *The Complete Idiot's Guide to Palmistry* (Alpha Books, 1999), has read palms since he was 15. Born to metaphysically-oriented parents, he was given access to a good library, including palmistry subjects, at an early age. At 30 years of age, Mr. Gile was gifted with a student who sought him out "to learn to read palms," and during this wonderful opportunity the teacher, Mr. Gile, learned as much as the student, and made a gradual transition to full-time professional palm reading over the next seven years. He's read thousands upon thousands of hands, traveling across the country for many years to do so.

Mr. Gile has taught palmistry to many students, some of whom showed real merit and even genius inherent when they applied themselves. Mr. Gile is also a student of the Tarot. He travels extensively in his work, and is especially prone to gravitate to the Puget Sound area of the country. He has made his home in Albuquerque, New Mexico, for the last 27 years.

"To foretell the future is my passion and goal. In a society that seldom looks beyond the weekly lottery number or the fidelity of a prospective partner, the fortune-teller doesn't receive much recognition. True, I have clients who ask about the outcome of an election, which judge will preside over a case, or which portfolio will perform better in the next year. These utilizations of my talents are very refreshing and give me a satisfying scope for my talents.

"Still, the dynamic of change a society will experience as the millennium turns... now *that* is an intriguing endeavor. I am not a doomsayer who feels that a cataclysm will sweep this country and create a new order. I *do* believe strongly that a new order of consciousness is being built, as values, priorities, and mores are changing around us rapidly. Further, I believe that these changes are deep, lasting, and profound.

"Crimes that were once locally denied, unrecorded, and covered up are today given national notice and prosecution. The rights of people, animals, and nature have taken on a new value and realm of support. True, the critic may state that more crimes go unrecorded than ever come to light, and I will concede the point. Change is accomplished as a series of waves in a rising tide. The turn of 1999 into 2000 (or 2000 to 2001, the true beginning of the next millennium) is significant because we give it significance: the collective conscious concept of change, a new beginning, and fresh opportunity. These are invaluable ideas that are shared by many—perhaps even, in a small way, a majority.

"Thoughts are things, thoughts have great power, and we as a society, a consciousness, and a world are thinking in new, more philanthropic, less selfish, less biased ways. The results of this change in attitude will be most obvious in our children's children. But today, how exciting, how invigorating to watch the rise and evolution and acceptance of these values and mores.

"Palmistry is one of many techniques to view the individual consciousness, values, and goals. Because I've practiced this technique across the country and on thousands of hands, I have a unique and valid view of this country and the people in it.

"Relax, enjoy—and by all means, detach. The tide will rise a long time."

Numerologist Kay Lagerquist

Kay Lagerquist is a professional numerologist, counselor, workshop leader, and published author, most recently of the soon-to-be-published *The Complete Idiot's Guide to Numerology* (Alpha Books, 1999). Her varied background includes pioneering a successful private tutoring agency; 30 years of teaching; and extensive studies in a variety of disciplines, including interpersonal communication, learning styles, literature, psychology, and alternative health. She is currently working on her Ph.D. in metaphysics. Kay lives in a quiet country home on Whidbey Island, Washington, in the majestic Pacific Northwest.

"Numerology is a unique system that gives each person who cares to look a map for his or her life. So many people are questioning their purpose in life now, and as we enter into a whole new time, it seems to me that people will be looking for direction, guidelines, and tools for knowing what to make of this new time. Numerology gives us insight into why we came here to this Earth and what our purpose is. Insightful information is only as far away as your name and birthday.

"Numerology is a spiritual link to the mystery called life. Since there has been an awakening on a conscious level to the spiritual nature in all of us, numerology seems important, more than ever, as a tool for helping people make the link to spiritual understanding.

"Why was I drawn to numerology? First of all, back in 1979, I began looking for good, solid tools for personal growth. I have been investigating metaphysics and psychology for the last 20 years, but after much searching became enamored with numerology. Numerology spoke to me because of its practical application and its connection to the mystical and the mystery of life. Numerology has guided me to insights about purpose and meaning for my life. I love the spiritual emphasis of this metaphysical art with its revelation of the Soul Number, Life Lessons, and Life Path, as well as its application to psychology. I also appreciate numerology's teach-ability.

"I have always been fascinated by symbolic systems, so the fact that numerology gave meaning to numbers was an instant draw for me. I love being able to tell what the theme is for each year so that I can maximize my efforts and live in harmony with the natural flow of the year. Numerology offers this—and much more.

"I also value the predictive nature of this study of numbers. It has allowed me to make good, timely decisions about relationships, business, health, and real estate.

"Numerology, for me, and for the clients I serve, has helped to identify direction and meaning of the major life transitions we all face."

Psychic Intuitive Lynn A. Robinson

Lynn A. Robinson is an articulate and down-to-earth intuitive coach, professional speaker, and co-author of *The Complete Idiot's Guide to Being Psychic* (Alpha Books, 1999). She works as a consultant to business leaders, health care professionals, and those on a path of spiritual and personal growth. She has worked as a professional intuitive since 1983. She publishes a free monthly intuition newsletter, available at her Web site: **www.lynnrobinson.com**.

Boston Magazine voted her "Best Psychic," and the *Boston Globe* reported, "Whatever one's vision of a psychic might be, Lynn Robinson is probably not it. There is a practical quality to what she offers, and at the same time she has been known to have some extraordinary 'seeings' into the specifics of a client's life."

Consultations with Lynn have a practical blend of psychology, metaphysics, and spirituality, combined with her background in business and marketing. Her work is not based on detailed predictions, although future events will be discussed. She believes we have a great deal of free will in determining our future. In an intuitive session with Lynn you are asked to work with her so she can assist you in identifying your goals and show you the path that will take you there.

Lynn has produced an audiotape series of guided meditations to assist people in developing their intuition. She is a popular and sought-after seminar leader, teaching workshops on such topics as "Developing Your Intuition," "Creating the Life You Want," and "Creating Abundance." She was Administrative Director of Interface, an adult education center focusing on the education of the body, mind, and spirit.

Her company, Intuitive Consulting & Communication (IC&C), provides training and consulting, and produces intuition-related booklets and audio tapes.

"Why am I participating in this book? I love to share my ideas with others!

"Why is intuition relevant to the new millennium? In the new millennium, we will have many more choices to make in order to create the life we want. I believe that intuition is guidance from our Higher Self that helps us make the right decisions. Trusting and acting on our intuitive guidance helps us to live our lives more fully. It assists us in being on the right path to fulfill not only our own destiny but to be of service to others. Intuition provides us with valuable insight. When it's combined with our rational abilities, it creates a winning decision-making combination that can help guide us as we approach this new exciting era."

Tarot Reader Arlene Tognetti

Arlene Tognetti, co-author of *The Complete Idiot's Guide to Tarot and Fortune-Telling* (Alpha Books, 1999) grew up in a home where religion and spiritual ideas came together. Her mother, a traditional Catholic, and her father, a more Edgar Cayce type of individual, helped her to understand that there's more to this world than what's obvious. Arlene began studying the Tarot and astrology in the 1970s and started her own practice in 1980. She began teaching the Tarot in 1982 at the University of Washington in the Experimental College, and currently teaches the Tarot and astrology at Pierce College in Tacoma, Washington. Arlene's focus is on enlightening her students and clients: "I want everyone to learn what Tarot and astrology are all about and how these tools can help them grow and look at the choices and alternatives in their lives." Arlene lives in the Seattle area.

"I'm participating in this book because I've seen what the Tarot can do for people, and I'm eager to share my knowledge with as many people as I can. I love to help others learn how to make their own choices, and the Tarot is a wonderful tool for doing just this.

"The Tarot is relevant to the new millennium because it's a New Age tool. More and more people every day use the Tarot to find out about themselves and to get answers to their big questions—and their little questions. The Tarot has been used for millennia, so it's only natural that it will be used in the new millennium as well. The next thousand years will demonstrate the integration of science and intuition as humankind explores more fully the whole mind/body connection. The Tarot is a wonderful way to explore the inner self as we all make the transition to the year 2000."

Writer Lisa Lenard

Lisa Lenard has co-authored, with Madeline Gerwick-Brodeur, *The Complete Idiot's Guide to Astrology* (Alpha Books, 1997) and *The Pocket Idiot's Guide to Horoscopes* (Alpha Books, 1997); with Arlene Tognetti, *The Complete Idiot's Guide to Tarot and Fortune-Telling*; with Robin Gile, *The Complete Idiot's Guide to Palmistry*; and with Kay Lagerquist, *The Complete Idiot's Guide to Numerology*. She's also written award-winning short stories, as well as five novels, and numerous articles and essays on a variety of topics. She lives in Corrales, New Mexico.

"Participating in this book seemed a natural extension of the ones I'd written with some of its authors. I've learned so much from each and every one of these experts—both in writing those books and this one—and am delighted to be able to showcase all of their work in one book."

Ask Spaceship Earth

Looking to the future means exploring both our past and our present. As with anything, we can learn much about what may happen by looking at what has already occurred.

The Future Enters into Us

The future enters into us in order to transform itself in us, long before it happens.
—Rainer Maria Rilke, *Letters to a Young Poet*

As we'll discuss in the next chapter, humans have been fascinated with the future as long as we've been aware that a future existed. Scientists and New Age experts aren't the only ones who have looked into their crystal balls: Artists, poets, composers, and writers have all tried to define the elusive nature of that which we haven't yet experienced.

What do you believe is possible in the future? Do you believe that the future is in all of our hands? We do. This book will show you how, together, we can create a new millennium full of promise and joy for all of us.

The Least You Need to Know

➤ This book is a natural outgrowth of new millennium interest in New Age intuitive arts.

➤ The intuitive arts and rational science have more in common than you may think.

➤ The New Age Collective is truly a country wide compendium.

➤ Looking to the future means exploring both our past and our present.

Chapter 2

Humankind Through the Millennia

In This Chapter

➤ Our fascination with the future

➤ When does the millennium *really* begin?

➤ A millennial timeline

➤ A look at the last thousand years

➤ A look at the next thousand years

What's the big deal about a millennium change, anyway? Is it somehow connected with our continuing fascination (some might say "obsession") with the future? Maybe, as historians suggest, we can use our past to help us look at our future.

In this chapter, we're going to examine how some 20th-century artists, writers, and films have looked at the future that's fast approaching. We'll also take a look at just when the new millennium begins through a brief history of the calendar, and then we'll take a look back to help us look forward more wisely.

Our 20th-Century Fascination with the Future

Humans have always wanted to know the future: In Biblical times, for example, Joseph became the Pharaoh's counselor because of his talent for divining events through dream interpretation. But it's only in more recent times that the arts have become the media for expressing our fascination with the future. Science fiction is a brainchild of the 19th century; the cubist art movement and filmmaking, the 20th.

Poets, writers, artists, and filmmakers seem to have an uncanny ability to foretell the future—even when that's not their intention. The year 1984 may have come and gone, and 2001 may be close at hand—but the events they depicted may be more than just science fiction.

1984, Brave New World, 2001: A Space Odyssey

George Orwell's novel *1984* is probably best known for the catch phrase "Big Brother is watching you." In actuality, an entire vocabulary comes to us from this tale of a totalitarian *dystopia*, where the Party slogan is "Who controls the past controls the future: Who controls the present controls the past."

Orwell's *1984* hero, Winston Smith, works for the Ministry of Truth, where his job is to adjust the past depending on what's going on in the present; in other words, he alters history. Winston Smith's problem is that, unlike his peers, he has a memory, and so begins to question Big Brother's policies.

While the real 1984 has come and gone without the Western world succumbing to Big Brother-ism, other aspects of Orwell's chilling portrait have become commonplace. The Party's "doublespeak" is synonymous with the "spin" of today, to cite just one example. The line between documentary and entertainment, blurred so effectively in films such as Oliver Stone's *JFK*, have edged a new "virtual reality" between fact and fiction.

Speaking Y2K

A **dystopia**, the opposite of a utopia, is a society where the conditions of life are dreadful.

Another book, Aldous Huxley's *Brave New World*, written in 1932, depicts a world six hundred years in the future—and yet many of its seemingly impossible prophecies have already come to pass. In Huxley's novel, the leaders create a "utopia" founded on happiness—to be unhappy is illegal.

Mass happiness is induced with the help of a drug called *soma*, and babies are made, not the old-fashioned way, but in enormous factories—cloned for a particular caste, from the elite Alphas who run the world, to the brain-damaged Epsilons who do the dirty work.

Time Capsule

Huxley himself noted in the 1950s that his book had been far more prescient than even he could have imagined. Whether or not a government can impose a "utopia" through what amounts to mass hypnosis remains a hypothetical question—but test-tube babies, and cloning, as we'll discuss in Chapter 26, are very much a reality.

When Stanley Kubrick's film *2001: A Space Odyssey* (based on a book by Arthur C. Clarke) first appeared in 1968, many were baffled by its images. What were those black obelisks supposed to *be*, anyway? It turns out that they were a kind of self-aware robot—a form of self-reproducing artificial intelligence sent as an advance team to scout our solar system for potentially inhabitable planets and moons, one of which they found in Europa, a moon of Saturn.

Many scientists believe that such self-aware, self-reproducing (that is, they can build others in their own image) robots—androids, if you prefer—are less than a century away here on Earth. Among them are Russian astronomer Nikolai Kardashev and Princeton physicist Freeman Dyson, who have defined a system of three types of civilizations—Types I, II, and III—ordered by how they utilize available energy:

➤ Type I civilizations can control the natural resources of their planet, including changing the weather, mining the oceans, and using the energy at their planet's core.

➤ Type II civilizations use the energy of their sun. Not only do they collect it from planet-based receivers, they have harnessed it directly, using force-field-like technology to enclose it and direct it.

➤ Type III civilizations use the energy of neighboring star systems and galaxies.

Where are we now? Kardashev and Dyson say we're still a Type 0 civilization: We use coal and oil—dead plants, in other words—to fuel our world. The civilization that sent probes to Stone-Age Earth and present-day Europa in *2001* was probably a Type III. Kardashev and Dyson say it may take us another 10,000 years to arrive there!

From Cubism to Andy Warhol to... ?

Is it art? Even at the end of the 20th century, there are those who look at the work of cubists such as Pablo Picasso and Georges Braque and shake their heads in confusion. If it doesn't depict something they can "see," it isn't art.

But what cubism really does is look at things from more than one angle. Take, for example, Picasso's "Girl Before a Mirror," painted in 1932. Instead of the traditional portrait and reflection, we see what seems to be a jumble of perspectives and viewpoints. The painting, which hangs in the Museum of Modern Art in New York City, depicts a woman looking at her own image in a mirror. The masterpiece shows the woman's *movement*, the woman in more than one moment. It also shows, by use of metaphor, the woman's interior and exterior perceptions of her own appearance in the glass.

Time Capsule

Time and perception are fragmented into moments and impressions that resonate to build one shimmering and ever-changing whole—with a blending of reality and reflection thrown in. The woman embraces her reflection, unifying the experience, real and perceived, across the picture plane. Circles, a symbol of the feminine, appear throughout the composition; and the woman's swelling abdomen suggests that she is pregnant—this is a moment filled with creative potential and possibility.

Picasso's "Girl Before a Mirror" was painted at a time of great advances in physics and quantum-mechanical theory. German physicist W.K. Heisenberg would shortly advance his uncertainty principle: the notion that measuring either of two related quantities, such as energy and time or position and momentum, produces an uncertainty in the measurement of the other. The physics of cubism!

Time Capsule

You could think of cubism as a reflection of the industrial revolution and seeing more than one perspective simultaneously. More than that, though, cubism is a mirror of our speeded-up society. It's like those time-lapse photos, where headlights appear as streaks of light. It's "fast-mo." It's the shape of things to come.

Artist Andy Warhol claimed that anything is art, that whatever gets your attention—whether it's advertising, the news, or a realistic reproduction of Campbell's soup cans—can be art. By this definition, a Web page is art. The way you arrange your desk is art. Even those *real* Campbell's soup cans, stacked on the shelf of your 24-hour super-duper supermarket, are art.

The traditional definition of art is "creative work," so it follows that the creativity of a particular time will reflect the time itself. Michelangelo's Sistine Ceiling at the Vatican in Rome, for example, reflects the church-oriented art patronage of his time. What will the art of the 21st century be? If Warhol is right, it will be everything and anything, combining the aesthetics of form with the practicality of everyday function.

Through advances in computer technology, the art of the 21st century will likely come alive. It will move and interact with spectators in ways we can only imagine at present, taking them to far-flung places and incredible situations. Art and experience will fuse in time to create a "virtual reality." As the ads for a major software company read, "Where would you like to go today?"

Just When Does the New Millennium Begin?

2001.

No, really. There was no year "0" when the Council of Nicea reconfigured the calendar in A.D. 325, so the first year *anno domini* was 1. That means that the first millennium ran from 1 to 1000. The second ran from 2 to 2000. And the third begins on January 1, 2001. In addition, so many people have futzed with the calendar that even that date has little real meaning.

It may help to consider where these numbers came from in the first place. So let's take a look at where our present-day calendar comes from.

A Brief History of the Calendar

Entire books have been written about just one particular calendar, but we're going to try to give you a brief history of the calendar in a few paragraphs.

In the beginning, the Sumerians, an agriculture-based civilization, created a *calendar* with a 360-day year, comprised of 12 lunar cycles, or months of 30 days each. Sounds nice and tidy, doesn't it? But the Sumerians soon encountered the problem that has plagued calendar-makers ever since—the seasons kept getting out of whack.

Speaking Y2K

The word **calendar** comes from the Latin word *kalendae.* In early Rome, priests dictated the months by following the *calends,* the days of the new moons.

Later, the movements of stars and planets were added into the equation—certain planets and stars appeared in certain parts of the sky at certain times of year. This is also the basis of astrology, by the way.

We use these terms day in and day out, but let's take a look at their origins:

➤ *Months* are based on the lunar cycle (month = moon). Today's astronomers calculate a lunar month as the length of time between two new moons: 29 days, 12 hours, 44 minutes, and 2.8 seconds.

➤ *Days* are based on the length of time from sunset to sunset. Our seven days got their names from the early Romans, who derived them from the seven known celestial bodies (other than Earth): Sun, Moon, Mars, Mercury, Jupiter, Venus, and Saturn.

➤ *Years* are the time from spring equinox to spring equinox.

Let's fast-forward to the Romans. When the early Romans first created a calendar of their own, it contained 10 months in a 304-day year:

➤ Martius (named for the god of war, Mars)

➤ Aprilus (from the verb *aperire*, to open)

➤ Maius (named for Maia, the goddess of fertility)

➤ Junius (for Juno, the goddess of the moon)

➤ Quintillus, Sextilis, September, October, November, and December—the Roman numbers 5 to 10

January, named for Janus, the god of doorways, and February, named for the festival of purification, were added in the 8th century B.C., and the year beginning was changed from March 1 to January 1 in 153 B.C.

Ask Spaceship Earth

Naturally, Julius had to name a month for himself, so Quintillus was re-named Julius. Not to be outdone, his nephew-successor, Augustus, re-named Sextilis as well.

Of course, as we've already mentioned, the seasons were still getting out of whack, and extra months had to be thrown in periodically to knock the year back into shape. When Julius Caesar went to Egypt (he met Cleopatra there, but that's another story), he learned about the Egyptian calendar from the astronomer Sosigenes (which is based on the flooding of the Nile), and came back to Rome eager to fix his own. Thus began the solar calendar with leap years, also known as the Julian calendar, adopted in 46 B.C.

When all was said and done, Julius Caesar's year 1 AUC (don't ask—it's more Latin) became the date of the founding of Rome, in our current numbering, 753 B.C.

It all seemed to work well, but then, in what's now A.D. 325, the Christians decided that the calendar should reflect the birth of Christ, not the birth of Rome. That's when the Council of Nicea stepped in, picked a time for Easter (the first Sunday after the full moon after the vernal equinox)—and for the birth of Christ.

The seasons still wouldn't quite stay in place, even after all this, and by the Middle Ages, the Popes were stepping in regularly to fix things up. The problem was, not every country changed over at the same time, and, to compound this, when they did, some countries leaped over weeks, while others added days—or even months.

Pope Gregory XIII dropped 10 days from the calendar, going straight from October 4, 1582, to October 15, 1582. The new calendar was dubbed the Gregorian calendar; Caesar's Julian calendar became designated as the Old Style (o.s.).

Newly Protestant countries didn't give a fig what the Pope wanted and were even slower to change over from the Old Style. In 1700, the Protestants had a leap year and the Catholics didn't. Sweden tried to catch up by skipping all leap years until 1740. England and America skipped from September 2 to September 14 in 1752.

Still other countries didn't actually make the change from the Old Style to the Gregorian calendar until this century. China shifted in 1912, Bulgaria in 1915, and Turkey in 1917. Russia, in fact, didn't change over until after their October Revolution in 1917, which means that the October Revolution was really in November!

Maybe the lesson here is that the millennium's got nothing to do with the calendar. But that doesn't mean we're not excited.

Out of Time

Oops! Turns out they were wrong. Herod actually ruled from 11 B.C. to 4 B.C. So if we actually date our current date from the birth of Christ, the millennium probably began in 1995!

Out of Time

Did you know that George Washington was really born February 11, 1731? When England and America changed over to the new calendar in 1752, his old birthday became February 22, 1732 o.s. (Old Style). That would explain President's Day!

More Calendars

Jewish	Years are designated A.M. for *anno mundi*, which means "year of the world" in Latin. This calendar follows the ancient Babylonian lunar calendar and adds a 13th month seven times in each 19-year cycle.
Chinese	This calendar is based on the phases of the moon. Each month has the name of an animal: rat, ox, tiger, hare, dragon, snake, horse, sheep, monkey, fowl, dog, and swine.
Muslim	Based on the teachings of the Koran, this calendar does not follow lunar cycles for its organization. Months shift and cycle through the seasons.

My, Oh, Maya!

Another famous calendar in history is the one devised by the ancient Maya of South America. Mayan culture spans the period from roughly 300 B.C. to A.D. 900 (Gregorian time, that is!). The Mayans calculated time according to astronomical cycles and based upon multiples of 20.

Mayan Time

Gregorian Calendar Days	Mayan Equivalent
1 day	kin
20 days	uinal
360 days	tun
7,200 days	katun
144,000 days	baktun

In Mayan time, January 1, 2000 is 12.19.6.15.2 (or 12 baktuns, 19 katuns, 6 tuns, 15 uinals, and 2 kin). The Mayans Long Count cycle, beginning at 0.0.0.0.0., has been calculated to end with the winter solstice of December 2012 (some place the date at December 21 and others at December 23). That day, or 13.0.0.0.0., has a significance to Mayan culture that scholars are still working to understand. You'll find out more about this date and the Mayans in Chapter 22.

Some New Age thinkers pinpoint the end of the Mayan Long Count as the time when the earth's electromagnetic field will shift in a dramatic way. We'll see! For now, you can have fun with the Mayan calendar by surfing the Internet. Search on "Mayan calendar" and you'll find several sites that will convert any date from our Gregorian calendar to the ancient Mayan system.

Set Your Clocks!

Officially, the first place in the world where the millennium will change is at the international date line, with the first land the islands of Micronesia. People in Guam, Truk, and Palau will be the first to experience the new century. No matter where you experience the new millennium, though, you'll want to make sure your clock is set to the second, so you won't miss a minute of it.

Passages: Millennial, That Is

Each thousand-year cycle of calendar time has presented new, exciting, and potentially thorny challenges to humankind. We've created a table to track the major lessons and achievements of the millennia and the centuries within them.

Millennium or Century	Challenge	Achievement
1000–1 B.C.	Accumulation of knowledge, which is shared among cultures	Height of ancient civilizations with advances in philosophy, medicine, science, the arts
A.D. 1–1000	Dark Ages in Europe	Surviving the fall of the Roman Empire; the plague spreads from Egypt and Rome to Britain
1200–1400	Bubonic plague	Universities founded; Dante writes the *Divine Comedy;* Marco Polo explores; Petrarch is born
1400–1500	European world exploration begins	Gutenberg introduces the printed book; Leonardo invents the parachute; Aztec culture flourishes; Columbus discovers the Americas
1500–1600	High Renaissance; Protestant Reformation	Breakthroughs in science, art, and medicine to rival the ancients
1600–1700		Isaac Newton measures the orbit of the moon
1700–1800	Age of Reason	Fall of monarchies—the French and American Revolutions
1800–1900	Industrial Revolution	Railroads introduced; Edison invents phonograph, telegraph, and produces electric light bulb; telephone invented
1900–2000	World wars; Atomic Age begins; rise and fall of Communism; emergence of a global economy	Rapid strides in science: the automobile, airplane, and the computer; humankind travels to the moon
2000–2100	The Information Age; spread of Global democracy; space exploration	Let's see!

The Last Thousand Years: From Morse Code to Satellites

Did you know that the Morse Code did not become the globally accepted disaster transmission until after the Titanic sank? Sure, the great ship probably would have gone down even if it had been using up-to-the-minute technology, and in fact, that's our point. Even up-to-the-minute technology is fallible.

In 1998, in fact, millions of pagers and cell phones didn't work when solar flares disrupted satellite transmissions all over the world. And what if a meteorite hit a satellite? How would we be able to watch *Frasier* and *Dateline*, let alone call our cousin in Kuwait? Satellites are now used to transmit disaster messages across the globe to alert rescuers.

The Next Thousand Years: From Y2K to... ?

Disaster scenarios for Y2K computer problems range from a few hours of inconvenience to worldwide breakdowns of everything from power plants to delivery systems. By the time you read this book, most of the lingering problems may well be solved, but even the best computer minds admit that having a couple hundred bucks on hand before the year 2000 strikes might not be a bad idea—"just in case your bank card doesn't work for a little while," to quote one bank computer director.

Meanwhile, on the high plains of western New Mexico, the Very Large Array patiently searches the universe for extra-terrestrial life (you may remember this line-up of enormous satellite dishes from the film *Contact*).

Futurists from astronomer Carl Sagan to astrologer Noel Tyl predict that life from another planet will be contacting us very, very soon. As author Arthur C. Clarke has said, "Two possibilities exist: Either we are alone in the universe or we are not. Both are equally terrifying."

One thing that *is* certain is that humans are the decision-makers when it comes to this planet—at least for now. Fortunately, with the new millennium, we're more aware of the fragile ecosystem that supports us, and, as we'll discuss in Chapter 26, we're learning to undo the chauvinistic errors of our past.

Our future lies not just in the stars, but on our own planet. We have much to learn about living together on Earth before we can achieve a "United Federation of Planets" to "boldly go where no one has gone before." But we've clearly learned a lot already, as the statistics in the next chapter will show.

The Least You Need to Know

➤ Humans have always been fascinated by the future.

➤ The millennium really begins January 1, 2001!

➤ Technology is not infallible.

➤ We're looking to the stars—and to our own planet.

Chapter 3

New Millennium Oracle

In This Chapter

➤ Stats about the American lifestyle

➤ Stats about people of the world

➤ Stats about the earth

➤ Stats about the universe

Like every oracle, this book bases itself in the firm foundation of the past and present, and what better way to do that than taking a look at statistics?

In this chapter, we examine what the statistics have to say about us in all our various guises—whether we're Americans, residents of planet Earth, or denizens of the universe.

What's a Book on the New Millennium Without Statistics?

The 20th century could well be dubbed the century of the statistic. You can't open a newspaper or turn on the TV news without hearing the latest numbers on everything from science to sex.

Before we explore some new millennium statistics, let's take a look back a hundred years and compare where we are now with where we were then:

➤ In 1900, 41 percent of Americans worked or lived on farms. In 2000, less than 2 percent of our population is rural.

➤ In 1910, 12 percent of Americans lived in suburbs. In 1995, 52 percent lived in suburbs.

➤ In 1900, 90 percent of African-Americans lived in the south. Today, 53 percent of African-Americans live in the south.

➤ From 1880 to 1924, 26 million legal immigrants came to America, most of them from southern and eastern Europe. From 1961 to 1995, 20 million legal immigrants arrived, this time mostly of Asian and Hispanic descent.

It's clear the demographic face of our country is changing. Next, let's take a look at our lifestyles, and see what we're doing.

Stats About the American Lifestyle

In 1990, 125.8 million Americans had jobs. In June 1998, that number was almost 137.5 million. Meanwhile, unemployment fell from 5.6 percent in 1990 to less than 4.5 percent in mid 1998, and continues to drop as we write this.

The average worker in the U.S. earned close to $13.00/hour by the middle of 1998, compared with about $6.50/hour at the beginning of the decade. That same worker averaged just over 34 hours/week, which leaves her (assuming eight hours of sleep per night) with over 77 hours per week in which to pursue the leisure time activities of her choice.

And, of course, there are statistics about those, too!

At Our Leisure

So what are we doing with that leisure time? Here are the top 20 leisure-time activities, adapted from the U.S. Statistical Abstract 1996:

Activity	Total Instances	Number of People (in Millions)
Walking	1,168.2	70.8
Swimming	995.0	60.3
Biking	821.7	49.8
Vacation travel days	781.0	47.3
Equipment exercise	722.7	43.8
Camping	707.9	42.9
Amateur softball	693.0	42.0
Pleasure trip days	671.0	40.6
Bowling	615.4	37.3

Fishing	511.0	36.0
Basketball playing	465.3	28.2
Golf	464.8	24.6
Hiking	417.4	25.3
Aerobics	382.8	23.2
Jogging	339.9	20.6
Tennis	308.5	18.7
Softball	298.7	18.1
Volleyball	287.1	17.4
Hunting	236.0	16.4
Football playing	257.4	15.6

Surprised? How many of these activities did you engage in recently? Interestingly, attending various professional sports events appears much farther down on the list. Major League baseball scored the highest, at 71.2 million instances and 5 million people; NFL football attendance is 14.7 million instances and .9 million people; and those attending NBA games didn't even make the top 40—and this was before the strike.

Time Capsule

What about TV? We turned to TV-Free America's (TVFA) Web page (**www.tvfa.org**) to get some quick numbers:

➤ Percentage of U.S. households with at least one television: 98

➤ Percentage of U.S. households with at least one VCR: 84

➤ Hours per day that TV is on in average U.S. home: 7 hours, 12 minutes

➤ Number of TV commercials seen in a year by an average child: 30,000

➤ Number of videos rented daily in U.S.: 6 million

➤ Number of public library items checked out daily: 3 million

An Aging America

What else do statistics have to say about this American life? As a whole, we're slowly aging. In 2012, the first of the baby boomers will reach retirement age, while the number of workers per retiree will drop from 5 in 1990 to about 2.6 in 2030.

By that same year, 21 percent of the American population will be over 65—and there will be more people over 65 than there are under 18. And, by 2050, there will be six times as many people who are over 85 as there will be in the year 2000.

Cultural Diversity

The majority of Americans today may be Caucasian, but this demographic is changing rapidly, as more and more non-white immigrants move to the United States:

➤ In the year 2000, immigrants will account for one in four households in the United States.

➤ Hispanics will surpass African-Americans as the largest minority group in the United States in 2015.

➤ By 2040, 50 percent of the people in California will be of Hispanic descent.

➤ By 2088, minority populations will form the majority in the United States.

Ask Spaceship Earth

In 2020, Mexico City will remain the world's largest metropolitan area, but at the same time, most Asians will be concentrated in huge megacities with populations over eight million.

Meanwhile, if all these people are coming to America, what's going on in the rest of the world? Let's look at some numbers from the United Nations.

Stats About Countries and Cultures All Over the World

It may look as if everyone's pouring into this country, but the truth is, plenty of people are staying in their countries of origin as well. But, just as here, enormous rural-to-urban population shifts are taking place. The problem is, not all countries are well-equipped to handle the change.

By some estimates, 1.5 billion people will be added to the already burgeoning Asian urban centers by the year 2020. This includes megalopolises like Tokyo and Singapore, as well as cities less prepared to handle the strain like New Delhi and Jakarta.

An Aging World, Too

The United States won't be alone in its aging population, either. According to the U.N., fertility will continue to decline while life expectancy will increase throughout the world through 2050. Here's a table from the U.N.'s Population Division of its Department of Economic and Social Affairs, showing median age in various regions of the world in 1950, 1998, and 2050.

Median Age by Major Area: 1950, 1998, and 2050

Area	Median Age (Years)		
	1950	1998	2050
World total	23.5	26.1	37.8
More developed regions	28.6	36.8	45.6
Less developed regions	21.3	23.9	36.7
Africa	18.7	18.3	30.7
Asia	21.9	25.6	39.3
Europe	29.2	37.1	47.4
Latin America/Caribbean	20.1	23.9	37.8
Northern America	29.8	35.2	42.1
Oceania	27.9	30.7	39.3

Source: United Nations Population Division, World Population Prospects: The 1998 Revision

Stats About World Population and People

When we checked the U.S. Census Bureau's running clock (www.census.gov/main/www/popclock.html) on February 26, 1999 at 11:41 a.m. MST, these were the numbers:

U.S. Population	World Population
271,957,703	5,969,808,627

Source: U.S. Census Bureau

The Census Bureau updates these numbers *every five minutes*, so you may want to check back when you read this book and see how much they've gone up. After all, the United Nations predicts that the world population will reach six billion sometime in 1999 (we'd say, looking at the number above, any minute now . . .), and that it will be close to nine billion by 2050.

But don't take our word for it. Here's the United Nation's population numbers from Year 1 to Year 2050:

Out of Time

While it took more than 1,600 years for the world population to double from about 300 million people in the year 1 to an estimated 600 million in 1600, it took only another 300 for it to more than double, to 1,650 million, by 1900. And the world's current rapid rate of population growth didn't even begin until 1950!

Year	Population (in Billions)
1	0.30
1000	0.31
1250	0.40
1500	0.50
1750	0.79
1800	0.98
1850	1.26
1900	1.65
1910	1.75
1920	1.86
1930	2.07
1940	2.30
1950	2.52
1960	3.02
1970	3.70
1980	4.44
1990	5.27
2000	6.06
2010	6.79
2020	7.50
2030	8.11
2040	8.58
2050	8.91

Source: World Population Prospects: The 1998 Revision

One more thing: In 1950, nine countries accounted for 60 percent of the world population. But by 2050, five countries will account for almost half.

1950 Top Nine Countries by Population (in Millions)

1	China	554,760
2	India	357,561
3	United States	157,813
4	Russian Fed.	102,192
5	Japan	83,625
6	Indonesia	79,538

7	Germany	68,376
8	Brazil	53,975
9	United Kingdom	<u>50,616</u>
Total		1,508,456
	% of World Population	59.8

2050 Top Five Countries by Population (in Millions)

1	India	1,528,853
2	China	1,477,730
3	United States	349,318
4	Pakistan	345,484
5	Indonesia	<u>311,857</u>
Total		4,013,242
	% of World Population	45.2

Stats About the Earth

Naturally, there are stats about our planet, too. First, its measurements:

➤ Earth's diameter at the equator: 7,926.68 miles

➤ Earth's diameter at the Poles: 7,899.98 miles

➤ Weight: 6,600,000,000,000,000,000,000 tons!

➤ Distance from center of the earth to its surface: 3,950 miles

➤ Thickness of its atmosphere: 500 miles

Next, some time measurements:

➤ Time for Earth to make one rotation on its axis: 23 hours, 54 minutes

➤ Length of Earth's orbit around the Sun: 600 million miles

➤ Time it takes for that orbit: 365.24219 days

➤ Speed at which the earth travels around Sun: $18^1/_2$ miles per second (that's 66,600 miles per hour!)

Lastly, let's look at some distances:

➤ Distance from Earth to its Moon: 238,857 miles

➤ Distance from Earth to its Sun: 93,000,000 miles

Now, armed with that data, let's look at some more staggering numbers: some stats about the universe.

Stats About the Universe

Our solar system consists of nine planets (including Pluto, which survived an attempt to demote it early in 1999, and Earth, which is the third from the Sun), along with their 31 moons, and hundreds of asteroids and meteors. All these bodies orbit around a large star we call the Sun.

Halfway from the center of our galaxy lies a band we call the Milky Way. Our solar system is actually one of many that are part of the Milky Way galaxy, which in turn is one of thousands of galaxies that make up the universe.

➤ The Sun, the star nearest to us, is, as we noted above, a mere 93,000,000 miles away. Its diameter is 860,000 miles.

➤ There are, as the late, great astronomer Carl Sagan so eloquently reminded us, "billions and billions of stars."

➤ Stars other than our Sun are so far away that we measure their distance in *light years* rather than miles.

➤ The next nearest star, Alpha Centauri, is 4.3 light years (or 26 million million miles) away from Earth.

➤ Our galaxy is believed to be 80,000 light years in diameter.

➤ There are millions and millions of other galaxies besides our own.

Feeling suitably humbled? That's the wonder of the universe—that each of us could be so small and yet so important at the same time. Because we are important, each and every one of us!

Speaking Y2K

A **light year** is the distance that light travels in one year, moving at its speed of 186,000 miles per second. One light year equals six million million miles.

Our Great Human Adventure

As we'll discuss in Chapter 26, the possibility of intelligent life elsewhere in the universe is a very good one. But where are these societies in relation to where we are in our evolution?

Just recently, scientists have discovered ice (which is, as you know, one form of water) not just on our Moon but on Mars as well. Water is considered the essential ingredient for life to develop. Does that mean that the Moon and Mars are in the incubation state Earth was millions of years ago? Or perhaps life once existed on those planets, and those small caps of ice are all that's left.

Our human adventure may be just one of many intelligent species' in the universe, and the new millennium is one more step in our great human adventure. What lies beyond the year 2000? It's time to find out.

The Least You Need to Know

➤ Americans lead lives of leisure—and we're getting collectively older.

➤ The world's population will probably reach close to nine billion people by 2050.

➤ The earth is the third planet in a solar system of nine planets that orbit around our Sun.

➤ Our solar system is one of millions and millions.

➤ Our human adventure may be just one of many intelligent species' in the universe.

Part 2

Meet the Dawn: Astrology

Using the ancient science of astrology, we look to the synergy of heaven and earth to explore some astrological cycles for the 21st century. From planetary pairs and their archetypal invitations to key cycles for the millennium, astrology can help us see what our millennial challenges will be.

Chapter 4

An Astro Primer

In This Chapter

➤ Astrology is a symbolic language of interconnectedness

➤ Signs are the "how" of astrology

➤ Energies, qualities, and elements show how each sign approaches activity

"Star light, star bright, first star I see tonight... "

Does this childhood chant bring back the thrill of seeing the stars on dark, clear nights? Did you once believe you *could* wish upon a star? When did you lose that childhood faith? And, more important, why? The truth is, humans feel awed and deeply moved by the stars and the night sky, and that's what astrology is all about.

Our guide for these chapters is counseling astrologer Sheila Belanger, whose areas of expertise include transpersonal psychology, ceremony, and shamanism.

Astrology Basics

Astrology is an ancient spiritual art that explores the relationship between the heavenly bodies in the sky and human experience here on Earth. As long as we've been here, we've been stargazers, seeking to find meaning in the cycles of the planets and stars in the sky. Our words and concepts for time in the western world derive from planetary cycles:

➤ A day is equal to the earth's cycle around its axis.

➤ A month is equal to the Moon's cycle around the Sun.

➤ A year is the equal to the earth's cycle around the Sun.

Speaking Y2K

Astrology is the study of planetary cycles and their connection to events and people on Earth.

In fact, it was only with the scientific revolution of the 17th century that the concepts behind astrology began to be questioned. Up until then, humans believed that the planets and stars were gods and goddesses. They watched the daily, monthly, yearly, and longer cycles of the planets to see what the gods were up to and what their messages to us were.

Time Capsule

It's part of human nature to create rituals and ceremonies to speak to the gods about our needs. In the darkest part of winter, for example, our ancestors gathered around bright fires to chant and pray to the Sun goddess and voice their longing for the return of her light and warmth. Warriors made offerings and petitioned the red planet Mars to connect to his strength and power, and young women gathered flowers in thanksgiving to Venus for their beauty and youth. It's only in modern times that we've lost our connection with the universe around us.

An Intuitive Art of the Spirit

As "modern" people, we may scoff at the "superstitions" of our ancestors. As our lives become more technologically advanced, we've lost our faith in a key philosophical belief of our ancestors: that all things, including humans and the heavenly bodies, are interconnected in a dynamic, spiritual, and energetic relationship. Modern science has made the once-wondrous lights in the sky lifeless chunks of matter circling the Sun.

As an intuitive art of the spirit, astrology is a symbolic language whose philosophical foundation is, "As above, so below; as within, so without." Astrologers carry the ancient world belief of interconnectedness forward into the 21st century. Like the ancient peoples, they track the location of the planets in the sky and their cyclic movements and interpret meanings in those locations and cycles.

Are You in Synch?

The symbolic basis of astrology actually has a scientific basis as well: *synchronicity*. This concept, the idea that coincidences are not accidental, comes from psychoanalysis pioneer Carl Jung. When astrologers say that what's happening overhead is a reflection of what's happening on Earth, they're talking about synchronous events.

Jung also discussed another concept that's important to astrology. While today the planets are no longer seen as gods, we can and do look at them as *archetypes*, which Jung called universal figures present in every person and culture. Arche-types are dynamic, instinctual patterns held by all humans, much like all birds hold the instinctual pattern of nest building within their natures.

Where our ancestors petitioned planetary gods for help in resolving physical challenges—such as getting the crops to grow successfully or helping find the migrating deer for winter food—modern astrologers seek communication with, and understanding of, the planetary archetypes to further growth in consciousness on both a personal and collective level. In Part 2 we'll show you every-

Speaking Y2K

Synchronicity is the concept, first discussed by psychoanalyst Carl Jung, that everything in the universe is interrelated. "As above, so below," is a synchronous concept.

Speaking Y2K

Archetype is a term used by psychoanalyst Carl Jung to represent patterns of the psyche, such as characters that have universal meaning. The Hero is an archetype, for example, and so is the Villain. Other archetypes include the Trickster, the Mentor, and the Sidekick (we're not making this up).

thing you need to know about astrology to find out how humankind will grow in the new century—and how *you* will too!

Planets Live in Signs and Houses

The main components of the astrology language are the planets, the 12 zodiac or Sun signs, and the 12 houses:

➤ The *planets* are the *what* of astrology. They symbolize key characters that live within your own personality and also within the culture at large as archetypes, or universal patterns. The planets are those heavenly bodies that, from our perspective on Earth, appear to rotate around us. The planets are the Sun, the Moon, Mercury, Venus, Mars, Jupiter, Saturn, Uranus, Neptune, and Pluto. In addition, we'll also include the comet Chiron and the North and South Nodes (which aren't actual planets) because all three are archetypes of evolution and dynamic change.

➤ The *zodiac* is the name of the circular path through the stars against which the earth travels in its annual orbit of the Sun. The zodiac is divided into 12 equal segments called the *zodiac signs.* From our perspective on Earth, it looks like the planets are circling around us as they move against the backdrop of the zodiac.

➤ The *signs* are the *how* of astrology. They are descriptions of how the planetary characters express their energies. The 12 zodiac signs are: Aries, Taurus, Gemini, Cancer, Leo, Virgo, Libra, Scorpio, Sagittarius, Capricorn, Aquarius, and Pisces.

➤ The *houses,* the *where* of astrology, are symbolic territories in your life in which the planetary characters hang out. Like rooms in your home, they're places where different activities take place: You sleep in the bedroom; eat in the dining room; socialize in the living room, and so on. Each of the 12 houses encompasses a specific arena of life and is the stage where the drama of the planets unfolds.

For example, the phrase "Mars in Scorpio in the 7th house" describes (what) the Warrior archetype (Mars), expressing itself (how) with emotional intensity (Scorpio) through the act of relating (where: the 7th house).

Astrology uses a set of symbols to represent key concepts. Astrologers "read" their language using a unique set of symbols for the planets and zodiac signs.

Ask Spaceship Earth

A spoken and written language combines nouns, verbs, and adjectives to form meaningful data. In astrology's language, you can think of the planets as nouns, and the signs and houses as verbs and adjectives that tell the unique story of the planetary characters in your personality and in the culture.

Astrological Signs and Their Symbols

Aries	♈		Libra	♎
Taurus	♉		Scorpio	♏
Gemini	♊		Sagittarius	♐
Cancer	♋		Capricorn	♑
Leo	♌		Aquarius	♒
Virgo	♍		Pisces	♓

Heavenly Bodies and Their Symbols

Sun	☉
Moon	☽
Mercury	☿
Venus	♀
Mars	♂
Jupiter	♃
Saturn	♄
Uranus	♅
Neptune	♆
Pluto	♇
North Node	☊
South Node	☋
Chiron	⚷

Time Capsule

Astrologers often use the analogy of a theatrical play to explain the three key components of the planets, the 12 zodiac or Sun signs, and the 12 houses. The planets are the performers, each playing a role that gives voice to a part of your personality and/or the culture. The signs are the costumes the actors wear in their roles. The houses are the areas of your life and in the culture in which they play out their parts.

Signs and Wonders

Now, let's examine the signs in more depth to discover the 12 different kinds of costumes the planets can wear in our personal and collective lives. Remember that the signs are sections of the zodiac, an imaginary band of the sky through which all the planets appear to move (including the Sun). From our perspective on Earth, the Sun travels through different signs in each of the four seasons. Each of the 12 *Sun signs* is divided into different categories that define their seasonal essence: *energies, qualities,* and *elements*.

➤ The twelve *Sun signs*—Aries ♈, Taurus ♉, Gemini ♊, Cancer ♋, Leo ♌, Virgo ♍, Libra ♎, Scorpio ♏, Sagittarius ♐, Capricorn ♑, Aquarius ♒, and Pisces ♓— describe how planetary characters express their energies.

➤ The two *energies*—*yin* and *yang*—describe the universal balancing act between the active and passive components of life.

➤ The three *qualities*—cardinal, fixed, and mutable—describe a three-fold developmental process that shows a sign's mode of operation.

➤ The four *elements*—fire, earth, air, and water—are the four basic components of life on the earth.

Energies: A Little Give and Take

Just as there are two sides to every coin, a sign can be either *yin* or *yang*. *Yin* represents indirect, receptive, female energy; while *yang* represents direct, active, male energy.

Astrological Signs and Their Energies

YIN	Taurus ♉
	Cancer ♋
	Virgo ♍
	Scorpio ♏
	Capricorn ♑
	Pisces ♓
YANG	Aries ♈
	Gemini ♊
	Leo ♌
	Libra ♎
	Sagittarius ♐
	Aquarius ♒

Qualities: Initiators, Stabilizers, and Adapters

The three qualities express a universal three-fold developmental process for cyclic growth. In life, something is created (born), develops its potential (grows), and then dies (transforms). The three qualities express that natural cycle. There are three qualities, cardinal, fixed, and mutable, each related to where in a season a sign falls.

The Qualities of Astrological Signs

CARDINAL	Aries ♈
	Cancer ♋
	Libra ♎
	Capricorn ♑
FIXED	Taurus ♉
	Leo ♌
	Scorpio ♏
	Aquarius ♒
MUTABLE	Gemini ♊
	Virgo ♍
	Sagittarius ♐
	Pisces ♓

➤ *Cardinal* signs, which begin each season, *initiate*. The cardinal signs are Aries in spring, Cancer in summer, Libra in autumn, and Capricorn in winter. People with cardinal signs are often the idea people: Independent, quick to start things, and often impatient. Don't expect these people to see a project through to its end—they're the ones who will get the ball rolling.

➤ *Fixed* signs, which occur at mid-season, *stabilize*. The fixed signs are Taurus in spring, Leo in summer, Scorpio in autumn, and Aquarius in winter. People with fixed signs are the persistent, reliable, determined folks of the zodiac. Once cardinal sign people have gotten that ball rolling, the fixed sign folks will make sure it keeps up its momentum.

➤ *Mutable* signs, which end each season, *change and adapt*. The mutable signs are Gemini in spring, Virgo in summer, Sagittarius in autumn, and Pisces in winter. People with mutable signs are problem-solvers. They're the ones who can find out why the ball's stopped rolling and get it rolling again, because they're adapters—flexible and resourceful.

Out of Time

Yin and *yang* don't correspond to "good" or "bad." It may be hard to conceive of positive and negative energies without those words, but that's precisely what *yin* and *yang* are all about. Your batteries always have a positive and negative connection, and they're not good or bad, are they? You can think of *yin* and *yang* the same way.

Elements: Smooth Operators

The four elements are like life's building blocks: earth in the bones of our skeletal system and flesh of our bodies; water in the blood that circulates through us; air moving through our lungs and relating us to the outside world; and fire in the spark of life essence that keeps us alive.

Astrological Signs and Their Elements

FIRE	Aries ♈
	Leo ♌
	Sagittarius ♐
EARTH	Taurus ♉
	Virgo ♍
	Capricorn ♑
AIR	Gemini ♊
	Libra ♎
	Aquarius ♒
WATER	Cancer ♋
	Scorpio ♏
	Pisces ♓

➤ The three *fire signs*, Aries, Leo, and Sagittarius, *inspire* and *enliven*. You'll find that people with these signs operate on an active, spirited level. High-energy idealists, they're unafraid of asserting themselves, and are often courageous and enthusiastic as well.

➤ People with *earth signs*, Taurus, Virgo, and Capricorn, *ground* and *embody*. These are literally the down-to-earth folks who operate on a physical level. They can come up with the best of systems to keep things running efficiently—the practical good managers among us.

➤ The *air signs*, Gemini, Libra, and Aquarius, *relate* and *create dialogue*. Here you'll find people who operate on a mental plane—the thinkers, talkers, and connectors.

➤ The *water signs*, Cancer, Scorpio, and Pisces, operate on the *emotional* plane. These are the intuitive romantics among us—the imaginative artists, the passionate lovers, and the compassionate caretakers and nurturers.

More About Sun Signs

What's the brightest light in the sky? The Sun ☉. It's so bright that, when it's daytime, it blocks our ability to see the stars and other planets (except for the Moon ☽). As an astrological archetype, the Sun symbolizes your conscious self and identity. Your conscious ego self usually blocks out awareness of your unconscious self just as the Sun blocks out the other planets.

You may not know much else about astrology, but you probably already know your Sun sign (the segment of the zodiac in which the Sun was traveling at the time of your birth). In case you don't, though, here's a zodiac to help you find it.

The zodiac: finding your Sun sign.

Your Universal Signature in Time and Space

Your *birth chart* (also called an astrological chart or natal chart) is a metaphor for you, and shows the position of the planets in their signs and houses for the moment you were born. A birth chart is created using the time, place, and date of your birth, and

Speaking Y2K

Your **birth chart** uses the date, time, and place of your birth to show the positions of the planets in their signs and houses at the moment of your birth. It creates a unique symbolic map of who you are.

Ask Spaceship Earth

You can think of your birth chart as a map of your potentials and possibilities. You may have the potential to be a great salesperson, for example, but are working as a research assistant. Knowing what your potentials and possibilities are can help you discover your personal path to happiness.

Speaking Y2K

An **event chart** uses the time, date, and place of an event to calculate its potentials and possibilities.

represents a symbolic outer map of your inner territory and life journey. In the birth chart, each of the planets (archetypal characters) are in a sign (role) and house (stage on which to express their unique identity in you).

To interpret the relationship between the "above" of the planets and the "below" of human experience on Earth, astrologers create your birth chart. The symbols in your birth chart represent the locations of the planets on that map. In the upcoming section "The Astrological Mandala: What Does a Chart Look Like?" we'll show you what a birth chart looks like.

Events Have Astrological Signatures, Too

Astrologers can calculate a birth chart for anything that is "born" in time and space. Naturally, we're most interested in the chart for our own birth and what it reveals about our life journey, but significant events in history also are "births" in time and space, and so they have birth charts, too.

For example, astrologers can interpret the personality and purpose of a country based on the time, date, and location that it was first created, whether through declaration, legislation, or even coup. An event like the signing of a peace treaty would carry the birth chart for the date, time, and location on Earth where the treaty was signed.

Astrologers can also calculate and interpret "events" in the sky, such as the time of a total solar eclipse or the coming together of several planets in one zodiac sign. These kinds of *event charts* symbolize messages from the planetary archetypes that describe current spiritual invitations to change and evolve on a collective level. In the next few chapters, we'll be looking at chart events and significant astrological cycles that will shed light on what's to come in the new millennium.

Just as your birth chart is calculated using the place of your birth, an event chart is calculated using the place on Earth where you want to examine the repercussions of such a collective invitation.

For example, if astrologers want to explore the key challenges and gifts of the next eclipse of the Sun as it impacts the United States, they would calculate the exact moment of the eclipse for Washington, D.C., the nation's capital. Washington, in other words, becomes the metaphoric representation for the United States.

The Astrological Mandala: What Does a Chart Look Like?

Now that you understand that a chart can be created for an event as well as a person, we'd like to show you what a chart looks like by showing you an event that's central to this book: the birth of the new millennium. Because we're especially interested in how the new millennium is going to impact the United States, we've created a chart for January 1, 2000 at 12:00 a.m. EST for Washington, D.C.

Natal Chart
Jan 1 2000
0:00 AM EST +5:00
Washington DC
38N54 077W02
Geocentric
Tropical
Placidus
True Node

Chart for the new millennium: the planets in their signs and houses at 12:00 a.m. EST, January 1, 2000.

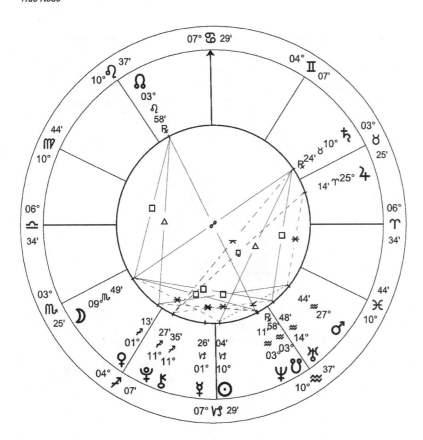

Note that we're using January 1, 2000 to signal the beginning of the new millennium because of the transition in numerology from a 1,000-year period of the "1" vibration to a 1,000-year period of the "2" vibration. (For more on numerology and the new millennium, see Part 3.) Some people use January 1, 2001 to mark the start of the new millennium.

Notice the symbols in each of the pie slices of this chart. The pie slices are the 12 houses, and the symbols represent the planets and signs. Note also that there are numbers next to the symbols. These represent the degree measurement of where in the sign each planet was located at the time of the event. While you don't need to understand these highly technical concepts, you may want to know more. If you do, we'd recommend *The Complete Idiot's Guide to Astrology* by Madeline Gerwick-Brodeur and Lisa Lenard (Alpha Books, 1997).

Circling the Zodiac: From Aries to Pisces

Before we go any further, let's take a look at some basic characteristics for each Sun sign. It's important to note here that Western astrology uses the seasons to determine Sun signs, not the location of constellations in the sky. This is because constellations have shifted over time.

Around two thousand years ago, the zodiac sign and the corresponding constellation of the same name were in the same place in the sky. This was at the time of the Greek Hellenistic civilization, with its focus on mathematics and logic. Modern Western astrology has its roots in that patriarchal Greek world view and has kept the same sign designation for the seasons that was true at that time. In other words, the constellations have shifted, but the seasonal metaphors they represent haven't.

We can learn more about each Sun sign's behavior by exploring the activities that occur in the corresponding season for that Sun sign.

♈ Aries, the Ram: March 21 to April 20

Aries represents **cardinal, fire,** *yang* energy. It's the initiating sign of spring, when we break ground for new projects, plant seeds in the earth, and generally feel frisky and rarin' to go after winter's dark and cold stillness. Here's the first sign out of the starting gate, the person who's always racing to get ahead.

People with an Aries Sun sign are courageous pioneers; so courageous, in fact, that they can sometimes be foolhardy. Their directness makes them cut straight to the heart of things—which can sometimes make them appear tactless or rude, sort of like a young bulb thrusting itself up through the dirt to demand space in the garden.

Because they like challenges, you'll often find Arians in leadership positions. It's a good place for these energetic, take-charge people; their enthusiasm inspires others to follow their lead.

♉ *Taurus, the Bull: April 20 to May 21*

Taurus represents **fixed**, **earth**, *yin* energy. It's the stabilizing sign of spring, when fruit trees are flowering, bees are buzzing, and the garden is filled with the luscious fragrances of the earth awakening. People with Taurus Sun signs are both sensual and grounded. In a no-nonsense way, they claim their space in the garden and settle in to grow those roots deep down into the earth. They know how to hold on to what they've got.

There's no reason for Taureans to change, though: They've got good jobs, material comfort, a love of the senses, and down-to-earth values. They can, in fact, be down-right stubborn if you do try to shake up their world.

Time Capsule

Do you know any bull? Chances are, you do know a bull story or two. Maybe it's simply a bull in a ring or field, or maybe it's a story with larger mythological implications, such as the story of the Minotaur. Whatever the story, it serves to illustrate the archetypal motifs by which we identify Taurus: groundedness, stubbornness, and a strength born of fortitude.

♊ *Gemini, the Twins: May 21 to June 22*

Gemini represents **mutable**, **air**, *yang* energy. It's the adapting sign of spring, when we juggle the many tasks required to maintain the garden: watering, weeding, fertilizing, and so on. This translates to people who are adaptable, quick, and dynamic—and people with Gemini Sun signs are indeed the rapid movers of the zodiac.

This is also the time of children impatiently awaiting the end of school and all the fun activities of summer. This is the sign of quick wit and glib words, but Geminis can also be impatient at times. Inventive and clever, these folks are always eager to try something new—even if it means dropping something old in the process. This trait sometimes causes them to be scattered and flighty—overwhelmed by too many details.

Because they're clever, Geminis are resourceful, good at coming at problems from angles others may not have considered. They help us remember to try new options and experiment with life.

♋ *Cancer, the Crab: June 22 to July 23*

Cancer represents **cardinal**, **water**, *yin* energy. This is the initiating sign of summer, when we focus on the family and our emotional "clan": summer vacations, family reunions, barbeques at the beach, and neighborhood Fourth-of-July block parties. At heart, Cancerians are nurturers and seek to feel emotionally safe and settled. Cancer folk happily can give their family and home all the warmth and attention they need.

At the same time, Cancer natives' initiating nature empowers them to reach out for support and ask for the same warmth and attention for themselves. Though, like their namesake crab, they may hide their emotions behind a hard shell, they are dependable and loving as well as oversensitive and moody. Life with a Cancer will have its ups and downs—as well as its sideways and backwards—but deep emotional warmth and love is their gift.

♌ *Leo, the Lion: July 23 to August 22*

Leo represents **fixed**, **fire**, *yang* energy: inspiration + stability + activity. It's the sign at the heart of summer, when we embrace all the joys of that delicious season: splashing in a city pool; necking in the cornfields; gobbling down ice cream sundaes; and enjoying a picnic in the park while a band plays on. Leos are the fun-loving, charismatic leaders of the zodiac, who know how to fall in love with life.

Charisma is a by-product of self-confidence, a trait Leos have in abundance. These are creative and willful people, and they can be both courageous and demanding. They're also loyal—and so expect loyalty in return.

Ask Spaceship Earth

Leo's a lion, so if you remember the traits that are archetypally associated with lions, you'll have no trouble remembering the traits of Leos: courage, strength, pride, and regalness.

One of the strongest traits of those with Leo Sun signs is their tenacity—they're not likely to let go of what they've got a hold of, whether it's a friend or an idea. They're also good at grabbing and holding the spotlight; in fact, they fully expect that it will shine on them, and most often it does, deservedly so.

♍ *Virgo, the Virgin: August 22 to September 22*

Virgo represents **mutable**, **earth**, *yin* energy, another of the zodiac's more intriguing combinations, perfect for the adapting sign of summer. It's time to wrap up the Leo party and prepare for the beginning of the school term and the garden's harvest. People with Virgo Sun signs are resourceful and practical, able to discern what's truly important. This is the time to separate the wheat from the chaff, to recognize what's necessary to sustain us through autumn and winter.

What this translates to are people who examine everything in great detail in order to discover the best way to make things better. Virgo is all about service, and, more specifically, service to a greater good and holistic healing.

People with Virgo Sun signs may appear calm, but inside, they can be cauldrons of restless energy. "Analyze, improve, and heal" is their mantra, and if their world seems perfect for the moment, they'll seek to improve yours. Organization and detail are their forte, and they'll be delighted to mold your world to their specifications. Virgo natives are challenged to not just sacrifice themselves in service to others and the earth, but to also be willing to receive help and support from others.

♎ *Libra, the Scales: September 22 to October 23*

In Libra, we find **cardinal, air,** *yang* energy. It's the initiating sign of autumn, when we seek to restore balance to our world after the joyous chaos of summer. The days grow shorter and colder; birds migrate to warmer climates; the autumn leaves display glorious, brilliant colors in their simple dying process; we amend the garden soil to bring it into balance.

This is also the time when we return to the shelter of homes, restaurants, and local coffeehouses to socialize and catch up with our friends and community. Librans like to actively promote relationships and social activities; in fact, they're the charmers of the zodiac. They seek harmony and balance in all things, thus their representation by the scales.

Partnership is a byword of Libra, and its natives have many friends. They're also high-principled, but weigh every issue carefully, on its merits and demerits. Sometimes, in fact, people with Libra Sun signs can seem indecisive as they continually look at both sides of an issue. It's hard to please all the people all the time, but if anyone will try, it's Libra.

♏ *Scorpio, the Scorpion: October 23 to November 22*

Scorpio combines **fixed, water,** *yin* energy, adding up to focused, deep-seated emotion. It's the stabilizing sign of autumn, when we get serious about making it through the winter. The light is dying, and we add mulch and cover tender plants to protect them from fierce winter winds. Behind the surface of ghost costumes, apple bobbing, and Halloween parties, there's a hint of the unearthly and mysterious in the night air. True to the heart of autumn, Scorpios are the most intense of the zodiac, with their power rooted in passion.

That word, passion, is a key word in the Scorpio person's resume. You'll sometimes find Scorpio and sex coupled, and there's no doubt this is true. But there's more to it than that: The Scorpio Sun sign is seeking something deep and powerful, and it's not always something they understand.

♐ *Sagittarius, the Archer: November 22 to December 22*

Sagittarius represents **mutable, fire,** *yang* energy, and its natives are lively, inspired, and philosophical as they search for the truth of things with a capital "T." Sagittarius is the adapting sign at the end of autumn, the time to celebrate and honor the harvest and gifts of the past seasons. We think about the meaning of life, offer thanks for abundance, and reach out to our fellow humans. Equally, we get into high gear as we race from one holiday party to another. This is the paradox of Sagittarius.

The high spirits of people with Sagittarius Sun signs make them a lot of fun, and their enthusiasm is contagious. They seek the freedom to explore their world through ideas, travel, sports, and higher education.

Honest and direct (their symbol's an archer, after all), Sagittarius folk believe in truth, especially universal truths. Their challenge is not to climb on the soapbox of dogmatic belief that their truth is the only one. Sometimes their search for The Answer can make them interested in ideas that others question, but seeking is the Sagittarian's *raison d'être.*

♑ *Capricorn, the Sea-Goat: December 22 to January 21*

Capricorn's energies are **cardinal, earth,** and *yin,* and this makes them determined, systematic, and ever the achiever. It's the initiating sign of winter, when we organize ourselves for the coming New Year with resolutions and a commitment to disciplined self-improvement. The Capricorn native is both goal-oriented and intense, resulting in a singular command and self-control. The challenge for these adept natives is not to take on too much responsibility, or misuse power by inappropriately controlling others.

Being a Capricorn Sun sign is all about responsibility, whether it's for one's children or society as a whole. Capricorns are determined to build for the future, and it's this determination that leads to their efficiency in all they do. But just like their symbol, the sea-goat (a goat with a dolphin's tail), they can also have a hidden nature that is sensitive and deeply connected to the earth's rhythms.

Even as they seek their pinnacle of stability, Capricorns may surprise others with their dolphin's tail in the waters of wit and humor. They can be pessimists, too, but this cynicism can contribute to the power their responsible organization can engender.

♒ *Aquarius, the Water Bearer: January 21 to February 19*

In Aquarius we find **fixed, air,** *yang* energy. It's the stabilizing sign of winter, when we settle in with a hot cup of tea and a good book to navigate through the heart of winter. While our bodies are quietly resting indoors, our minds are racing with new ideas, staying connected to the community through phone and e-mail, and envisioning new projects for the upcoming spring. Aquarius natives carry inventive idealism coupled with a certain eccentricity: They're the crazy inventors of the zodiac, and some of its more famous residents include Mozart and Virginia Woolf.

Because this is a fixed sign, people with Aquarius Sun signs are both persistent and determined—even if what they're after is a little off the beaten path. Aquarius natives are particularly known to be both progressive and open-minded, yet at the same time quite stubborn about what they believe in. Sometimes their motto is "My mind's made up, don't confuse me with the facts."

Ask Spaceship Earth

Why is Aquarius an air sign rather than a water sign? Because it's the water *bearer*, not the water itself.

Aquarians are the humanitarians of the zodiac, but they also appear aloof or apart. That's because they've so often got their heads literally in the clouds. Radicals, renegades, or revolutionaries, in one way or another, they're always ahead of their time in their thinking.

♓ *Pisces, the Fishes: February 19–March 21*

Pisces represents **mutable, water, *yin*** energy, making this an adaptable, deep, and passive sign. It's the adapting sign of winter, coming at the end of the seasonal year, between the worlds of death and life. The earliest spring bulbs just poke out, reminding us of rebirth after the death process of winter. We celebrate resurrection of life at Easter and the exodus of the Jews from Egypt at Passover, and feel grateful for surviving another passage through the darkness.

Pisces natives recognize that two worlds can coexist beside one another, sometimes leading to confusion about which reality is the most important one. They can be deeply spiritual and compassionate, connected to the world of dreams and imagination.

At the same time, though, Pisceans may live too much in their imagination, and there can be a danger of dependence on one drug or another, whether it's another person or alcohol or cigarettes. Still, their connection to the "other realm" can make them the most sympathetic of listeners and the most caring of friends.

In our modern "rational" world, it's a little harder for those who live by faith. No one goes by faith more than those with a Pisces Sun. Dreamy and spiritual, Pisceans may seem impractical as well, but they're often seeing the other worlds that exist beside our own.

Little Fish in a Big Universe

To use a Piscean metaphor, now that we know more about our own Sun sign characteristics and birth chart signatures, let's take a look at how broader cycles and patterns in the heavens can reveal what's happening here on Earth. You'll be able to use what you've learned in this chapter and the next to understand just how we all fit into the universe as the new millennium begins.

The Least You Need to Know

➤ The signs are the "how" of astrology.

➤ Planets live in signs and houses.

➤ A birth chart represents a moment in time and space.

➤ Your Sun sign is a metaphor for who you are.

➤ Events can have a birth chart too.

Chapter 5

Heaven on Earth

In This Chapter

➤ Planets are the "what" and houses are the "where" of astrology

➤ All about retrogrades

➤ Aspecting the future

➤ Transiting planets are symbolic change agents

➤ Paired planetary cycles are symbolic maps of the times

➤ The Nodes are karmic portals

We'd like you to think of the planets as symbolic characters who behave in certain ways, for example, Venus as a Lover or Mars as a Warrior. This means that once you understand a particular planet's dynamic, you can begin to explore interplanetary relationships as well.

The birth chart is similarly a metaphor for planetary interaction. As planets move through their orbits in the sky, they enter into relationships with each other, which are represented on the chart of a moment. Charting moments can help us plan for the future, and so, plan for the new millennium as well.

The Soul Has Many Mansions: The 12 Houses

We looked briefly at the houses in your birth chart in Chapter 4, but now we'd like to explore them a little more fully. Remember that your birth chart is a kind of symbolic "soul map" of your life journey, describing your personal potentials, challenges, and unique personality. Each of the 12 houses represents an area of your life, the various rooms where your story unfolds. From the 1st house of the self to the 12th house of the unconscious, every possible location for your life's story is represented. The following chart shows the houses and their corresponding areas of life.

The 12 houses of the zodiac.

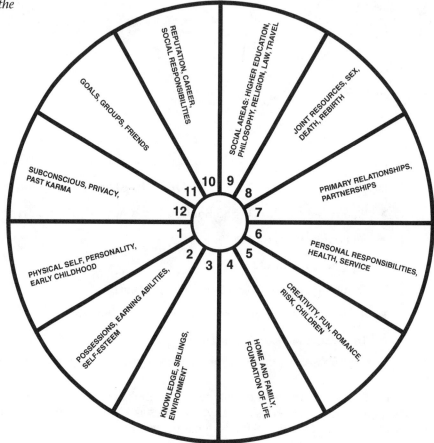

When an astrologer calculates the houses for your birth chart, she uses the actual physical location of your birthplace on Earth. The chart is a symbolic "snapshot" of the sky as viewed from your birthplace at the moment of your birth. You can think of the chart as a large spoked bicycle wheel containing 12 segments, which stands perpendicular to the earth and is superimposed onto the sky as if half of the wheel were above the horizon and the other half hidden below the horizon.

In this example, the person at your birthplace (let's say it's you) is standing on the earth at the hub of the bicycle wheel. The straight lines that radiate out from the hub divide the semicircle of the visible sky into six segments. The lower half of the wheel also divides the hidden part of the sky below the horizon into six segments.

The segment that begins at the eastern horizon and sweeps out downward to go below the earth is designated the 1st house. The next segment you come to as you move below the earth is called the 2nd house. The third segment that would end at the point directly below the earth is the 3rd house, and so on.

You keep moving counterclockwise from segment to segment down below the earth toward the western horizon, then above it around to the zenith (the point directly above the earth), and finishing up back at the eastern horizon point, until a total of 12 houses have been described. The 1st through 6th houses lie below the earth's horizon; the 7th through 12th houses lie above the earth's horizon. The zodiac signs and planets appear to move through these houses (bicycle wheel segments).

An Earth's-Eye View of the Solar System

Another way to think of the zodiac wheel is as a giant roulette wheel in the sky. If you stargaze on a clear night and watch the eastern horizon, over time you'll see stars rise up in the east and gradually move across the night sky toward the west. Depending on how far north you live, the zodiac "roulette wheel" will spin directly overhead or appear at a tilted angle. Instead of numbered slots, the zodiac roulette wheel is divided into the 12 equal slots that are the zodiac signs, each one encompassing 30 degrees of the 360-degree wheel.

From your perspective as stargazer, the planets also appear to rise in the east and go around the sky and set in the west. The planets are like balls spinning against the backdrop of the roulette wheel. If we freeze that roulette wheel for a moment in time, the "balls" (planets) fall into a segment of the wheel (a zodiac sign). So when someone says "My Sun sign is Virgo," it means that, from our perspective on Earth, when that person was born, the Sun "ball" appeared to fall into the "slot" of the zodiac sign of Virgo.

The Sun, the Moon, the Nodes, and the Planets

It's helpful to think of *planets* (which in astrology include the Sun and the Moon) as different archetypal energies within us. Some of these energies are personal (Sun ☉, Moon ☽, Mercury ☿, Venus ♀, and Mars ♂); some are social (Jupiter ♃ and Saturn ♄); and some are transpersonal (Uranus ♅, Neptune ♆, and Pluto ♇). All together, the planets are the "what" of astrology.

The following table introduces the planets, including their symbols and energies. You may want to tab this page for future reference.

Speaking Y2K

The **planets** are the "what" of astrology. They represent the different archetypal energies within us all.

The Planets

The Personal Planets

Sun ☉	Your self and your will
Moon ☽	Your feminine energies and instinctive side
Mercury ☿	Your thinking and communication
Venus ♀	Your approach to values, art, and possessions
Mars ♂	Your masculine energy, courage, action, and physical energy

The Social Planets

Jupiter ♃	Your luck, philosophy, and growth
Saturn ♄	Your rules and regulations

The Transpersonal Planets

Uranus ♅	Your originality and the unexpected
Neptune ♆	Your idealism, spirituality, and dreams
Pluto ♇	Your capacity for transformation

It will be helpful for you to remember that every planet tells a story. Some of these stories you may already know, such as that of the warrior Mars or the sea deity Neptune. These stories relate how a planet seems to "behave," and that, in turn, when combined with signs in houses, can tell stories about personal and collective behavior.

Like the Sun and the Moon, the *Nodes* aren't planets either, but their energies are included when we talk about human behavior. The paired North Node ☊ and South Node ☋ are karmic portals, doorways to your spiritual past and future.

Think of the South Node as lessons you've already learned. We like to call this the doorway to the known or past, or the path of least resistance. The North Node represents your possibilities, the doorway to your future. It's in these areas that you'll find your potential for growth, along with the challenges that may come with it. Some astrologers interpret the South Node to represent the skills and tendencies you acquired in past lives and the North Node to represent the areas your soul wants to explore to evolve for future lives.

Speaking Y2K

The **Nodes**, North and South, are a paired set of points that relate to the Moon's orbit around the earth. Their energies show what behaviors you've inherited and where your potential for growth lies.

What's a Retrograde?

Planets move at different speeds, and when one planet is moving faster than another, there's a period of time when from the vantage point of one, the other appears to be moving backward. When other planets appear from our earthly perspective to be moving backward, they are said to be *retrograde*.

Speaking Y2K

When planets are **retrograde**, their motion from our perspective on Earth appears to be backward. Planets do not actually move backwards, though.

The concept of retrograde planets is important because our perceptions of the energies of the planets change when this happens. The planets are symbolically inviting us to slow down, review, and reflect on their energies and stories. In most cases, their energies seem to be reversed: Mars appears to become more passive, for example; Mercury slower to communicate. Retrogrades aren't "bad," but we do need to be aware of when they're occurring so we can review and plan for things that may not go as they ordinarily would.

Transiting retrogrades, which occur in our day-to-day lives, naturally affect all of us. Something will feel different when a particular planet is retrograde. Your normally amenable partner may seem to be picking fights all the time when Venus is retrograde, for example.

Time Capsule

Ever been in a speeding car that passed a train going in the same direction? At first, the train is ahead of you. Then your car catches up and overtakes the train. As you pass the train, it appears to move backwards, even though it is still moving in the same direction as you. This is a case of a retrograde train.

A *personal retrograde* is a fancy way of saying that a planet was retrograde at the moment you were born. That means that its reversed energies may hold special keys about why you behave the way you do. People with personal retrograde planets, in fact, often need to focus internally with the retrograde planet's energies first before expressing its energies in an outward way.

Speaking Y2K

Transiting retrogrades, which occur in our day-to-day lives, occur according to the movements of the planets, and affect us all. A **personal retrograde** is a fancy way of saying that a planet was retrograde at the moment you were born.

Speaking Y2K

An **aspect** between two planets in your birth chart is a measurement of the spatial relationship between the two planets in the sky for the moment you were born. Astrologers also track the spatial relationship between different planets as they move in their orbit around the Sun, and how they **aspect** one another at any given moment in time.

When Planets Are in Aspect to Each Other

An *aspect* between two planets in your birth chart is a measurement of the spatial relationship between the two planets in the sky for the moment you were born. Remember, your chart is like a freeze-frame snapshot of the planets in the sky at the moment of your birth. Planets move at different speeds as they orbit around the Sun. This causes their spatial relationship to one another to constantly change. In addition to the "snapshot" of your birth chart, astrologers track the spatial relationships (aspects) between the planets themselves as they orbit the Sun.

Aspects are all about relationships. How far apart was Venus from Mars on the day of your birth? And what does that symbolize about the inner relationship between the Warrior (Mars) and the Lover (Venus) inside of you? What happens when transiting Mars conjuncts the place in the zodiac where Mars was located at your birth (also called a "Mars return")?

While there are quite a few aspects, only six of them are considered major, and those are the ones we'll be concentrating on here. Aspects are literally the degrees between planets on the circle of your birth chart. A circle is 360 degrees, and aspects form angles on that circle.

Here are the six most important aspects, their angles, and their meanings.

The Six Major Aspects

Aspect	Angle	Meaning
Conjunction	0°	Strength, emphasis, unity
Square (1st quarter)	90°	Challenge, initiate external action for change and growth
Square (3rd quarter)	270°	Challenge, initiate internal action for change and release
Opposition	180°	Negotiation, need for balance
Trine	120°	Harmony, ease
Sextile	60°	Opportunity, attraction

Every planet in our solar system moves around the Sun, each one with a different orbital period, which is the time it takes for the planet to complete one orbit around the Sun. The big giant Jupiter takes about 12 years to go once around the Sun. In contrast, cold tiny Pluto at the fringes of the solar system takes about 248 years for its orbital period. In short, each planet has its own rhythm in its dance around the Sun.

Personal Planets	*Orbit*
Mercury ☿	88 days
Venus ♀	225 days
Mars ♂	2 years
Social Planets	*Orbit*
Jupiter ♃	12 years
Saturn ♄	29$\frac{1}{2}$ years
Transpersonal Planets/Points	*Orbit*
Chiron ⚷	50$\frac{1}{2}$ years
Uranus ♅	84 years
Neptune ♆	164 years
Pluto ♇	248 years
North/South Nodes ☊/☋	18$\frac{1}{2}$ years

What this means is that different planets will aspect one another in the sky in accordance with the cycles specific to their orbital periods. It also means that, over time, a planet can make different aspects to its own position in your birth chart. For example, if Jupiter was in the zodiac sign of Libra at the time of your birth, then approximately six years after your birth (one half of Jupiter's 12-year orbital period), Jupiter will be in the zodiac sign of Aries and oppose itself (be 180 degrees away from its position in the sky at your birth). It sounds confusing, but it's really not—and it provides important keys about why certain things happen to you at certain times.

Paired Planetary Cycles Are Symbolic Maps of the Times

Far more than a study of fixed moments in time, astrology is a study of cycles, whether of planets, societies, or individual lives. You can think of planetary cycles, in fact, as corresponding to cycles of human consciousness. Astrologers are interested in tracking the synchronistic link between what the planets were doing in the "above" at the time that important personal and collective human events were occurring on the "below" of the earth.

Speaking Y2K

Planetary pairs are two planets that have a unique timeline for completing their cycles with each other.

As we noted in the previous section, each planet has its own timetable to complete one orbit around the Sun. Similarly, each set of *planetary pairs* has its own timeline for com-pleting its cycle with one another. For example, Jupiter and Saturn come together in the same place in the sky (a conjunction) about every 20 years, while Neptune and Pluto come together in the same place in the sky only about every 493 years.

By tracking the time periods and corresponding events in history for the various paired planetary cycles, astrologers can interpret the current collective status of the relationship between the two planets in question. This information helps us all to know the invitations from the planetary archetypes to evolve and transform, both collectively and personally.

Planets That Are Symbolic Change Agents for the 21st Century

A change agent is someone who shakes up the status quo and catalyzes change and transformation. Some planets carry more weight as symbolic change agents for human-kind than others. Astrologers look at the transpersonal planets (Pluto, Neptune, and Uranus) and the social planets (Jupiter and Saturn) far more closely than the inner planets. Why not the personal planets as change agents? Closer to both the Sun and Earth, these planets transit more quickly. This means that their effects are not so globally profound as those of the outer planets.

First, let's take a quick look at how each of the transpersonal planets' transits affects both the individual and the larger world. The mythic archetype corresponding to each of these three planets is a deity whose territory lies outside the realm of human control (*transpersonal* means "beyond the personal ego"). Uranus is a sky deity; Neptune is a deity of the sea; and Pluto is a deity of the Underworld or inside the earth. If you're interested in learning more about transits, we once again refer you to *The Complete Idiot's Guide to Astrology*.

Planet	Transit Effect
Pluto ♇	Deep and lasting change; transformation of power and intimacy issues; conscious dying
Neptune ♆	Imagination; transcendence; dissolving of illusions, addictions, and fear
Uranus ♅	Innovation; unexpected changes; liberation from the status quo

The Social Planets: Jupiter and Saturn

Saturn and Jupiter are called the social planets because they symbolize the balance between expansion and contraction, growth and appropriate limitation. This balancing act is at the heart of any society's rules of conduct. To live successfully with other people, after all, we each have to give a little and take a little.

Transiting Saturn is all about integrity and self-authority, the capacity to take charge and organize your life. Transiting Saturn corresponds to times of assessing your life: Is it on track and working for you? And what, if anything, is your responsibility to improve it?

Transiting Jupiter involves expansion and education, and that translates to anything from travel to making friends. This may be a time when you go back to school or join a new church or synagogue. The house in which the Jupiter transit occurs in your birth chart can indicate where in your life the invitation to grow and expand is developing.

Globally, transiting Saturn and Jupiter have similar effects, but on a larger scale. Saturn transits invite global reassessment and the challenge to be self-responsible, while transiting Jupiter invites broadening global perspectives and philosophical understanding.

Wild Card Ambassadors: Chiron and the Centaurs, the Comets

In November of 1977, astronomer Charles Kowal discovered a small heavenly body orbiting between the planets Saturn and Uranus, which appeared to be a small planet (a planetoid) or an asteroid. Kowal named it Chiron, after the mythical centaur (half-man, half-horse), a gifted warrior, teacher, and healer.

Eleven years after that discovery, astronomers recognized that Chiron was actually an unusually large comet. Astronomers believe that Chiron originated in the Kuiper belt, which lies on the fringes of our solar system, beyond the orbits of Neptune and Pluto, and contains the remains of the nebula that originally formed our solar system.

More recently, astronomers have discovered several other Chiron-like comets in the Kuiper belt, which they call the "centaurs." The centaurs are symbolic ambassadors from the edges of our known solar system. Chiron and the centaurs are like wild cards from beyond the frontiers (from the wilderness) of our own solar system, symbolically inviting us to cross over into uncharted territories.

Time Capsule

Chiron has an orbital period of around $50^1/_2$ years. Its orbit is shaped like an egg and is inclined to the plane of the solar system. As it orbits around the Sun, Chiron actually crosses the orbits of both Saturn and Uranus (the astrological gateway to the transpersonal planets). Chiron bridges the realities between Saturn (consensus reality) and Uranus (liberating, alternative realities). It's the symbolic bridge between the known (Saturn) and the unknown (Uranus).

A shapeshifter is someone who is able to change identities at will. Chiron acts like a shapeshifter, so we call it a "symbolic shapeshifter." Consider: Is this body an asteroid or a comet? Where does it come from? This small comet is causing quite a stir in the astronomical community. Its very nature is forcing astronomers to change how they view our solar system. They need to make room in their reality for objects, which originate from the edge of our solar system.

At the same time, Chiron is a symbolic wounded healer and shaman. The mythic Chiron was an immortal healer who couldn't heal himself from a physical wound and chose to die to relinquish his woundedness. And shamans are shapeshifters who actively move between different spiritual realities to effect healing and to restore balance and harmony to their communities. Shamans can do this because of their own personal initiation with woundedness.

In his myth, Chiron worked to unite his unruly and violent fellow centaurs with the civilizing influence of reason and peace. Because he's part animal, Chiron knows intimately the path of animal wisdom. In his struggle to heal himself of his own woundedness, Chiron's story is one of a shamanic healing crisis.

As a comet, Chiron shape-shifts between asteroid and comet form, and, like a skilled shaman, catalyzes his people (astronomers) to awaken to new realities.

Chiron's myth presents the spiritual quest to make a paradigm shift from a wounded belief system into a healed one. Often in that journey, you must face your darker self and in so doing become reborn into a new self. The path of healing through transmutation of our woundedness is a familiar one to many who are on a conscious evolutionary journey. Chiron the mythical healer symbolizes the human process of shape shifting woundedness into wholeness by changing our consciousness (entering into a paradigm shift) about our woundedness.

Transpersonal Planets: Uranus, Neptune, and Pluto

The transpersonal planets are Uranus, Neptune, and Pluto. They are the three outer-most planets in our solar system and are not visible to the naked eye. The following table shows the archetypal energy of these planets.

Transpersonal Planet	Archetypal Energy
Uranus ♅	Liberation
Neptune ♆	Visioning
Pluto ♇	Death or transformation

Uranus is named after a sky deity and symbolizes the principle of sudden and radical change. Uranus is also connected to mythic Prometheus, who in Greek myth stole fire from the gods for the benefit of humankind. Communing with Uranus is like dancing with the cosmic trickster: Reality just isn't what it used to be.

Uranus is symbolic of the energies of freedom, breakthrough, and unexpected change. Change agent Uranus calls you to integrate radically different parts of yourself into your conscious life. These are the parts of you that don't behave or follow the consensus rules of the family or culture. When Uranus is around, you often need to break free from being the duti-ful son or well-behaved daughter. The spiritual gift of Uranus is *ego liberation*, to explore the other dimensions of your self that allow for authentic self-expression.

Neptune is named after an ocean deity and represents the force to dissolve consensus reality and honor vision, dreams, and spirituality. An invitation from change agent Neptune is like a mystical sea nymph beckoning you to submerge into your emotional depths. Will you find ecstasy, artistic power, sorrow, vision, fear, and/or the Divine itself there?

Neptune's issues connect with dreams, visions, universal truths, self-deception, escapism, addic-tions, psychic phenomena, imagination, and other aspects of non-ordinary reality. Neptune brings the gift of *ego dissolution*, so that you can explore your relationship to oneness and merging with all life.

> **Speaking Y2K**
>
> Ego is our conscious identity, or the roles we take on in our family or culture. In **ego liberation,** we ac-tively take off those roles and experi-ment with others, for example, the stockbroker who chucks it all to open a B & B in Vermont. In contrast, **ego dissolution** is when you release or surrender those behaviors, such as when you stop worrying—or stop arguing with your mother-in-law.

Pluto is symbolically the "Lord of the Underworld," representing the capacity to die, trans-mute, and regenerate. Pluto is also Kali, the Goddess of Destruction and Rebirth. Pluto is the guide to the Underworld, through whom you confront issues of death and regen-eration, along with, according to astrologer Jeffrey Green, the evolution of your soul.

Change agent Pluto invites you to confront disempowerment on inner and outer levels and to face and integrate the major shadow aspects of yourself. Pluto calls you to the task of ego transmutation and purification by examining issues of mortality and your willingness to release the false self that was created in response to family and cultural expectations. Pluto helps you to seek deep emotional honesty in all facets of life.

Karmic Portals: The Nodes

As we've discussed, the Nodes are points in the sky that symbolize the intersection of the earth's orbit around the Sun and the Moon's orbit around the earth.

Let's first think of the Moon as symbolic of our deepest emotional and instinctive needs—the infant within us who needs to be safe; the animal within us who needs to be wild. The earth, in turn, symbolizes our experience in earthly, or material, form. The Moon's Nodes symbolize the patterns we need to release and heal in order to evolve on our karmic path through the process of our earthly incarnation.

As we discuss the potential of the new millennium, the Moon's Nodes will play an important part in that unfolding.

The Least You Need to Know

➤ The planets are the "what" of astrology.

➤ The houses are the "where" of astrology.

➤ Retrograde planets' energies appear to be reversed.

➤ Planetary aspects explore planetary relationships.

➤ Paired planetary cycles are symbolic maps of the times.

➤ Planets are symbolic change agents.

 **Astrological Cycles for the 21st Century**

In This Chapter

➤ Planetary aspects are symbolic gateways to consciousness

➤ Planetary cycles are roadmaps for individual and collective growth

➤ Jupiter–Saturn aspects translate to social change and manifestation

➤ Cycles with the transpersonal planets translate to profound transformation of the personal ego

➤ Birth charts for the millennia

As we noted in Chapter 5, each set of transiting planetary pairs has its own timeline for completing the cycle between one another. Remember that astrologers track the timeline and position of a planetary pair's cycle to interpret the current status of the relationship between the two planets in question. For example, we can examine the current phase of the cycle between Saturn (the Builder) and the Pluto (the Transformer) to discover the cosmic invitation to transform our current personal and collective life structures.

Once we understand them, planetary cycles can be like roadmaps that guide us to understand current opportunities for individual and global evolution. In this chapter, we'll explore in more detail the various combinations of planetary pairs as roadmaps for the new millennium.

Gateways of Initiation for Each Paired Planetary Cycle

Two planets in relationship to one another (called, as we discussed in Chapter 5, a *planetary pair)* follow natural cycles as they move against the backdrop of the zodiac wheel and come together, separate, and rejoin one another in the sky. Most of us already know or watch the most important paired planetary cycle of all, that of the Sun and the Moon.

A Quick Trip Through the Moon's Phases

Humans track four major phases of the Moon: the New Moon, First Quarter, Full Moon, and Last Quarter. These phases correspond to the apparent movement of the Moon with respect to the Sun in a 360-degree circle. The Moon is in waxing phase when it is 0 to 180 degrees away from the Sun, and it's in waning phase when it is 180 to 360 degrees away from the Sun.

A New Moon occurs when the Sun and Moon are in the same place in the sky, which, as you may recall from Chapter 5, is called a conjunction. The First Quarter phase occurs when the Sun and Moon are 90 degrees away from one another; the Full Moon occurs when they're opposite (180 degrees away from) one another; and the Third Quarter (also called Last Quarter) phase occurs when the Sun and the Moon are 270 degrees apart.

Time Capsule

These four major Sun/Moon phases happen every month. More rare are solar (New Moon) and lunar (Full Moon) eclipses, which occur a few times a year. In Chapter 7, we discuss the significant solar eclipse of August 1999, that leads to the denouement of the old millennium, and the rare New Moon of May 2000 that ushers us into the new millennium.

Other Planetary Pair Cycles

Other planetary pairs have similar cycles with one another. For example, a *Jupiter-Saturn conjunction* cycle occurs approximately every 20 years and happens when Jupiter and Saturn appear to be in the same place in the sky, just like the Sun and Moon during a New Moon phase. A *First Quarter Saturn Square Neptune* cycle occurs when Saturn has moved 90 degrees (a Square angle) away from Neptune in the sky, which means these planets are one-fourth of the zodiac wheel away from one another. This Saturn-Neptune cycle point is like the First Quarter Moon phase, also called a waxing square phase.

Another example is a *Uranus-Pluto opposition* cycle, which occurs when Uranus is exactly opposite from Pluto in the sky, corresponding with the Full Moon phase. As a fourth example, a *Third Quarter Chiron Square Neptune* cycle occurs when Chiron has moved 270 degrees away from Neptune, and these planets are three-fourths of the zodiac wheel away from one another. This Chiron-Neptune cycle point is like the Last Quarter Moon phase, also called a waning square phase.

Ask Spaceship Earth

Humans measure the aspect between the Sun and Moon in a lunar cycle by symbolically holding the Sun stationary and measuring the number of degrees the Moon has traveled away from it with respect to the 360-degree circle. Astrologers calculate the aspect between two paired planets in the same way. We hold the slowest moving planet stationary and measure the number of degrees of separation between it and the second planet in question to determine the aspect between them.

Aspect	Phase	Comparable Moon
Conjunction	New	New
First Quarter Square	First Quarter	First Quarter
Opposition	Full	Full
Third Quarter Square	Third Quarter	Last Quarter

Hard Aspects: Symbolic Invitations to Shift Consciousness

Astrologers call the conjunction, the two Squares, and the opposition *hard aspects*, because they symbolically invite deep change and adjustment processes. Although the sextile (60 degrees) and the trine (120 degrees) are also important aspects to track between two planets, they don't carry the same kind of invitation to shift consciousness. Their invitation is to stay the course and enjoy the current harmony between the two planets in question.

Each time two planets come together in one of these four hard aspects, they're symbolically inviting us to come through a gateway of

Speaking Y2K

Hard aspects, the conjunction, Squares, and opposition, are so called because they symbolically invite deep change and adjustment processes.

initiation of consciousness, and the type of aspect (conjunction, Square, or opposition) indicates what kind of initiation is being offered. In addition, the zodiac sign that each planet is in at the time of the hard aspect describes the nature of the initiation.

Let's use a gardening metaphor to make these gateways clearer:

Conjunction	Plant new seeds in the Earth
First Quarter Square	Thin out the seedlings to make room for growth
Opposition	First harvest and full utilization of the herbs; fruits and flowers produced
Third Quarter Square	Last harvest; composting time; let fields go fallow; prepare the beds to rest and be ready for new seeds to come

It's also important to see how the symbol for each aspect helps tell the story of what's happening:

- ☌ The conjunction aspect is symbolized by a line of attachment coming a circle.
- ☐ A square box symbolizes the First and Third Quarter Square aspects.
- ☍ Two circles joined together by a line symbolize the opposition aspect.

Conjunction: The Seed Gate ☌

When two planets come together to form a conjunction in the sky, they're metaphorically starting all over with one another. It may be helpful to think of a conjunction between two planets as the beginning of a new cycle of dialogue between the two characters. Symbolically, the conjunction is a seed gate. It marks a time for each of us to start a new cycle of dialogue between these characters within (on a personal level) and without (on a collective level).

Time Capsule

During a conjunction, the two planets appear to be next to one another in the sky. This represents a time of seeding a new way to express these two archetypes in our personal and collective lives, akin to the planting phase of the garden's growth. During a conjunction we scatter the seeds of many ideas and new directions, and then wait to see what develops and grows.

First Quarter Square: The Action Gate □

During a First Quarter square, the two planets are in an energy dynamic called "crisis in action" (the phrase comes from astrologer-philosopher Dane Rudhyar). Think of this as the thinning phase of the garden's growth: Some seedlings need to die so that the remaining ones can grow. In the same way, some ideas and projects begun at the time of the previous conjunction must now be let go so that other ideas seeded at the conjunction can evolve fully to completion.

If connected by an imaginary carpenter's square, at this time the two planets would appear to be 90 degrees apart. This represents a time of assessing the relationship between the two planetary energies in our lives with respect to what was seeded at the time of their previous conjunction. It's also a time to release patterns that don't work and to strengthen patterns that do.

Opposition: The Harvest Gate ☍

When they're in opposition, the two planets face one another, allowing for full illumination, so they can "see" everything about one another. The spiritual/karmic task of this cycle is to create balance and harmony between the two archetypal energies.

Time Capsule

Akin to the first harvest and continuing care and feeding phase of the garden's growth, it's time to pick the first fruits and flowers, and to keep weeding, fertilizing, and watering to maintain the beauty and productivity of the plants. During this time, we should harvest the "fruits" of the ideas, actions, and projects begun at the previous conjunction of the two planets so that the next phase of their development can occur.

Facing one another in opposition, the two planets appear to be 180 degrees apart from one another. Now we can see the full picture of the dialogue and relationship of the planetary pair that was seeded at the conjunction, and it's time to bring balance between the two energies.

Third Quarter Square: The Reflection Gate □

During a Third Quarter square, the two planets are in an energy dynamic called "crisis in consciousness" (this phrase, too, comes from astrologer-philosopher Dane Rudhyar).

Time Capsule

Like the composting phase of the garden's growth, the symbolic fruits and flowers of the planets have been harvested, and it's time to distill down the essence of their gifts: To make preserves and wine, dry the fruit, press apples for cider, and dry flowers for decoration and herbs for teas. We're also getting the garden ready for winter and its natural death process, so it will once more be ready for spring and the new seeds to come.

Similarly, ideas and projects begun at the previous conjunction are now naturally wrapping up. The spiritual and karmic tasks of this cycle are to reflect on what's been learned in the past years of the current cycle (since the last conjunction between the two planets occurred). From this internal reflection process, we can determine which beliefs, ideas, and attitudes must be changed to adapt to the lesson learned from the whole cycle so far.

During a Third Quarter square, the two planets appear to be 270 degrees apart, carving out an image of three-fourths of a pie. It's a time to reflect on the relationship of the two planetary energies that was seeded at the past conjunction to determine the "attitude adjustments" required and to begin to wrap up the lessons of this cycle.

Cycles to Look Forward To

Not surprisingly, the major planetary cycles of the end of the 20th century and the beginning of the 21st century carry some profound invitations from the cosmos to transform our core belief systems and relationship patterns between humans and with the earth itself. Please note that these are descriptions of the cycles in the sky and have no reference to any events on Earth. The only link to the earth is the location at which we cast the chart for the cosmic event, i.e., Washington, D.C.

In the rest of this chapter, we'll be interpreting our sense of what's to come. Admittedly, we bring our own filters and biases to these interpretations. Other astrologers might conclude that more difficult or negative events could occur in response to these planetary invitations.

We prefer a more positive spin, and here's why: We believe in the ability of humans to change their consciousness and wake up to greater awareness of the ancient truth of our inter-relatedness to all life, including other humans, animals, plants, the earth itself, and the cosmos around us. We hope that on both a personal and collective level, people can make self-empowered choices to honor simultaneously their own individuality and the greater good of the world. The new millennium (of the number "2" vibration underscored by the number "3"—read more about this in Part 3) beckons us to answer the call to deeply transform the patterns and attitudes that keep us in separation.

With that invitation in mind, let's explore the nature of the individual paired planetary cycles and the unique cosmic invitations they offer to all of us on Earth.

Jupiter-Saturn: Social Change and Manifestation

It takes 20 years for Jupiter and Saturn to complete one cycle and return to a seed point of conjunction. Jupiter symbolizes the Quester or Philosopher, the part of our inner and outer selves that seeks to expand knowledge and growth. Saturn symbolizes the Builder and Manifestor, the part of our nature that seeks to stabilize and create solid game plans and foundations.

Together, their cyclic dance describes the natural personal and collective process of expansion and contraction. We must be able to build a solid foundation to support our aspirations and desires to quest and grow. After going on an adventurous and expansive trip, after all, the next step is to come home and live with the changes we've made in our everyday lives.

Time Capsule

In our own culture, the rhythmic process with Jupiter (expansion) and Saturn (contraction or appropriate limitation) is represented by "boom and bust" business cycles and by the bull and bear cycles of the stock market.

Astrologer Noel Tyl links the Jupiter-Saturn cycle to corresponding key developments of history on the collective level and to dominating "focus points" for life development on a personal level. He notes that the Jupiter-Saturn conjunctions take place in the same zodiacal element (i.e., fire, earth, air, or water) for approximately 170 years before transitioning into another element family over the course of several decades. During this transition time, a conjunction (called a Grand Mutation conjunction) occurs in the zodiac sign of the new element to portend the next cycle of conjunctions in the new element.

When the element of the Jupiter-Saturn conjunction shifts, it symbolizes the invitation to shift our developmental focus to a new area of our personal and collective lives.

According to his research on historical cycles, Noel Tyl suggests these are the key areas of human development for the corresponding elements (the dates of the most recent element cycles are listed):

➤ *Water.* Humans explore and develop religious concepts and belief systems (1425 to 1603).

➤ *Fire.* Humans explore colonization, militancy, and the enforcement of religious positions (1603 to 1802).

➤ *Earth.* Humans explore the importance of a government figure or monarch, codes of conduct, and administrative powers (1802 to 1980).

➤ *Air.* Humans explore social concerns, rebellions, and the need for equality (1980 to 2160).

It should be no surprise that we're living in a Grand Mutation cycle right now. The Jupiter-Saturn conjunction of 1980 occurred in the air sign of Libra after 178 years of the cycle occurring in earth signs. The conjunction of 2000 is the last one to occur in an earth sign (Taurus) before the subsequent conjunctions move into air signs.

So, as we enter into the next millennium, we're collectively moving from the expansion and establishment of governmental structures and physical security systems into exploration and manifestation of new social systems that are revolutionary and egalitarian.

We'll talk more about the five Jupiter-Saturn cycles of the third millennium, our new millennium, in Chapter 7.

Saturn Cycles: Laying a Foundation and Building on It

Saturn cycles invite us to grow up and mature. Saturn, as an archetype of the Elder or responsible one, invites us to do a "reality check" on the issues relating to its current cycles. Is your life stable and working on a material level? Do you have a functional game plan for your life? Do you feel that you are in control of your life?

A **Saturn-Chiron** cycle invites a dialogue between the Builder and the Shaman. What world structures (governmental, personal, financial, and physical) require a paradigm shift in order to heal old wounds?

The current Saturn-Chiron cycle began with the seed gate of 1966 when Saturn was in conjunction with Chiron in the sign of Pisces. Pisces is a mutable, yin, water sign that represents the world of intuition, dreams, and spirituality. The conjunction in Pisces symbolizes the need to shift wounded beliefs (Chiron) that separate the spiritual and receptive principles of life (Pisces) from the functional, accomplished aspects of our nature (Saturn).

On the outer level, this seed point began a cycle that calls on us to instill spiritual and compassionate values into our business and government structures. On an inner level, it beckons us to dissolve old wounded illusions about outer authorities having control over our lives and to create inner authority based on authentic faith and beliefs.

This conjunction occurred at the same time as the spiritual revolutionary cycle of the Uranus-Pluto conjunction (which we'll discuss in a few pages). We saw its many manifestations in everything from the peace movement to the rise of the drug culture and acid rock. The year 1966 was also the year of China's "cultural revolution."

A **Saturn-Uranus** cycle lasts for about 45 years and invites a dialogue between the Builder and the Revolutionary. What external and internal rules need to be broken now for the liberation of the authentic self and community?

The current Saturn-Uranus cycle began with the seed gate of 1988 when Saturn and Uranus conjoined in the sign of Sagittarius. Sagittarius is a mutable, yang, fire sign that represents the enthusiastic search for meaning and the "Truth." The conjunction in Sagittarius symbolizes the invitation to create new philosophical systems that synthesize diverse beliefs and cultural truths into a whole understanding.

Examples from that time include the increased interest in alternative healing, channeling, and Eastern religions. But more specifically, 1988 included a cease-fire agreement in Nicaragua, an Iran-Iraq peace plan, the recognition of Israel by the Palestine Liberation Organization, and Mikhail Gorbachev's first step toward reducing Soviet troop presence in Europe.

A **Saturn-Neptune** cycle lasts for about 35 years and invites a dialogue between the Builder and the Mystic. How can the desire to merge with the Divine and the transcendental combine with the need to be grounded and competent in the "real" world? On a collective level, this seed point invites us to dissolve old authoritarian and constrictive structures and open to new dreams of unity and imagination.

The current Saturn-Neptune cycle began with the seed gate of 1989 when Saturn and Neptune conjoined in the sign of Capricorn. Capricorn is a cardinal, yin, earth sign that represents the world of achievement and impeccable use of life resources such as time and money.

The conjunction in Capricorn symbolizes the invitation to dissolve illusionary and deceptive institutions and the experience of being victims to external authoritarian systems. During this most recent Saturn-Neptune conjunction, both the Tianammen Square uprising and the dismantling of the Berlin Wall occurred. As we note numerologically in Chapter 9, 1989 was quite a year.

A **Saturn-Pluto** cycle lasts for about 32 years and invites a dialogue between the Builder and the Transformer. How can the desire to release and let die old patterns of misuse of power and manipulation combine with the need to have some kind of external social and personal structure and set of rules under which to operate? On a collective level, this seed point invites us to address the misuse of power and violent manipulative tendencies of any inner and outer dictators.

The current Saturn-Pluto cycle began with the seed gate of 1982 when Saturn conjoined Pluto in the sign of Libra, a cardinal, yang, air sign that represents the need to create balance, fairness, and justice in our relationships. The conjunction in Libra symbolizes the challenge to address injustice between the sexes, races, and socioeconomic groups.

In the U.S., 1982 marked the beginning of the Reagan years and attempting to get things back in balance financially, as well as the growth of feminism in the culture. It was also the year of the Falklands War between England and Argentina, and the year Israel withdrew its troops from the Sinai Peninsula according to its peace agreement with Egypt.

Chiron Cycles: Paradigm Shifts into Greater Healing

Chiron, symbolically the wounded healer who creates paradigm shifts of consciousness, initiates cycles where the Shaman meets each respective planet's archetype to heal and restore its issues.

A **Chiron-Uranus** cycle invites a dialogue between the Shaman and the Revolutionary. The current Chiron-Uranus cycle began with the seed gate of 1898 when Chiron conjoined Uranus in the sign of Sagittarius. Their seed gate beckons us to open to radical new ways to shift our consciousness about the nature of reality so as to heal old wounds.

Remember that Sagittarius is the sign of synthesizing diverse truths into new philosophical systems of wholeness. The challenging side of Sagittarius is the tendency to be dogmatic and self-righteous about personal and national beliefs. Witness the conflicts of the 20th century that are due to the intolerance of another's viewpoint.

Astrologer-philosopher E. Alan Meece notes that during the 1890s, humankind invented amazing new devices that essentially launched us into our mass media world (such as the airplane, radio, telegraph, and newspapers). The inventions of the decade of the 1890s radically transformed our planet and moved us out of the consciousness of separation and into that of interconnected realities.

A **Chiron-Neptune** cycle tracks the dance between the Shaman and the Mystic. The current Chiron-Neptune cycle began with the seed gate of August 1945, when Chiron conjoined Neptune in the sign of Libra. That conjunction invites us to enter the process of healing unfair religious and spiritual beliefs. The wounded side of Neptune is the Addict or Victim. With Libra as the costume for this encounter, what new paradigms of balance and justice can aid in transforming victimized patterns of relationships?

In August of 1945, the United States dropped two atomic bombs on Japan, thereby catalyzing the end of World War II (which was healing to many), but simultaneously creating a precedent for our capacity as humans to destroy our world. The end of this war also revealed the extent and horror of the Holocaust to the world for the first time, reminding us all too graphically of our capacity for hatred and destruction.

A **Chiron-Pluto** cycle explores what happens when the Shaman meets the Transformer and invites us to enter the gateway of healing by using power wisely and by cleaning up hidden manipulative patterns. The current Chiron-Pluto cycle of the last half of the 20th century began with the seed gate of July 1941, when Chiron conjoined Pluto in the sign of Leo. The wounded side of Pluto is the Rapist or rageful Destroyer. It was in 1941 that Hitler's armies invaded Russia, Italy and Germany invaded Egypt, the Japanese attacked Pearl Harbor, and the U.S. entered World War II.

Leo is a fixed, yang, fire sign that represents the need to express yourself and be visible with your gifts. The challenging side of Leo is the tendency to be narcissistic and arrogant. What new paradigms of creative self-expression and open-heartedness (Leo as the costume for this encounter) can aid in transforming violent patterns of selfish destructiveness into the capacity to honor and support each person's unique gifts and talents, no matter their race, culture, or sex?

The next seed gate for the Chiron-Pluto cycle ushers in the new millennium as the two heavenly bodies are conjunct in the sign of Sagittarius on Dec. 30, 1999. More on this in the sections of the chart for January 1, 2000.

Uranus Cycles: Liberation into Authenticity

Uranus represents the archetypal Revolutionary, and its cycles with other planets relate to liberating and freeing the other planet's particular energy.

A **Uranus-Neptune** cycle lasts about 172 years. The current Uranus-Neptune cycle began with the seed gate of 1993 when they conjoined in the sign of Capricorn. The Revolutionary meets the Mystic, with a concurrent dialogue about radical new spiritual and creative systems to liberate humanity's dreams and visions.

Remember that Capricorn represents the need to have integrity and do things right in accordance with personal and societal ethics. The conjunction in Capricorn symbolizes the invitation to create new dreams of freedom and change that aspire to liberate all peoples from outer controlling governmental and institutional systems and inner restrictive and punitive authority voices.

E. Alan Meece links the Uranus-Neptune cycle to the formation of cultural patterns and the challenge to alter our most cherished collective and personal beliefs. He notes that the key current challenge of our times is the established global ethnic conflicts, which could sabotage the movement into a true "new world order" where all of humanity unites as a common people.

A **Uranus-Pluto** cycle lasts an average of 127 years. The Revolutionary meets the Transformer—and all hell breaks loose. Their archetypal dialogue is about blowing up entrenched status quo systems, like corrupt governments or manipulative family patterns, so that everyone involved can be more authentic.

The current Uranus-Pluto cycle began with the seed gate of 1966 when they conjoined in the sign of Virgo. Some of us are old enough to remember the volatile, revolutionary wake-up calls of the hippie movement, from which came the call for peace, women's liberation, deeper ecological healing, and the transmutation of the corrupt and restrictive patterns of the status quo establishment values.

Out of Time

In 1966, Lyndon Johnson's administration escalated its secret troop build-up in Viet Nam. This single event would ultimately lead to the anti-war movement, the confrontations at the 1968 Democratic convention in Chicago, and ultimately, the decision of LBJ to not run for another term. Uranus-Pluto cycles transform, but they don't do it gently.

Virgo is a mutable, yin, earth sign that represents the desire for holistic physical forms and systems that allow for the individual and society to be in congruence with their own natures, with a place for everything and everything in its place. Virgo is deeply connected to physical healing and the capacity to make things whole. The challenging voice of Virgo is cranky perfectionism where no one is doing it right or correctly. The wounded side of the hippie movement often carried a judgmental intolerance of another's perspective: "You're either with the revolution or against it," and "Don't trust anyone over 30."

E. Alan Meece describes the invitation of this 1966 conjunction as calling the individual to be in creative interdependent relationship with society and the earth. As this is a 127-year cycle, we've clearly still got much to learn.

Neptune Cycles: Dissolving Illusions, Embracing the Spirit

A **Neptune-Pluto** cycle, which lasts about 493 years, is where the Mystic meets the Transformer. Their archetypal dialogue is about dissolving old power bases and social structures and opening to new visions of change and rebirth. E. Alan Meece links these large cycles to the rise and fall of major civilizations like the Roman Empire and Renaissance Europe. The current Neptune-Pluto cycle began with the seed gate of 1892 when Neptune conjoined Pluto in the sign of Gemini.

Gemini is a mutable, yang air sign that represents the need for communication and dialogue about diversity and alternative ways to do things. It is a costume of change and adaptability. The challenging side of Gemini is to go into dualistic (black and white) positions or to get overwhelmed by the quantity of ideas and options and just "check out" or become fragmented.

Consider, for example, the pain of fragmentation that's overwhelming our western lifestyle and world since the creation of all the communication devices and inventions of the late 1890s. It's made for radical social transformation in the past 100 years—but at what cost?

Pluto Cycles: Detoxing from the Old, Empowering into the New

Pluto cycles invite deep transformation of old aspects of our personal and collective lives. Sometimes these cycles feel as if a clogged up drain is cleaned out thoroughly and completely.

You can review Pluto's dance with the social and transpersonal planets in the previous sections.

Birth Charts for Two Centuries

As we discussed in Chapter 4, any given moment in time has a birth chart. In order to understand the close of the 20th century, we'd like to begin by looking at its beginning. Each of these century event charts is a symbolic map of what the archetypal invitation was from the planets for that moment in time.

The Cosmic Job Description for 1,000 Years

When a new century begins in our western calendars, we create the event chart for that moment when the numbers in the calendar change. Because we're writing this book in the United States, we've cast the charts for Washington, D.C., the capital of that country, in order to find the U.S.'s "century or millennium growth assignments." The event chart becomes a symbolic map of the job description for the next hundred or thousand years of growth on both a personal and collective level.

Astrologers interpret an event chart by looking for prominent aspects and the archetypal stories told by the planets. Let's see how we did this century.

January 1, 1900

At first glance, you'll note a pattern of symbols for the planets like a seesaw, with a large grouping of planets at the bottom of the chart (in the sign of Sagittarius ♐) and three at the top part of the chart (in the sign of Gemini ♊). The dialogue between Gemini (the desire for options, communication, and restless change) and Sagittarius (the desire to learn and synthesize and gain greater understanding) is about moving from being a student to being a teacher.

The biggest challenge here is to avoid getting into communication processes involving dogmatic philosophical positions (the dark side of both Mercury and Chiron together in the sign of Sagittarius in the 3rd house). Consider how many 20th-century wars were fought due to national dogmas and intolerance for another's point of view.

Event chart for January 1, 1900.

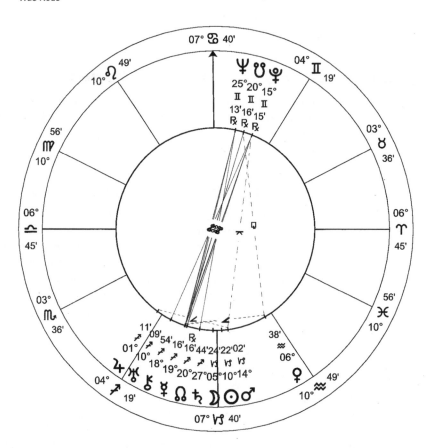

Natal Chart
Jan 1 1900
0:00 AM EST +5:00
Washington DC
38N54 077W02
Geocentric
Tropical
Placidus
True Node

The second point of interest is that there were no planets in a water sign at the time of this event. Remember that water signs symbolize the ability to have deep feelings. The lack of water indicates a challenge to 1) not overindulge in emotionality; and 2) not become unfeeling and machine-like.

The third point is that the Sun and the Moon were both in Capricorn and just about 10 hours away from joining each other in a New Moon phase. Astrologers call this a dark moon (or balsamic) phase between the two planets. This Sun-Moon signature suggests an assignment to release Capricorn structures (like governments and family systems) that would limit the exploration of the new Gemini options and ideas coming forward.

The planet Mars was also in conjunction with both the Sun and the Moon in this event chart, symbolizing the challenge not to use war and violence (Mars as the symbolic Warrior archetype) to maintain authoritarian institutions and systems (dark side of Capricorn).

Another point of interest is that the South Node (past patterns) was between Neptune and Pluto in Gemini. This symbolizes the need to move beyond old ways of destroying (Pluto ♀) due to religious (Neptune ♆) differences of opinion (Gemini ♊). The North Node ☊ is in Sagittarius ♐ conjunct to Chiron ⚷ and Mercury ☿, inviting us to evolve healed forms (Chiron ⚷) of dialogue and thinking (Mercury ☿) about our wisdom and "truths" (Sagittarius ♐).

January 1, 2000

Natal Chart
Jan 1 2000
0:00 AM EST +5:00
Washington DC
38N54 077W02
Geocentric
Tropical
Placidus
True Node

Event chart for January 1, 2000.

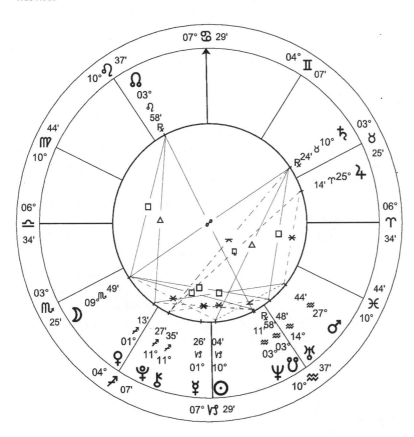

Here's the same chart we looked at in Chapter 4. This event chart was once again calculated for Washington D.C. since we're interested in the "growth assignments" for the new millennium for the United States.

At first glance, you'll note how a lineup of symbols creates a box formation, which astrologers call a "grand square." The Moon in Scorpio in the 2nd house is in an opposite line from Saturn in Taurus in the 8th house. The North Node in Leo in the 10th house is in an opposite line from Neptune in conjunction with the South Node, both of which are in Aquarius in the 4th house.

All four of these groupings in the sky form a big square in the event chart. The Grand Square is an invitation to make some decisive changes to move forward with respect to the issues represented by the planets.

The need for intimacy with emotional and yin components of our lives (Moon in Scorpio) wants to balance with the need for responsibility to our physical and financial security issues (Saturn in Taurus). The South Node–Neptune combination invites us to remember our spiritual and compassionate sides as we become more creative and respectful of everyone's worthiness.

A key point in this chart is the conjunction between Chiron and Pluto in Sagittarius. The Shaman meets the Transformer in the sign of seeking greater truths and understanding. We begin a new cycle (seed point) of examining the wounds of our dogmatic belief systems. The Moon and Saturn placements (in the 2nd and 8th houses, respectively) suggest the need to heal the wounds of hoarding resources from a greedy and violent perspective (dark side of the Moon in Scorpio and Saturn in Taurus).

In this cycle, the corporate and consumer culture pattern of controlling through grabbing up all the resources will be deeply challenged. As will our old patterns (South Node) and illusions (Neptune) that we can figure it all out in our heads or through technology (Aquarius) without any dialogue with Mother Earth (Moon) about the right use of her waters and oil (Scorpio is a water sign). We'll also discover as Americans that we're paying too high a price to ignore the essential dignity and worthiness (North Node in Leo) of each member of our American society (Aquarius).

This Aquarius pattern of overconfidence in technology is also linked to the challenge of the Y2K computer problem that will possibly affect our technological world on a global level. The Y2K issue can also be symbolized with the First Quarter Square pattern between Saturn in Taurus (earth resources) and Uranus in Aquarius (technology).

As this book is being written, people throughout the country are already meeting in small regional groups to prepare and organize (Saturn) for potential disasters in their communities as they attempt to create radical new forms (Uranus) of community. The call to live as interconnected beings in our world is being voiced through the Y2K issue.

The Least You Need to Know

➤ Planetary aspects are symbolic gateways to consciousness.

➤ Planetary cycles are roadmaps for individual and collective growth.

➤ Jupiter-Saturn aspects translate to social change and manifestation.

➤ Saturn cycles lay down foundations, while Chiron cycles shift us into healings.

➤ Uranus cycles free us to be authentic; Neptune cycles dissolve illusions; and Pluto cycles transform us into releasing old patterns.

Chapter 7

How Planetary Cycles in the New Millennium Affect *Your* Birth Chart

---

In This Chapter

➤ How to get and interpret your birth chart

➤ Connecting your birth chart to event charts

➤ Generational planetary cycles and you

➤ Your grandchildren's future

In Chapter 4, you learned that your birth chart is a metaphor for you, as well as a roadmap that uses your birth date, time, and place to show the positions of the planets in their signs at the time of your birth.

In this chapter, we'll be discussing some of the major astrological events of the new millennium by designating their sign and degree location in the zodiac—and so creating birth charts for them. With a copy of your birth chart, and a basic understanding of which signs are in which houses in your chart, you can pinpoint the area of your life in which these astrological events will most influence you.

Have You Had Your Birth Chart Done?

If you haven't had your birth chart done yet, you'll probably want to do so now. This chapter is all about using your birth chart to find out how various events will affect you personally, and your birth chart will be an important tool in that discovery.

Getting your birth chart done is as easy as picking up the phone. But what information do you need before you do that? Read on.

How to Get Your Chart Done

If you don't already have a copy of your chart, here's what you need to get it done: accurate data on the date, time, and location of your birth. Most people know their birth date and the city or town they were born in. But sometimes the birth time is a little bit trickier.

The first place to look for the birth time is your birth certificate, if you have a copy of it. If not, check with the department of vital statistics for the city or state of your birth to get a copy of your birth certificate. Not all birth certificates have times, though. If that's the case, ask your parents or any family members if they remember. Check a baby book or family bible for records of your birth. It's important to get as accurate a birth time as possible, because as little as one minute can change the house or sign a planet appears in.

What happens if you just can't come up with an accurate birth time? Don't panic. You can ask an astrologer to do a *rectification* of your birth chart. During this session, you'll tell the astrologer important things that happened in your life as well as how you behave in certain situations. Using this information, the astrologer will figure out the exact time of your birth.

Speaking Y2K

A **rectification** of your birth chart is done when you don't know the exact time of your birth. An astrologer will use important events in your life and how you behave in certain situations to determine the time you were born.

Once you have accurate birth data, you can get your chart calculated via a computer program. Contact a local metaphysical bookstore (look in the Yellow Pages under "Metaphysical Bookstores and Supplies") and ask them their fee for producing a copy of your chart. This can usually be done in five minutes.

The other option is to contact a local astrologer (look under "Astrologers" in the Yellow Pages) to find out if they will run your chart for you and their fee for this service. The fee should be around five dollars. An astrologer can also interpret your chart for you in a professional consultation. The fee for that varies but is similar to the fee for a session with a counselor or therapist.

Time Capsule

You don't need a copy of your birth chart in front of you to continue reading this chapter. We'll describe in general the cosmic invitation of each astrological event on a collective level. In addition, we'll offer the specifics of the astrological events as they connect to each house in a chart. If you do have your birth chart, though, you can determine the corresponding house location in your chart for each event. We'll also analyze the impact of the upcoming Jupiter-Saturn conjunctions of the 21st century for each of the 12 Sun signs—and you already know your own.

Basic Birth Chart Interpretations You Can Make Yourself

You can make your own general interpretations of how an astrological event of the new millennium impacts your chart. To do this, you need to determine the house location in your chart for the key zodiac degrees of an event chart.

Let's use the birth chart of Hillary Rodham Clinton as an example. She is an important figure in American society at the turning of the millennium. Hillary will appear in later chapters in examples of the applications of other intuitive arts.

Let's say we want to find out how the solar eclipse of August 1999 at 19 degrees of Leo might impact Hillary (later on in this chapter, we'll tell you more about this eclipse). First we need to determine in which house the zodiac sign of Leo is located in Hillary's chart. Remember that Leo has to do with will, reputation and the desire to love and be loved.

In Hillary's chart, the arrow points to the edge of the third house (astrologers call this a *cusp*) of her chart. At the cusp of her third house, you see the number 10, followed by the symbol for Leo, and then the number 03. This means that the third house of Hillary's chart begins at 10 degrees of Leo and 5 minutes (remember that each degree of arc in the sky is made up of 60 minutes).

Speaking Y2K

In astrology a **cusp** refers to the beginning of each house.

When you look at this chart, you'll note that the cusp for Hillary's fourth house is at 5 degrees of Virgo and 07 minutes. Therefore, 19 degrees of Leo falls into Hillary's third house (19 degrees of Leo is between 10 degrees of Leo and 5 degrees of Virgo). If you want more information on the more technical parts of zodiac degrees and house cusps, we refer you to *The Complete Idiot's Guide to Astrology*.

Birth chart for Hillary Rodham Clinton.

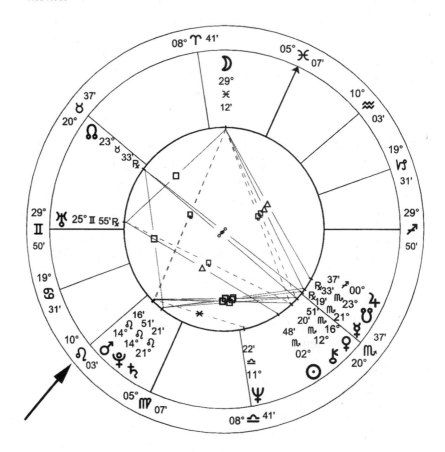

Hillary Rodham Clinton
Natal Chart
Oct 26 1947
8:00 PM CST +6:00
Chicago IL, USA
41N52 087W39
Geocentric
Tropical
Placidus
True Node

Now remember, a solar eclipse occurs when the Moon and Sun are together in the sky in a New Moon phase. In certain areas on the Earth, the Moon's shadow blocks the Sun's disc, causing us to see a portion of a dark disc over the Sun.

➤ Solar eclipses happen several times a year and symbolically invite us to eclipse (or block out) our conscious mental perspective on things. It's a seed gate of initiation between the Sun (conscious Hero or Heroine) and the Moon (instinctive Wild Man or Woman).

➤ The third house is the area of life in which you explore your communication style and your willingness to pursue new ideas and knowledge. In the next section, we define the meanings of the 12 houses.

A Closer Look at Hillary Rodham Clinton's Birth Chart

Hillary Clinton has the planets Mars (Warrior), Pluto (Transformer), and Saturn (Builder), all in Leo in her third house. Mars and Pluto are at 15 degrees of Leo (rounded up) and Saturn is at 22 degrees of Leo. These placements suggest:

1. That Hillary is able to fight for (Mars) ideas and experiments (3rd house) that create new structures (Saturn) for deep and lasting change (Pluto).

2. She goes about this with charisma, style, and self-confidence (Leo).

3. She can express the shadow side of these placements by willfully (Leo) using power (Pluto) and authority (Saturn) in an aggressive way (Mars).

In August 1999, the solar eclipse in Leo invites Hillary to release old patterns of how she willfully expresses her power and authority in a decisive way. In the first two years of her husband's presidency, some politicians and members of the American public branded her as being too aggressive. She may resurrect (Pluto) herself as a political figure in August of 1999 by remaking her communication style.

Interpreting Events in Your Own Chart

We used Hillary's chart as an example for how to track the placement of key astrological events. Let's review the steps for how you interpret the impact of those events in your own life journey:

1. Locate the sign and degree location in the zodiac for the designated event. (For the August 1999 solar eclipse, for example, this is 19 degrees of Leo.)

2. Determine the house in which that zodiac degree is located in your own birth chart. Use the table in this chapter to determine the meaning of the house. (For Hillary, this is in her 3rd house.)

3. Determine if there are any planets in your birth chart within 10 degrees of either side of the event degree. You may emphasize these archetypal parts of your nature during the astrological event. (For Hillary, these are Mars, Pluto, and Saturn.)

4. Summarize the key invitation for growth of the new millennium astrological event in question (these invitations are summarized later on in this chapter). (For the solar eclipse, it is to release old patterns of will, self-worth, and reputation.)

5. Recognize that you are being asked to explore that growth opportunity in the area of life that corresponds to the particular house of your chart in which the event is located. (For Hillary, this is in the third house of communication issues.)

Synthesizing Your Own Chart with the Bigger Picture

As you become more comfortable tracking individual parts of an event chart in your chart, you can challenge yourself to synthesize the bigger picture of the event chart as it connects to your chart.

Again, let's use Hillary's chart as an example. For comparison, we've made a double wheel with Hillary's chart in the center and the chart for the solar eclipse as the outer wheel. At a glance, you can see that the North Node, Sun, and Moon in Leo of the eclipse chart fall into Hillary's third house, close to her natal Mars, Pluto, and Saturn. We just discussed the Sun and Moon connections.

Comparison Chart for Hillary Rodham Clinton with August, 1999 Solar Eclipse.

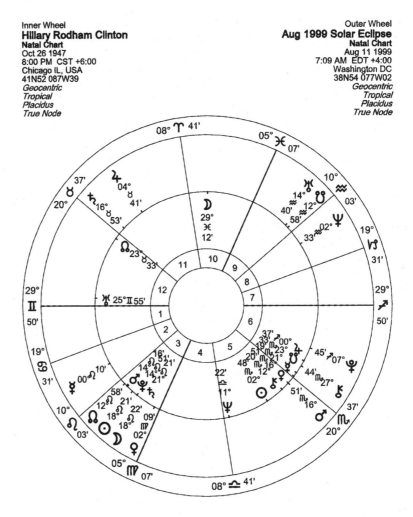

Inner Wheel
Hillary Rodham Clinton
Natal Chart
Oct 26 1947
8:00 PM CST +6:00
Chicago IL, USA
41N52 087W39
Geocentric
Tropical
Placidus
True Node

Outer Wheel
Aug 1999 Solar Eclipse
Natal Chart
Aug 11 1999
7:09 AM EDT +4:00
Washington DC
38N54 077W02
Geocentric
Tropical
Placidus
True Node

Here are some of the planetary invitations that we note:

1. The solar eclipse Mars in Scorpio is exactly next to Venus and close to Chiron in Hillary's chart in her 5th house.

2. The solar eclipse Chiron in Scorpio falls close to Hillary's Mercury and South Node in her 6th house.

3. The solar eclipse Pluto in Sagittarius is close to Hillary's Jupiter in her 6th house.

4. The solar eclipse Saturn in Taurus is close to Hillary's North Node in her 12th house.

5. The solar eclipse North Node in Leo is close to Hillary's Mars and Pluto in her 3rd house.

Whew! The planets are rocking and rolling with Ms. Clinton in the summer of 1999. The planetary invitations above suggest the following:

1. Mars invites Hillary to take action on healing wounds (Chiron) around love relationships and values (Venus).

2. Chiron as change agent challenges her to heal past patterns (South Node) of communicating (Mercury) in a self-sacrificing way (6th house).

3. Pluto calls her to transmute old beliefs (Jupiter) about work and service (6th house).

4. Saturn asks her to take up the challenge of her evolutionary purpose (North Node) to ground, and be a good steward for (Taurus) her life visions and spirituality (12th house).

5. And the North Node invites her to follow her destiny to express (3rd house) her commitment to take a stand for change (Pluto) for issues with heart and meaning for her (Leo).

House Definitions

As we've already discussed, each house covers a specific area of your life. The following table provides you with this information in an easy reference format. You may want to tab this page for future reference.

House	Meaning
1	Your sense of personal identity; physical self; outer personality
2	Your sense of self-worth; personal value systems; money and possessions
3	Your communication style; relationship to siblings; pursuit of new ideas and knowledge

continues

continued

House	Meaning
4	Your home and roots; emotional foundation and security; family-of-origin
5	Your sense of fun; children (artistic creations as well as offspring); romance
6	Your day-to-day routines; personal health; work and service; sense of wholeness
7	Your primary relationships; important partnerships; sense of aesthetics
8	Your willingness to change; intimacy; joint resources; sexuality; death and rebirth
9	Your belief systems; personal philosophy; travel; higher education; legal issues
10	Your ethics; reputation; career; social responsibilities; administrative self
11	Your sense of belonging to larger community; rebellious side; life goals; freedom needs
12	Your sense of the divine; unconscious patterns; victimization issues; life visions

Important Astrological Events as Transits to Your Birth Chart

The key astrological events of the new millennium are actually transits to your own birth chart. Recall that the planets are constantly moving around the Sun in their orbits, transiting through the degrees of the zodiac wheel. These planetary transits are frozen "moments in time" that appear as event charts for that moment in time.

In the following sections, we'll describe the key astrological events of the new millennium. You can take the important degree locations of the event charts and place them in your own chart to see where the event is transiting your own chart.

First, let's get a larger perspective on the planetary dance. We'll begin with the three key conjunctions that occurred between transpersonal planets in the 19th and 20th centuries.

Neptune-Pluto Conjunction of 1892

Remember from our discussion in Chapter 6 that a Neptune-Pluto cycle lasts about 493 years. At their seed gate (conjunction), on an archetypal level, the Mystic and the Transformer dialogue about the dissolution of old civilization paradigms and the rebirth of new ones.

Astrologer E. Alan Meece has calculated an event chart for the Neptune-Pluto conjunction as shown below. He calls it the "Horoscope of Modern Humanity." Because Neptune and Pluto move so slowly, it's difficult to set the exact time of their conjunction. Meece calculates their conjunction to the solar eclipse in Taurus that occurred in April, 1892.

Remember from our previous discussion in this chapter that a Solar eclipse invites us to eclipse our conscious, mental perspective on things.

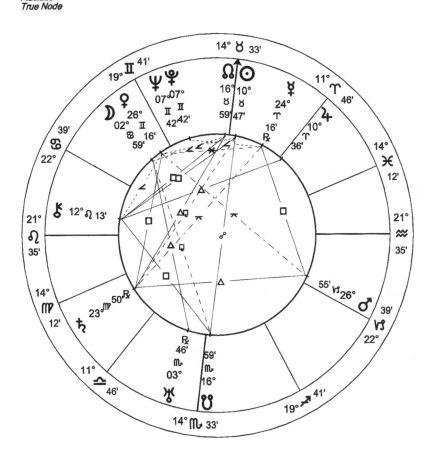

Neptune–Pluto Conjunction
Natal Chart
Apr 30 1892
5:20 PM GMT +0:00
Washington DC
38N54 077W02
Geocentric
Tropical
Placidus
True Node

The Neptune-Pluto conjunction of April, 1892.

95

In this event chart, the solar eclipse in Taurus suggests that in the next 500 years of human civilization, we'll explore new ways to communicate (Gemini) about the earth's resources (Taurus). Remember that the challenge of Gemini is polarity and fragmentation, both of which have occurred in the 20th century regarding resources, with the contrast between the rich developed nations and the poorer Third World nations.

The Nodes of this chart are at 16 degrees of Taurus and Scorpio. The North Node of growth and evolution is in Taurus, inviting us to be good managers of physical resources (money, possessions, and the earth itself). The South Node of past patterns is in Scorpio, inviting us to release automatic tendencies to misuse power and manipulate joint resources for our own gain.

Chiron is at 12 degrees of Leo, forming a square aspect to both of the Nodes. The Shaman invites us to heal self-worth wounds by:

1. Accepting that others (those of different cultures, religions, economic classes, etc.) are just as worthy as we are

2. Recognizing our own value and not accepting disrespectful treatment

Some of the key astrological events of the end of the 20th century and the beginning of the 21st century reflect back to this seminal Neptune-Pluto chart.

Uranus-Pluto Conjunction of 1965–1966

Uranus and Pluto formed an exact conjunction (seed gate) in late 1965 and the first half of 1966 at 16 to 17 degrees of Virgo. The Revolutionary and the Transformer sent out the volatile, revolutionary wake-up call to transmute the corrupt and restrictive patterns of the status quo establishment values.

Determine which house in your chart contains 16 to 17 degrees of Virgo to determine where in your life the wake-up call sounded. This is where you are seeking an inner and outer peace movement, equality for all aspects of your nature, and the need for physical forms and systems (Virgo) that are truly authentic for you. If you were not yet born in 1966, the 16- and 17-degree Virgo point in your birth chart indicates the area of your life where you want to make deep, lasting changes (Pluto) to be radically authentic (Uranus).

Uranus–Pluto Conjunction
Natal Chart
Jun 30 1966
9:49 AM GMT +0:00
Washington DC
38N54 077W02
Geocentric
Tropical
Placidus
True Node

The Uranus-Pluto conjunction of June, 1966.

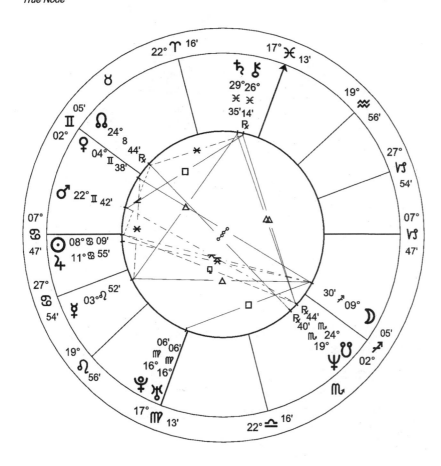

Uranus-Neptune Conjunction of 1993

Uranus and Neptune formed an exact conjunction (seed gate) three times in 1993 at 18 to 19 degrees of Capricorn. The Revolutionary and the Mystic invited us to radical new spiritual and creative systems. As we noted in Chapter 6, the Uranus-Neptune cycle symbolizes the challenge to create alternative cultural patterns and collective and personal beliefs.

The Uranus-Neptune conjunction of October, 1993.

Uranus–Neptune Conjunction
Natal Chart
Oct 24 1993
8:19 PM GMT +0:00
Washington DC
38N54 077W02
Geocentric
Tropical
Placidus
True Node

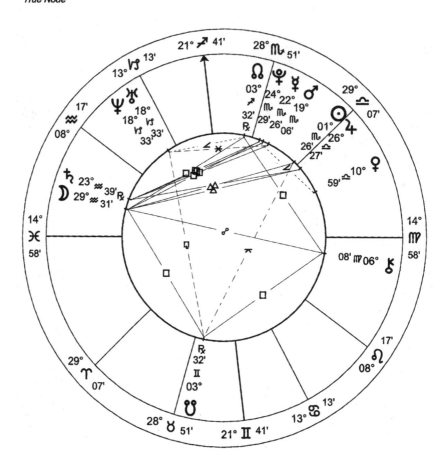

Determine which house in your chart contains 18 to 19 degrees of Capricorn to determine where you are challenged to envision new life structures and rules (Capricorn). This is where you are seeking to be authentic and to liberate yourself from inner and outer restrictive and punitive authority voices.

New Moon Solar Eclipse of August, 1999

The solar eclipse on August 11, 1999, occurs at 18 degrees of Leo. Notice that this event chart contains a Grand Square, where four groupings of planets form a box in the sky.

98

In this chart, the Sun, Moon, and North Node are in Leo in an opposite line to Uranus and the South Node in Aquarius. Saturn is in Taurus in an opposite line to Mars in Scorpio. These two lines intersect one another to form a big square pattern. Remember that squares symbolize the challenge to initiate change for release and growth.

Aug 1999 Solar Eclipse
Natal Chart
Aug 11 1999
7:09 AM EDT +4:00
Washington DC
38N54 077W02
Geocentric
Tropical
Placidus
True Node

New Moon (solar) eclipse of August, 1999.

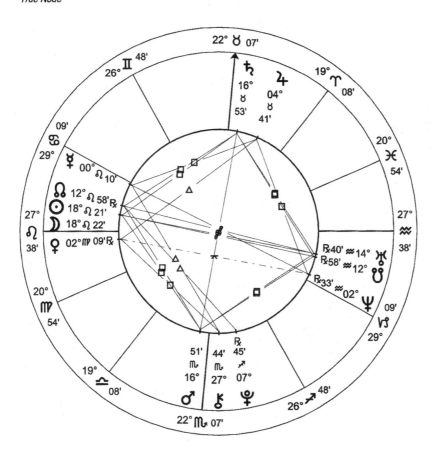

Here's the eclipse story. The conscious Heroine (Sun) and the instinctive Wild Woman (Moon) join together to take up the spiritual challenge (North Node) to be creative, loving, and playful with each other (Leo). The Revolutionary (Uranus) insists that an old pattern (South Node) of unexpected change and disruption of the status quo

(Aquarius) be factored into the Sun-Moon union. Don't compromise your personal freedom and authenticity (Aquarius) to be loved and recognized by others (Leo).

The Responsible One (Saturn) insists on holding tight to the status quo and physical and financial security (Taurus). The Warrior (Mars) passionately takes a stand for the right to fight corruption and hidden manipulative games (Scorpio) of external authorities.

The solar eclipse (at 18 degrees of Leo) is an invitation to release old conscious patterns about compromising your self-worth for the sake of others' approval. The Uranus-South Node voice of personal "freedom at all costs" is at 12 to 14 degrees of Aquarius. Saturn's invitation to keep the status quo and be good resource managers comes from 16 degrees of Taurus. Mars' feisty "change or die" battle call sounds off at 16 degrees of Scorpio.

The North Node degree point (12 degrees of Leo) in this solar eclipse chart is the same as the location of Chiron in the Neptune-Pluto conjunction chart. The evolutionary purpose (North Node) of this eclipse event is to assist us to deepen the healing work (Chiron) about love and self-worth (Leo) that's at the heart of the current information civilization.

Chiron-Pluto Conjunction of December 30, 1999

Chiron and Pluto conjunct (are together in the same place in the sky) on December 30, 1999, at 12 degrees of Sagittarius. This is a key astrological signature of the new millennium chart. Remember that a Chiron-Pluto cycle explores what happens when the Shaman meets the Transformer and invites us to enter the gateway of healing by using power wisely and by cleaning up hidden manipulative patterns.

New Moon of May 2000

The New Moon on May 4, 2000, occurs at 14 degrees of Taurus. This event chart carries an unusual pattern in that the seven visible planets in our solar system are within 28 degrees of one another in the sky. All but one (Mars) are in Taurus, the sign of Earth resources and physical security and sensuality. The planets are:

➤ Venus ♀ (Lover)

➤ Mercury ☿ (Communicator)

➤ Sun ☉ (Heroine)

➤ Moon ☽ (Wild Woman)

➤ Jupiter ♃ (Philosopher)

➤ Saturn ♄ (Builder)

➤ Mars ♂ (Warrior)

Chiron and Pluto continue their dance in Sagittarius.

Chiron–Pluto Conjunction
Natal Chart
Dec 30 1999
4:59 AM EST +5:00
Washington DC
38N54 077W02
Geocentric
Tropical
Placidus
True Node

The Chiron-Pluto conjunc-tion of December, 1999.

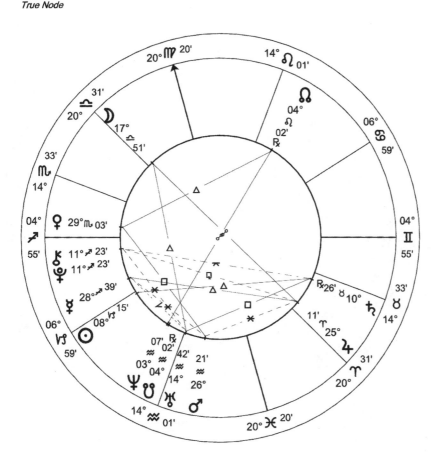

This New Moon calls us to a time of reckoning about our ability to be secure and stable. Are we loving, dialoguing, honoring, feeling, seeking wisdom from, being accountable to, and taking a stand for Mother Earth? Or, in our wounded dogmatic beliefs about the earth and physicality, are we polluting the earth with our judgments and religious wars? Look at where Taurus falls in your chart to determine in what areas of your life you need to ask these questions.

New Moon of May, 2000.

May 2000 New Moon
Natal Chart
May 4 2000
0:12 AM EDT +4:00
Washington DC
38N54 077W02
Geocentric
Tropical
Placidus
True Node

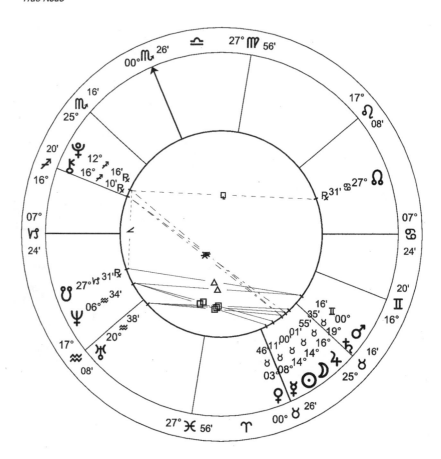

The Saturn–Jupiter Challenges and Opportunities for Each Sun Sign in the 21st Century

It takes 20 years for the social planets Jupiter and Saturn to complete one cycle and return to a seed point of conjunction. In their cycle, the expanding Philosopher dances with the grounded Builder to explore personal and collective processes of growth and contraction. During the 20 years of their cycle, they invite us to change our patterns of socialization with one another and our world. The sign in which the conjunction

102

occurs is like the sound of a tuning fork that keeps us in tune with our current tasks of balancing between give and take.

There are five Jupiter-Saturn conjunctions of the 21st century. Recall from Chapter 6 that we're currently in a Grand Mutation cycle as the conjunctions are moving from occurring in an earth element to an air element. We're leaving behind the growth and stabilization of government and personal security systems as we explore more equal and experimental social systems.

In the next few sections, we'll explore the key challenges of the five Jupiter-Saturn conjunctions as they impact each of the Sun signs.

2000 to 2020: Aries ♈ *to Pisces* ♓

The Jupiter-Saturn conjunction occurs at 23 degrees of Taurus on May 28, 2000. This is the last conjunction to take place in the earth sign cycle that began in 1802. The other recent conjunctions in Taurus were in 1881 and in 1940–41. The key challenge of this conjunction is to both expand and stabilize with respect to the right use of personal and social resources.

➤ The three *fire* signs are invited to ground their fiery natures. **Aries** ♈ Sun signs need to slow down, get rooted, and claim ownership of their life. **Leo** ♌ Sun signs need to recognize their own authority and ability to maturely administrate their lives. **Sagittarius** ♐ Sun signs need to focus on personal health and self-care in a consistent and supportive way.

➤ The three *earth* signs are challenged to loosen up and invest in their own creative and enthusiastic sides. **Taurus** ♉ Sun signs need to assess where their possessions and resources are truly reflective of their individual natures. **Virgo** ♍ Sun signs need to consider their personal truths and philosophy about money and resources. **Capricorn** ♑ Sun signs need to invest resources in their own creative and self-expressive sides.

➤ The three *air* signs are invited to make changes in their relationships to reflect their emotional needs. **Gemini** ♊ Sun signs need to address the emotional overwhelming caused by doing too many things with too many people at one time. **Libra** ♎ Sun signs are challenged to become more intimate and committed in their relationships. **Aquarius** ♒ Sun signs need to confront their fear of losing personal freedom if they say yes to settling down and growing roots.

➤ The three *water* signs are challenged to get a more dispassionate perspective on their emotional lives. **Cancer** ♋ Sun signs need to explore new communities and friendships that support their value systems. **Scorpio** ♏ Sun signs need to embrace fairness and equality in relationships to balance out their tendency to dive in with both feet. **Pisces** ♓ Sun signs need to explore alternative ways to communicate their intuitive and sensitive natures.

The Jupiter-Saturn conjunction of May, 2000.

Jupiter–Saturn Conjunction
Natal Chart
May 28 2000
11:05 AM EDT +4:00
Washington DC
38N54 077W02
Geocentric
Tropical
Placidus
True Node

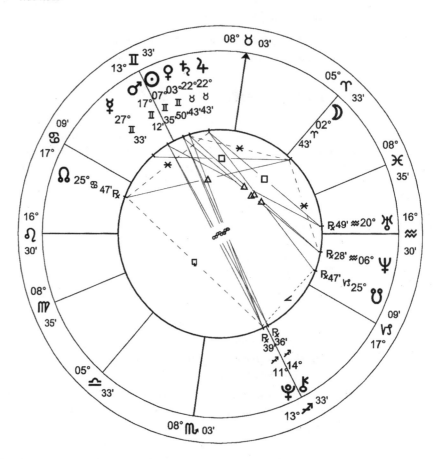

2020 to 2040: Aries ♈ to Pisces ♓

The Jupiter-Saturn conjunction occurs at 1 degree of Aquarius on December 21, 2020. The invitation is to explore ways to create a larger global community that is humanitarian and innovative in nature. How do we collectively form societies that are diverse and open to change, yet stable enough to include and support all members of its groups?

➤ The three *fire* signs are invited to bring their fiery enthusiasm to dialogue and relate with others. **Aries ♈** Sun signs need to initiate new ways to form community and take some risks to manifest their life dreams. **Leo** ♌ Sun signs need to focus on fair and equal partnerships and restoring balance to their lives. **Sagittarius** ♐ Sun signs need to explore new perspectives in their personal philosophy.

Jupiter–Saturn Conjunction
Natal Chart
Dec 21 2020
12:22 PM EST +5:00
Washington DC
38N54 077W02
Geocentric
Tropical
Placidus
True Node

The Jupiter-Saturn conjunction of December, 2020.

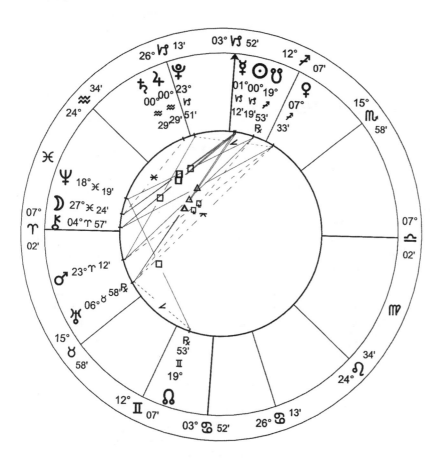

➤ The three *earth* signs are encouraged to stabilize and solidify their physical structures and game plans. **Taurus** ♉ Sun signs need to claim their capable management skills and be willing to take charge as administrators of resources. **Virgo** ♍ Sun signs need to find work and service that truly uses their abundant skills and gifts in a fair and supportive way. **Capricorn** ♑ Sun signs need to organize their own

105

physical resources and possessions and attune their financial situations with their value systems.

➤ The three *air* signs are invited to get moving on manifesting and expressing their ideas and passions. **Gemini** ♊ Sun signs need to take some time to synthesize their ideas and vast amount of data into a more concise belief system. **Libra** ♎ Sun signs need to explore fun and playfulness in their relationships. **Aquarius** ♒ Sun signs need to actualize more of their uniqueness and take some risks to be independent and self-reliant.

➤ The three *water* signs are challenged to explore how to deepen their own emotional expression and attune to their sensitivity in social situations. **Cancer** ♋ Sun signs need to become emotionally honest about the price they pay to be caretakers for others and to be willing to ask others to support them, too. **Scorpio** ♏ Sun signs need to release old emotional patterns from family dynamics so that they can have a more intimate experience of home. **Pisces** ♓ Sun signs need to recognize their intuitive and visionary natures and create ways to honor them.

2040 to 2060: Aries ♈ *to Pisces* ♓

The Jupiter-Saturn conjunction occurs at 18 degrees of Libra on October 31, 2040. This 20-year cycle explores social structures that are equal and balanced, yet also creative and artistic.

➤ The three *fire* signs are challenged to mentally understand decisions before they leap into action. **Aries** ♈ Sun signs need to be willing to see the other guy's point of view and to explore partnerships with equals. **Leo** ♌ Sun signs need to share in dialogue with the world their creativity and full-heartedness and not be attached to being special. **Sagittarius** ♐ Sun signs need to explore communities with kindred spirits that share similar life dreams and goals.

➤ The three *earth* signs are challenged to participate in relationships that are prag-0matic and grounded. **Taurus** ♉ Sun signs need to create daily routines that are balanced with work and self-care and to explore service that is worthwhile. **Virgo** ♍ Sun signs need to create a functional and practical way to manage their finances and resources. **Capricorn** ♑ Sun signs need to explore career paths that allow for their natural leadership abilities to be in balance with their creative needs.

➤ The three *air* signs are invited to become enthusiastic and fired up about their relationships. **Gemini** ♊ Sun signs need to discover creative ways to express their diverse interests. **Libra** ♎ Sun signs are challenged to become more selfish in an appropriate way and not always defer to the other guy's needs and wants. **Aquarius** ♒ Sun signs need to explore their personal truths and beliefs about equal relationships.

➤ The three *water* signs are challenged to honor their authentic emotional natures in their relationships. **Cancer** ♋ Sun signs need to nest and create emotionally secure relationships. **Scorpio** ♏ Sun signs need to release their need to control and to seek the more subtle and spiritual dimensions in relationships. **Pisces** ♓ Sun signs need to explore the ability to establish clear emotional boundaries and dialogue about power issues in relationships.

Jupiter–Saturn Conjunction
Natal Chart
Oct 31 2040
6:50 AM EST +5:00
Washington DC
38N54 077W02
Geocentric
Tropical
Placidus
True Node

The Jupiter-Saturn conjunction of October, 2040.

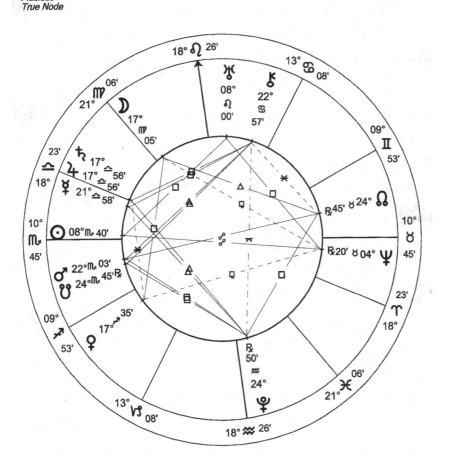

2060 to 2080: Aries ♈ to Pisces ♓

The Jupiter-Saturn conjunction occurs at 1 degree of Gemini on April 7, 2060. This is close to the Neptune-Pluto conjunction degree of 1892 (see page 95), so this

Jupiter-Saturn cycle links us back to the seed gate of the current civilization. This 20-year cycle invites us to explore and create new structures for using data and information in an impeccable way.

The Jupiter-Saturn conjunction of April, 2060.

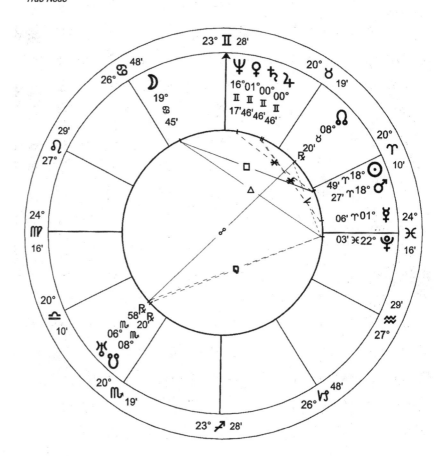

Jupiter–Saturn Conjunction
Natal Chart
Apr 7 2060
4:32 PM EST +5:00
Washington DC
38N54 077W02
Geocentric
Tropical
Placidus
True Node

➤ The three *fire* signs are invited to intensify their spirited natures and develop new forms to communicate their uniqueness. **Aries** ♈ Sun signs need to discover how to best articulate their pioneering and courageous ideas. **Leo** ♌ Sun signs need to create communities and friendships in which personal creativity and skills are mutually shared. **Sagittarius** ♐ Sun signs need to release judgment and dogmatic stances in relationships and be willing to learn deeper truths from others.

➤ The three *earth* signs are challenged to explore innovative new ways to manage and administrate technological and communication resources. **Taurus** ♉ Sun signs need to create physical and financial security through appropriate dialogue with others. **Virgo** ♍ Sun signs are invited to step forward with their analytical skills to help administrate and organize ways to manage resources. **Capricorn** ♑ Sun signs need to analyze personal and collective strategies for the healthy maintenance of whole systems.

➤ The three *air* signs are invited to actively pursue their intellectual and communication gifts in new ways. **Gemini** ♊ Sun signs need to take risks to step out in new directions to express their ideas and knowledge. **Libra** ♎ Sun signs are challenged to reflect on their philosophy about relationships and to quest for greater beauty in their lives. **Aquarius** ♒ Sun signs need to come out of their heads and explore playfulness and their willingness to reveal their creative gifts to others.

➤ The three *water* signs are invited to communicate their emotional truths and to explore new paths with personal intimacy. **Cancer** ♋ Sun signs need to develop their intuitive and psychic natures and explore the union of spirituality with emotionality. **Scorpio** ♏ Sun signs need to develop the ability to share honest dialogue about issues of power and emotional intimacy with others. **Pisces** ♓ Sun signs need to explore how to make a safe home in the world for their mystical and sensitive natures.

2080 to 2100: Aries ♈ to Pisces ♓

The Jupiter-Saturn conjunction occurs at 12 degrees of Aquarius on March 15, 2080. As the 21st century comes to a close, the Jupiter-Saturn dance again occurs in Aquarius (the conjunction in 2020 was also in Aquarius). We return to the challenge of how to create an open and free, yet also stable society that honors the uniqueness of all its members yet is also organized, functional, and efficient.

➤ The three *fire* signs are invited to bring their fire to their world on an intellectual and relational level with others. **Aries** ♈ Sun signs need to seek out friendships and group experiences that honor their courage and strong individuality. **Leo** ♌ Sun signs need to seek balance and harmony in their lives. **Sagittarius** ♐ Sun signs need to quest for new understanding about their personal truths.

➤ The three *earth* signs are encouraged to get their lives grounded and functional in experimental new ways. **Taurus** ♉ Sun signs need to organize their personal resources in efficient and functional ways. **Virgo** ♍ Sun signs need to analyze and discern the most effective way to maintain their health and stability. **Capricorn** ♑ Sun signs need to clarify how best to manage their personal physical and financial resources.

The Jupiter-Saturn conjunction of March, 2080.

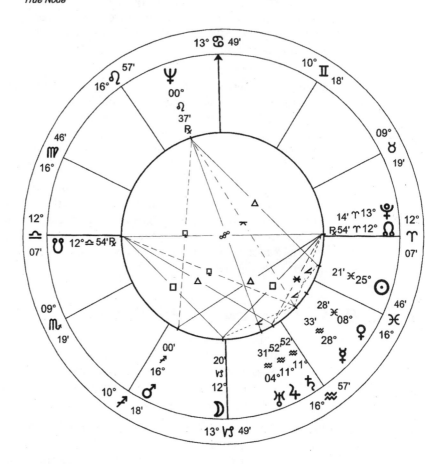

Jupiter–Saturn Conjunction
Natal Chart
Mar 14 2080
7:34 PM EST +5:00
Washington DC
38N54 077W02
Geocentric
Tropical
Placidus
True Node

➤ The three *air* signs are called to get inspired about participation in community and group processes. **Gemini** ♊ Sun signs need to explore new belief systems that can assist them in communicating their wisdom. **Libra** ♎ Sun signs need to celebrate their special gifts of heart and creativity. **Aquarius** ♒ Sun signs need to follow their own drummer and to claim more fully their individual natures in the world.

➤ The three *water* signs are challenged to express their emotional truths with friends and community. **Cancer** ♋ Sun signs need to explore emotional intimacy with self and others. **Scorpio** ♏ Sun signs need to explore new visions of family and home in which their passionate natures are honored. **Pisces** ♓ Sun signs need to seek spiritual and contemplative experiences with their friends and community.

The Evolutionary Tasks of Four Generations

Just as each generation expands and furthers the wisdom, evolutionary growth, and understanding of preceding generations, children carry the baton of progress into the next phase of cultural change initiated by their parents.

Time Capsule

Astrologers who are interested in the key evolutionary and spiritual tasks of a generation use the location of the transpersonal planets in the birth chart to map these tasks. Remember that these planets take a relatively long time to orbit the Sun. Uranus, for example, takes about seven years to transit through one sign. Therefore, millions of people will be born in a seven-year period who all have Uranus located in the same zodiac sign in their birth chart. Remember that the archetypal energies of Uranus connect us to radical change and liberation; Neptune connects us to spiritual visions, surrendering ego control, and victimization issues; Pluto connects us to issues with power and death-rebirth.

We've made up four sample charts for four generations of family members to use as examples to explore the evolutionary tasks of different generations. These are not charts of "real" people we know (although somewhere on Earth there are probably people who really were born—or will be born—on these dates, times, and locations), but rather imaginary charts made up to tell a multi-generational story.

Parent Born January 1, 1940

Here is the imaginary birth chart for a parent born in 1940. At this time, Uranus was in Taurus, Neptune was in Virgo, and Pluto was in Leo.

This chart represents a generation of individuals who explore how to revolutionize and seek personal freedom (Uranus) through their experience of personal values and money (Taurus). They also want to dissolve and re-envision (Neptune) new ways to work and offer service (Virgo) to their world. Additionally, they seek to empower themselves (Pluto) by honoring their own individuality and creative gifts (Leo).

Birth chart for January 1, 1940.

Natal Chart
Jan 1 1940
12:00 PM EST +5:00
New York NY, USA
40N45 073W57
Geocentric
Tropical
Placidus
True Node

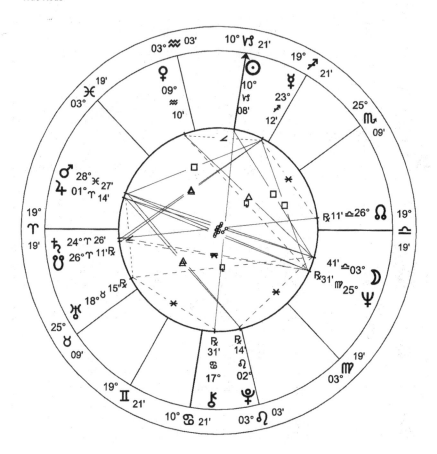

Time Capsule

Astrologers associate the Pluto-in-Leo generation with the Baby Boomers and the "me" generation because so many of them have transmuted old patterns of self-sacrifice and insisted on their own worthiness and birthrights. This generation's tasks blend together the earth (Taurus and Virgo) and fire (Leo) elements and call for them to ground their fiery natures.

Natal Chart
Apr 1 1970
12:00 PM EST +5:00
Miami FL, USA
25N47 080W11
Geocentric
Tropical
Placidus
True Node

Birth chart for April 1, 1970.

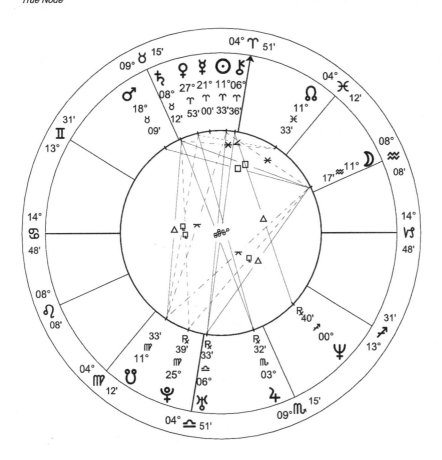

Child Born April 1, 1970

Now let's contrast these life lessons with that of the parent's child born in 1970. The chart for this April Fool's child has Uranus in Libra, Neptune at the beginning of Sagittarius, and Pluto in Virgo. This generation's tasks blend together the air (Libra), earth (Virgo), and fire (Sagittarius) elements and challenge them to ground their ideas and enthusiastic natures.

People of this generation seek to liberate from (Uranus) old gender-assigned roles and experiment with more equal forms of relationships (Libra). They also quest for understanding and deeper truths (Sagittarius) about spirituality and the mystical

(Neptune). Where this child's parent sought to dissolve patterns of self-sacrifice, the child takes that to the next step and wants to clean up and change collective patterns of misuse of power (Pluto) in the areas of work, service, and health (Virgo).

Grandchild Born July 4, 2000

The chart for the Independence Day grandchild in this imaginary family system carries Uranus and Neptune both in Aquarius and Pluto in Sagittarius. This generation focuses on the air (Aquarius) and fire (Sagittarius) elements and suggests a group that will pursue progress and change wholeheartedly.

Birth chart for July 4, 2000.

Natal Chart
Jul 4 2000
12:00 PM PDT +7:00
Los Angeles CA
34N00 118W10
Geocentric
Tropical
Placidus
True Node

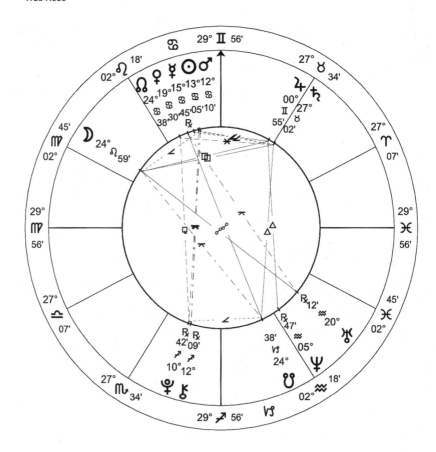

This will be a generation of change agents as they seek to be their authentic and radical selves (Uranus) and pursue their dreams and intuitive visions (Neptune) in experimental and innovative community and group associations (Aquarius). Whereas their parent (born in 1970 with Neptune in Sagittarius) sought new truths about spirituality, this generation will seek to deeply transform metaphysical beliefs that are dogmatic and disempowering (Pluto in Sagittarius).

Great-Grandchild Born October 31, 2030

To complete our family story, we made up a chart for the great-grandchild of the person born in 1940. This Halloween baby will have Uranus in Gemini, Neptune in Aries, and Pluto in Aquarius. Again we have a generation whose elemental signature as change agents is with air (Gemini and Aquarius) and fire (Aries).

Natal Chart
Oct 31 2030
12:00 PM PST +8:00
Seattle WA, USA
47N36 122W20
Geocentric
Tropical
Placidus
True Node

Birth chart for October 31, 2030.

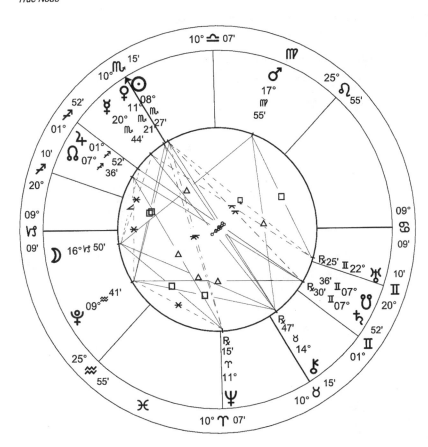

This generation will seek radical and liberating (Uranus) experiences with communication devices and languages (Gemini). They will be visionary and spiritual (Neptune) pioneers and risk-takers (Aries). Perhaps they are the ones who will live in space stations and explore planets. They will seek to clean up and transmute (Pluto) corrupt misuse of technology and social group processes.

Now that you've had a glimpse of how events can affect you personally, it's time to move on to some of the major astrological events of the 21st century. Don't put your birth chart away yet—the best is yet to come.

The Least You Need to Know

➤ You can use your birth chart to analyze a planetary cycle's personal message.

➤ The Neptune-Pluto cycle that began in 1892 marked the birth of modern civilization.

➤ The 1966 Uranus-Pluto seed gate was a revolutionary wake-up call, and the 1993 Uranus-Neptune seed gate was a call to create new spiritual and creative systems.

➤ Saturn-Jupiter cycles of the 21st century offer us the opportunity to explore more equal and experimental social systems.

➤ Each generation has an evolutionary task all its members share.

Chapter 8

Predictions, Visions, Challenges, and Weavings

In This Chapter

➤ Your 21st-century cosmic growth assignments

➤ The dawning of the Age of Aquarius

➤ Healing the mind/body split

➤ Return of the Goddess

In this chapter, we're going to summarize the major planetary cycles of the 21st century. That means we'll be reviewing the chart for the new millennium to check our collective and personal growth assignments as well as tracking how the key trans-personal cycles of Neptune-Pluto, Uranus-Pluto, and Uranus-Neptune unfold in the near future. Each cycle of a planetary pair is like a colorful thread in a beautiful tapestry, so let's take some time to stand back and admire the whole tapestry of important cycles in the next century.

We'll also be honoring the presence of the Goddess (an archetype of the divine feminine) as she makes her voice heard throughout the 21st century. Are you ready to put *your* 21st century together?

Are You Ready to Change?: 21st-Century Cosmic Growth Assignments

At the end of Chapter 6, we offered an interpretation of the birth chart for the 21st century. You may recall that Chiron and Pluto are conjunct in the fire sign of

Ask Spaceship Earth

Our task is to change the past patterns (South Node) of the Aquarius experience (which we'll discuss in the next section). This means we face up to destructive social alienation that happens when everyone is "doing their own thing" without considering how those actions impact the greater whole.

Sagittarius as we enter the new millennium. Their seed gate initiates us into the challenge to heal and transform the wounds of dogmatic belief systems. Another key pattern in this chart is a Grand Square formation in the sky between Saturn in Taurus (earth) opposite the Moon in Scorpio (water), both of whom are squared to Uranus, Neptune, *and* the South Node in Aquarius (air) opposite the North Node in Leo (fire). Wow! No wonder it's called a "grand square."

A major growth assignment of the 21st century is to transmute the old dogmatic pattern of:

➤ misusing our collective and personal physical (Taurus) and emotional (Scorpio) resources

➤ carrying an arrogant belief in the primacy of the individual need for freedom (Aquarius) at all costs

➤ the accompanying narcissistic attitude of spoiled children (Leo) who do not have to "clean up their room" and "do their chores" like everyone else.

We're collectively challenged to grow up and embrace the next level of spiritual maturity and accountability with respect to our impact on the web of life in which we're all interconnected.

Saturn in Taurus calls us to be accountable to our stewardship of earth resources. The Moon in Scorpio calls us to stop lying to ourselves emotionally about the destructive consequences of our misuse of power in the realm of finances, relationship intimacy, and shared resources amongst people.

This invitation to shift wounded Aquarius patterns comes as we enter the Age of Aquarius.

The Age of Aquarius: What Is It and When Does It Start?

The Age of Aquarius is one of 12 zodiacal ages created by the effect of the earth's motion as it turns on its axis. The axis of the earth is tilted approximately 23 degrees from vertical, and, as it rotates, the earth appears to wobble, like a spinning top.

If we project the line of the North Pole of the earth upward into the heavens, the earth's axis would point to a star. Currently, this star is Polaris (the North Star). Over a period of about 26,000 years, due to the earth's wobble, its North Pole carves out a circle projected onto the heavens. That means that, over time, the North Pole points to other stars in the universe. For example, it pointed to the star Vega approximately 13,000 years ago. And, in about 26,000 years, it will again point to Polaris.

What does this have to do with the Age of Aquarius? The Ages are named according to where in the zodiac the Sun is located at spring equinox. Because the earth's axis is tilted 23 degrees, we experience the seasons. When the earth's axis points toward the Sun, we have summer. When it points away, we have winter. When the axis is between those extremes, we experience spring or fall equinox, the time when the days and nights are of equal length.

As the earth wobbles, the Sun's apparent location at spring moves backwards in the zodiac. Around 2,000 years ago, the Sun was in Pisces at the time of spring equinox and the Age of Pisces began. Around 2100, the Sun will be in the physical constellation of Aquarius at the spring equinox. Because of that, astronomers designate this as the beginning of the Age of Aquarius. This apparent motion of the Sun moving into different zodiac signs at different ages is called the *precession of the equinoxes*.

The zodiac sign for the astrological age symbolizes the overall nature and characteristics of human developments during that age. We're just completing about 2,000 years of the Age of Pisces, when the dominant characteristics involved spiritual faith, empathy, and compassion. But the challenging side of Pisces was also very present in dogmatic religious wars, victimization of indigenous and underdog populations, and addictions with alcohol and painful unconscious family-of-origin patterns.

Speaking Y2K

The **precession of the equinoxes** is the term given to describe the Sun's apparent motion into different zodiac signs through the ages. Because of the slow motion of this cycle, its effects are felt a few hundred years before the actual astronomical event occurs.

The Age of Aquarius lasts until about the year 4300, and will carry the traits of humanitarianism, experimentation with social and community forms, and the urge for individual freedom. The challenging side will be with intellectual dogmatism, disassociation from the physical, and destructive anarchy.

Healing the Split Between Body and Mind

A primary challenge in the new millennium chart is the First Quarter square between Saturn in Taurus (an earth sign) and Uranus in Aquarius (an air sign). This action gate initiation asks us to make important decisions about how we can build structures (Saturn) to support and ground innovative new ideas and group processes (Uranus).

In Chapter 4 we introduced the four elements as akin to life's building blocks. The earth element connects to the physical and material part of life; the air element connects to the mental part of life. An important theme in the next century is the union of the body and mind (earth and air).

Out of Time

In the chart for the 21st century, three planets (Neptune, Uranus, and Mars) and the South Node are in Aquarius (air sign). Three planets are in earth signs (Sun and Mercury in Capricorn and Saturn in Taurus). The challenge to combine mental technological advancements (Aquarius) with good physical stewardship of the earth (Capricorn and Taurus) is a key issue for the next century.

The theme of initiating new ways to honor, and live respectfully on, the earth is emphasized by the New Moon of May 2000 (see Chapter 7). The century begins with that seed point between the solar and lunar luminaries in our sky inviting us to find new ways to create practical resource management. Remember—there are four other planets accompanying the Sun and Moon in Taurus.

Planetary Dances in the 21st Century

Throughout the 21st century, **Jupiter**, **Saturn**, and **Pluto** continue to emphasize the earth-air dance in their movements through the zodiac wheel. The Philosopher, Builder, and Transformer invite us to keep working on uniting the body and the mind.

Previously, we discussed how the 20-year **Jupiter-Saturn** cycle ushers in new paradigms for social contracts and the balance between expansion and limitation in human developments. At the turning of the millennium, they come together in a Grand Mutation conjunction, where they are shifting the element emphasis for their cycle from earth into air (see Chapter 6).

Pluto is in Capricorn (earth) from 2008 until 2024 and in Aquarius (air) from 2024 until 2043, so for about the first half of the century, the Transformer beckons us to let die old patterns with physical structures and social and community processes.

Saturn Can Dance!: Saturn Cycles in the 21st Century

Saturn, the ally of accountability, does a seed dance in earth and air signs with several key planets. In Chapter 6, we described the nature of Saturn cycles with its relationship to other planets. We've already discussed the Grand Mutation Jupiter-Saturn cycle from earth into air signs.

2028: Saturn-Chiron conjunction at 3 degrees of Taurus. The Builder and the Shaman begin a new cycle of creating paradigms for healed foundations and game plans to honor the human experience of ownership of property, money, and physical security.

The two Saturn-Uranus conjunctions alternate between air and earth signs. The Builder and the Liberator beckon us to create radical new structures that allow for innovative and practical ideas to manifest. They come together in 2032 at 29 degrees Gemini, inviting us to explore new forms of communication and dialogue. Their meeting in 2079 is at 30 degrees of Capricorn, calling us to actualize unique new forms of government and business.

Saturn-Neptune Conjunctions: The Builder and the Visionary. The Builder and Visionary challenge us to create spiritual and compassionate forms of government and social rules. Their conjunction in 2026 is in Aries. Their conjunction in 2061 occurs in an air sign at 21 degrees Gemini (spiritual communication forms). At the end of the 21st century, they create a seed in 2096 at 9 degrees of the earth sign of Virgo (impeccable forms of spiritual service).

Saturn-Pluto Conjunctions: The Builder and the Transformer. The first Saturn-Pluto seed gate of the new millennium occurs at 23 degrees of Capricorn in 2020. Again the planetary change agents (the Builder and Transformer) call us to seek new ways to structure our world (Capricorn) and be empowered administrators of human experience on Earth. The subsequent two conjunctions will be in 2053 in Pisces (water) and in 2086 in Aries (fire).

Transpersonal Invitations to Evolve: The Cycles of Uranus, Neptune, and Pluto

We've observed the specific color theme of air and earth in some of the cycles of shorter duration in our cosmic tapestry. Let's follow the unfolding of the significant cycles with the three transpersonal planets, whose cycles have longer periods. Because their cycles last much longer than those of Jupiter or Saturn, their colored threads form a large border on our astrological tapestry that frames the other planetary cycles we have noted.

In Chapter 5, we discussed how the three transpersonal planets act as change agents who invite us to go beyond our personal ego control and evolve to a greater level of spiritual maturity. Uranus brings innovative and unexpected changes and liberation of the authentic self. Neptune brings transcendent and spiritual experiences along with increased sensitivity to personal illusions, addictions, and fear. Pluto brings deep and lasting change and the opportunity to transform issues with power and intimacy.

Let's track how the "big three" transpersonal cycles unfold their evolutionary gifts to humankind.

Liberation from Illusions

In Chapter 7, we discussed the seed gate (conjunction) of Uranus and Neptune, which occurred in 1993 in **Capricorn**. This conjunction calls you to follow new visions (Neptune) of radical authenticity and to liberate yourself (Uranus) from inappropriate inner and outer authority voices (Capricorn). Remember that it takes 172 years for these two planets to complete one cycle. As their cycle develops, their key initiatory gates repeat the challenging themes of the Grand Square in the 21st century chart.

The action gate of their journey occurs on October 3, 2039. Uranus is at 3 degrees Leo in a First Quarter square to Neptune at 3 degrees of **Taurus**. The Liberator is asking for creative self-expression in dialogue with the Visionary, who wants spiritual grounding. The seed gate occurred in Capricorn, sign of government systems and personal structures. This could be a time of creative and heartfelt innovative solutions (Uranus in Leo) to the dream (Neptune) of healed financial and physical environments (Taurus). It could also speak to an environmental crisis around those issues.

Ask Spaceship Earth

Astrologer E. Alan Meece notes that this Uranus-Neptune opposition of 2081 could be a time when radical political change could occur based on spiritual ideals.

The harvest gate of their cycle happens in 2081. Uranus is at 5 degrees **Aquarius** opposing Neptune at 5 degrees of **Leo**. The Liberator faces the Visionary across the sky as they seek balance between the needs of the individual (Leo) and those of the collective (Aquarius).

The reflection gate of their cycle happens in 2126. Uranus is at 13 **Leo** in a Third Quarter square to Neptune at 13 degrees of **Scorpio**. They call us to an "attitude adjustment" in combining individuality (Leo) and shared resources of power (Scorpio).

The Hippie Legacy: The Continuing Cycle of the Uranus-Pluto Seed Gate of 1966

In Chapter 7, we discussed the seed gate (conjunction) of Uranus and Pluto, which occurred in 1966 in **Virgo**. Remember that it takes an average of 127 years for these two planets to complete one cycle. The invitation is to create physical forms and daily habits (Virgo) that allow for transformational changes (Pluto) to be radically authentic (Uranus). This current cycle develops in signs with the qualities of cardinal (taking action) and mutable (being adaptable).

The action gate of their journey occurs on March 17, 2015. Uranus is at 15 degrees **Aries** in a First Quarter square to Pluto at 15 degrees of **Capricorn**. Time to take action on the revolution of the individual with the death-rebirth of collective structures.

The harvest gate of their cycle happens on September 22, 2046. Uranus is at 4 degrees **Virgo** opposing Pluto at 4 degrees of **Pisces**. They illuminate how transformational spiritual processes can balance unusual technical practices.

The reflection gate of their cycle happens in 2073. Uranus is at 6 degrees **Capricorn** in a Third Quarter square to Pluto at 4 degrees of **Aries**. They invite us to shift consciousness about combining radical new life structures that support the empowerment of the individual.

The Civilization of Information: The Continuing Cycle of the Neptune-Pluto Seed Gate of 1892

In Chapter 7, we discussed the seed gate (conjunction) of Neptune and Pluto, which occurred in 1892 in Gemini. Remember that it takes 493 years for these two planets to complete one cycle, and that 1892 Neptune-Pluto conjunction marked the birth of the modern civilization in which we're currently living. The two planets conjoined at 8 degrees of Gemini, inviting us to initiate new ways to communicate and explore diverse kinds of information.

The action gate of their journey occurs in 2062. Neptune is at 23 degrees **Gemini** in a First Quarter square to Pluto at 23 degrees of **Pisces**. This is the only initiation gate (as we have defined them in Chapter 6) of the 21st century. The potential of addiction to information (Neptune in Gemini) needs to be balanced with the penetrating call of the intuitive and emotional (Pluto in Pisces). E. Alan Meece expects this to be a crisis time period with issues involving the environment, possible epidemics, and ethnic struggles.

The harvest gate of their cycle happens in 2138. Neptune is at 9 degrees **Sagittarius** opposing Pluto at 9 degrees of **Gemini**. Pluto will have returned to the point of the 1892 conjunction calling for deep change with dualistic thought processes balancing with Neptune's call for synthesizing, integrative belief systems.

The reflection gate of their cycle happens in early 2309. Neptune is at 25 degrees of **Sagittarius** in a Third Quarter square to Pluto at 25 degrees of **Pisces**. We'll be called to shift our consciousness about expansive spiritual belief systems (Neptune in Sagittarius) and powerful mystical and empathetic awareness (Pluto in Pisces).

Neptune and Pluto will conjoin again in 2385.

> **Ask Spaceship Earth**
>
> Each of the subsequent Neptune-Pluto initiation gates occur in mutable signs, symbolizing the evolutionary challenge of the "information civilization" to continue to adapt and change in a fluid and open way.

When God Was a Woman

The Goddess is an ancient symbol of the earth as a divine presence that humans have worshipped for eons. In their book on the Goddess, *The Great Cosmic Mother* (Harper and Row, 1987), authors Monica Sjoo and Barbara Mor concluded that "God" was a female for at least the first 200,000 years of human existence. Images of the Goddess found in cave paintings and carved statues in stone, clay, and bone show that humans attributed magical power to the earth itself as the "Mother of Life and Death." Here are the ancient roots of our modern concept of Mother Earth.

The worship of the Goddess focused on the cyclic nature of physical life where vegetation and newborn animals emerged after the death processes of winter. Sjoo and Mor note that in the world's oldest creation myths, the Goddess is the Great Mother who births the world out of herself and remains immanent and alive in her creation. This is in contrast to the more recent images of the divine masculine with God the Father being separate from, and having power over, the physical earth.

Time Capsule

In her pioneering research, archaeologist Marija Gimbutas traced the development of Goddess-centered art on ancient artifacts found throughout Europe. She discovered that this art contained no images of warfare and male domination, indicating instead a non-violent, Earth-centered agricultural culture. In her book, *The Language of the Goddess* (HarperCollins, 1989), she focused on the continuity of art images and symbols found on art in Western Europe from the period of about 4500 to 2500 BC. This is approximately the period of the astrological Age of Taurus (4200 to 2100 BC).

In the Age of Taurus, agricultural humans focused on the physical and sensual aspects of life with fertility of crops, animal domestication, and procreation of life. People lived in harmony with the natural cycles of the earth. The Age of Aries, with its aggressive invasions by warriors and establishment of dominating war-based empires, did not arrive until the period of 2100 BC to AD 1.

The Return of the Goddess

The 21st century marks our collective entry into the Age of Aquarius with humanitarian values and innovative new forms of community. As we do so, the characteristics of the Age of Taurus are re-emerging in our cultural awareness as tools to help us create new societal forms. There has been an explosion of books and interest on the Goddess and matriarchal, non-warrior civilizations.

This "return of the Goddess" in our collective Western psyche coincides with the recent conjunctions of Saturn-Uranus (at 29 degrees of Sagittarius) in 1988 and Saturn-Neptune (at 11 degrees of Capricorn) in 1989. The Builder, Liberator, and Mystic danced together to invite us to create new philosophical belief structures (Sagittarius) and new spiritual ground rules (Capricorn) at the turning of the millennium.

The Goddess as a figure of the divine symbolizes a spirituality of interconnectedness with all life on Earth. She is a presence of vital necessity at this turning of the ages when humans grapple with crises in the areas of ecology, nuclear weapons, and the imbalance of Earth resources of food and goods.

Writer Caitlin Matthews notes that Goddess consciousness can be seen in the rise of feminism, the ecological movement, the re-emergence of Mother Mary as a key aspect of the divine in Christian theology; and Gaia theory in science, which we'll discuss in Chapter 25.

The Primacy of Mother Earth: Cycles in Taurus

The next century begins and ends with two important cycles in Taurus, symbolizing that in the 21st century we will remember the primacy of Mother Earth. On May 3, 2000 (just before the New Moon in Taurus mentioned earlier), there's a rare alignment of the seven original planets (those visible to the ancients) in Taurus. They are the Sun, Moon, Mercury, Venus, Mars, Jupiter, and Saturn.

At the end of the 21st century, Pluto enters Taurus. The Transformer and archetype of death and resurrection enters Taurus for the first time since 1851, when a Uranus-Pluto conjunction occurred at 1 degree of Taurus. This coincided with mass revolutions in the industrial world around the issue of fair distribution of resources and goods—and marked the birth of the socialist movement.

So, as the next century ends, Pluto returns to Taurus and the resurrection of the issue of a healed and empowered relationship to the physical world re-emerges as primary. This echoes the ancient spiritual belief that the earth is the Great Mother of life and death. The primacy of Mother Earth means that no matter how technologically astute and innovative we get, we can't escape our link to our senses and the interdependent ecology of our Earth environment.

Out of Time

Astrologer Tem Tarriktar calls this seven-planet alignment a "continental divide" on the human timescape because it links with major changes in global financial structure (like the creation of a new global economic system). He notes that there may be big corporate mergers or cooperation between countries due to a security crisis that may occur at the time of the Leo solar eclipse in August of 1999.

The Yin Experience at Mid-Century

Remember from Chapter 4 that the earth and water elements are considered to be *yin*, (receptive or feminine) parts of our nature. The cycles of the middle part of the next century emphasize these two elements, once again inviting us to honor the presence of the feminine aspect of life.

The Pluto-Uranus opposition of June 30, 2048.

Pluto-Uranus Opposition
Natal Chart
Jun 30 2048
2:24 AM GMT +0:00
Washington DC
38N54 077W02
Geocentric
Tropical
Placidus
True Node

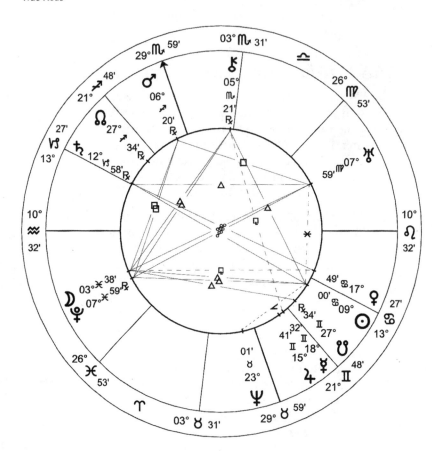

In 2048, the harvest gate of the Uranus-Pluto cycle occurs. Uranus is at 8 degrees Virgo opposite Pluto at 8 degrees Pisces. The Liberator and Transformer seek to balance precise, grounded forms for expressing the spiritual, intuitive sides of human nature. Additionally, all of the planets beyond and including Saturn are in either an earth or water sign. Saturn is in Capricorn, Chiron is in Scorpio, and Neptune is in Taurus, for example.

At mid-century, there's a *grand earth trine* between Saturn, Uranus, and Neptune. Recall from Chapter 4 that a trine aspect is when two planets are about 120 degrees away from one another in the sky. A trine symbolizes a relationship of harmony and ease between the two archetypal energies. A grand earth trine occurs when three planets in earth signs form an equal triangle in the sky so that each of them is about 120 degrees from one another. Saturn in Capricorn (build impeccable structures) dances with Uranus in Virgo (express authentic forms of service and healing) and Neptune in Taurus (spiritualize money and the material world).

Speaking Y2K

A **grand earth trine** occurs when all three earth element planets are about 120 degrees away from each other in the sky.

Take Up the Challenge: Be a Conscious Weaver with the Gods

As you've learned, astrology is a study of how the cycles of the planets correspond to cycles of human consciousness. In addition, you can see how the synchronistic link between what the planets are doing in the "above" of the sky at the time of important human events mirrors what is happening in the "below" of the earth. And you've learned how to interpret some of the key spiritual weavings of "above and below" that will occur as we enter the next millennium.

Unlike our ancestors, we no longer petition the planets as gods and goddesses to grant us our survival. Still, through the lens of astrology, we do recognize the planets as important archetypal companions in the evolution of human consciousness.

Time Capsule

At its core, the human study of astrology is an attempt to ascertain how to live in harmony with our personal and collective destinies. But astrology is not an instrument of fate, through which the planets control us and we have nothing to say in the matter. Rather, it's an intuitive art of the spirit, through which we can honor and celebrate the dynamic spiritual dance of interconnection between humans, the heavenly bodies, and the earth itself.

The deepest challenge of the new millennium is inherent in its "2" vibration: to live in sacred relationship with the earth, one another, and the greater universe to which we all belong. We respectfully challenge *you* to take this astrological wisdom on the planetary cycles and use it in the best way possible to make deep and lasting changes in *your* life.

Honor the call of the planetary change agents to wake up and shift your consciousness from the narrow focus of "everyone for themselves" to the expansive and healing focus of "many hands make light work." It's time to move from the independent "1" vibration of the heroic explorer and conqueror to the conscious, mutually supportive partnership of the "2" vibration (supported by the "3" vibration for the third millennium that begins in the year 2000). It's time to honor the return of the Goddess as the divine feminine in all beings that seeks to belong and make union with others in an interdependent and cooperative way.

Let us co-create with the universe a tapestry of a healed ecology, spiritual beauty, personal authenticity, world peace, and dynamic and passionate creativity.

The Least You Need to Know

➤ We all have 21st-century cosmic growth assignments to complete.

➤ The dawning of the Age of Aquarius will turn us to humanitarian tasks.

➤ Healing the mind/body split is our most important cosmic growth assignment.

➤ The return of the Goddess heralds a return to a more holistic global understanding.

Part 3
Two's Company: Numerology

Numerology, the language of numbers, is an accessible tool for exploring both global and personal challenges for the 21st century. We'll introduce you to the numbers of the new millennium. You'll also learn how to find your own numbers and put them together to find out how your millennium will shape up by the numbers.

Chapter 9

Numerology and the Language of Numbers

In This Chapter

➤ The symbolic language of numbers

➤ Numbers give us insight into the human condition

➤ The old millennium was under the number 1

➤ The new millennium is under the number 2

➤ Two is the number of peace, harmony, balance, cooperation, and relationships

---

Now that we've got some astrological insights into the new millennium under our collective belts, it's time to move on to the equally fascinating intuitive art of numerology. You can think of numerology as the language of numbers—what they mean, how they affect us, and how we can use our knowledge of them to improve our lives. Our resident expert for this section is Kay Lagerquist, numerologist, teacher, and life-planning counselor.

The numerological connection to the new millennium is readily apparent: We'll be moving from the 1 to the 2. But the meanings behind those numbers may not be familiar to you. In this chapter, we'll walk you from the old (1) to the new (2), and discover exactly what this change calls for, by the numbers.

Numerology Is the Language of Numbers

Let's begin by looking at exactly what *numerology* is. As a system of relating names and numbers, numerology is based on Pythagoras' (the father of mathematics and music) theories that all things in the universe are actually harmonic vibrations.

Numerology is an amazingly simple system of adding numbers, names, and dates to find their symbolic meanings. Once we know the symbolic meaning of any number, we have a practical and spiritual system of relating numbers to our lives.

Numerology can help you understand:

Speaking Y2K

Numerology is a system of relating names and numbers to gain insight into the human condition.

➤ Events in your life

➤ Psychological conditions

➤ Feelings and hunches

➤ Cycles in your life

➤ Your challenges

➤ Your strengths and talents

How can numbers reveal so many things? Read on: They're symbols of vibration.

Numbers Are Symbols of Vibration and Energy

To understand the language of numbers, let's begin by looking at the meaning of the numbers 1 to 9 and their energy. Besides having symbolic meaning, each number generates a certain kind of energy. Each of these number's symbolic meaning is universal in its application. We call this energy a *vibration*.

Energy of Numbers

Numerologists have been studying the energy of the numbers 1 through 9 for more than just this millennium. In fact, you may know more than you realize about the numbers' energy already. Read on and see:

Number 1. The energy of the number 1 is intensely active, with a driving determination to get ahead. There's a mental vigor here, and it results in goal-oriented, masculine expression. Slackers need not apply.

Number 2. Number 2 energy wants nothing so much as to merge, and it's patient while it waits for this to happen. In fact, 2 energy moves to a slower rhythm, and is subtle and gentle, with light from within. There's also a heightened sensitivity to light and sound, and a capacity for balance, as 2 dwells in both beauty and things of spirit. The 2 energy is quiet and intuitive, and psychic activities are more prominent here than in most of the other numbers.

Number 3. The energy of the 3 is intensely creative. It also naturally follows that it's excitable, enthusiastic, and vital. Here's an energy that incubates imaginative ideas but depends on other numbers to put them into form and action. The 3 energy positively bursts forth.

Number 4. The energy of the 4 grounds the energy of the other numbers with its practical planning. Here's the energy that creates patterns from the material, by forming, building, enduring, preserving, and systematizing. The 4 energy is solid and stable.

Number 5. The energy of the 5 is active, energetic, speedy, and curious. Quick to promote, quick to perceive, this is an energy where you'll find both a sense of adventure and a quick-change artist. The 5 energy likes to investigate everything, and its action as it does is both impulsive and spontaneous. The energy of the 5 is not afraid to take risks.

Number 6. Here you'll find an energy that's nurturing, loving, and concerned. The 6 energy is caretaker of what's already been formed, and this number is both humanitarian and service-oriented. The 6 demands balance and fights for ideals and principles, while at the same time being conventional—there's a good business sense here. Sometimes called "the cosmic mother," the 6 provides and protects, and, like your real mother, is pretty darned good at problem-solving as well.

Number 7. The 7 energy is about rest and rejuvenation, and turns inward to reevaluate and discover inner truths. Here you'll find serene contemplation, an energy that finds the soul in all things. The energy of the 7 is about restoration, and the healing that comes from nature, solitude, and spiritual focus. This energy is a law unto itself; it seeks the unusual, and is skeptical, analytical, and reticent in its approach to outer world matters. "Withdraw," says the energy of the 7, "and you shall heal."

Speaking Y2K

A number's **vibration** is its intensity of energy, or the emotional response associated with the number.

Number 8. The energy of the 8 is strength, power, and vision. Here's the energy of authority and expansion, and its playing field is the material world. However, judicial action is called for where higher principles are brought to bear upon the material world of money, power, and achievement. Achievement-oriented, the energy of the 8 works on bigger issues that affect the whole, all the time demanding organization. This energy wants both to execute things envisioned in the 7 and to lead toward a larger vision for life.

Number 9. The energy of the 9 represents the beginning and the end, and it's here that the energy sphere widens from local to global, with great achievements possible. The 9 wants to promote improvement for mankind; after all, it's a service energy, especially for philanthropic endeavors. But because it's also an emotional energy, the 9 puts its deep convictions into action, and generosity, sympathy, a loving nature, and idealism abound. The energy of the 9 is challenged by the need for compassionate, tolerant, forgiving, and deeply transformational understanding. Energy runs deep here, moving all along the path of transformation. Whether it's from destruction, loss, sorrow, suffering, pain, or from great achievement, earned reward, or intense spiritual awakening, the energy *is* intense with this number. It's said to have the power of all the other numbers within its vibration, and it brings completion, ending, and conclusion to any cycle.

We're Picking Up Good Vibrations

Once we know what a number's energy translates to, we're also aware of the numerological "vibe" we're getting from someone—or something.

Sound complicated? It's not, really. All this means is that numbers tell us what we can expect vibrationally. So when we look at, say, the new millennium, we can ask questions like:

➤ What can we expect with the number 2 heading up the next millennium?

➤ What's the meaning of the number 2000? And all those zeroes?

➤ What vibes will we be living with?

➤ What are the emotional components of this number 2000?

See what we mean?

Time Capsule

The bigger the number, the more intense the vibration. For example, a number 4 is less intense than an 8. Of course, 2000 is a pretty big number, so it's a very intense vibration.

Raising Our Vibration from the 1 to the 2

In millennium 2000, we'll be leaving the number 1 behind and changing over to the number 2. To put it another way, we've just been knowing life under the millennium 1000, or the *1*. The millennium number is the "1" in the number 1990. When 1999 turns into the year 2000, we'll move from the vibration of the number 1 to the vibration 2—as in 2000, or the *2 millennium*.

Moving from the 1 to the 2 means that we'll be changing vibrations. And because 2 is greater than 1, we'll be living under a higher vibration.

What It Means to Raise Our Vibration

When we change vibrational frequencies, we begin to change our lives because our perceptions begin to change. This change may be referenced differently by various disciplines. The new "vibration" of millennium 2000 might be called:

➤ In earth sciences: it might be seen as change in planetary frequency, and magnetic field shift

➤ In medical sciences: biochemical and cellular change, shifts in DNA coding, more emphasis on energy medicine

➤ In esoteric disciplines: it may be referred to as "moving toward the light," "the coming of the New Age," Or "living in the positive vibration" (instead of the fear-based negative vibration of the last 1000 years)

Speaking Y2K

The **1 millennium** governs years 1000–1999 (it's what we're leaving behind). The **2 millennium** governs years 2000–2999. Because it's a higher number, we're raising the vibration with this move.

We'll be restructuring our bodies and our lives in subtle yet profound ways, too. All of this is part of the adaptation process that we'll come to know as we begin to assimilate this higher frequency. Simply put, come the new millennium, we will evolve!

Changing Channels: Moving from the 1 to the 2

The new millennium begins our long, intimate experience with the number 2. The year 2000's numerical composition is 2 + 0 + 0 + 0, so numerologically, it will be a 2 year (2 + 0 + 0 + 0 = 2). Still, as we move through the years and numbers throughout this millennium, we'll always be under the influence of the 2, because that's the number of the millennium.

To give you a better feel for how a number influences an entire millennium, we're going to look at three millennia (that's the plural of millennium)—the 1000s, the 2000s, and the 3000s—and explore the meanings behind their numbers.

Millennium Numbers: Millennium 1000

The time span of millennium 1000 covers the years from 1000 to 1999, and this is the millennium we're leaving behind. The predominant number, millennially, is the number 1. Using the symbolic meaning of the number 1, we might say that we've been in a thousand-year period of beginnings. This has also been a time of establishing independence, innovation, self-starting, determination, and leadership, and it has required courage, daring, will, and intelligence. That's a pretty good thousand-year beginning! All these words are properties and vibrations of the number 1.

Ask Spaceship Earth

When 1 is the dominating energy, it feels like we're in a start-up phase—in the larger picture.

The number 1 is very much about the energy of birthing, beginning, and starting anew—even when this 1 gets coupled with other numbers, such as the 9 in 1999. The 1 remains the dominant theme running throughout the thousand-year cycle.

Time Capsule

It's interesting to note that, when you reduce it, the year 1999 is a 1 universal year. To reduce, add the numbers together:

   1 + 9 + 9 + 9 = 28

Now, keep adding:

   2 + 8 = 10

Finally, add the last two numbers:

   1 + 0 = 1

This means that the millennium 1000 ends with 1 energy—looking forward to new beginnings.

As you recall, we have just finished the 20th century. Here we see the number 2 showing up in concert with the one of this millennium. So our old millennium, 1000, in all its self-sufficiency and independence, is asked to begin to factor in the 2. What about relating and learning to work together? The 2 reminds us to find a place in our lives for the "other": to begin to know the value of connecting (the 2). This is because, when dealing with numbers, symbolically, a sneak preview is always given of what's to come, and so, at the end of any cycle, we're given a taste of what the next vibrational pattern will be.

As a result, this millennium of 1000, and specifically the 20th century, is spiced with issues of cooperation, patience, and peacemaking, all reminders that 1 doesn't stand alone, but is in relationship to its kin number, the 2.

Millennium 2000

This time span covers years 2000 to 2999, and the predominant number of this millennium is the number 2, which means this is a thousand-year time period under the influence and vibration of the energy of the 2. We might say that we'll live in a time that's about harmony, balance, and relating. And, even though we'll have many numbered years in this new millennium, we'll always be striving for the bigger picture of blending, harmonizing, and balancing.

This millennium is called the 3rd millennium, and within it we find that we enter into it with the 21st century (21 = 2 + 1 = 3). Just as the 2 made itself felt during the 1, we now see the 3 operating under the influence of the predominant energy of the 2 of this millennium.

If the 2 is about balance, harmony, and relationships, then the 3 reminds us, as a subtle influence, that we can 1) find joy and happiness in this time of the 2, and 2) that we'll be given many opportunities to express ourselves, and to say our truth (these are the issues of the 3), all while we're learning about relationships, balancing our lives, and living harmonically with life forms of this planet.

The High Priestess is Tarot's Major Arcana card number 2. It is the card of intuition and balance.

THE HIGH PRIESTESS

Astrologically, as you already discovered in Chapters 4 through 8, we'll be experiencing paradigm shifts into "greater healing" and balance. From the Tarot, which we'll be exploring in Chapters 12 through 17, you'll learn that the number 2 is the High Priestess card, the card of intuitive knowing. In this millennium 2000, we'll learn to resolve duality, achieve balance, and live in relationships harmonically.

Millennium 3000

As you've probably guessed, this time span covers the years 3000 to 3999 and is under the predominant influence of the number 3. This would be the time we've all been waiting for—living in the vibration of joy and happiness, with positive, creative energy surrounding us.

Astrologically, this millennium appears to be a time of resurrection of Mother Earth, and from the Tarot, we're reminded that the 3 is the card of the Empress and her nurturing mother energy. It would seem, then, that this will be a time of abundance, fertility, creativity, and joy. Don't forget, this will also be the 4th millennium, so we'll be grounding this happy energy, and creating form for this new vibration of ecstasy. We can't wait! Let's hope we find our way back here to enjoy this.

The Empress is Tarot's Major Arcana card number 3. It is the card of abundance, creativity, and fertility.

THE EMPRESS.

Legacy of the 1: Where We've Been

Numerologically, as you've just learned, the time we've just completed was under the number 1. This means that the 1 has been the dominant theme of the last 1,000 years. This was a time under the masculine principle, a patriarchal time, and so, naturally, this masculine number embodies the male qualities of drive, courage, and single focus.

The negative and positive expressions of the number 1 have set the stage for the new millennium. But first, let's take a look at how those expressions have played out over the past 1,000 years, and see if anything looks familiar.

Out of Time

Each number can have both a positive and a negative influence. Well-balanced, a number's energy will of course be positive. But when the qualities of the same number aren't balanced, it becomes negatively expressed.

Positive Expression of Number 1

At its best, the number 1 is original, inventive, and pioneering. It governs things which are being initiated and so encourages courage, will, determination, and competition. The 1 likes action and wants instant results, to lead and begin. You know: instant breakfast, instant banking, wrinkle-free cream that promises instant results…

The ultimate goal of the 1 is to learn leadership and independence. All of these can be the positive expression of this number's influence, but when we push too far, become too invested in getting results, or when we just plain go too fast, it creates an imbalance that will bring out the negative expression of this number.

Negative Expression of Number 1

At its worst, the number 1 is competitive, narcissistic, driven, willful, self-centered, opinionated, single-minded, and impatient. The negative 1 likes to handle the big picture, but cares little for the details. How many times have we seen this in the past century? An example: Did it occur to any of the big-picture folks that damming the Everglades might lead to the extinction of an entire ecosystem?

Negative 1 expression lacks diplomacy, mainly because it rushes on to achieve the goal, or to get the lead. The 1 in this form often forgets that it's in relationship with others instead; the eye is on the prize.

Many of these negative traits of the 1 have been dominant in the last century of the millennium 1000 and have left us pretty disheartened. We can't help but long for compassion, consideration, and cooperation. We wonder if it's even possible to have a time where people are sensitive, gentle, caring, and not driven.

Fear not! We bring on the 2—the next millennium. And just in time, too!

Leaping to the Number 2: Where We're Going

We won't be leaving the 1 totally behind as we slide into this new millennium. In its earliest years, we'll be making the transition from the 1 to the 2. Like getting a divorce or a new coach, it will take time to get used to the new one.

The number 2 has its positive and negative qualities also, of course. It will be up to us, collectively, to work with achieving the best the 2 has to offer, but to get there, we'll have to work our way through the worst first.

Negative Expression of Number 2

The challenge of the 2 focuses mainly around having to cooperate, but we can't work with each other using the old model of the 1. The 2 says add the ingredient "sensitivity." However, too much sensitivity, which is the opposite of too much narcissism, puts us out of balance. When we're out of balance, we express negative energy. At its most negative, the 2 governs easily hurt feelings, emotionalism, and hypersensitivity in all forms, including allergens to the body (we've all been sneezing a little more lately...).

People, the environment—even the economy—become too sensitive and are easily disrupted because of this delicate nature. The emotional body, the environmental body, and all other "bodies" at present seem to be saturated with the negative legacy of the 1. It's clearly a time to move on, but in order to do that, the 2 says "get in balance." To achieve balance, we'll all have to go through the stages of sensitivity in order to realign ourselves with a healthier model.

We've already experienced some of this in the 20th century (which, we remind you, century-wise is the 2), but when the 2 is the dominant theme, we'll be immersed in the issues of relating, cooperating, and finding the balance. If the negative 2 expression is what we're working out, then we'll have these sensitivity issues "in the face" in the following ways:

➤ Timidity

➤ Fear

➤ Aloneness

➤ Discord

➤ Too much detail

➤ Loss of time

➤ Unhappiness

➤ Nitpicking (who? not me!)

➤ Divided

➤ Aloneness

➤ Weakness

➤ Passive abdication of one's power, needs, well-being

How might we see these negative issues show up in work, family, business, the Y2K situation, global negotiations, and personal relationships? These will be the testing grounds where the growth will be felt. Remember, though, as we work through the negative aspects of the number 2, we'll begin to embrace the positive influence of this number. And none too soon, thank you!

Positive Expression of the Number 2

At its best, the number 2 brings harmony (yes, freedom from conflict), balance, and peace. But these states are not achieved via a push-through-it, driven, reach-the-goal-at-all-costs consciousness. This is not, after all, the aggressive nature of the 1 anymore. No, we arrive at this blessed state of balance and peace through the *subtle*.

It's so hard for us to grasp subtle notions like energy, vibrations, perceptivity, and gentleness—all characteristics of the 2—and yet, it's from these subtle influences that we'll see a heightened capacity for relating and partnering, for agreement and cooperation, for diplomacy and mediation. This is precisely how we will change the vibration of the old to the new.

The positive influence of the 2 will result in:

➤ Merging

➤ Finding our true tribe and community

➤ Heightened sensitivity to others, world problems, communication and the environment

➤ Heightened awareness to the psychic, telepathic, subconscious communications

➤ Developing a sense of what's needed without waiting to be told

➤ Joining together to solve problems

➤ Developing a slower, more sane rhythm for how we execute business and live our lives

➤ Honoring of the feminine in all things, which then honors the gentle, sensitive, and the subtle

And remember, all of this "2-ness" prepares us for the 3 of the following millennium. It's in the 3 that we'll get to live in a stabilized vibration of happiness, love, joy, and ecstasy. But first, we have to learn to get along, which is the bottom-line message of the number 2.

The Least You Need to Know

➤ Numbers are a symbolic language with universal application.

➤ Numbers give us insight into the human condition.

➤ The old millennium was under the number 1.

➤ The new millennium is under the number 2.

➤ Two is the number of peace, harmony, balance, cooperation, and relationship.

Chapter 10

New Millenium Numbers at a Glance

In This Chapter

➤ The new millennium is a 2

➤ The 2 means we'll be blending and harmonizing previously opposing forces

➤ Y2K translates to 11/2—a master number

➤ The Year 2000 has 3 zeroes

➤ The new millennium began January 1, 1999, numerologically

The new millennium means a move from the self-interested 1 to the sensitive 2. How we approach this 2 millennium individually can help us together create a universe beyond our wildest dreams. The 2 vibration is giving us the opportunity to move to the next level of consciousness, but it's up to us to seize it. How? Read on.

Living with the 2

As the new millennium with all its unknowns approaches, one thing we *can* count on is that the number of the millennium won't change—and that there are certain truths that belong to this number. The number of the new millennium is, of course, the *number 2*, as in 2000.

Within our own lifetimes, we'll be doing the dance with the 2 from 2000 through 2100. Our kids, grandkids, and great-grandkids, of course, will see years with other numbers in them (2306, 2752, 2984 . . .), but these years too are under the millennium number 2. Because of this, we thought it would be helpful to bone up on what it means to live with the 2, so we'll be prepared for all its promise—and problems.

Getting Connected

First of all, the number 2 governs all aspects of connecting. This means that together, we'll be facing a time of finding a "tribe"; merging; achieving balance and cooperative consensus-building; a return to honoring the feminine; and, most importantly, enhancing the quality of relationships and partnerships. Ultimately, this represents a shift from the "me" to the "we"—from "mine" to "ours," in other words.

Living with the 2 will encourage new paradigms in diplomacy, relationships, and community, as well as new patterns of relating. The 2 also means we'll begin to stress the more subtle means of acquiring information, such as intuition, psychic energy, telepathy, and various other sensitivities we're not currently using. It means more attentiveness to our bodies as indicators of environmental health.

It's not all sunshine and roses, of course; no number is perfect. One of the more bothersome features of the 2 is that it can bring delays or a slower rhythm. This is a time for "being," which will be a big jolt after the go-get-'em, do-it-fast mentality we've become accustomed to during the last 100 years of the 1.

Blending, Merging, and Getting Balanced: Ø Opposition

Under the 2, we'll be blending and harmonizing previously opposing forces. Some examples:

➤ Male/Female

➤ Science/Spirituality

➤ Traditional Medicine/Alternative Medicine

➤ Self/Community

➤ Us/Them Mentality

➤ Left/Right (whether political viewpoints or brain functions)

➤ Dogs/Cats (just seeing if you're paying attention . . .)

The point of the 2 is that, even when they seem to be opposing forces, we'll be called upon to find a way to create harmony between the two. In theory, we'll fully realize the best of each without discounting the other. To find the balance point, we'll learn not to sacrifice the one for the other, or the 1 for the 2, for that matter. It's the blend that we'll be after.

We're required to make room for the coming of more feminine presence in our lives, for cooperation instead of control, consensus instead of authority. In short, it will be the co-mingling of opposing energies. It will be about having "both" instead of "either/or."

Out of Time

Don't be fooled—"balanced" doesn't mean "either/or" consciousness. It's a third space—a space of wholeness.

In other words, the new paradigm for the new millennium is something really, really new. Most of us probably can't even imagine what this is, and it will take both courage and creativity to move to this new place. But while the 2 will be ever present in its demand for balance, it will also be what's helping us to learn and create the balance it's demanding.

The New Millennium Model

What can we expect on our new 2 adventure? To find a way to belong, live in harmony, embrace new paradigms, a new model of relationship, new concepts of time, and the power of interdependence. But let's look at each of these, one at a time.

Finding a "Tribe"

This new age favors the "brotherhood of mankind," where we will each be called to find our true "tribe" or family. It's a time for community—and for finding a community of kindred souls. We'll be shifting away from customary notions of community and family, toward people of like consciousness to call family, to hang with, to grow with, and to build a better world with.

The 2 will find us looking for connection and group belonging, which will be quite an adjustment for all those loners, separatists, "I-don't-need-anybody" folks out there. But as the 2 vibration takes hold, even the most rugged of individualists will begin to seek connection. After all, it's only in community and relationships that we can begin to live in harmony—and *harmony* is going to be the name of the game.

Return to the Feminine: The Age of Gaia

The ultimate feminine force in our lives is Mother Earth, and in the last decade we've become newly aware of our relationship to the earth and her people. In the new millennium, also called the Age of Gaia (which we'll discuss in Chapter 25), "Earth will no longer support inharmonious patterns of fear, hate, prejudice, greed, and polarity," according to Gregg Braden in *Awakening to Zero Point* (Radio Bookstore Press, 1997).

After all, as we've said before, this will be a time of blending and learning to live in harmony.

We think the ultimate goal of this new millennium is to balance and heal the earth, which includes all of us working to achieve balance in our lives that will then sustain that healing. For this, we turn to the sensitive, loving, healing energy of the feminine.

Numerologically, the return to the feminine comes from the gentle vibration of the 2, which is about tenderness, psychic knowing, and intuitiveness. This means relying on our higher senses—to govern, to make decisions, to create policy, and for our personal lifestyle choices. The feminine aspects of the 2 ask us to allow things to emerge, rather than make them happen, to learn to "be," rather than to live consumed with "doing."

This 2 is a receptive energy, which means we shift to being more open to emerging possibilities rather than demanding, driving, and depleting. We learn to respect these qualities of the feminine within ourselves and from there we honor our planet as sensitive, caring creatures coexisting on this living, breathing globe.

Time Capsule

Some say that this new millennium is the opening of the heart chakra, yoga's center of energy located near the heart, on a mass scale, while others say it's the end of the patriarchal system. Either way, it's a return to the more sensitive, feminine traits—a kinder, gentler humanity that must emerge to honor and care for this finite planet of dwindling resources.

It's important to note that the "return of the feminine" is not a *trading* of the patriarchal for the matriarchal; it's not an exchange of the one for the other. Rather, it's about blending, about bringing the 1 into the 2 rather than just perpetuating the "male" versus "female" opposition.

New Paradigms for the New Millennium

One change that can be expected from the influence of the 2 is a movement toward more active integration of our intuitive abilities and our psychic awareness. As we become more sensitized in our thinking-feeling responses, we'll come to understand and utilize our intuition in more profound ways. From this juncture we'll see paradigm shifts in our attitudes.

Old Paradigm Attitudes	New Paradigm Attitudes
Millennium 1000	**Millennium 2000**
Make it happen	Allowing it to emerge
"Get it done now"	It will happen at the right time
Impatience	Patience (become saints, we will!)
Mistrust	Trust
Hurried life	Slower rhythm
Penetrating, pushing	Receiving, emerging
Disregard for timing ("pushing the envelope")	Timely action, living in the flow
Overt	Subtle
Outer, external focus (disregard for the inner)	Inner focus, taken into relationship with others
Loss of meaning	Return of meaningful
Disregarding body signs	Living in tune with our bodies
Loss of self in relationship	Valuing the individual in relationship
Insensitivity and lack of awareness	Attuned to inner sensitivities

During the 2 vibration, we can expect energy medicine to become more popular with its medical intuitives becoming more involved with diagnostic medicine. Also, it follows that with the gentle influence of the 2, non-invasive procedures will become the norm rather the exception. Doctors and patients alike will become more sensitive about how we deal with the human body. In fact, we've already seen the emergence of this trend in energy-medicine pioneer Carolyn Myss' work, *Anatomy of Spirit* and *Why People Don't Heal* (Random House, 1998).

On the more far-out side, the 2 vibration will allow us to create more light for ourselves—everything from solar power to "inner" light will be favored. Remember, light is a higher vibration.

Relationships: The New Dynamic

Naturally, the 2 is` at home in relationships, so not surprisingly, along with all the other changing paradigms we find yet another one about how we'll approach relationships. Where the old paradigm for partnering was "Two halves make a whole," the new relationship paradigm is "Two wholes make something greater than the separate individuals." To write it mathematically:

Old relationship paradigm model: $1/2 + 1/2 = 1$
(not whole without the other half)

New relationship paradigm model: $1 + 1 = 1$
(wholeness—and something greater than ourselves)

147

This "blended" relationship paradigm asks us to see one another as whole, individualized people, and to be more mature, wise, and responsible toward the value of wholeness in forming partnerships.

Slower Rhythm: Kairos Time

We all live within two different concepts of time, though we don't often think about it. There's clock time, called by the Greek word, *chronos*; and there's transcendent time, called *kairos*.

Part of the 1 millennium has been a tendency to honor *chronos* at the expense of *kairos*, although humans have never satiated their longing for *kairos*. Think about how time flies when you're having a good time, and how it seems to drag when you're not.

Chronos is time of the clock, the morning alarm, the daytimer, the beeper, the agenda, and schedules. With *chronos*, in other words, we keep track of time. *Kairos* is transmuted time, connected with infinity, the flow, and letting go. Naturally, we'll find *kairos* in love—when time stands still, when we're having the high of peak experiences, or when we're in the throes of joy and passion. *Kairos* is spiritual time, so it's natural that these moments should feel sacred to us.

As we make the transition to the new millennium, we're coming to the end of the exaltation of *chronos*, because it's the time of the 1 vibration: hurried, masculine, driven, competitive—all to meet the equally masculine "schedule." In the days to come when the 2 will lead the millennium, we'll become more intimate with *kairos*, the energy of the 2. This is a slower rhythm, one more in tune with the cosmos.

How will we live with this new sense of time? In her inspired book *Simple Abundance* (Warner, 1995), Sarah Ban Breathnach describes these two concepts of time beautifully. Here are some things she reminds us to keep in mind as we make the transition from old time paradigm to the new:

➤ Slow down

➤ Concentrate on one thing at a time

➤ Realize that time is what we make it

➤ Make time

➤ Take time

➤ Stop running and listen

➤ Learn to "be"

Ban Breathnach also suggests that to prepare for the new millennium, we should do 3 things:

1. Decide what we need, not want.

2. Set boundaries.

3. Spend 2 hours a day on spiritual and self-development. In other words, spend time with *kairos*!

One thing's for sure, it won't be an easy transition. Those of us on 1 time will keep trying to run over 2 time. But in the end (let's hope it's not the far end!), we'll come to live with the balance of *chronos* and *kairos*. But first, we have to learn to keep time with *kairos*.

Interdependence: We Are Family

Last but not least, the 2 millennium will lead us to live interdependently. To do this, of course, we'll have to forego sacred cows such as: "Authority knows best," "The power is outside of me," and the ideas of "It's my view, (property, child, money, etc.), right or wrong." The 2 will challenge us to understand the connectedness of dependence and independence of all things—not as mutually-exclusive concepts, but as mutually-inclusive realities.

Interdependence will force us to find the courage to take responsibility for the whole—for seeing all of the various social, political, and economic issues from a larger perspective. After all, as U.S. poet and dramatist Archibald MacLeish pointed out: "We are all passengers on the spaceship Earth."

"Interdependence" has at its very root an assumption that two are going to work together. Therefore, a 1 joins with another 1 and together these independent, whole beings (whether individuals, companies, or countries) join forces to mutually achieve success. The trick with interdependence is to not lose oneself in the union (just like the new paradigm for relationship and community), and to honor the spirit of each other as individuals in joint effort.

Time Capsule

Interdependence requires mutual trust and stems from mutual need. There's nothing wrong with "need," after all, and it will actually be a lot easier to act interdependently when we get it through our heads that we're no longer living in a separate, isolated world!

Interdependence can be a curse as well as a blessing and it will show both of those faces in the first year of our new millennium—in the year 2000. Y2K brings us the curse of interdependence, namely that all systems are affected by each other—so the weakest link can bring down the whole chain. No matter which link proves to break the chain, the blessing is that we'll learn how to need each other and how to solve the puzzle—together.

Year 2000: The Big One

Most think the new millennium begins January 1, 2000, but from a numerological standpoint, we would argue that the real beginning was January 1, 1999. Why? Well, for starters, in 1999, we began a universal cycle of 9 years. The year 1999 was a 1 year (new beginning, the start, the first), the beginning of a new 9-year cycle that coincidentally leads us into the new millennium.

So having said that the beginning was in 1999, let's get down to what the year 2000 is all about. As we said earlier, this year is made up of a 2 and three 0s. This means that symbolically the year will be dominated by the vibration of the 2 and 000.

2000 Has 3 Zeroes

The meaning of the zero is that it is about a vibration that is unformed; it signifies something that is full and empty at the same time because the zero is the symbol of an "open channel" to higher forces. Simply put, these zeroes mean that we'll have lots of free will in how we craft this year. Further, it's believed that because of this many zeroes, we'll receive "Divine" assistance as well.

There's something sacred present here, and something unknown about the way this year will shape up. Yes, it will be powerful. Can it mean a higher connection among ourselves? It's part of the great mystery.

The 2 in 2000

We've been talking about the influence of the 2 on the new millennium, but in the year 2000, the 2 will be emphasized more than any other year. In Y2K, the 2 will be backed by all those zeroes, which will serve to enhance the properties of the 2: the need for connectedness, having to find balance, working together, finding new ways to relate and form partnerships, interdependence, and finding a slower rhythm. Let's call it harmonic resonance instead of the not-so-harmonic convergence of last millennium.

Ask Spaceship Earth

One thing to keep in mind is, we won't see 3 zeroes again for another 1,000 years—when the Y3K rolls around.

The Math Behind "Y2K"

What's the meaning behind this quaint way of referring to the year 2000? If we were to use numerology to explain the meaning of "Y2K," first we'd need to do a little quick addition.

In numerology, all letters of the alphabet have assigned numbers. When we add the numbers from each letter together, we come to a single number, and this final number is the telling one. To illustrate, let's see what "Y2K" means, numerologically.

Number Assignments for the 26 Letters of the Alphabet

1	2	3	4	5	6	7	8	9
A	B	C	D	E	F	G	H	I
J	K	L	M	N	O	P	Q	R
S	T	U	V	W	X	Y	Z	

From this chart, we find that "Y" = 7 and "K" = 2. If we were to write out Y2K together, it would look like this:

Y 2 K = Year 2000

Or

7 + 2 + 2 = 11

This last number is the numerological meaning of "Y2K." So what does this 11 mean? Very interesting! The 11 is a *master number*.

The master number 11 is written "11/2." That's because if you add the 1s in the 11 together, you get 2 (1 + 1 = 2 or 11 = 2). However, the thing to remember with master numbers is that you must never reduce them, so instead of reducing the 11 to a 2, we write it as 11/2. Now what happens is that we must look to see what the 11 means as well as the 2. Both are important.

Speaking Y2K

Master numbers are thought to be stronger and more charged with energy than numbers 1 to 9. Master numbers are 11, 22, 33, 44, and so on. In other words, master numbers have identical double digits.

Like any 11 master number, Y2K is an 11/2, which means it has the properties of both the 11 and the 2. Using the following key words, you can figure out just what Y2K means.

Properties of the 2:

➤ Willing to share

➤ Wants to be supportive

➤ Governs delays, waiting

➤ Can be healing

➤ Is deeply sensitive

➤ Is tender, gentle, subtle

➤ Attends to details

➤ Wants to cooperate

➤ Seeks balance

Properties of the 11:

➤ Brings inspiration to others

➤ Is intuitive

➤ Is the "spiritual messenger"

➤ May have psychic properties

➤ Deals with aviation and electricity

➤ Wants to explore things with deeper meaning

➤ Is a metaphysical number

➤ Has intense, very demanding energy

➤ Has will and determination (of the two 1s in 11)

➤ Is stronger than the other "2" numbers (2, 20, 200, 2000)

➤ Is a natural leader

➤ Rules dealing with the masses and spiritual integrity is demanded when the 11 is present

Therefore, we might say that symbolically, Y2K will be a time, an event, or a moment in history, when we have the opportunity to share and support while being led by inspiration, intuition, and spiritual energy. Hey—not bad for "doomsday!"

If the year 2000 (Y2K) plays out as predicted, it will be a time of mutual interdependence and concern for something larger than individual gain. We'll feel a need to be connected—by phone, fax, Internet, proximity, or in spirit. The irony in Y2K is that we're being thrust up against the issues of the 1 (isolation, independence, separation, self-focus) just when we get to the 2. What better way to make the transition—we have no choice but to work together to solve disruptions!

The First Millennium Cycle, by the Numbers

As we venture into the new millennium both astrologically and numerologically, we become deeply aware of nature, our resources, and our physical bodies. While we're beckoned to become good stewards of the earth, we face challenges in legions, and experience a crisis in philosophy as old patterns end. We learn we must trust, and, worst of all, we must develop that airy, scary thing called "faith." It all seems so intangible. What ever happened to good ol' concrete "Rambo" style?

Well, to quote one of our old millennium prophets, Bob Dylan, "The times, they are a changin'." One of the best things about numerology is that it helps us make sense of the future. Very simply, we can know what lies ahead by looking at the meaning of each number for each year.

Numerological Cycles

In western numerology, things evolve in cycles of 9 years (in Chinese numerology, things move in 7-year cycles). That means there's a definite pattern and rhythm to a 9-year period of time, and in our case, it means we can make some sense of the first 9-year cycle (years 1999–2007) of the new millennium, before it happens.

Cycles are based on universal years, which we find by adding a given year's numbers together (see Chapter 9). In turn, the universal year tells of the collective energy available to us in that particular year. For example, in year 2034 we'll be in a 9 year $(2 + 0 + 3 + 4 = 9)$. From this number, we know that 2034 will be a year of endings. A cycle will be closing, so it won't be a time to begin new things. The energy of closure, the natural flow of energy for that year, will be all around us. To align ourselves with this natural flow, we'll want to look to things that need to be finished.

Now that you've got the basic idea, let's take a peek at what lies ahead.

The First Nine Years of the New Millennium: 1999–2007

1999 = 1

As we said before, numerologically, the new millennium begins January 1, 1999. This 1 universal year is a time of beginning anew. However, because of the presence of three 9s, we'll be mainly ending things so the new can begin. A 1 year is a time for planting seeds, so we might say that the seeds for the new millennium were planted in 1999.

2000 = 2

The year 2000 is pure 2 energy, because the 2 is coupled with 3 zeroes. When we add in the universal nickname for the year "Y2K," we find we're also symbolically dealing with energy of the master number 11/2. Numerologically, we would say this is a year of managing details, dealing with delays, and using diplomacy and cooperation. It entails partnership, for the 2 favors working together rather than individually. Problems in marriage and any form of partnership

Ask Spaceship Earth

Take a lead from the greatest basket-ball player in the history of the game: Michael Jordan. Michael announced his retirement from the game in January 1999, saying he's 99.9 per-cent sure (a whole lot of 9s again for transformation!) this second retire-ment will stick. Seems like Michael is in sync with the numbers. How can you transform your own life toward new beginnings in 1999?

may show up, and this is not a year to pull away and try to be independent; it's a year to get along with others. The emphasis will be on achieving harmony among people and balance in all forms. The presence of 3 zeroes magnifies all these qualities tri-fold. In fact, with this many zeroes, we can expect Divine intervention.

2001 = 3

The year 2001 is under the vibration of the 3 (2 + 0 + 0 + 1 = 3). This year will call for creative teamwork and will offer good opportunities for communication and expressing feelings. It's also a good money year, although there may be delays. Emotions will have to be kept under control.

2002 = 4

A 4 universal year is a year of hard work. It brings the laying of foundations, hard work, and putting the ideas of the previous year into form. Because we'll still be recovering from Y2K, we can expect to be putting effort into building new systems and setting down a new root structure for the future. What's built and formed in this year will be the foundation of the next five years. But again, because this year encompasses two 2s, we'll be working to achieve balance, harmony, and connection everywhere in our lives. By the way, expect delays this year.

2003 = 5

This is a universal year of change. The entire planet will experience changes, some sudden and unexpected. Besides the usual emphasis on cooperation and teamwork, we will find a theme of having to say our truth and express ourselves, creatively as well as emotionally. This very expression will bring about change. It's in this 5 year that it looks like we'll be coming out of the Y2K situation and things will really begin to change. We may feel a sense of freedom from the restrictions of the previous year. No matter what, a transition is at hand.

2004 = 6

The 6 universal year brings an emphasis on duties and responsibilities wherever we have care of children, relatives, or property. This year finds our energy being put on matters of the home, remodeling, and family—the domestic issues. It's a year of service, so personal interest won't be served well this year. Instead, this time of caring and nurturing will favor community connections. In fact, it's here that people will begin to find their real "tribes." It's also a good money year—as long as the money's gained through service. Financial success and happiness are hallmarks of this year when life is lived from the heart. The sobering truth is, this 6 year will require doing hard work on relationships or family issues. The goal will be to get balance in these two areas of our lives.

2005 = 7

The 7 universal year favors educational and scientific pursuits and will be a time of reevaluation and reflection. People tend to hold on to their money in a 7 year, reviewing their goals and waiting until next year for spending. This year will draw interest to metaphysics, spirituality, and the hidden forces of nature, as it's not a material year. There will be changes in this year as well as a call for unification and balance, and it's this year that the separatist-isolationist mentality will be put to the test. Balance will be sought for any organizations or philosophies that seem too far to the right or left, spiritually. The universe is calling for harmony.

2006 = 8

This 8 universal year will bring financial abundance and prosperity. Hopefully, we'll have learned something since the last 8 universal year (1997). This year will bring our attention to harmony at the domestic level, within partnerships (especially business relations), and to community services. The theme of the year will be to achieve power, money, and success through selfless service and sensitivity to others.

2007 = 9

This year marks the end of the first cycle of the new millennium. The 9 year brings completion, reward, and a sense of finishing a chapter. We'll have a more galactic consciousness, as promised astrologically; and at this point, we would expect to be working together in a truly cooperative manner on a global scale.

Of course, this is only the first cycle of the new millennium. Our global and galactic achievements will be one small step for mankind, rather than a giant leap. But they will be unmistakable galactic strides as we move toward more universal harmony under the 2.

The Birthday and Life Path of the New Millennium

On January 1, we will have a new birthday for the new millennium. For all practical purposes, the collective population of our world will call the first day of January, 2000, the birthday of the new millennium. So we might consider what this new birthday tells us, numerologically, that is.

January 1, 2000 = 4 Life Path

If we add the numbers together (1 + 1 + 2 = 0 + 0 + 0 = 4) we see that our new millennium will follow the path of the 4. With 4 as the Life Path, we can know that this millennium will be governed by the principles of order and form. The energy of the 2 millennium (harmony and peace) will have the assistance of the 4—the ability to put these energies into physical form and order. With a 4 Life Path, we might expect that this will be a time of building, constructing and establishing solid roots for this predicted time of harmony and cooperation. We can expect tangible, concrete, real results.

The 4 Life Path tells that the destiny of the new millennium will be one of hard work. Numerous opportunities will abound for the use of our practical, down-to-earth know-how to meet the challenges of our new time. It will be through endurance, persistence and determination that we will achieve the promise of this time of tranquility.

It will be a time to be organized, to plan, to be dependable, efficient and good managers of resources (read this as environmental as well as monetary). The 4 tells us that the lessons will be to learn to be flexible yet steadfast, to proceed with purpose, to get the job done efficiently yet not box in or restrict this newly emerging energy of the 2. The 4 indicates that things will proceed methodically, carefully, with much planning as we try on this new time of cooperating, belonging, and balancing.

A 4 Life Path ensures that the much hoped for "brotherhood of man," this time of peace and tranquillity, will come into form. The 4 lends its energy to the quiet, subtle, unassuming 2 and focuses the energy. It will be a time of building, and constructing systems that will house all that the 2 generates.

Having a 4 Life Path for our new millennium gives great hope for what is to come. It means that all that is promised by the 2 will be more than just a promise. The 4 ensures that our Millennium 2000 will be healthy, solidly constructed, firmly planted, and systematically shaped and ordered. Numerologically, it is the stability we would hope for.

As a result, we can begin our 21st century with confidence that we are on solid ground—the number 4 will guide our path into the new millennium.

The Least You Need to Know

➤ The new millennium is a 2.

➤ The 2 means we'll be blending and harmonizing previously opposing forces.

➤ Y2K is a chance to be guided by intuition, inspiration, and spiritual energy.

➤ The year 2000 is influenced by 3 zeroes.

Chapter 11

Your Personal Numbers for the New Millennium

In This Chapter

➤ Every year has a theme

➤ Your personal year has a message just for you

➤ The calendar year is called the universal year

➤ Your balance number tells your ability to deal with challenges

➤ Knowing your numbers helps you embrace the new millennium

Now that we've discussed the meaning of the numbers of the new millennium, it's time to talk about a number that will have direct impact on *your* life under this new millennium. We're talking about your personal year number.

As we've discussed in Chapters 9 and 10, each year has its own number, called a universal year. In addition, each of us has a personal year number and theme, both of which connect to the nine basic numbers of numerology. Lastly, we've each got a balance number, based on our initials. Let's take a look at the numbers themselves—and what their meanings hold for *you*.

Basic Meanings of Numbers 1–9

Before we get into what personal years are and their particular meanings for you, let's review the meanings of the numbers 1 through 9.

Number	Key Words
1	Beginning, independence, innovation, leadership, masculine principle
2	Balance, harmony, unity, relationships, cooperation, feminine principle
3	Saying one's truth, imagination, optimism, happiness, creativity
4	Building, formation, hard work, endurance, seriousness
5	Progressive, resourceful, unrestricted, change, versatility
6	Domestic vs. work issues, nurturing, service-oriented, responsibility and duty, family focus, marriage and divorce number
7	Research, inner analysis, science-minded, solitude, wisdom, spiritual focus, investigates the mysteries, the mystical, the metaphysical
8	Authority, power, finances, business, successful, material wealth, organization
9	Vision, tolerance, endings, transformation, spiritual consciousness, cosmic teachings, global awareness, perfection

Speaking Y2K

The **personal year number** tells the theme of each year for you personally.

Let's Get Personal

Now that you've learned in Chapter 9 about the energy of each number, and seen in Chapter 10 what the numbers mean for the new millennium, let's get personal, and find out what the personal year can reveal about you.

In numerology, we can determine the number and theme of each year for you personally. A *personal year* number tells the trend of events to be unfolded during that year.

The personal year number can be a:

➤ Prophecy

➤ Forewarning

➤ Guide on how to direct personal affairs

➤ Message on how to live in harmony with your own natural rhythm

Where a universal year number will tell the general direction the world is moving, a personal year number will show the direction *you* will want to take for yourself during the year. Needless to say, the personal year is considered one of the most useful and highly important aspects of numerology.

Time Capsule

A personal year is not the same as a universal year. The personal year number is your individual theme during the universal year.

The Message of the Personal Year

Once you know the number of your personal year, you can determine the message that year has for you—the lesson that you're meant to learn during that 12-month period.

Being aware of the theme and number of any given year will allow you to plan ahead and understand what to expect, as well as help explain why certain things seem to be happening in your life at a certain time.

Figuring Your Personal Year Number

To compute your personal year number, you'll want to look at the month and day you were born. It doesn't matter what year you were born when figuring the personal year—the year that *does* matter in a personal year calculation is the *calendar year*.

Here's how you find your current personal year:

Add the month you were born to the day you were born and then add it to the calendar year. (As always, you'll reduce the final number to a single digit in the end.)

Here's what this formula looks like:

Birth month + day of birth + current calendar year = personal year

Here's an example:

For September 14 in the year 2000:

9 (September) + 1 + 4 + 2 + 0 + 0 + 0 = 16 = 1 + 6 = 7

Figuring the Calendar Year

To find a given calendar year's number, add all of its numbers together, then reduce to a single number. For example:

$$1999 = 1 + 9 + 9 + 9 = 28$$

The result, 28, is still two digits, so you want to reduce it to a single digit. Add $2 + 8 = 10 = 1 + 0 = 1$. So 1999 is a 1 calendar year.

Here are some examples where we've done the figuring for you:

$2000 = 2 + 0 + 0 + 0 = 2$ calendar year

$2001 = 2 + 0 + 0 + 1 = 3$ calendar year

$2035 = 2 + 0 + 3 + 5 = 10 = 1 + 0 = 1$ calendar year

Get the idea? It's easy: month + birth date + calendar year!

Out of Time

When figuring your personal year number, DO NOT use the year you were born. The year number to use for the personal year is the calendar year we're currently in.

Months by the Numbers

Every month has a number, too. You probably know them already, but if not, you can use the following numbers to find the number for your month of birth.

Birth Month	Number
January	1
February	2
March	3
April	4
May	5
June	6
July	7
August	8
September	9
October	10 = 1
November	11 = 2
December	12 = 3

One Example of a Personal Year

Let's try an example. What personal year was Princess Diana in when she died? Diana was born July 1st, so we'll add 7 (for July) to 1 (day of birth) to 1997 (the year she died).

First, we find the number for the calendar year, 1997:

$$1 + 9 + 9 + 7 = 26$$

Then reduce the 26 to a single digit:

$$2 + 6 = 8$$

So, the calendar year when Princess Diana died was an 8 (of course, this means that 1997's universal year was 8 as well, because it's the same thing).

Next, we add Diana's personal numbers to the calendar year number:

$$7 \text{ (for July)} + 1 + 8 \text{ (for the year)} = 16$$

Lastly, we reduce 16:

$$1 + 6 = 7$$

So Princess Diana died during a 7 personal year.

What does this mean? It's believed that when a person is in a 7 personal year, the veil to the other side is at its thinnest. This means that a soul can then make the decision to stay or leave this earthly existence. In addition, a 7 is a year when one wants to be alone, to be private, to withdraw, and spend a great deal of time reevaluating his or her life. We can see from the stories told of Diana's last months that she was very much living out the 7 personal year.

Figuring *Your* Personal Year Numbers from 2000 to 2009

The following is a table of calendar year numbers translated to universal years. You can figure this yourself, too, of course, but we thought we'd make it a little simpler.

To find your personal year number, just add the month and date of your birth to any of these numbers. Remember, the universal year number is the same as the calendar year. Just use the universal year number, and add it to your month and day of birth.

Calendar Year	Universal Year Number
2000	2
2001	3
2002	4
2003	5
2004	6
2005	7
2006	8
2007	9
2008	10 = 1
2009	11 = 2

To add your birthday to this, remember that if your birthday is a double-digit number, you need to add the numbers together to get a single number. For example, if you were born on the 14th, add 1 + 4 to get 5 as your day of birth number.

Now you try it. You can do it, just go slowly. It's quite easy, really.

My birth month _____ + my day of birth _____ + year in question_____

Added together:

Month _____ + day _____ (**be sure to reduce it!**) + calendar year _____(**reduce this too!**) = _____ my personal year

See, wasn't so bad, was it? Now let's try another.

If you were born August 23 and you want to know what personal year it would be for you in 2004, just add 8 (for August) + 2 + 3 (for the birthday) and + 6 (for 2004) = 15 = 1 + 5 = 6. Got it? Good.

Now let's see what all this means.

Personal Year Themes

Just like every number you calculate, your personal year number reveals a certain theme. You can think of this as a 9-year cycle, which begins in your 1 year and ends in your 9 year. Once you're aware of this cycle, you'll begin to see why certain years seem to follow certain themes. It's not as random as you may have thought.

Ask Spaceship Earth

Formula for figuring the personal year: birth month + day of birth + calendar year = personal year number (universal year).

1 Personal Year: Beginnings and Knowing the Self

The 1 personal year is one of new beginnings, a time to start, to plant, to bring in the new. This 1 year is the beginning of a new 9-year cycle, so what you seed is what you will sow in the next 9 years. It's a time to be a leader, to learn to stand on your own, and to do all kinds of self-improvement. In a 1 personal year, the focus is on yourself. Take this time and make the most of it.

2 Personal Year: Relate and Cooperate

The 2 year is one of relationship, partnerships, and contracts, and the making and breaking of all of these. This is a time where you learn to be in relationships; however, at some point you may have to stay in the background and wait. Delays are part and parcel of this year, so be patient and don't push the river. The 2 year is the year of cooperation, diplomacy, and negotiation, and you may find yourself having to be the peacemaker in this year. It's also a time to handle the details, gather things—and learn the feeling of being at peace.

3 Personal Year: Express Yourself

A 3 year brings inspiration, creativity, and many opportunities to express yourself. Emotions can run high in this year as it's a time for speaking out, speaking up, or making your feelings known in some way. In addition, this is a time for friends and social activities, and it's considered the lucky number for money. This is also the year to incubate your ideas and dreams, but it's not the year to set them in motion. That's next year, in your 4 year.

4 Personal Year: Hard Work

This 4 year is where you put down roots and build a solid foundation on what you began in your 1 year, and it's also the year you put form to the ideas from your 3 year. It's a year of hard work, planning, setting up systems, and attending to health, and a time to be practical and economical. You're building this year, sort of like a remodeling project; it takes lots of determination and dedication. Keep at it—it will pay off.

5 Personal Year: Change

A 5 year brings change and transition. It's common in this year to feel confused, restless, and scattered. That's because it's a busy year, often bringing travel, a move, or change of some sort. Things are less restricted than last year (the 4 year), and you'll find you crave freedom from the restrictions of the 4 year, new information, and variety. It's a great time to promote yourself, advertise, and publish. In addition, the 5 favors sales.

6 Personal Year: Responsibility and Home

Now you center on home and family. The 6 personal year is a year of responsibility, service, and duty. It's not a time of self-interest; all good things come this year from being of service to others. A 6 year is a good time for remodeling your home, your marriage, or your environment, and it's considered the marriage and divorce year. You'll also find that you'll have to balance your work and home life.

7 Personal Year: Rest and Rejuvenate

The 7 year is the year to rest. It's a time for turning inward to study, specialize, follow intellectual pursuits, and to do mental housecleaning. At the same time, this is a prime year for spiritual advancement, but it's not a year for business expansion or starting new things. Instead, it's a time to pull in, withdraw, and draw upon your inner resources. This is, in fact, a great year for a sabbatical. Don't miss your chance to recharge—you don't get another 7 year for nine more years!

8 Personal Year: Achievement

Now's the time to expand and attend to business opportunities. The whole 8 year is one of managing business affairs. It requires a businesslike attitude, organization, planning, and vision. Money goes out in big chunks in an 8 year, but it comes in, too, in like proportion. This will be a very busy time, and a far cry from last year (your 7 year). Because expansion is the theme, you'll want to watch your weight this year. At the same time, it's a good year to get pregnant, so plan ahead.

9 Personal Year: Endings

This is the year of endings, completion, and letting go. It's a time of transformation and great rewards, and it can be very emotional because it may involve some kind of loss. This marks the end of the cycle, after all. It's a philanthropic year—giving back for what you've received in this 9-year cycle, and it's also the year to re-envision your dream. The tide is out, and this is not the year to begin anything new. Rest, wait, and dream. This is harvest time. Enjoy!

Personal Year Vibes Under the 2

No matter what personal year you're in, you'll also be influenced by the universal year number. In 2000, the universal year number is 2, the same 2 that will permeate the whole new millennium. Therefore, your personal year will be additionally influenced by the theme of cooperation, achieving harmony in all your relations, finding balance, and learning to be sensitive to the subtle vibes.

In order of importance, you'll feel your personal year more than the universal year vibration, but you must keep your eyes on the larger picture. Regardless of the theme of your personal year, we'll all be learning to get along more, better, and bigger in this new millennium of the 2.

The Balance Number: Your Ability to Deal with Difficult or Threatening Situations

Now let's look at a number that tells how you might deal with the challenges of the new millennium. It's called the *balance number*, and it comes from the initials of your full name. Use the initials of your current name.

To find this mysterious number, you'll add the initials of your name together. Here's how:

First, find the number that corresponds to the letters of your initials.

Number Assignments for the 26 Letters of the Alphabet

1	2	3	4	5	6	7	8	9
A	B	C	D	E	F	G	H	I
J	K	L	M	N	O	P	Q	R
S	T	U	V	W	X	Y	Z	

Add these numbers together to get a single number. Don't forget to reduce double-digit numbers!

What does this number mean for you? After you use the numbers in the table to find your balance number, use the following interpretations to find the answer.

Balance Number Interpretations

➤ **1 balance number.** With a 1 balance number, you'll tend to draw strength from yourself rather than from others. You may be a loner or isolated in some way. You'll also be very firm in your opinions. You have the ability to lead, to get results, to initiate, and will be great at the start-up phase. But you'll leave the process to someone else. A 1 balance number needs to allow others to have a viewpoint as well. In the Y2K disruption, you may, despite all indications to the contrary, continue to have a tendency to do everything by yourself.

➤ **2 balance number.** A 2 balance number indicates you'll be tactful, diplomatic, and good at details. You'll also be willing to compromise, but could be timid, fearful, or even a doormat for the more aggressive types. When afraid, you might

Speaking Y2K

The **balance number,** found by adding together the numbers for the initials of your name, tells how you might deal with the challenges of the new millennium.

165

be overly sensitive and nit-picky. But when you work for balance and harmony, you'll positively shine in the problem-solving department. A 2 balance number is the original "team-player," great to have on a committee, especially when Y2K arrives.

➤ **3 balance number.** A 3 balance number will bring humor to the situation. You're optimistic and charming, and can be persuasive with words. At the same time, you can be emo-tional or scattered when things get tough. There's also a tendency to become too subjective, so team up with the analytical, observant 7 for balance during Y2K.

➤ **4 balance number.** Discipline is the strength of this number. You know how to work hard, are honest, have integrity, and are highly practical. Sure, you can get lost in the details, or fail to see the bigger picture, and you might become rigid and controlling if feeling insecure. If you're the manager, though, with your know-how and thoroughness, you can throw yourself into the work, to the betterment of the whole Y2K project.

➤ **5 balance number.** The 5 balance number may be rebellious, restless, and try to avoid the challenge. You may want to escape through mind-altering substances to keep yourself from feeling the pain or conflict, but should instead tap into your quick-thinking mind for a highly creative solution to the problem. You're both resourceful and quick, and you bring a much-needed youthful spirit to the Y2K table.

➤ **6 balance number.** With a 6 balance number, your strength is in problem-solving and your understanding nature. A good counselor, you consider respon-sibility a key issue. Of course, you may accept too much of the responsibility, or may feel it's a burden, and can be codepen-dent if you're not careful. Still, you're the one who will draw the family together in a crisis, Y2K or otherwise.

➤ **7 balance number.** A 7 balance number indicates a keen analytical ability, with a knack for clarity and insight. You may have a tendency to withdraw, retreat, or turn to nature for solace, but you'll also bring spiritual philosophy to any challenging situation as well as your understanding of universal principles. You can be aloof and observing, rather than participating, but that can help you see a different way to solve the issue, especially challenging ones like Y2K.

➤ **8 balance number.** The 8 balance number brings power to the situation. You may well be the "boss," if 8's your balance number—you will, in any event, take a leadership role in any crisis. Yes, you can be manipulative and controlling, especially if you perceive that others aren't as strong, efficient, and competent, but isn't that what a boss is for? With your ability to organize, envision, and execute a plan, you'll be the one to show others the way to a trouble-free Y2K.

➤ **9 balance number.** A 9 balance number means you'll be sympathetic, compassionate, and gifted at seeing the broader picture. You may be very generous, a healer and teacher. You'll want to improve or remake the situation on a more idealistic model, and have a multitude of talents. You can also be intense and emotional. This one will want to solve everything from how to feed the people during the Y2K computer glitch to organizing day care for the little ones.

One Woman's Balance Number

Let's see how Hilary Rodham Clinton will handle the challenges of the new millennium. Her initials are H, R, and C:

H   R   C

8 + 9 + 3 = 20 = 2

What does this number mean when it comes to challenges for Hilary Rodham Clinton? Well, for starters, she's a tactful diplomat who knows the value of compromise. Clearly, rather than accentuating the doormat qualities in this case, Hilary has learned to work for balance and harmony in difficult situations. She has the best resilient qualities of the 2 balance number, and she's the consummate team player. Her keen eye for detail and diplomacy can only serve her well in the coming millennium. If a situation is truly threatening to her, she may feel the overly sensitive aspect of the 2, but she uses the balance point of negotiation to achieve peaceful resolution.

The Numbers and Your New Millennium

By now you can see that there's a wealth of information available to you through your numbers. This unique, sacred information is given to all of us to help us maximize our resources, energy, and achievements. Our numbers help us to both live and make choices with full knowledge of what's right for us—if we seize the positive aspects of the numbers and live accordingly.

The new millennium is a time for all of us to move up the spiral staircase of evolution and development. May the 2 guide all your days.

The Least You Need to Know

➤ Every year has a theme.

➤ Your personal year has a message for you.

➤ The calendar year is also called the universal year.

➤ Your balance number indicates your ability to deal with challenges.

➤ Knowing your numbers helps you embrace the new millennium.

Part 4
Picture This: The Tarot

The 78 cards of the Tarot deck afford us a unique opportunity to get the answers to questions both personal and global. After an introduction to the cards, we're going to do just that, and ask the cards some key questions about what the tarot has to tell us about everything from the economy to our own millennial challenges.

Chapter 12

What's in the Cards?

In This Chapter

➤ Why a picture is worth a thousand words

➤ Getting to know the cards

➤ Everything you need to know about the Tarot

➤ A journey through the Major Arcana

Hand-in-hand with astrology and numerology is the art of the Tarot, a 78-card excursion through the archetypal journey called Life. Our expert for the next five chapters is none other than the co-author of *The Complete Idiot's Guide to Tarot and Fortune-Telling*, Arlene Tognetti.

What's intriguing about the Tarot is that it can not only help us look into the future (as well as the past and present), it can help each of us look within ourselves to find the answers that lie within. How can a deck of cards do all that? Read on.

A Picture's Worth a Thousand Words

When it comes to the *Tarot*, a picture really *is* worth a thousand words. That's because the images of the Tarot cards are designed to explore every aspect of human life.

Speaking Y2K

The **Tarot** is an ancient method of fortune-telling, which uses the 78 cards of the **Tarot deck** to create a story of you—past, present, and future.

Let's begin by looking at the first card in the *Tarot deck*: the Fool. One of 22 *Major Arcana* cards, the Fool represents the archetypal first step in any journey, whether it's a new job, a new baby—or an actual trip.

In addition to the 22 Major Arcana cards, there are 56 *Minor Arcana* cards. Divided into four suits—Wands, Cups, Swords, and Pentacles—these cards represent everyday events, things like making ends meet and falling in love!

You can think of the Fool, the first of the 22 Major Arcana cards, as an archetypal representation of any first step you make.

THE FOOL.

Speaking Y2K

A Tarot deck contains 22 **Major Arcana** and 56 **Minor Arcana** cards. The Major Arcana depict an archetypal journey through life, while the Minor Arcana show everyday events.

When you first encounter a Tarot deck, it may be overwhelming for a number of reasons. First of all, the cards are bigger than everyday playing cards, so the deck is harder to handle. Second, there are 78 cards instead of the 52 you're used to, making it harder still to get your hands around—especially if your hands are small.

Then there's the matter of the imagery itself. It's only natural to be put off the first time you encounter cards like the Devil or Death. But these initially frightening images actually represent very real occurrences we all face again and again, whether it's the temptation depicted by the Devil, or the potential renewal offered by the Death card.

Death and the Devil, both Major Arcana cards, may seem scary the first time you see them. But Death actually shows renewal or rebirth, while the Devil represents temptation.

Take Some Time to Get to Know the Cards

The examples above are just two reasons why it's important to take some time to get to know the cards before you begin to ask the cards some questions. That's why, in the next three chapters, we're going to introduce you to each and every card, as well as some key words for understanding each card's possible meanings.

Bear in mind that the Tarot is an ancient art that takes practice and patience to master. What we can give you in this chapter is only an overview. If what's here whets your interest, however, you'll find more detail in *The Complete Idiot's Guide to Tarot and Fortune-Telling*.

Seeing Is Believing

One of the best ways to get to know the Tarot cards is to begin a Tarot journal. This can be a special notebook set aside for this purpose, scraps of paper you shove into the top drawer of your desk, or even a directory on your PC or Mac devoted to the Tarot. What's important is to keep a record of your impressions of the cards, and later, of your *Tarot spreads* and *readings* themselves.

Speaking Y2K

Tarot spreads are different methods of laying out the cards during a Tarot reading. **Tarot readings** occur when the cards are laid out to reveal a particular story, often in answer to a question.

We're going to begin your Tarot journal right now, by taking a look at one Major Arcana card and one Minor Arcana card. You don't need a deck of Tarot cards for this exercise, because we'll provide pictures of the cards (from the most often used Universal Waite deck) Bear in mind, however, that the color imagery on each card adds an important dimension to how you feel about the card.

First, spend some time just looking at the Sun card. Don't demand anything of yourself or the card, just look at it. What do you see? Write down what you notice about this card below.

The Sun is a Major Arcana card and the 4 of Swords is a Minor Arcana card.

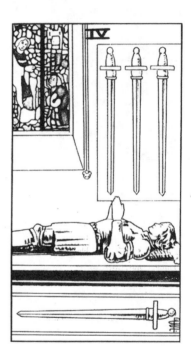

_____

_____

_____

_____

_____

_____

What did you notice about the Sun? Here are some of the things that we see when we look at this card. It's important to note that what *you* see is what matters to *you*, and that what *we* see is what matters to *us*—there's no right or wrong when it comes to what you see—or don't see—in a particular Tarot card.

➤ A large yellow sun in a deep blue sky dominates the upper half of the card (we know you can't see these colors unless you have a Universal Waite deck, but we thought we'd tell you what they are). The Sun has a sort of Mona Lisa smile, too.

➤ A beautiful, smiling child with golden curls is astride a white horse, carrying a flowing red banner.

➤ Bright yellow sunflowers grow above a tall wall.

Did you see these images? Chances are, you did. What else did you notice about the card that we didn't mention? The alternating shapes of the Sun's rays? The child's crown of sunflowers? No matter what you noticed, good for you!

Now, let's turn to the 4 of Swords. We chose this card because its images may initially frighten you, and we wanted to show you how to use your powers of observation to look beyond that fear.

What do you see when you first look at this card? Write your observations here.

_____

_____

_____

_____

_____

_____

Did you think the young man was dead? This is a common assumption many people make the first time they see this card. Here, however, is another possibility, what many Tarot readers see when they look at this card.

A young man is resting in a church, his hands folded in prayer. His own sword is at rest beneath him, while three swords protect him from above. Still more important protection comes from the brightly colored stained glass window in the upper left of the card: Here we find a joyful depiction of the Virgin Mary and a child.

When the 4 of Swords appears in a spread, most Tarot readers view it as well-earned rest after difficult times. Swords, as you'll learn when we discuss the Minor Arcana cards in a few pages, are the cards of activity and yes, conflict, and the 4 of Swords depicts the respite between the battles we all must fight.

Upright and Reversed Tarot Cards

Every time you shuffle the Tarot cards, turn the top half of the deck around so that the cards will be facing in the opposite direction. In this way, your Tarot deck will contain both *upright* and *reversed* cards the more you shuffle.

Speaking Y2K

Tarot cards may appear either **upright** or **reversed** in a spread. Reversed (upside-down) cards suggest that the lessons of that particular card may be more challenging for you at this particular time.

Every card has both an upright and reversed meaning, but the reversed meanings are not necessarily the opposite of the upright ones. Rather, they're telling us to pay special attention to the card's message. Here's an example:

Upright, the Page of Cups (Pages are messengers or messages, as you'll learn in a moment, and Cups are the cards of emotion) might mean the beginning of a romantic adventure. Reversed, however, it could indicate some hesitation or fear about a potential romance.

Here is the Page of Cups in its upright and reversed positions.

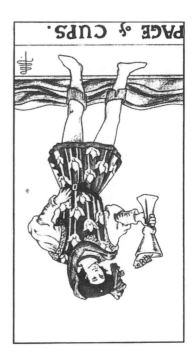

As we show you each of the cards in the sections that follow, we'll also give you brief interpretations of their reversed meanings. Note that when cards appear reversed in a spread, the capital letter "R" will appear after the card.

Tarot's Major Arcana

Are you ready to begin the archetypal journey of the Major Arcana? Each of these cards is a metaphor for a step in any human life, whether it's your first baby steps or a change of job or home. Beginning with the youthful innocence of the Fool and culminating with the success of the World, these 22 cards can serve as signposts along the journey of life.

Your Karma and Destiny Challenges

Most Tarot readers believe that the Major Arcana cards depict karma or destiny challenges—lessons that you need to learn in this life—while the Minor Arcana depict more down-to-earth matters.

Life lessons or challenges can take many guises. Perhaps you need to learn to be more patient. If that's the case, challenges to your patience will keep cropping up in your life until you learn the lesson—and the Temperance card, both in its upright and reversed positions, will appear again and again in your Tarot spreads until patience is second nature to you.

Ask Spaceship Earth

When a majority (more than half) of cards in any spread are Major Arcana cards, it indicates a life lesson or challenge that must be learned or met—whether you want to or not.

When it's your destiny to learn patience, the Temperance card may appear in your Tarot spreads.

Above all, the Major Arcana cards are a way of helping you see things about yourself more clearly. You can think of them as images that tell your story.

Keys 0 Through 21: From the Fool to the World

Here's what you've been waiting for: the cards themselves. So, without further ado, allow us to introduce the 22 Major Arcana cards.

The Fool (Key 0).

Upright meanings:
Beginnings
Innocence
A new adventure

Reversed meanings:
Foolhardiness
A rough start
Look before you leap!

The Magician (Key 1).

Upright meanings:
Creative power
The magic touch
Creating your own reality

Reversed meanings:
Hidden talents not being
*   used*
Not living up to full
*   potential*
Lack of enthusiasm

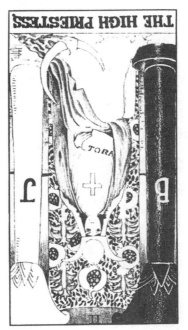

The High Priestess (Key 2).

Upright meanings:
Intuition
Psychic skills
Inner voice

Reversed meanings:
Mixed messages
Superstition
Look beneath the surface

179

The Empress (Key 3).

Upright meanings:
Abundance
Fertility
Maternal energy

Reversed meanings:
Problems at home
A poor harvest
Problems with the land

The Emperor (Key 4).

Upright meanings:
Rational solutions
Leadership ability
Paternal energy

Reversed meanings:
Dictatorial
Lack of control
An uncomfortable position

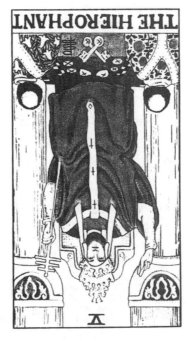

The Hierophant (Key 5).

Upright meanings:
Tradition
Conformity
Conventional wisdom

Reversed meanings:
Questioning authority
Non-conformity
Unconventionality

The Lovers (Key 6).

Upright meanings:
Choices
Romance
Inspiration

Reversed meanings:
Delays
Indecision
Learning to make the right
choices

181

The Chariot (Key 7).

Upright meanings:
Success
Victory after hardship
Stamina

Reversed meanings:
Lack of focus
Lack of vigor
Time to regroup and wait
for tomorrow

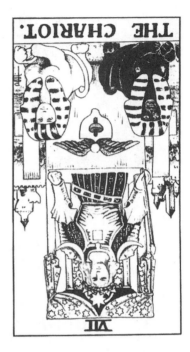

Strength (Key 8).

Upright meanings:
Compassion
Love conquers all
Unconditional love

Reversed meanings:
Overwhelming passions
Over-materiality
Time to calm down

THE HERMIT.

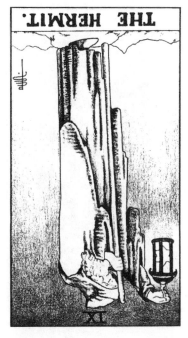

THE HERMIT.

The Hermit (Key 9).

Upright meanings:
The inner voice
Seeking the truth
Withdrawing to meditate

Reversed meanings:
Not listening to advice
Daydreaming
Not following your heart

WHEEL of FORTUNE.

WHEEL of FORTUNE.

Wheel of Fortune (Key 10).

Upright meanings:
Good luck
Fortune
A lucky cycle

Reversed meanings:
A turn for the worse
Stagnation
An unlucky cycle

Justice (Key 11).

Upright meanings:
Fairness
Equilibrium
Balanced judgment

Reversed meanings:
Lack of good counsel
Unwise decisions
Unfair systems

The Hanged Man (Key 12).

Upright meanings:
Time to move on
Spiritual growth
Self-sacrifice

Reversed meanings:
Hanging on to the past
Learning to let go
Hung up on fears of the future

Death (Key 13).

Upright meanings:
Transformation
Rebirth
Renewal

Reversed meanings:
Inertia
Just can't quit
The crisis continues

Time Capsule

"Not the Death card!" Many people are frightened the first time this card appears in a reading—but it's not the Grim Reaper it looks to be. This card shows up whenever you're going through a change of lifestyle or attitude, when you're starting to realize that the old must make way for the new. If the Death card appears upright, you're ready to move on, while if it's reversed, chances are you're still a little intimidated by the change you're thinking about making.

Temperance (Key 14).

Upright meanings:
Patience
Adaptation
Self-discipline

Reversed meanings:
Impatience
Lack of tolerance for others
Slow down and smell the
roses!

The Devil (Key 15).

Upright meanings:
Temptation
Addiction
Obsession

Reversed meanings:
Freedom from self-imposed
restrictions
Breaking a bad habit
Getting one's self back
together

The Tower (Key 16).

Upright meanings:
*A bolt from the blue
Expect the unexpected
    surprise!*

Reversed meanings:
*Putting an unexpected
    experience behind you
Feeling like life is conspir-
    ing against you
Feeling backed into a
    corner*

The Star (Key 17).

Upright meanings:
*Hope
Faith
Dreams come true*

Reversed meanings:
*Doubt and pessimism
Lack of faith
Feeling ill-at-ease*

The Moon (Key 18).

Upright meanings:
Imagination
Psychic development
Look beneath the surface

Reversed meanings:
Common sense rules
   imagination
Caution over haste
The practical side wins

The Sun (Key 19).

Upright meanings:
Contentment
Happy unions and
   partnerships
Pleasure and satisfaction

Reversed meanings:
Delayed success
Put on a happy face
Look the issue over again

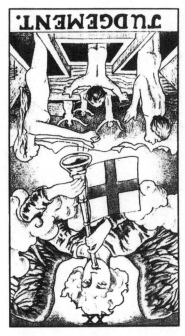

Judgement (Key 20).

Upright meanings:
A shift in consciousness
An awakening
The great a-ha!

Reversed meanings:
Denying the inevitable
A lack of spirituality
Fear of failure

The World (Key 21).

Upright meanings:
Final attainment
Liberation
Complete triumph

Reversed meanings:
*Refusal to learn from
    experiences*
*The end of the journey
    postponed*
Fear of change

The Least You Need to Know

➤ The 78 cards of the Tarot deck are divided into 22 Major Arcana cards and 56 Minor Arcana cards.

➤ When it comes to the Tarot, a picture really is worth a thousand words.

➤ Take some time to get to know the cards.

➤ The Major Arcana cards depict an archetypal journey through life—from the Fool to the World.

Chapter 13

Tarot's Minor Arcana: Wands and Cups

In This Chapter

➤ A who's who of the Minor Arcana

➤ Everyday cards of your free will

➤ Wands—the cards of enterprise

➤ Cups—the cards of emotion

The Major Arcana are just the beginning of the Tarot's journey: The 56 Minor Arcana cards are the everyday cards of your own free will.

Whether it's the enterprise of Wands, the emotions of Cups, the action of Swords, or the prosperity of Pentacles, when it comes to your day-to-day life, the Minor Arcana tell the story.

Tarot's Minor Arcana

There are 56 Minor Arcana cards, divided into four suits of 14 cards each, 10 numbered cards, and 4 royal cards: the Page, Knight, Queen, and King. Each numbered and royal card has a specific role, which, when combined with a specific suit, adds up to an everyday occurrence—or even a person!

The following table shows you each Minor Arcana suit, the corresponding suit in a regular deck of playing cards, a key word to remember the suit by, and an image we think may be helpful in identifying it.

Tarot Suit	Regular Deck	Key Word	Image
Wands	Clubs	Enterprise	A magic wand
Cups	Hearts	Emotion	Cupful of joy
Swords	Spades	Action	Sword fight
Pentacles	Diamonds	Money	Coins

Next, let's look at what each number represents. Remember, a card's suit has as much bearing on its meaning as its number. Whether a card is upright or reversed can affect its meaning as well.

Card Number	Meaning
1	Beginnings
2	Partnerships/Decisions
3	Gatherings
4	Foundations
5	Regroupings
6	Reviews
7	Choices
8	Fears and hopes
9	Final preparations
10	Culminations
Page	A young person or note
Knight	A message or messenger
Queen	A woman
King	A man

Your Everyday Choices and Challenges

Just as the Major Arcana cards represent karma or destiny, the Minor Arcana cards represent your free will and the choices you make every day. Sometimes your choices will be about matters of enterprise (Wands), sometimes matters of the heart (Cups), sometimes matters of activity (Swords), and sometimes matters of money (Pentacles). We'll be discussing Wands and Cups in this chapter, and Swords and Pentacles in the next one.

Time Capsule

Sometimes people are disappointed when there are more Minor Arcana cards than Major Arcana cards in a reading. It's important to remember, though, that when the majority of cards in a reading are Minor Arcana cards, your decisions are up to you, not fated or destined. This can mean, for example, that you haven't got a karmic lesson about a certain type of guy, or that you're not destined to learn to read between the lines. Lots of Minor Arcana cards can mean lots of choices—but they're all up to you!

Wands: Your Enterprise

Wands, the first of the four Minor Arcana suits, are all about enterprise and growth. Whenever you're asking about an activity, work, or something that goes through stages of development, Wands will appear to address your question.

Wands are also the cards of new projects and potential travel, as well as your creativity and enthusiasm for new projects. If you're ambitious and competitive, you'll also find Wands showing up, because these are the cards with the passion and the power to get the job done.

Speaking Y2K

Wands are the minor arcana cards which show your enterprise, growth, and development.

Ace of Wands.

Upright meanings:
New energy
Ready to face the day
Good self-esteem

Reversed meanings:
*Are you missing
    something?*
Back to the drawing board
Time to regroup

2 of Wands.

Upright meanings:
Waiting for results
Someone to watch over you
Patience and focus

Reversed meanings:
*Lack of movement toward
    goal*
Delays and frustration
*May be time to change the
    plan*

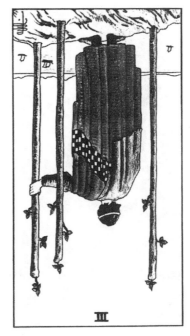

3 of Wands.

Upright meanings:
Cooperation from others
Everyone's involved in the effort
Pride in accomplishments

Reversed meanings:
Strong competition
Wasted energy
Not seeing the big picture

4 of Wands.

Upright meanings:
A bountiful harvest
A reunion with loved ones
Work well-done and rewarded
Reversed meanings:
Unseen blessings
Appreciate the little things
Time to give thanks for help of others

5 of Wands.

Upright meanings:
Struggles and opposition
Stress of disorganization
Something's gone wrong

Reversed meanings:
Harmony again prevails
Working out differences
Compromise and
  negotiation

6 of Wands.

Upright meanings:
Just rewards
Problems will be solved
Reunion or travel

Reversed meanings:
Tired of the battle
Don't overreact
Delayed journey

7 of Wands.

Upright meanings:
*Inner strength and
    stamina
Advantage despite
    adversity
Fighting for ideals*

Reversed meanings:
*Threats have passed
Competition wasn't so
    strong
The rough part is past*

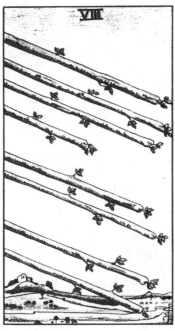

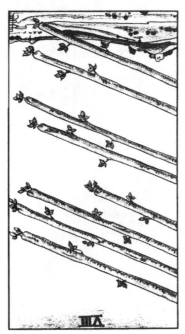

8 of Wands.

Upright meanings:
*Success and forward
    motion
Positive progress toward
    goal
Keep moving in the same
    direction*

Reversed meanings:
*Keep a handle on your
    feelings
Don't force an issue
Stand back and reassess*

9 of Wands.

Upright meanings:
Prepared to face adversity
Protecting what you've
    worked for
Hold on to what you
    believe in

Reversed meanings:
Need for R & R
Unprepared
Worry or feeling let down

10 of Wands.

Upright meanings:
Too many burdens
What's really important?
Keep your priorities
    straight

Reversed meanings:
Letting go of a burden
Someone making others
    carry the load
Don't pass the buck

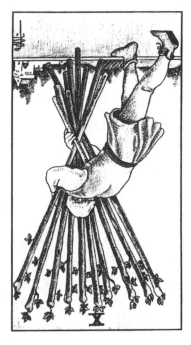

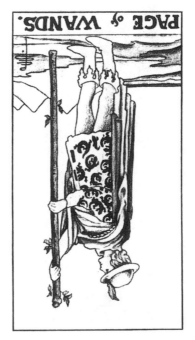

Page of Wands.

Upright meanings:
Good news!
A young person
Enthusiasm for life

Reversed meanings:
Delayed or unwanted
  message
Superficiality
Disappointing news

Knight of Wands.

Upright meanings:
A generous friend
A new adventure
An enthusiastic person

Reversed meanings:
Postponed journey
Narrow-minded or jealous
  person
Disorganization

Queen of Wands.

Upright meanings:
Strong leadership
Forward motion and growth
An ambitious woman

Reversed meanings:
Bossiness or arrogance
Aggression
A pushy woman

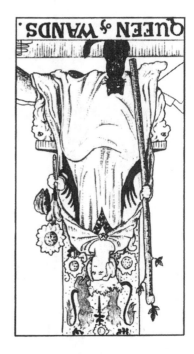

King of Wands.

Upright meanings:
Enthusiasm for life
Someone who encourages others' potential
A man of authority and confidence

Reversed meanings:
Low self-esteem
Feelings of inadequacy
A detached man

Cups: Your Emotion

Cups explore every aspect of your emotional lives and creativity. It's here you'll find your heart's desire, as well as romance and your soulmate.

Like everything in life, love and creativity have their ups and downs. Upright and reversed, Cups reflect the reality of day-to-day life.

Speaking Y2K

Cups are the Minor Arcana suit that explores your emotional life and creativity.

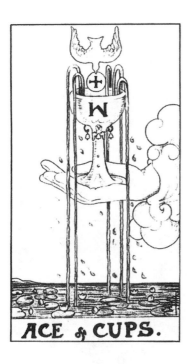

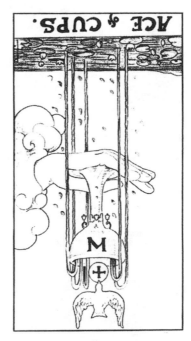

Ace of Cups.

Upright meanings:
New happiness
New love
Fertility and conception

Reversed meanings:
Insecurity about new
   relationship
Tired of the same old,
   same old
Frustrating contacts

201

2 of Cups.

Upright meanings:
Beginning of a friendship
Understanding and
    cooperation
Kindness and
    thoughtfulness

Reversed meanings:
Misunderstandings
Someone being stubborn
Jealousy or possessiveness

3 of Cups.

Upright meanings:
Celebration time!
Individual talents
Good family and friends

Reversed meanings:
Overindulgence
Possibility of gossip
Time to apologize

4 of Cups.

Upright meanings:
Detachment from world
Boredom
Need for reevaluation

Reversed meanings:
Time to try something new
Renewed motivation
Renewed ambition

5 of Cups.

Upright meanings:
Loss or heartache
Time to let emotions out
Disillusionment

Reversed meanings:
Energy increasing
Renewed hope
Learning from past
  mistakes

6 of Cups.

Upright meanings:
Good memories of the past
A gift from an admirer
Something or someone
    from the past returns

Reversed meanings:
An unhappy memory
Dwelling on the past
Disappointment with
    family

7 of Cups.

Upright meanings:
Too many choices!
A difficult decision
Confusion about choosing

Reversed meanings:
Finally a decision
Commitment to following
    through
Your plan is right!

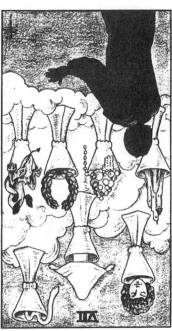

204

8 of Cups.

Upright meanings:
A desire to move on
Leaving the material world
*   behind*
Seeking something
*   different*

Reversed meanings:
Return to the material
*   world*
Renewed interest in people
Desire for adventure and
*   passion*

9 of Cups.

Upright meanings:
The wish card!
Your dreams come true
Your heart's desire

Reversed meanings:
Not today…
Too much of a good thing
Don't push what you want

10 of Cups.

Upright meanings:
Happily ever after
Marriage or reunion
New home or new baby

Reversed meanings:
*Contentment's around the
corner*
*Some delays before
contentment*
Possible loss of reputation

Page of Cups.

Upright meanings:
A message about romance
Good news in the mail
A birth or young person

Reversed meanings:
*Happy message doesn't
arrive*
*I don't want to talk about
it!*
A moody or unhappy child

Knight of Cups.

Upright meanings:
The beginning of romance
Learning to love
A romantic dreamer

Reversed meanings:
Fear of commitment
Weary of relationships
A person who's afraid to
    tell the truth

Queen of Cups.

Upright meanings:
Someone who nurtures
    others
A sensitive, intuitive
    woman
A powerful imagination

Reversed meanings:
Someone who worries too
    much
An overemotional woman
Heart over head

207

King of Cups.

Upright meanings:
A quiet, devoted man
Someone who understands
others
Humanitarian work

Reversed meanings:
Loss of perspective
Inability to express
emotions
Secrecy or shyness

Now you've explored your enterprise and emotions. In the next chapter, we'll take you on a tour of Swords and Pentacles, the cards that reveal your everyday trials—and successes.

The Least You Need to Know

➤ The Minor Arcana depict everyday events.

➤ Wands are the suit of enterprise.

➤ Cups are the suit of emotions.

Chapter 14

Tarot's Minor Arcana: Swords and Pentacles

In This Chapter

➤ More about the Minor Arcana

➤ Swords, the cards of action

➤ Pentacles, the cards of prosperity

➤ How to ask the cards a question

The last two Minor Arcana suits explore how you interact with the world around you. Swords are the cards of action and aggression, while Pentacles are the cards of wealth, possessions, and security. In this chapter, we'll take you on a tour of these Minor Arcana cards.

You and Me Against the World

While the enterprise of Wands and the emotions of Cups are very personal matters, when it comes to Swords and Pentacles, you're out there in the world of others. Swords depict the world of action and aggression—and yes, war—while Pentacles are about both making money and the things that money can buy. Let's see what these two Minor Arcana suits have to reveal about you.

Speaking Y2K

Swords are the suit of the Minor Arcana that reveal how you deal with conflict, obstacles, and aggression.

Swords: Your Action

Life isn't always Wands and Cups, and *Swords* represent strife and aggression, those everyday conflicts and problems that we all must face.

One important thing to remember about Swords is that they can cut both ways—they can be used for good as well as harm. Sometimes you can force a bad situation to a good ending, and sometimes the war is worth the battles you must fight.

Ace of Swords.

Upright meanings:
A new undertaking that will succeed
Birth of a leader
A feeling of power and control

Reversed meanings:
Too much force
Try not to push so hard
Use common sense and be diplomatic

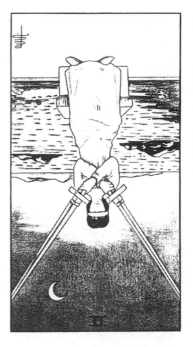

2 of Swords.

Upright meanings:
Need for well-balanced life
A point of indecision
Blind choices

Reversed meanings:
A decision has been made
Forward movement
Renewed confidence
toward goal

3 of Swords.

Upright meanings:
An argument
Heartache or breakup of
friendship
Separation

Reversed meanings:
Dissatisfaction of a
passing nature
Working through a
difficult time
An apology may be
forthcoming

211

4 of Swords.

Upright meanings:
Time to rest and think
   about the future
A retreat or vacation
A calming period before
   the next storm

Reversed meanings:
Ready to return to action
Renewed energy
Political upheaval

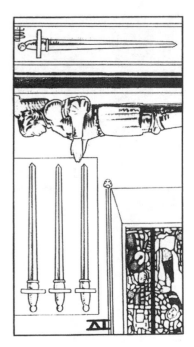

5 of Swords.

Upright meanings:
Lack of concern for others
Legal complications
Deception or manipulation

Reversed meanings:
Sneaky behavior
A loss
Gossip

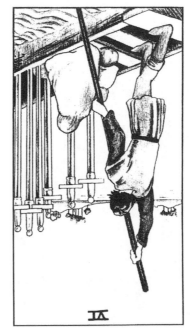

6 of Swords.

Upright meanings:
A difficult cycle is ending
A journey away from a sad
*   condition*
Recovery from difficulties

Reversed meanings:
Stuck in a negative
*   situation*
Need to wait for circum-
*   stances to improve*
Postponement of decision

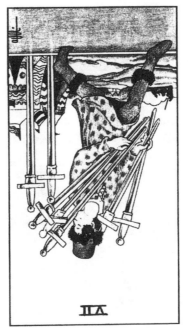

7 of Swords.

Upright meanings:
Someone's being sneaky
Things not working out as
*   planned*
Unreliability or deception

Reversed meanings:
The truth is at hand
An apology is forthcoming
Stolen goods are returned

8 of Swords.

Upright meanings:
Fears can render you
   helpless
Indecision
Inability to cope

Reversed meanings:
Letting go of fears
Pressures leaving
Hope and inspiration
   return

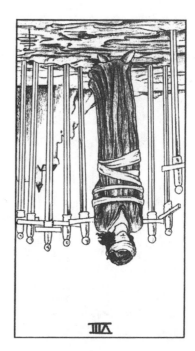

9 of Swords.

Upright meanings:
The nightmare card
Depression and
   desperation
Despair and anxiety

Reversed meanings:
Getting through the
   trauma
Help is on the way
Developing strength of
   character

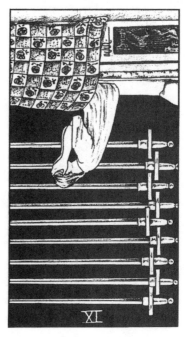

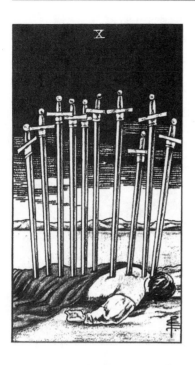

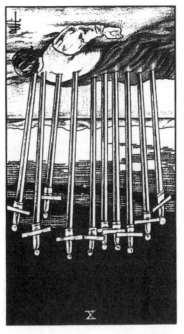

10 of Swords.

Upright meanings:
The end of a cycle
Past obligations completed
You can't beat a dead horse

Reversed meanings:
The light at the end of the tunnel
A steady improvement
Ready to move on to new challenges

Page of Swords.

Upright meanings:
A message to heed
Information that requires courage to face
A quick-thinking young person

Reversed meanings:
Truthful information
Strange events turn out for the best
A silver lining to the dark cloud

Knight of Swords.

Upright meanings:
Something important you
 need to know
Sharp wit and direct focus
Someone who wants to
 know the truth

Reversed meanings:
Someone spoiling for a
 fight
Delays, apprehension,
 conflicts
Just plain worn out

Queen of Swords.

Upright meanings:
A keen observer and good
 listener
A woman who's learned to
 bear sorrow
A strong and direct woman

Reversed meanings:
A narrow-minded woman
Someone who only sees
 one side
A tendency to be
 judgmental

King of Swords.

Upright meanings:
A strong leader and
   authority
Good counsel and advice
A just and honorable man

Reversed meanings:
Someone who's preoccu-
   pied with his own
   troubles
A lack of diplomacy or
   good judgment
An overly opinionated,
   dogmatic man

Pentacles: Your Money

The last of the Minor Arcana suits, *Pentacles* are the cards of wealth, possessions, and security. It's here where you'll find the things that you own, as well as your money and your home itself—including your family and security.

If you have a Tarot deck of your own, you may notice that Pentacles are often yellow or another cheery color. That's because these are the cards of well-earned success. You've come through the Swords now—so you've earned it!

Speaking Y2K

Pentacles are the Minor Arcana suit that reveal your role within your material and financial world.

Ace of Pentacles.

Upright meanings:
The beginning of
  prosperity
A new business
A new career direction

Reversed meanings:
Look at the new venture
  before you leap
Are you really prepared?
A false sense of security

2 of Pentacles.

Upright meanings:
A balancing act
Handling several things at
  once
Helpful advice will arrive

Reversed meanings:
Too many irons in the fire
Disorganization causes
  delays
Don't try to handle so
  much

3 of Pentacles.

Upright meanings:
Recognition for skill or
*   ability*
Congratulations are due
Material gain through
*   hard work*

Reversed meanings:
Inability to do best job
Contract disagreements
Lack of good workmanship

4 of Pentacles.

Upright meanings:
Attachment to money and
*   possessions*
A comfortable financial
*   position*
A little too stingy?

Reversed meanings:
Chance of losing money or
*   possessions*
A delay in getting the
*   money*
Overextending oneself
*   financially*

5 of Pentacles.

Upright meanings:
Financial or spiritual
 difficulty
A feeling of loss or
 abandonment
Left out in the cold

Reversed meanings:
The bad luck is reversed
Acceptance of loss and
 moving on
Courage and hope return
 anew

6 of Pentacles.

Upright meanings:
A raise or promotion
Receiving what's rightfully
 yours
A sharing of alms

Reversed meanings:
Smaller bonus or gift than
 expected
Unfair distribution of
 wealth
Lack of recognition for
 work

7 of Pentacles.

Upright meanings:
A good return on
 investment
Solid accomplishment
You're almost ready for the
 harvest

Reversed meanings:
Hard work but little profit
Larger factors work against
 you
Possible poor speculation

8 of Pentacles.

Upright meanings:
Diverse talents
Ability to achieve profit
 and recognition
Doing well in career

Reversed meanings:
Mediocre work or
 workplace
Delayed production or loss
 of profit
Training for new career

9 of Pentacles.

Upright meanings:
Self-sufficiency,
 independence
Prosperity has arrived
A strong connection to the
environment

Reversed meanings:
Fear about current
 finances
Fear of losing all one's
 worked for
Too much dependence on
 others' money

10 of Pentacles.

Upright meanings:
The success of a lifetime's
 work
Purchase of a home or car
A stable foundation

Reversed meanings:
Dispute over inheritance or
 control
Hard time making ends
 meet
Financial loss or poor
 investment

Page of Pentacles.

Upright meanings:
A young student
Someone who's enthusiastic about learning
A message of good financial luck

Reversed meanings:
Delay of financial message
A young person who doesn't listen
A procrastinator

Knight of Pentacles.

Upright meanings:
Someone who helps others get ahead
A new job offer or pay increase
Good news about finances

Reversed meanings:
Financial progress at a standstill
Someone who needs encouragement to get the job done
A loner or malcontent

Queen of Pentacles.

Upright meanings:
A creative woman
A charitable woman
Someone who takes care of
  others

Reversed meanings:
Someone who's suspicious
  of others
A moody person who's
  dependent on others
Someone who's overex-
  tended herself

King of Pentacles.

Upright meanings:
A good financial advisor
A financially secure man
A decisive, logical person

Reversed meanings:
Someone who wants
  financial security
  without working for it
A stubborn person
Bad choices about money
  matters

Interpreting Tarot Spreads and Doing Readings

You don't have to memorize all the cards to interpret a Tarot spread or do a Tarot reading. With a tool like these three chapters, all you need are the cards and a question.

The most important thing about doing Tarot readings is to not jump to conclusions. In fact, we recommend that in the beginning, you simply write your cards down in your Tarot journal and not demand an interpretation of them. Sure, you can look up their meanings and come to some conclusions, but it takes time and practice to see the bigger picture a Tarot spread represents. Or, you may insist the cards "say" what you want them to, and ignore what they're really trying to tell you.

When You're Reading Someone's (or Your Own!) Y2K Cards

Whether you're giving or getting a Tarot reading, keep an open mind. Relax, don't fight it, and concentrate on what you want to know and how the cards can help you know it.

If you've got a specific question you'd like answered, ask it in the right way to get the answer you're really looking for. If you want to know if you'll get that promotion or transfer, ask specifically about that promotion, such as:

➤ Will I be promoted to Vice President of Big Truck Company in three months?

➤ Will I be transferred to Portland to head the cybernetics division in May?

➤ Is my employer a survivor in the Y2K transition or will I be looking for a new job in the year 2000?

See how specific our questions are? If we just asked, "Will I get a promotion?" the answer would be less specific—and might even answer for a promotion we'd already gotten—or might be getting years down the road!

A Karma Spread for the 21st Century

A karma spread is a simple four-card spread that shows your (or, in this case, the 21st century's!) current karmic lessons. For this spread, we use only the Major Arcana cards, taking them from the Tarot deck and setting the 56 Minor Arcana aside.

As we shuffle the cards, we ask the question. When we are ready, we lay out the cards. Here is how the cards are laid out for a karma spread:

The Karma Spread.

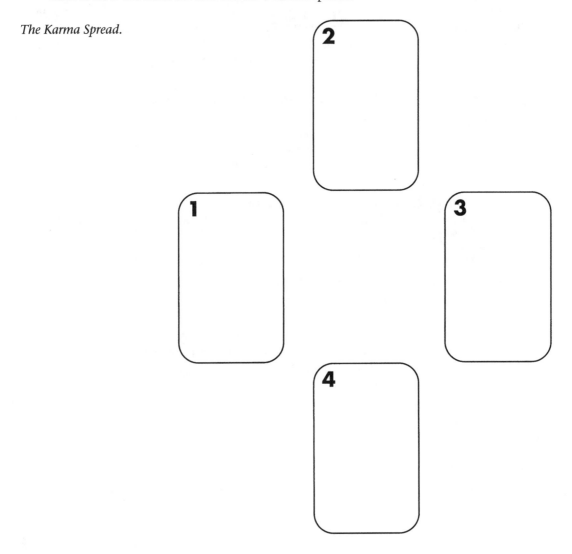

Now, here are the cards that came up when we asked the question, "What are the karmic lessons for the 21st century?"

What are the karmic lessons for the 21st century?

1st Card: World R. One of the big lessons of the 21st century will be that we'll sense many changes, which may make us feel uneasy. We may be afraid of what's to come, or fear that our homes or environment can be threatened in some way. The World R can represent a lack of vision or a refusal to listen to the lessons of the past. Maybe we won't want to remember history, or think we could have been better in the past. What's important to remember is that we still *can* improve, but first, we'll have to work harder and concentrate on our goals.

2nd Card: Strength. The Strength card shows our need to learn to trust ourselves and develop self-confidence. "Learn compassion and unconditional love," this card says. "She who tames her fears will be rewarded." The Lion represents our fears or passions,

227

Out of Time

We all know that history can repeat itself. If, as the World R suggests, we refuse to pay attention to cycles or the lessons we've gone through before, we may have to learn them all over again. Or, as George Santayana said, "Those who cannot remember the past are condemned to repeat it."

which, if out of control, could render us helpless. Courage and inner spiritual strength will win against fear and ignorance. The lesson in this card is to have compassion for other people's losses and to have an understanding mind and heart when others go through loss or traumas.

3rd Card: The Lovers. The lesson of the Lovers is to learn about our intimate relationships, sexual energy, and choosing the appropriate relationships in our lives. The Lovers reminds us that we must make choices and evaluate whom and what we need to develop in ourselves in order to find the right "loves" of our lives. In the 21st century, the Lovers tells us, we will desire to choose our friends and partners wisely. Some kind of sexual or social revolution could occur in this next cycle, allowing us to choose relationships in a manner that creates peace. The desire of this card is to find both physical and spiritual happiness in all of our relationships. In the 21st century, we'll be on a quest for the higher ideals of romance and intimacy.

4th Card: The Hierophant R. The old conventions and traditions of the 20th century will be looked at and deliberated over in the 21st century, and what was once considered traditional will become the non-traditional. For example, traditional medicine may merge with non-traditional medicine. Or, there may be new ways of looking at marriage, a new appearance to law and politics, or traditional religions experiencing dramatic changes and transformations to suit the new needs of society. Some traditional ideals and religions will remain, of course, but not without undergoing some kind of overhaul and change from the old ways of thinking, educating, and believing.

So what does this karma spread say overall about our collective 21st-century karma? Clearly, we'll be going through a process where what seems unusual, different, or revolutionary will become part of the norm. We'll be faced with hard choices, and we'll need to remember to pay attention to old lessons so we don't have to repeat them. In the end, though, new inventions, new religions, and new forms of education are coming!

Now, are you ready to find out more about what the Tarot has to say about the new millennium? In Chapter 15, we'll ask about money, society, and politics. In Chapter 16, we'll look at technology, medicine, and the environment. And, in Chapter 17, we'll take a look at what the cards have to say about *your* new millennium!

The Least You Need to Know

➤ Swords are the suit of activity.

➤ Pentacles are the suit of money.

➤ You can use the Tarot to find out your past, present, and future.

➤ Our karma spread reveals tough choices for the new millennium.

Chapter 15

Questions, Questions, Questions

Now that you've learned the basics of the Tarot, it's time to put the cards to work. In this chapter, we've asked the Tarot questions about everything from the future of the stock market to the possibility of a woman president.

Are you ready to see what the cards have to say about our financial, social, and political future? It's time to find out what all the buzz is about.

Everybody's Curious About the New Millennium

As you've already discovered, there's a lot of excitement about the beginning of the millennium, but there's fear as well. People have questions about everything from their leaders to the possibilities for new medicines and cures—as well as the potential for extraterrestrial life and interplanetary exploration!

In the next three chapters, we'll be using the Tarot as a medium to explore our curiosity about some of the possibilities for the new millennium. Remember, anything is possible: We human beings create what will come simply by our desires or our fears—and the Tarot can show us what those desires and fears are.

So, using the Tarot as our guide, let's peek into the year 2000 and beyond, taking an eagle's-eye view of the possibilities and trends that we've already started somewhere in our collective consciousness.

Keep a Tarot Journal of Your Questions and Answers

As we've already mentioned, it's very important to keep your readings recorded in any way you think would help. That's because it's easy to forget the readings, not just six months or a year later, but five minutes after you've put the cards away!

Whether you keep a written journal, tape your readings on cassette, or save your readings on your computer, you'll find the history of your readings a helpful tool not just for recall, but for generating more insight by hindsight.

Here's a sample journal page:

March 15, 1999   Celtic Cross

Will I get the raise this month?

1. *Queen of Swords*
2. *2 of Wands*
3. *2 of Swords*
4. *Knight of Cups R*
5. *Knight of Pentacles*
6. *Ace of Pentacles*
7. *Page of Cups R*
8. *7 of Cups*
9. *Queen of Pentacles*
10. *9 of Cups!*

This person did get the raise that month—can you see the answer in the cards? What else do you notice about the spread? Use the following space to make some notes about your thoughts before you go on.

_____

_____

_____

_____

Looking back at the cards after the fact can help you learn more about what certain cards mean for you personally. Or, if a specific card seems to come up again and again in your readings, keeping a journal can help you see the patterns and examine them for the future. When it comes to the Tarot, hindsight can be foresight.

Remember, Fate Is What You Make It

The Tarot is a tool you can use to make your life decisions resonate closer to your heart's desire—because it's about getting in touch with your own energy and then using that energy to live up to your fullest potential. At the same time, however, it's important to note that the Tarot reveals potentials and probabilities—not certainties.

The only things certain in life are that:

➤ We are alive now.

➤ *You* create your future.

It follows that if, #1, you believe you can do something, and, #2, you're proactive enough to create the steps to attain those goals, you will succeed. Fate, in other words, is what *you* make it.

As an example, let's say you don't like your job because there's a lot of gossip and in-fighting amongst your work group, and negative energy surrounds the workplace. Maybe you choose to complain, or gossip yourself. Perhaps you get depressed, or just drag yourself to work: It's better than the unknown and the paycheck covers the bills.

If any of these instances are the case, you've made a deal with the conditions at hand. You don't really want to change because of fear, but at the same time, you're always unhappy—and you really want out! Then, one of these days, a situation will develop to get you out of that workplace. Perhaps you'll get fired or laid off. Or you'll actually create a situation where you could get fired because there's a part of yourself that says, "To heck with this place!"

Did you create your release from this job? And, if so, did you do it the easy way or the hard way? The Tarot can allow you to not only know that you're tired of the job, but to go about getting out of it—or any difficult situation—in a more positive way. As one of Arlene's wonderful Tarot teachers used to say: "There are two ways of doing anything in life, the hard way or the graceful way!"

233

Ask Away!: Questions About Money

Everyone wants to know about money, whether it's how their investments are doing, or how they can accumulate more cold, hard cash. Let's face it: We live in a material world, and even though we never forget our spiritual natures, there's nothing wrong with developing our financial potentials in life as well.

So what do you want to know about the economic future? Here are some of the new millennium money questions we thought might be interesting to ask the cards.

How Strong Will the Global Economy Be in 2000–2005?

For this question, as we will for many of the questions throughout these chapters, we used a Celtic Cross, the most commonly used Tarot spread. In a Celtic Cross, each card represents a specific aspect of the question, covering its past, present, and future. Here's the meaning of the cards in a Celtic Cross Spread.

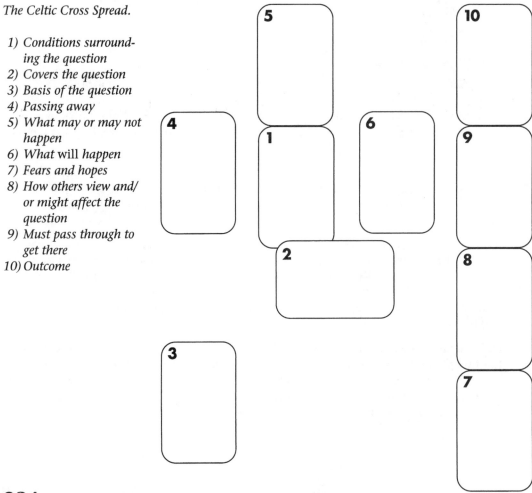

The Celtic Cross Spread.

1) Conditions surrounding the question
2) Covers the question
3) Basis of the question
4) Passing away
5) What may or may not happen
6) What will happen
7) Fears and hopes
8) How others view and/ or might affect the question
9) Must pass through to get there
10) Outcome

Now, here are the cards that came up when we asked the question, "How strong will the global economy be in 2000–2005?" Remember, the following spread will relate to global conditions, not just those in the U.S.

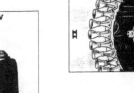

How strong will the global economy be between 2000 and 2005?

1) *Knight of Cups*
2) *9 of Cups*
3) *5 of Cups*
4) *5 of Pentacles*
5) *Wheel of Fortune*
6) *3 of Cups R*
7) *The Star*
8) *8 of Cups*
9) *Page of Cups*
10) *5 of Swords*

235

1st card (conditions surrounding the question): Knight of Cups. This card indicates the beginning of good movement ahead. The Knight offers up hope and inspiration, the desire for a positive economy, and genuine concern for trade and movement forward (when upright, the Knight's horse always represents movement in a positive direction).

2nd card (covering the question): 9 of Cups. Wishes are coming true! The beginning of the cycle from 2000 to 2005 looks pretty good: Things will start to look up in different parts of world economy or trade. Remember, Cups show the emotional desire to attain happiness, so this card suggests that the world will be planning in a hopeful way to attain more material goods. Plus, there's no opposition from the global marketplace for those who want to do well.

3rd card (basis of the question): 5 of Cups. As we already know by 2000, there are regrets in the global economy about the fact that others have not been able to make it, or that some countries' economies have actually slid backward instead of forward. This card suggests that some marketplaces will not do well, either because of living in the past or because of economic losses due to old habits. It's also possible that some parts of the global community have inherited poor conditions or are still recuperating from former losses.

4th card (passing away): 5 of Pentacles. In the past global cycle, some economies were poverty-stricken, some had their money devalued, and others were beaten down by Mother Nature. No matter what the cause, these countries can't get out of their past impoverishment. This card could also represent that the global economy will have its ups and downs, so 2000 to 2005 could be a period when the global economy goes from one extreme to another. Or, it could indicate that some countries are always going to be better off than others.

5th card (what may or may not happen): Wheel of Fortune. The Wheel of Fortune represents a possible positive turnaround in the global economy, and negative events and cycles have the potential to be turned around between 2000 and 2002. This card indicates that potential success could be realized—but first, the world community has to notice the good cycle and go into it!

6th card (what will happen): 3 of Cups R. This card indicates that the economy may have a sudden boom, and that the collective groups may overindulge or think, "Hey! We can really have a great party here! Things are looking up!" The 3 of Cups R represents an event that *will* come to pass, probably by the middle of this cycle. It says that we'll feel good, or even overly optimistic, about the global economy—but caution is advised to guard against overdoing a good thing. It might also mean that a good cycle could only last a short while, and that we'll need to keep our perspective about where we really are.

Time Capsule

If you look at the cards in this Celtic Cross without considering the question, you'll notice that the cards go from a good picture to an unhappy picture, back and forth, up and down. Note, too, all the fives in the spread. They represent a constant state of fluctuation; in this case, in the global marketplace for the period from 2000 to 2005. Lastly, there are quite a few Cups here as well, which indicates that we'll all be emotional about that five-year cycle. Maybe that's because the global economy will never be quite settled during those five years!

7th card (our attitude toward the question): The Star. Fortunately, we seem to have an optimistic, hopeful, and forward-looking attitude toward this question. It's great to have a good card like the Star in the seventh position, because it's the position of how we're feeling, in this case toward what's going on with the economy. This card doesn't show overall fear or anxiety, but instead looks toward the possibility that despite all the ups and downs, we can create a good global economy in these five years.

8th card (how others view or might affect the question): 8 of Cups. The 8 of Cups suggests walking away from the material world or abandoning old thinking and old ideals for the new. Perhaps the world will start to abandon what doesn't work for us in the global marketplace and try new ways of trade, commerce, or changing money themes. There's also the possibility we might get rid of our old ways of handling economic trends and start something totally new. Spiritual insight will come from others as well. Perhaps some new leaders in the 2000–2005 cycle will bring new hope and encouraging direction, either away from old ideals or obsolete ways.

9th card (must pass through to get there): Page of Cups. Here we have the desire for the global market to do wonderful things. This is the card of happy messages, good energy, and compassion. The Page of Cups understands that what the world needs will come from the world's youth. It's possible that our young hold the key to success in this five-year cycle.

10th card (outcome): 5 of Swords. This card indicates that our global economy will be threatened either by small wars or civil unrest in different countries at different times. Challenges may come from unrest, legal, or political upheavals in various parts of the world. This is a difficult card, so we *covered* it, and got the 4 of Cups R. The 4 of Cups R can help a 5 of Swords turn around. In the cycle of 2000-2005, we will have different crises in the world, crises which either threaten or slow down global economy, conditions of bad weather, and/or a lack of political leadership in certain countries

Speaking Y2K

When a particular card doesn't seem to give the whole answer, it may be *covered* by selecting another card from the deck (either from the top of the deck, or selecting it from a fanned-out deck), to get more information.

which will create negative trade issues. Still, the 4 of Cups R indicates a change for the better (even in the difficult countries) by 2002-2005.

The 4 of Cups R suggests that we'll get out of our contemplative phase and take action about the things that are disturbing us. This card shows that we'll be motivated toward a goal (and it's true that war and upheaval of any kind can certainly get us motivated!), try new things, and get our act together to find a new approach to an old problem. This card suggests that there will be a great desire to accomplish new ideals, such as new trade agreements, or even a new way of dealing with the economy worldwide.

This spread shows that between 2000 and 2005 the global economy may well be on a roller coaster, but after that short cycle, we as a group will want to stabilize it and smooth it out. Plan on rough waters at times, perhaps from 2000 to 2002, then a smoothing out, and then a rough period again. This spread suggests that the last rough cycle may be the one (before 2005) that moves the whole world into initiating a whole new cycle that could last a lot longer than five years!

Time Capsule

This reading suggests that we'll put up with the ups and downs for two to five years, but in the long run, the global community won't want the roller coaster ride to continue. Many places around the world may ask for help in times of disasters (whether man-made or caused by nature). This may well be a time when we face much introspection, but ultimately, victory through adversity seems to be the outcome of the global economy from 2000 to 2005.

How Will the U.S. Stock Market Do from February 1999 Through 2001?

For this question, we used a Celtic Cover Spread. In a Celtic Cover Spread, a second card covers each of the first 10 cards, in reverse order, to enhance their meaning.

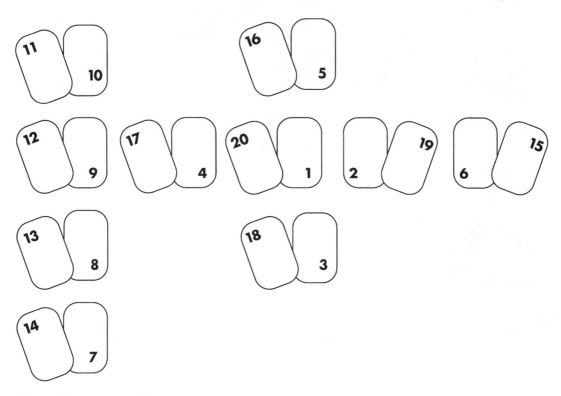

The Celtic Cover Spread.

1) Lovers R
2) 10 of Pentacles
3) Sun R
4) 6 of Cups
5) 8 of Cups
6) Knight of Swords
7) The Devil
8) 2 Swords
9) Ace of Wands
10) Queen of Swords

20) 3 of Pentacles R
19) 2 of Wands
18) 3 of Wands
17) Queen of Cups
16) King of Swords
15) Ace of Cups
14) The Star R
13) 4 of Swords
12) 3 of Cups
11) 7 of Swords R

How will the U.S. stock market do from February 1999 through 2001?

1st/20th cards: The Lovers R/3 Pentacles R. These cards suggest that the stock market will have conditions around it having to do with negative choices, poor speculation on companies, people making poor choices, a cycle of ups and downs, poor conditions in other parts of the world, or over-enthusiasm that causes a loss. Not a good beginning!

2nd/19th cards: 10 of Pentacles/2 of Wands. The market will still have a firm foundation to stand on through 1999, as the desire of new investors shows in these cards. Companies that have stayed conservative with their growth will stay sound as well.

3rd/18th cards: The Sun R/3 of Wands. The foundation of the spread is the Sun, which, when reversed, indicates unrest, uneasiness, and uncertainty. The Sun R tells the Tarot reader that the general public feels the future of the stock market from the end of 1999 to 2001 is in question, and may not trust that the market has a solid foundation during this time period. The 3 of Wands suggests that we'll take a wait-and-see attitude, however.

4th/17th cards: 6 of Cups/Queen of Cups. The 6 of Cups represents our recent past with the stock market, and, as we all know, the stock market has been quite profitable in the recent past. The cover card here, the Queen of Cups, says exactly the same thing!

5th/16th cards: 8 of Cups/King of Swords. The 8 of Cups indicates that people may give up on the market or that the average person may not go into the market from October 1999 to April 2000. The King of Swords may be a political person or someone like Allen Greenspan saying things to keep people balanced for the time of unease.

6th/15th cards: Knight of Swords/Ace of Cups. There will be a good turn in the market in the early part of 2000. The sixth position is what *will* come about—and these cards are both good news!

7th/14th cards: The Devil/The Star R. These cards reveal the fears that some will feel about the market being over-valued, leading to ups and downs from October 1999 through 2001.

8th/13th cards: 2 of Swords/4 of Swords. This position is how others outside our country see our stock market. The 2 and 4 of Swords suggest that others are taking a cautious approach and haven't made a decision about our market from October 1999 through February 2000. Others are resting or just keeping an eye on us but without much comment or action toward our market. It's almost as if the whole world is waiting to see what we'll do or how we'll handle differing conditions in our own economy.

9th/12th cards: Ace of Wands/3 of Cups. The Ace of Wands and the 3 of Cups show our collective attitude is for growth and success, and that our desire in our marketplace is to be #1 with new growth, new stocks, and continued success in general for the market itself. The ninth card always predicts our collective attitude or goals toward the question at hand, and when it comes to the stock market, we clearly have a good attitude and optimistic focus!

Out of Time

This reading, like the previous one, indicates a roller coaster effect—down from late 1999 to early 2000, up and then back down again by fall of 2001. At the same time, however, this reading doesn't indicate a dramatic crash but rather the ups and downs we're already seeing in the stock market.

10th/11th cards: Queen of Swords/7 of Swords R. The Queen of Swords represents Libra, or the fall season, and this card could mean that by the fall of 1999, the market could drop. People may be scared or unsure, and in fact this fear could cause the market to fall! If the market indeed falls in the October 1999 through February 2000 period, it will come back up again after February 2000, because the 7 of Swords R indicates good legal or political counsel will be given. Of course, the roller coaster may roll back down a little once more, and then come up again in 2001.

Will Social Security Still Be Around When You Need It?

Will Social Security still be around when you need it? We asked the question for the period through 2001, and the cards looked good! For this question we used a Seven-Card Spread to indicate a yes or no answer. Cards are laid out one through seven from left to right. The cards that came up were:

1) The Star R
2) 2 of Cups R
3) 9 of Wands R
4) 6 of Wands
5) High Priestess
6) Knight of Pentacles
7) 6 of Pentacles

Will Social Security still be around when you need it?

These cards look like a "yes" to us! There may be some changes in the system, whether in distribution or how we put our money into it. Still, Social Security will continue to maintain the general theme of getting some of your money back out of the system.

How Will Attitudes Toward Money and Finance Evolve?

Here's a Three-Card Spread looking at how U.S. attitudes toward money and finance will evolve. A Three-Card Spread simply takes three cards and puts them together to get an answer. The cards are laid out one through three from left to right. Take a look at the cards we got and see what you think.

1) *Ace of Swords*
2) *9 of Cups*
3) *6 of Cups*

How will attitudes toward money and finance evolve?

What do you think? Some of the possibilities we come up with for these cards include a more heart-centered attitude toward money and finance (the same holds true for the first two readings in this section, too). Maybe we'll be more compassionate when it comes to money, which could mean sharing resources in our communities, or sharing with others in other ways. No matter what, these are nice cards!

Ask Away!: Questions About Society and Politics

But enough about money. What about a woman president? What about the Pope? It's time to ask some questions about society and politics. We put Arlene's Winter 1999 Tarot class to work to see what kind of answers they came up with for these questions.

Will the Battle of the Sexes Continue in the 21st Century?

We were curious: How would men relate to women in the 21st century? So we asked the cards, and here's what they had to say.

1) *7 of Cups*
2) *7 of Pentacles*
3) *Ace of Swords*
4) *The Tower*
5) *8 of Swords R*
6) *2 of Swords*
7) *10 of Wands*
8) *The Fool*
9) *The Hanged Man*
10) *The Magician*

How will men relate to women in the 21st century?

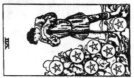

1st card: 7 of Cups. Right now, men don't know how to help women, and they feel confused about how to relate to women, too. "Which way do I go?" they wonder. "Do I open the door or do I not open the door for her?" At the same time, men have fantasies about women—but those fantasies don't necessarily tie into what women really are.

2nd card: 7 of Pentacles. In opposition, when men speculate about women, they wonder how to relate to them, too. In the past, they've related better financially than emotionally—taking care of women materially was enough in the old days. Men believed, like the man in the 7 of Pentacles, that hard work and effort toward their goal would be enough. But when it comes to women, it's not!

3rd card: Ace of Swords. The foundation of the matter is that men are thinking they've done the right thing. There's a desire to communicate with women, and in fact men are talking more and communicating better than they have in the past. The Ace of Swords' victory is intellectual—and this will hold into the 21st century.

4th card: The Tower. The foundation of where men came from got blown up—the past got disintegrated! Men were shocked that they had to change their whole concept about how to relate to women, and not only did women surprise them, they surprised themselves as well. Family dynamics changed, people changed their minds, and a revolution in male/female relationships occurred in the last part of the 20th century.

5th card: 8 of Swords R. Men are learning to release their fears about women, and they're in the process of letting go of old conditioning and old dynamics about their relationships with women.

6th card: 2 of Swords. Here's a literal pause. Men are thinking, "Okay? What now? We know how to communicate, but which way should we go?" They're going to observe, think about, and analyze women to see what to do next. They know that women are smart (and that men are smart, too). They're being cautious and guarded, and waiting to see what happens next.

7th card: 10 of Wands. Men are afraid of being overwhelmed, or maybe have a sense that they may fail in their relationships with women in the future. There's a lot of apprehension about being responsible, but what will the burdens be? Again, caution is advised with this card.

8th card: The Fool. Somehow, something's going to happen to men which allows them to feel like they have the freedom to be who they are. That's because this card indicates a new journey for men with women in the 21st century. Men will shed their old fears, move into a new dimension, and start anew with women. Plus, some outside influence will cause this to happen.

9th card: The Hanged Man. A change in consciousness *will* occur. Men *have to* pass through a letting go of an old dynamic or paradigm and change their consciousness and awareness toward women. They *will* let go in order to make way for a higher consciousness about this issue.

10th card: The Magician. Heaven and Earth! Men will be able to connect to women better, and re-create themselves in the process! Men and women won't be frightened by each other any more, and the differences between men and women will no

Ask Spaceship Earth

Arlene and Lisa were discussing this reading on the phone on the last day we were working on this book, and suddenly we noticed that every card in this reading is male. Even the Cup, in a "female" suit, has a man in the picture! How appropriate for a reading that's for the men.

longer even be thought about. The new paradigm will be non-threatening, where symbolic roles no longer matter. Our ability to create our own reality will result in a whole new dynamic. We can't wait!

It Takes a Village: Family Values

When it came to family values, we wanted to ask as specific a question as possible, so we asked the cards, "How will we handle family values and ideals in the next 10 years?" Here are the cards that came up:

1) *Queen of Cups*
2) *7 of Cups*
3) *5 of Wands*
4) *3 of Swords*
5) *8 of Cups*
6) *The Magician*
7) *The Hierophant*
8) *Death*
9) *The Tower*
10) *The Lovers*

How will we handle family values and ideals in the next 10 years?

246

1st card: Queen of Cups. In the position of conditions around the situation, it's clear that women will be the focal point of family values, and that good female energy or nurturing will be a focus. This isn't just taking care of family and children, but taking a nurturing approach to the situation (of course, men can be nurturing, too!). In this case, the Queen of Cups represents how we're going to handle family, whether a woman or a man is the head of household.

2nd card: 7 of Cups. On the other hand, we may have difficulty trying to raise our families in a new and different world. This may be like trying to play soccer on a foggy field: We know both teams are good, but how can we go about our game if the fog gets in the way? We're beginning to raise families differently than before, and as we move into the 21st century, the playing field will change still more. As our values change, we'll need to adapt to those conditions. So, while we're familiar with the game, the new weather's throwing us for a loop.

3rd card: 5 of Wands. The foundation of this reading is the ongoing struggle regarding how we handle family values. For example, kids do their thing and parents do theirs—and while sometimes it works, other times it leads to families that are scattered or even shattered. We've worked through a lot of struggle with family values and we still have to get a handle on it now.

4th card: 3 of Swords. Recent sorrow or separation of family values is in our past. More families than at any other time in history have gone through either divorce or loss of children through societal troubles. In our recent past (let's say from 1980 to 2000), we've seen a lot of change in the way families are structured, as well as changes in how we discipline (or don't discipline) our children. Could it be "the American Dream" was never more than a dream in the first place? In any event, we've had a lot of pain as we struggle to come to terms with our families.

Ask Spaceship Earth

When you study the cards for this reading, note that in the first five, we have three Cups, which indicates that this is very much a heart-centered issue. The last five cards are all Major Arcana, which suggests that we're evolving without any personal control over what happens. Natural evolution, in other words, will occur.

5th card: 8 of Cups. This card indicates that we may walk away from something we've held dear. Maybe we'll give up our old ideals and look for something to replace them. It's clear that we're seeking a higher level of consciousness and that we want to create families that are different than before so that we can have more peace and spiritual connection to each other.

6th card: The Magician. We're going to create a dynamic new family, one where everyone contributes creatively in some way. Extended family will become more important, as will outsiders. After all, the Major Arcana represent touching outside one's own community.

7th card: The Hierophant. There's a fear of falling back to the traditional dynamics, which worked for a while, but no longer do. There's also a fear of traditionalism or a conservative backlash, such as the fundamental right trying to take control of how we handle our families. It's possible that many people may even go that way for a while. After all, that's what they know.

8th card: Death. Here's transformation—with an outside influence. "You must change!" says the Death card. Something outside of the family, larger than ourselves in some way, is going to make us reexamine everything. In fact, we'd guess this card suggests a change of consciousness in all of us—or the awareness that old ways of doing and operating our world and systems in this world have to change.

Out of Time

Interestingly, this major transformation brought on by something outside of us scenario has come up in many of the readings for this book. The question is, what's coming? Aliens again? War? Ecological threat? Time will tell!

9th card: The Tower. Here we are, getting blown up again! This card indicates the end of a cycle: We're going to start anew. It's clear we can't live in the old paradigm anymore. We'll agree to change, with this card here in the 9th position.

10th card: The Lovers. The final outcome is a better world, a better life, a better family, and a true balance between male and female energy! The right choices will be made and peace will once again reign in family relationships. Give it 25 more years, and we'll be living happily ever after!

Will There Be a Woman President?

Nine students were in class on Monday, February 22, 1999, to ask and answer the question: "Will there be a woman elected to the U.S. presidency or vice-presidency before 2005?" A Celtic Cross Spread was used.

Wow! What an answer! Here's how Arlene's class interpreted these cards!

1st card (present atmosphere around the question): 6 of Wands R. This card indicates delays in accepting the idea of a woman president. Maybe there's interest, but the public isn't ready to take any action toward a woman in that position at the present.

2nd card (cover card): 4 of Swords. This cover card can represent any opposition toward a woman in office, and the 4 of Swords shows that people may be thinking about it while they rest from recent political strife. The 4 of Swords can indicate that we will contemplate a woman in office, or, that we'll think toward that end. But we may not take any action toward it at the present.

1) *6 of Wands R*
2) *4 of Swords*
3) *The Fool*
4) *The Emperor*
5) *Queen of Cups R*
6) *Queen of Wands R*
7) *10 of Wands*
8) *Temperance*
9) *6 of Pentacles R*
10) *2 of Cups/5 of Wands*

Will there be a woman elected to the U.S. presidency or vice-presidency before 2005?

3rd card (basis of the question): The Fool. This is the card of the foundation of the question, and with the Fool in this position, it's clear that we the public will be open-minded toward this issue. We're ready for a new beginning, says the Fool.

4th card (past, passing away): The Emperor. Here's the card of our collective past, where we've gotten used to men presidents. Further, as members of Arlene's class pointed out, we're used to a married man, not a single or divorced one. Maybe, someone suggested, a married couple should be in the office! (Of course, that wasn't the question, but…) As a collective society, this card says, we've needed an Emperor rather than an Empress. But remember, the 4th card indicates passing away…

5th card (possible future energy): Queen of Cups R. The energy of the 5th card may or may not occur. Well. This certainly shows that a woman or women are thinking about running for this office or position… Arlene's class mentioned Geraldine Ferraro might be the Queen of Cups R. Or maybe it's Elizabeth Dole or Hillary Clinton. After all, the Queen of Cups R has known her emotional ups and downs.

6th card (will happen in the future): Queen of Wands R. Some woman will make a try at it for sure, Arlene's class said. She might appear bold, strong-willed, and fiery—and she'll sure be able to get the crowds going. But reversed, the class just wasn't sure if she would be accepted by the public wholeheartedly. Some comments from class members:

"The best women leaders the world has known have been women like Indira Gandhi, Margaret Thatcher, and Golda Meir, so our country won't pick a woman as president unless those women's qualities are there."

"There will be a woman or two making a run for it this next two to four years for sure!"

The class agreed with both these statements, but even the future cards looked doubtful before 2005. So—after 2005, they said.

7th card (attitudes toward question): 10 of Wands. This card represents our collective fears or attitude toward the question. The burdens of the 10 of Wands suggest that even if a woman wins an election on her own, she'll have too many burdens from the old conditioning that continues to affect society. Maybe we're not ready yet, suggested the class, or maybe there will be too many other changes going on and we won't be able to adjust to yet another "first."

8th card (others): Temperance R. This card shows what we collectively think of the idea of a woman as president. This card indicates that the public might need more time before it accepts a woman as president—or even the idea of a woman president. Arlene's class contemplated this question further, however, and decided that this card is about public misconceptions regarding a woman's ability to handle everything from business to the military. In fact, people might worry whether a woman could handle anything without her temper getting out of control. But hey—can a man?

9th card (must go through to get there): 6 of Pentacles R. This is the card of what we have to go through to get to the goal of a woman in office. At this time, according to the 6 of Pentacles R, there aren't enough resources to put toward a woman's election. Maybe the parties won't want to put a lot of money toward this venture now. Or there could be bribery or deception with money or funding with this card, or not enough support from the business world to support a party who takes on a woman now (1999–2002). Too bad!

10th card (outcome): 2 of Cups, covered by the 5 of Wands. Final outcome as of February 22, 1999. The class decided to cover this outcome card for clarification. Eventually, they decided, the 2 of Cups indicated that a woman would be accepted by the public and that she would have a good partner or running mate. The right pair could win the day! Still, the 5 of Wands indicates obstacles and frustration in the present. But, as we move through 2004 and beyond, Arlene's class agreed that a woman either will become president or become an accepted figure in the public eye. In the future, our society will be ready to accept a woman as a political leader. But sadly, we're not ready yet.

Will We Have a Pope or Not in 2000–2005?

To answer this question, Arlene's class used a seven-card spread for a yes-or-no answer. Here are the cards they came up with.

1) *Wheel of Fortune*
2) *The Star*
3) *Queen of Wands*
4) *10 of Cups R*
5) *Page of Pentacles*
6) *High Priestess*
7) *Hierophant*

Will we have a Pope or not in 2000–2005?

Everyone in the class thought these cards suggested that there will be a different kind of Pope! Perhaps she'll be a more High Priestess-style Pope—a woman, or someone more intuitive. This person would still hold a powerful position, but it would also be a unique position, like the Pope, but maybe not the Pope?

Possible change in the traditions of the Church—or even a total transformation away from the fundamental or strict teachings of the Church could be indicated, too, with more compassion and understanding as the Church changes with the times. Maybe the Church will split in two, with two separate leaders—one more traditional, one more contemporary. This may be a yes-or-no spread, but it's clearly not a yes-or-no answer!

Cultivating Patience and an Open Mind

If you want to try some spreads of your own, it's important to learn to be patient and to keep an open mind as you do the reading. Here's an example from a reading Arlene did for a young man named Donald in December of 1998:

1) *King of Wands*
2) *8 of Cups*
3) *Queen of Swords*
4) *2 of Wands*
5) *Knight of Cups*
6) *5 of Swords R*
7) *5 of Pentacles*
8) *Page of Wands*
9) *The Hierophant*
10) *Ace of Wands*

Donald asks: "What do I need to do to make more money in the next two years?"

As Arlene and Donald went through the cards, Donald was patient, and asked questions with an open mind to help Arlene interpret the reading.

1st card: King of Wands. This is the card Donald selected to represent himself. This is sometimes done for a Celtic Cross Spread—and Donald selected a card that represents a man who wants action.

2nd card: 8 of Cups. Donald had been unhappy with his job and wanted to quit—and this is the card that came up as the cover card for the question!

3rd card: Queen of Swords. Donald believed that this card represented his supportive wife, Betty, who has brown hair and brown eyes, like the Queen of Swords. Betty has a good job with the phone company.

4th card: 2 of Wands. In the past, Donald loved to run his own business, but he hadn't gotten it all together. In fact, Donald had been on hold, waiting for something to occur—and he was still waiting when the reading took place.

5th card: Knight of Cups. This is the card of future possibilities, and in this case, it indicates a possible offering of an artistic or creative type of job. Donald said he loves the travel industry, and, on the side, he told Arlene, "I love the horse!" Horses, remember, appear on all of the Knight cards.

6th card: 5 of Swords R. This is the card of what will come about. The 5 of Swords R suggests that delays or fears were holding Donald back from making new or better money. It can also indicate that losses would occur in some way, so that extra money he had saved might get spent on other things. In either event, delays in attaining the goal show up here.

7th card: 5 of Pentacles. These are Donald's fears regarding the question, and he was clearly afraid he wouldn't make his goals. Donald admitted this, but he said he didn't want to see that card. Arlene agreed it looked pretty difficult from a money angle, but reminded him that in this position, this is what's inside him, not what might happen.

8th card: Page of Wands. This is the card of others, and the Page of Wands indicates that new, hopeful messages about work and new jobs are coming in this year. Good news!

9th card: The Hierophant. Donald could end up working for a corporation or a business that has stable and conventional work for him. In the past, Donald had done union work, which offers very good money and benefits. This led Arlene to suggest that Donald connect back to a system or traditional job with the union or something related. He thought that over very carefully.

10th card: Ace of Wands. "Yes!" cried Arlene when this card came up. It indicates a new job offer coming which will bring optimism and success to Donald's original goal—and answers his question about making more money. This outcome card equals success!

The answer to Donald's question was that he would do better, and that soon there would be a job offering. The spring seemed like a possible time, because Wands rule springtime, and the majority of Minor Arcana cards in Donald's reading were Wands.

By January 30, 1999, Donald was working for a union house of boiler-makers. Now, he wants to go to school to develop his carpentry skills. *And*, he may want to take a part-time job as a census-taker this year—talk about traditional!

If you are patient with the cards and help them help you, you, like Donald, can find the answers you're seeking!

The Least You Need to Know

➤ Our economic future will have its ups and downs.

➤ Social Security will still be around in the new millennium!

➤ We will have a woman president—but not for several more years.

➤ Learning to cultivate patience and have an open mind can help the cards help you find the answers you seek.

Chapter 16

More Questions, Questions, Questions

In This Chapter

➤ We ask the cards about technology

➤ A question about Y2K

➤ Some questions about the future of health

➤ A question about the environment

➤ What about space travel? Will we boldly go where no one has gone before?

Now that you've had a taste of what the Tarot can tell you about the future, we're sure there are more questions you'd like the cards to answer. In this chapter, we take a look at the future of technology (including a question about Y2K), as well as what medical advances the new millennium may hold.

In addition, we'll see if we finally begin to heal our environment rather than hurt it, and then we'll go on to find out about space travel—in the 24th century!

We Know There's More You Want to Find Out

Tarot readers decide which spread to use based on what the question is. For example, in this chapter, Arlene decided that a seven-card spread for getting a "yes" or "no" answer was a good one for questions that didn't require more than that, while she used the Celtic Cross Spread when she felt more background on a question was needed.

In Chapter 17, we'll introduce you to some other Tarot spreads that you can try yourself, including the Horoscope Spread, Karmic Spread, Gypsy Wish Spread, and Decision Spread.

The more Tarot readings you do, the more comfortable you'll feel selecting the spread that's right for the question. But we know that right now there's more you want to find out—not just about the Tarot, but about the new millennium.

Ask Away!: Questions About Technology

Let's begin by taking a look at the technology of the future. In Chapter 25, we'll be taking a closer look at what some scientists predict for the new millennium. But first, we're going to ask the cards some questions. When you compare the following spreads with the predictions in Chapter 25, you'll see for yourself that the Tarot and science do have something in common!

Will the Y2K Crisis Be Our 21st-Century Titanic?

Here's a seven-card spread Arlene's class did in response to the question: "Will the Y2K crisis be our 21st-century *Titanic*?"

1) *4 of Swords R*
2) *Knight of Pentacles R*
3) *The World R*
4) *6 of Swords R*
5) *The Star R*
6) *6 of Pentacles*
7) *The Lovers R*

Will the Y2K crisis be our 21st-century Titanic?

Look at all those reversed cards! Your immediate reaction may be that the answer is "yes." When you look at these particular cards more closely, though—especially when you take into account the *wording of the question*—you'll realize that the answer is "no."

Time Capsule

How you word a question when you do a Tarot spread is very important when you inter-pret the answer the cards give you. In the example here, the question is phrased so that a "yes" answer would be a negative outcome; that is, the Y2K crisis *would* be our 21st-century *Titanic*!

These cards don't foretell a disaster. As Arlene's class discussed, the *Titanic* was thought to be unsinkable, so its crew wasn't prepared when the ship hit an iceberg. There weren't even enough lifeboats, for example—and no disaster plan was in place.

The Y2K problem is quite different—we *know* this ship could sink, so we're preparing to keep that from happening. In other words, when you're prepared, ready to work on meeting a problem head-on instead of avoiding it, it won't turn out to be a disaster.

How Will We Use Nuclear Technology?

For this question, we used a ten-card Celtic Cross Spread to look at the past, present, and future of nuclear technology.

Again, an interesting spread! Notice that, with one exception, *all* the Minor Arcana cards here are Cups, so this is clearly an emotional issue. Note, too, how the Major Arcana are placed throughout the spread. Some of this is out of our hands already.

1st card: 6 of Pentacles. At present, nuclear technology is being used in a practical way. The 6 of Pentacles shows that we're currently using nuclear energy for heat, electricity, and power, as well as medical research.

2nd card: The Emperor. The Emperor covering here stands in opposition to the 1st card. The Emperor rules political leadership in the world, and in this case, this card can be read as using nuclear technology for political gain, or even war for political control.

3rd card: The High Priestess R. The foundation of the question is a card which reversed represents deception or a secretive nature. Might this be people or countries who are using this technology for their own hidden agendas? It sure could be!

4th card: 9 of Cups. The Wish card in this position suggests that we've discovered how nuclear technology works and can be used to fulfill our wishes for whatever we want to do with it. As we've worked with this technology in the past, we've learned how to use it for good—as well as for our own selfish needs.

1) 6 of Pentacles
2) The Emperor
3) The High Priestess R
4) 9 of Cups
5) King of Pentacles
6) The Chariot R
7) 10 of Cups
8) 2 of Cups
9) Death
10) 4 of Cups

How will we use nuclear technology?

5th card: The King of Pentacles. A powerful leader, country, or even a research group could come up with something great regarding nuclear technology, something with the potential to become a great resource or a new inventive way to deal with nuclear technology that we haven't heard of before.

6th card: The Chariot R. A reversal of good fortune could occur with future use of this technology. While upright, the Chariot can represent travel, automobiles, or other high-tech travel; reversed it suggests that nuclear technology for those purposes may not be successful or cost-effective. This card can also indicate possible failure of plans if we try to use nuclear power for travel, cars, or any other form of transportation. It probably will be best if we look toward some other technology for more efficient energy use.

7th card: 10 of Cups. The 10 of Cups in the fears and attitudes position suggests that we have nothing to fear! We're able to work with nuclear technology with a hopeful attitude and for the good of the collective community. This card could also mean that we'll keep our technology to ourselves or in the family—close to home rather than spreading it to others.

8th card: 2 of Cups. There would be support from the public or organizations to a find a way to use nuclear technology for the benefit of people, in other words to help rather than harm. This might be medicine, or science for medical purposes. This card can also indicate that other countries may make new discoveries, such as finding some humanitarian ways to use nuclear technology.

9th card: Death. The desire to transform from our old ways of using nuclear power in order to get into something else is indicated by this card in this position. It's time to move away from the original reason we developed nuclear technology (that is, nuclear bombs) and to instead try something new, something more beneficial to all of us. The potential is there!

10th card: 4 of Cups. This card shows a man pondering what's being offered. It could indicate a new way of looking at this question—or does he just want to think about the potentials of nuclear technology for awhile? Sometimes, this card can mean the man really doesn't care about the subject at hand, or that he doesn't feel it will have any movement toward his objective. Perhaps nuclear technology won't really be the best way to solve our problems.

Out of Time

Did the Death card scare you in this spread? It *is* a frightening image. It's important to remember, though, that this card represents the potential for transformation. Change can be scary, like this card, but it can be worth it, too.

This could be saying we'll use nuclear technology, but it could also indicate that we could go in an entirely different direction in the next 10 years, and actually move away from nuclear technology because we discover something better. It could be that nuclear technology is only the beginning of discovering that something else. Warp drive, maybe?

Some Cards for Corporate America

While we were looking at the future of technology, we got curious about corporate America. We decided to take a look at corporate America's past, present, and future, using a Past, Present, Future Spread.

This spread requires a total of 21 cards, which are set out in three rows of seven cards each. Here's what the spread looks like:

The Past, Present, Future Spread.

And here are the cards that came up when we asked the question, "What's going on in corporate America?"

The present for this spread (represented by the middle row) was 1999 to 2000; the future is 2000 to 2005.

What's going on in corporate America?

A look at this spread told us that there would be rocky times around the middle of 1999, lasting all the way through the middle of the year 2000. This might begin with the 8 of Wands R, when corporate America might be considered the culprit, as people are laid off or changed around too often.

It's possible that corporations' policies will create jealousy or even domestic upheaval by the very ways they run their companies. Their methods of profit-making may not be ones that their employees approve of, for example.

Ask Spaceship Earth

In this Past, Present, Future Spread, note the King of Swords, smack in the middle of the middle row: He represents the corporate mentality—and he landed right where he wanted to!

The feeling from the last row for the future of the corporations in America is that the Lovers R and the World R represent a change from the way corporations have done things in the past. Perhaps corporate America will realize that they made poor choices about letting go of people with talents and abilities, or that they were too preoccupied with balancing money and profit against the employees' needs for recognition of their skills.

The good news is that the 3 of Cups is the final outcome. By 2005, corporate America will once again become more employee-friendly, and have a desire to connect to the larger community as well as its employees. Corporate America will have marked improvement in the way it handles employee and problems.

Ask Away!: Questions About Medicine and Health

As we'll be discussing in Chapter 25, the Human Genome Project offers us the potential to unlock the mystery of every disease, including our current scourges, cancer and AIDS. But will isolating the genes for these diseases truly result in their cures?

In addition, medicine is moving away from a concentration on fixing what's wrong to a more holistic focus on taking care of what's right. How will we heal—body, mind, and soul—in the 21st century? Let's see what the cards have to say.

Will There Be Cures for Cancer? For AIDS?

The first question we asked the cards is important to all of us: "Will there be cures for cancer and AIDS, and if so, when?" For this spread, we once again used a Celtic Cross.

Right off the bat, we noticed that this spread was dominated by Wands and Pentacles—that is, enterprise and money. It's clear that the fight to cure these diseases will take both.

1st card: 2 of Pentacles. This card represents the scientists and researchers who are trying to get a handle on this subject. At this time, they're juggling, analyzing, and weighing some of the discoveries and messages they've already found, and they're hopeful that more are on the way.

2nd card: 3 of Swords. This cover card says it all: We've had a lot of sorrow and pain over these two particular diseases—and there's continued pain and loss of life as we write this. The public wishes for these cures quickly, but as of this writing, more sorrow may come before they arrive.

3rd card: 8 of Wands R. This card represents the foundation of the question or why we asked it, and, in this case, yes, there has been difficulty in understanding these diseases. While we have found drugs that can keep these diseases at bay, or in some people can even put the diseases in remission, there aren't yet the cures we asked about. More work must be done, this card says. More research is needed to find these cures.

1) *2 of Pentacles*
2) *3 of Swords*
3) *8 of Wands R*
4) *5 of Pentacles*
5) *Ace of Pentacles R*
6) *7 of Wands R*
7) *Knight of Wands R*
8) *Death R*
9) *2 of Wands*
10) *The World R*

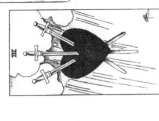

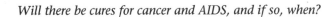

Will there be cures for cancer and AIDS, and if so, when?

4th card: 5 of Pentacles. This card describes a condition of some kind of impoverishment in the recent past. Is it a spiritual loss? A financial loss? Has there not been enough money put into research? This card refers to the fact that not enough resources have been put into curing these illnesses in the past 10 to 15 years. It can also mean that medicine that did help in the past doesn't help the patients like it used to.

5th card: Ace of Pentacles R. This seems to say there will be a desire for a new direction, new monies, and new research on these illnesses. Will there be a new start? With this card reversed, there could be delays due to lack of funds or research money. But remember that this card is a possibility, not a certainty.

Out of Time

Remember, if you have to have a negative card in a Celtic Cross Spread, it's best to have it here in the 4th position, where it's in the past, passing away—and not the outcome!

6th card: 7 of Wands R. This card is actually good reversed: It indicates that these diseases won't feel so threatening in the future. We'll get a handle (the wand!) on the reasons for these diseases, how they start and how they grow, so that the enemy will be gone. In addition, feelings of insecurity about the subjects at hand will pass away from us, and we'll feel more in control of accomplishing the goal of controlling or even getting rid of these diseases.

7th card: Knight of Wands R. This position represents our fears, and in this case, we fear that we'll never cure these diseases. Perhaps we'll yell out to the traditional medical establishment, "We fear you are taking too long to cure these diseases!" At times, we'll feel out of control and helpless, and our collective fears may even cause fighting, lawsuits, or mere restlessness in our society. More than anything, the Knight of Wands R tells us that we as a society are and will continue to be impatient for cures.

8th card: Death R. This is the card of outside influences, or how others help or hinder the situation. Could it be Death R in this position relates to what we all know: that these diseases are extremely hard to cure, or that we'll still wonder, even when we do get them under control? Could these diseases come back to haunt us somehow? Death R means stagnation of plans, and it's possible that initial cures may not be permanent solutions.

9th card: 2 of Wands. This card reveals what we wish to happen. We're all watching and waiting for a cure. We believe we can find a cure, and that's our hope and wish for this spread. We'll keep on studying and doing more and more research until we find a cure. We're very definite about that—and so is the 2 of Wands, standing firm on the hill overlooking the condition, holding the globe in his hand. The man in the 2 of Wands represents our collective wish to find cures, as well as the good attitude we have toward curing these diseases.

10th card: The World R. The World is the outcome—but it's reversed. What does that mean? This isn't a bad card: Reversed in this case indicates delays, and success that's yet to be won. As this is a Major Arcana card, it means we're destined to work on these major health problems worldwide, and because it's the World, it indicates that we're going for help from other countries to win the battle.

The World R can mean that we could be our own worst enemy. Maybe, because of a lack of resources or financial aid, we're not moving fast enough. Perhaps some types of cancer will be cured in a short period of time, but others won't be. The journey to find these cures will be a long one, but eventually, it will be successful.

Lastly, let's take a look at the timing on this question. It could take until 2005 or beyond to find permanent cures for cancer and AIDS. First of all, the 7 of Wands is in the 6th position, which represents what will happen. The number on the 6th card, in this case a 7, can give us an indication of timing—either seven months, seven years, or in 2007.

The other card we look at to determine timing is the 10th one. In this case, the card in that position is the World R, which indicates that there will be some success before 2005 for sure. However, because this card is reversed, it will also take beyond 2005 to feel that we're really making progress in finding lasting cures for these diseases.

How Will We Heal, Body, Mind, and Soul?

For our second spread about health and medicine, we decided to ask about how we'll heal. Rather than ask about specific ways of healing, however, we asked the cards, in a Celtic Cross Spread, to tell us how we might heal. Here are the cards that came up when we asked the question, "What can the Tarot tell us about how to heal the body, the mind, and the soul?"

What great cards these are! They're all about love, being like a kid, and getting back to the arts, music, and beauty—the artistic and creative sides of our natures, in other words. The answer here seems to be that we'll be moving toward understanding how meditation (the Hanged Man and the Hermit) and love (the Queen of Cups, 3 of Cups, Sun, and Ace of Cups) can help us heal ourselves.

The majority of the cards here are about developing our hearts and our creative sides, if for no other reason than keeping us positive. There's an old saying that humor cures all ills, and it's true: A good sense of humor can help bring about a lot of healing for all of us.

The arts have been proven to have a therapeutic effect for healing, whether it's the body, mind, or soul. Music and singing, for example, allow us to safely express our feelings and emotions. The arts can help us to let go of stress, and at the same time heal what ails us. All things that feed the soul are good medicine.

1) *Queen of Swords*
2) *7 of Pentacles*
3) *Judgement*
4) *The World R*
5) *The Hanged Man*
6) *The Hermit*
7) *The Queen of Cups*
8) *3 of Cups*
9) *The Sun*
10) *Ace of Cups*

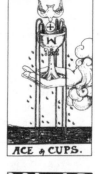

ACE of CUPS.

THE HANGED MAN.

THE SUN .

THE WORLD.

QUEEN of SWORDS.

THE HERMIT.

JUDGEMENT.

QUEEN of CUPS.

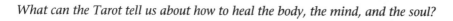

What can the Tarot tell us about how to heal the body, the mind, and the soul?

266

Ask Away!: Questions About Our Earth

We're all concerned with the future of our planet. From global warming to natural disasters, it seems as if we can't entirely depend on the planet we call home to keep us safe and secure. What will happen to the environment? Will we learn to take care of it so that it can take care of us?

Meanwhile, we're looking beyond our planet—not just to our own solar system but to the stars as well. Will we travel to other planets by the 24th century—the century of Captain Picard and the Enterprise IV crew? Let's see what the cards have to say.

What Will Happen to the Environment?

From oil spills to depletion of the rain forest to the continuing effects of global warming, concern about the environment is with us every day. What will happen to the environment in the new millennium? Will we begin to turn matters around and help our environment rather than continue to harm it?

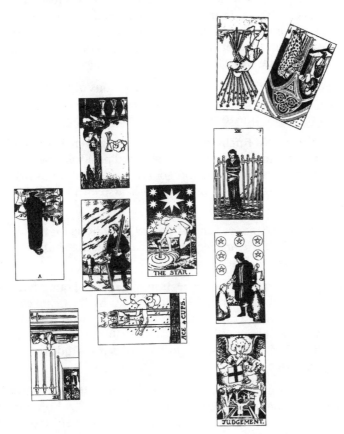

1) 5 of Swords
2) Ace of Cups
3) 4 of Swords R
4) 5 of Cups R
5) 4 of Cups R
6) The Star
7) Judgement
8) 6 of Pentacles
9) 8 of Swords
10) 10 of Wands R/ covered by 3 of Pentacles R

What will happen to the environment in the 21st century?

Here are the cards that came up when we did a Celtic Cross Spread, asking the question, "What will happen to the environment in the 21st century?"

Again, this was a very interesting response to the question. Right off the bat, we were excited to see the Star upright in the 6th position. Here's one of the most hopeful cards in the Tarot deck, one that's all about water and the earth—in the position that shows what will definitely happen. Good news for the environment!

But what does the rest of this spread say about the environment in the 21st century?

1st card: 5 of Swords. We've shown a lack of sensitivity for the environment—and the 5 of Swords makes no bones about it. This card can indicate selfishness, or a stealing away of energy. Clearly, the environment has been abused.

2nd card: Ace of Cups. Despite our use and abuse of the environment, Mother Nature continues to try to bless us with her abundance. The Ace of Cups represents blessings from above, and, in this case, from below as well. The earth can be a wonderful home—if we don't abuse it.

3rd card: 4 of Swords R. Enough R & R—the knight in the 4 of Swords is ready to get back into the action, and the basis of this question is that we're ready to focus on helping our environment rather than continuing to harm it. Working together, we can take positive action to change the environment for the better, but this card also cautions that political problems can stand in the way of progress.

4th card: 5 of Cups R. Reversed, the 5 of Cups represents the lessons of the past, and in this position, this card suggests that we now know enough. "Enough crying over spilled milk," says the 5 of Cups R. It's time to move on and start anew.

5th card: 4 of Cups R. It's possible we'll finally stop wishing things were better and do something about the environment. That's because in its reversed position, the 4 of Cups allows us to come out of our contemplation and go in a new direction. Newly motivated, in fact, we may well *want* to accomplish new work, goals, and ambitions for our environment.

6th card: The Star. As we mentioned, this card shows there's great hope for the environment in the future. Just look at the imagery on this card—all the abundance of Earth and sky is there for us—if we're there for them, too.

7th card: Judgement. We're afraid that if we don't begin to take care of our environment, we could destroy the very earth that's meant to support us. In *The Complete Idiot's Guide to Tarot and Fortune-Telling*, we say, "This card often comes up when you're trying to improve your health or well-being. It indicates a desire for something higher than where you are now." With this card in this 7th position of our attitude toward the question, we couldn't agree with ourselves more!

8th card: 6 of Pentacles. It will take money to help heal the wounds in the environment, but the money is there, from helpful others (such as Ted Turner?) who want to see the earth repaired before it's too late. In fact, the 6 of Pentacles can very specifically indicate charity, philanthropy, and sharing of wealth. People with money who care will be there when the environment needs them.

9th card: 8 of Swords. It will take time before we heal the environment, and we will feel entrapped by our own lack of vision. Our fears can render us helpless, says the 9 of Swords, and there may be times as we move toward healing our environment that we feel as if we're all bound up and unable to move forward. It's important to remember, however, that in this case we've created our own prison—and that we're the ones who hold the key.

10th card: 10 of Wands R/covered by 3 of Pentacles R. Finally, the burden will be lifted, but there may still be others who seek to undo the good work we all will have done to help the environment heal. There may be those who seek to shift the burden to others, such as those who do less than good work (3 of Pentacles R), or negotiations may be delayed because of disagreements.

All in all, this reading suggests that we'll be working together to improve the environment. But we'll have to be careful of those who would seek to undo what we've done— or who will continue to abuse the environment for their own ends.

Will We Travel to Other Planets by the 24th Century?

For this spread, we used a seven-card spread for a "yes" or "no" answer to the question: "Will we travel to other planets by the 24th century?" Here are the cards that came up for the answer:

1) 5 of Swords R
2) The Devil
3) The High Priestess
4) 8 of Cups R
5) Page of Wands
6) Knight of Cups
7) The Emperor

Will we travel to other planets by the 24th century?

Before we tell you if we think these cards say yes or no, we'd like you to go back to Chapters 12 to 14 to see what you think they say. No fair peeking ahead!

Okay—ready? Here's our interpretation:

The last two cards tell our answer: The Knight of Cups says not only will we travel to other planets, but we'll have romantic approach to it as well—that is, the idea of making the fantasy a reality is very appealing. In addition, the Emperor upright shows us that good leadership (whether through private enterprise or governmental bodies and science together) will help lead the way. Past delays are evidenced by the reversed cards, but this spread suggests that we may travel to other planets sooner than the 24th century—a Knight and a Page, plus an Emperor and a High Priestess. *Star Trek* becomes a reality!

What Happens to Art, Music, and Literature?

We thought it would be appropriate for Lisa to do this spread, since she's the writer in the family. Here are the cards that came up when she did a Celtic Cross Spread asking "What happens to art, music, and literature in the 21st century?"

1st card: Justice. Justice is a card of fairness and honesty, with the open-mindedness to weigh all factors and see that justice is done. In this 1st position of the Querent, this suggests to us that the arts have always sought to be honest and cut to the truth of the matter—no matter how difficult that can sometimes be.

2nd card: 2 of Cups. Covering the Querent card is the 2 of Cups, a card that shows understanding, good partnerships, and cooperation. The sharing of the 2 of Cups leads to still better things, which makes us think that there's great promise for art, literature, and music to forge connections to their audiences.

3rd card: 2 of Wands R. Another 2! As you'll recall from Chapter 9, 2s "want nothing so much as to merge . . . 2 energy moves to a slower rhythm, and . . . there's also a heightened sensitivity to light and sound, and a capacity for balance, as 2 dwells in both beauty and things of spirit. The 2 energy is quiet and intuitive, and psychic activities are more prominent here than in other numbers." The 2 of Wands is good news for the basis of the matter—even in its reversed position.

4th card: 6 of Wands. This is the card of coming home to success, but here in the 4th position, this situation is passing away. Does this mean that in the future, it will be harder for artists, writers, and musicians to achieve the success they deserve? Is it possible that as more and more artistic venues merge into larger corporations that fewer voices will be heard? All this is possible with the 6 of Wands in the 4th position.

1) *Justice*
2) *2 of Cups*
3) *2 of Wands R*
4) *6 of Wands*
5) *The Magician*
6) *Judgement*
7) *Temperance R*
8) *9 of Cups R*
9) *7 of Cups*
10) *Knight of Cups R*

What happens to art, music, and literature in the 21st century?

Time Capsule

This spread contains four Major Arcana cards, four Cups, and two Wands. What does this tell you about the response? First of all, that it's destined to occur (the Major Arcana cards); next, that it's about emotional issues (the Cups); and lastly, that much enterprise is involved (the Wands).

5th card: The Magician. In *The Complete Idiot's Guide to Tarot and Fortune-Telling*, one of the archetypes we use to define this card is "the artist in us all." What a great card to have for the 5th position of possible future energy! The energy exists for us to turn ideas into reality, whether it's the writer's words, the artist's canvas, or the musician's score.

6th card: Judgement. Good news here as well! In the definite future position is a cosmic wake-up call, indicating self-actualization and work well done. Suddenly people from all walks of life will understand what artists are trying to show them, and a greater global appreciation of the arts will happen as a result.

7th card: Temperance R. Of course, we're afraid, and in this spread, we're afraid of a lack of tolerance when we try new ways of expressing ourselves. Temperance R can indicate poor judgment or poor business management, and artists, writers, and musicians may be afraid of what will become of their work when they no longer have control over it.

8th card: 9 of Cups R. The last three cards in this spread are all Cups, indicating heightened emotions leading to the outcome of the reading. In its upright position, the 9 of Cups is called the Wish card, but reversed, it can represent a lack of resources, or that the wish won't be fulfilled right now. Coupled with the fears of Temperance R in the 7th position, this card could indicate that artists will have to stand alone, without the financial backing of others (such as the NEA, for example).

9th card: 7 of Cups. The 7 of Cups indicates too many choices, and to get to the outcome of this reading, artists, writers, and musicians may need to decide which route they want to take. Do they want to take the next step beyond post-modernism (and what would that be?)? Or do they want to return to the realism of the 20th century or the romanticism of the 19th century? This card can represent too much daydreaming and not enough work, too—something any artist can tell you goes with the territory.

10th card: Knight of Cups R. The Knight is reversed because we'll all want to create new artwork, music, and literature—but we'll be stuck in the emotions of the time. Every art form will undergo transformation in the 21st century, in ways that we can't even imagine. While this will be exciting, the beginning of the century will be resemble birthing a new baby for the arts. For example, there may not be enough funding, or the public may be more preoccupied with finances rather than art—but art is what we'll need. Ultimately, the arts will be our healing, and music, dance, and literature will all be transformed between 2000 and 2005 to get ready for the rest of that century.

Anything Goes?!

There are so many questions about technology, health, the environment, and space travel, it's very possible we haven't asked the ones you want to know the answers to.

If that's the case, get out your Tarot deck and ask away. What do you want to know about future technology? About our health and the health of our planet? Do you want to know if *you'll* be heading for space in the new millennium? With a Tarot deck to guide you, when it comes to the future, anything goes!

The Least You Need to Know

➤ The cards tell us to be careful with our technological advances.

➤ A look at some medical advances shows they'll take some time.

➤ Working together, we can improve the environment in the 21st century.

➤ What about space travel? Will we boldly go where no one has gone before?

➤ The arts will be our healing in the 21st century.

Chapter 17

What the Tarot Says About *You* in the New Millennium

In This Chapter

➤ Looking at your year 2000

➤ A Horoscope Spread of your own

➤ A Horoscope Spread for Hillary Rodham Clinton

➤ Finding your destiny and dreams in the cards

➤ Spinning the Wheel of Fortune

Now that we've explored what the cards have to say about our world in the 21st century, it's time to turn to someone who's very important to you—yourself! In this chapter, we'll introduce the Horoscope Spread, and show you how you can use it to look at your own new millennium.

We'll also do a Horoscope Spread of our own for Hillary Rodham Clinton, and see what the cards have to say about her future—especially her political future. Then, in the second half of this chapter, we've created a workbook for you to use the Tarot to find out some answers to your own questions about your new millennium.

A Fool's Journey to the Future

Like the Fool, we're all poised on the brink of an exciting new adventure. We're not certain what the future will bring, but we've packed our satchels (and our little dogs, too!), and we're taking that big first step toward the unknown.

The new millennium is a new adventure for the Fool—and for all of us.

We don't have to go forward blind. With the Tarot to guide us, we can ask intelligent questions about the future, and forearmed, can make the right decisions now to ensure that our futures will be all that we want them to be.

What Kind of Year Will 2000 Be for YOU?

Speaking Y2K

A *Horoscope Spread* is a yearly over-view for your life, using the format of an astrological chart as its basis.

When it comes to exploring how the year 2000 will be for you, no spread will do the trick quite so well as a *Horoscope Spread*. Just like your horoscope (see Chapter 4) is a pie chart divided into 12 houses, the horoscope spread uses 12 cards to show a specific 12 months in your life.

You may want to return to the astrological chart you tabbed in Chapter 4 to review what each of the 12 houses represents. In addition to those areas, each also represents a month in a Horoscope Spread. The 1st slice is January, the 2nd February, and so on, up through the 12th slice, which is December.

What You Want to Know (And Why?)

Do you have specific questions about your year 2000? It's possible you may just want to know what the future holds, and a Horoscope Spread is perfect for that. It's a perfect way to see how a year will go in general—and it's also a great way to get to know the Tarot cards better.

At the same time, however, a Horoscope Spread can help answer a specific question about a future year, as you'll see below, when we ask about Hillary Rodham Clinton's political future. Just as Ms. Clinton would want to know about her political future, *you* may want to know about your romantic future, or about your career.

Time Capsule

If you've got a specific question about the year 2000, be sure to phrase the question so that the cards will give the kind of answer you're looking for. Remember, though, that the cards "know" far more than you may say—and they'll often answer your unasked questions as well.

Your Year 2000 in a Horoscope Spread

As you shuffle the cards for your Horoscope Spread, think about what your next year will be like. If you've got a specific question, you'll want to think about that as you shuffle as well.

When you're ready, lay the cards out as shown below. Remember, each of the twelve "slices" represents both a specific house and a specific month in the year you asked about.

The Horoscope Spread.

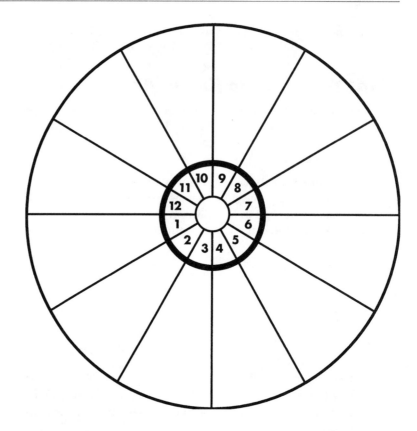

Before you begin to examine each card individually (using either Chapters 12–14 from this book or *The Complete Idiot's Guide to Tarot and Fortune-Telling* to help you), take a moment to look at your spread synergistically. If you'd like, think of the pictures on each of the cards as a chapter in a story—*your* story.

After you've looked at your spread as a whole, go ahead and look up each card's interpretation. We've provided room for you to write those interpretations below.

Your Horoscope Spread for the Year 2000

1st card: _____

Interpretation: _____

2nd card: _____

Interpretation: _____

3rd card: _____

Interpretation: _____

4th card: _____

Interpretation: _____

5th card: _____

Interpretation: _____

6th card: _____

Interpretation: _____

7th card: _____

Interpretation: _____

8th card: _____

Interpretation: _____

9th card: _____

Interpretation: _____

10th card: _____

Interpretation: _____

11th card: _____

Interpretation: _____

12th card: _____

Interpretation: _____

What did your Horoscope Spread reveal about your year 2000? We hope your future's bright!

A Sample Horoscope Spread: What the Cards Mean

To show you how a Horoscope Spread can show how a year will go, we decided to ask about Hillary Rodham Clinton's political future in the year 2000. Here are the cards that came up for Ms. Clinton:

1) 10 of Swords R
2) The Magician
3) 7 of Swords
4) Ace of Wands
5) King of Pentacles
6) 10 of Pentacles

7) 8 of Swords R
8) King of Swords R
9) 8 of Cups R
10) 5 of Cups R
11) 3 of Cups
12) The Hanged Man

How does the year 2000 look for Hillary Rodham Clinton's political future?

1st Card (house of the self, and what surrounds her): 10 of Swords R. This card indicates the cycle of change has finished. Now is the end of a karmic debt or struggle, and the proverbial light is at the end of the tunnel: Ms. Clinton will now begin to reap what she has personally sown. She will regain some personal power and strength to continue her life's goals.

2nd Card (house of money and finances): The Magician. Ms. Clinton has the power to manifest money or the ability to attain and create money for herself and her family. This card can also mean that she can develop her own business enterprise or create a new image which can become an asset to herself.

3rd Card (house of knowledge, siblings, and environment): 7 of Swords. Ms. Clinton may not tell us all that she feels for a while. She can keep many things to herself or even be a little deceptive about her plans. Sometimes, the 7 of Swords can indicate that someone or something is not clear, or that she may not know which way to go in her life. She may have a lot of indecision about where she should put herself in the public eye or how she became known in the first place.

4th Card (house of home and family): Ace of Wands. This card indicates the beginning of something new in the family. A new home, or a new environment and new conditions in the home, will start occurring in 2000, so she's off to a new start, either residence-wise or family-wise. This card in this position indicates a breath of fresh air.

5th Card (house of creativity, risks, and children): King of Pentacles. This is a King of wealth, business, and concern for Ms. Clinton. He falls in the area of speculation, social support, or possible friendship, and represents a man with dark hair and usually brown to hazel eyes who's kind and introspective, and gives wise advise about financial, business, and investment matters. He's also an easygoing person, who's both industrious and supportive of what Ms. Clinton may want to do. Good counsel comes from this man.

6th Card (house of job, health, and service to the public): 10 of Pentacles. Ms. Clinton will serve her community well. She'll be involved in community projects and possibly develop new funding for groups and organizations that perform public services. She also could receive an offer of a new job (!), which pays well and/or receives wide public recognition. Prosperity is hers, whether she wants to develop her own business or do service for the public good. She will be well-received in whatever she would like to do in the public arena!

7th Card (house of marriage and partnerships): 8 of Swords R. This card reversed is actually good for Ms. Clinton as it shows a woman releasing herself from a kind of bondage or restriction. It's possible she might release herself from a marriage or business partnership which doesn't serve her anymore! Or, it could mean she'll go in a new direction without fear. In *The Complete Idiot's Guide to Tarot and Fortune-Telling*, we note that the 8 of Swords R can mean "That an apology may be forthcoming, and the people involved will accept it. 'Sorry for causing so much trouble!'"

281

8th Card (house of hidden things or conditions she has not thought about): King of Swords R. This King represents a different man, who could cause her harm via legal or money issues. She shouldn't trust this man in anything having to do with investments, money, or advice. This reversed King can cause pain and is very secretive about what he does. He's very different than the other King in the 5th position in this spread. The King of Swords usually has brown to light brown hair, and blue to hazel eyes, and is involved in the law, politics, or government work. Now who might this be?

9th Card (house of attitude, philosophy, or beliefs for the year): 8 of Cups R. Now, this isn't a bad attitude at all. Ms. Clinton will turn to the world again and once again become active in the worldly things she would like to work with. She'll have a renewed interest in people and connections to her community, and get her passion back for life, and get back to do the work she believes in doing. As the months pass, into 2000 and beyond, she'll become stronger and stronger in her beliefs.

10th Card (house of public image, career ideals, or what she will contribute her society): 5 of Cups R. This card says that Ms. Clinton will return to feeling hopeful about her career and career contributions. She'll again get a breath of fresh air, and will do for herself what *she* wishes. Ms. Clinton will want to serve her community by working in a position in an area she's already familiar with (maybe law, education, or politics)—but how she returns will be her choice. This card suggests that she would be happy performing duties of her own choosing for the country, and even possibly the global community.

11th Card (house of friends, hopes, and desires): 3 of Cups. Ms. Clinton does and will continue to surround herself with good friends, as well as organizations that will support her desires and wishes. In fact, with the 3 of Cups in this position, it's clear she'll have a lot of luck through groups, organizations, public connections, and her friends. Success and celebration will come from others, and great support will be with her in 2000. People will feel for her, especially her closest friends and associates.

12th Card (house of karmic debt, or what she may have to work on, or her most difficult lesson in 2000): The Hanged Man. The Hanged Man means that Ms. Clinton will have to learn sacrifice, and to let go of an old lifestyle and move into a new lifestyle. She'll be learning to develop herself spiritually, and she may take on a new approach to life, or a new lifestyle. By accepting the situations she is attached to, whether they're good or difficult, she can learn to pass through difficulties with grace. Ultimately, she will find her place in the universe well, become satisfied with what she has accomplished, and continue to accomplish more.

All this could take awhile, however: Sometimes, the Hanged Man in the 12th house can mean the person has already been put on hold due to circumstances outside of her control. If that was the case, she wasn't able to move ahead with her own goals because of restrictions or blockages placed in her way.

Most of all, this spread says that through the year 2000 could still be a difficult time for Ms. Clinton, but she has the fortitude and insight to overcome her struggles and succeed on her own terms. We wish her much luck!

What's Your Destiny?

There are lots of different Tarot spreads you can try, depending on what you'd like to know about your future. In the remainder of this chapter, we're going to give you the tools to try a variety of spreads, in order to find out everything from your destiny to making your wishes come true.

First, let's see where your destiny lies. For this reading, you'll be using a Karmic Spread, a four card spread that reveals what lessons you're learning now.

Begin by selecting the 22 Major Arcana cards from your Tarot deck. Using only these 22 cards, shuffle as many times as you like, asking the question, "What lessons am I learning now?"

When you're ready, deal the cards into the Karmic Spread shown here:

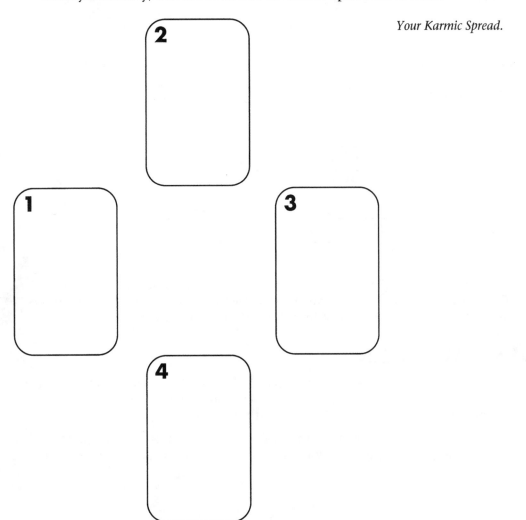

Your Karmic Spread.

Before you look up our interpretations of these cards, take a moment to meditate on the images. What do you think these cards have to say about your destiny?

_____

_____

_____

_____

After you've meditated on the images, go ahead and look up our interpretations. We've provided space below for you to write down your findings.

Your Karmic Spread

1st card: _____

Interpretation: _____

2nd card: _____

Interpretation: _____

3rd card: _____

Interpretation: _____

4th card: _____

Interpretation: _____

So, what's your karma? Were you surprised by what your karmic cards revealed? Chances are, if you think about, you know those karmic lessons all too well—because you'll keep on receiving them again and again, until you get them right!

What's Your Wish?

The next spread you may want to try is called a Gypsy Wish Spread. You'll once again be using all 78 cards in the Tarot deck for this spread, and its 15 cards are great for answering the simple question, "Will my wish come true?"

Do you want to know if you'll win the lottery? The girl next door? *A new car?* No matter what your wish, the Gypsy Wish Spread will show if your dreams will come true.

Before you begin your Gypsy Wish spread, select a card to represent you. This can be any card—a royal Minor Arcana card, or any other card that you feel represents the you that's asking about this particular wish. After you've selected this card, place it on the "W" in the following diagram.

Next, instead of shuffling your Tarot deck, spread it out in a fan so that all 77 of the remaining cards can be seen. Be sure they're face down—you don't want the faces of the cards to show!

Now, from the fanned-out deck, select 15 cards and set them aside. After you have 15 cards, shuffle them until you're ready to place them into the following spread.

Ask Spaceship Earth

If the 9 of Cups appears anywhere in your Gypsy Wish Spread, *your dreams will come true!* The 9 of Cups is the Wish Card, and if it shows up, your wishes are granted!

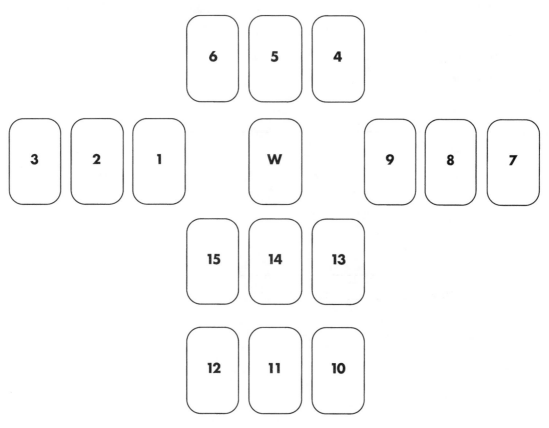

The Gypsy Wish Spread.

Well, is the 9 of Cups there? If so, your wish will definitely come true. If it's not, it doesn't necessarily mean you won't get your wish; you'll just need to interpret the cards to see how, when, and if it will come true. We've provided space below for you to do just that.

Your Gypsy Wish Spread

Your wish: _____

The card you selected to represent yourself: _____

1st card: _____

Interpretation: _____

2nd card: _____

Interpretation: _____

3rd card: _____

Interpretation: _____

4th card: _____

Interpretation: _____

5th card: _____

Interpretation: _____

6th card: _____

Interpretation: _____

7th card: _____

Interpretation: _____

8th card: _____

Interpretation: _____

9th card: _____

Interpretation: _____

10th card: _____

Interpretation: _____

11th card: _____

Interpretation: _____

12th card: _____

Interpretation: _____

13th card: _____

Interpretation: _____

14th card: _____

Interpretation: _____

15th card: _____

Interpretation: _____

Did your Gypsy Wish Spread reveal that your wish will come true? We hope so!

What Decisions Do You Need to Make?

Decisions, decisions, decisions. We all face them every day. Fortunately, there's a Tarot spread to help you make wise ones, by showing you not only past information and present conditions surrounding your decision, but the future directions you can take to arrive at the best decision possible.

Begin by shuffling your Tarot deck as you ask the question about your decision. Do you want to know whether to move to Rhode Island next June? Or whether to accept the job with FoolCorp.? Whatever your decision, be sure to phrase the question to get the specific answer you're seeking.

When you're ready, lay out three cards in a row, as shown in the diagram below. Then, lay three more over those, as shown, and lastly, three more over those. Your Decision Spread will look like this:

The Decision Spread.

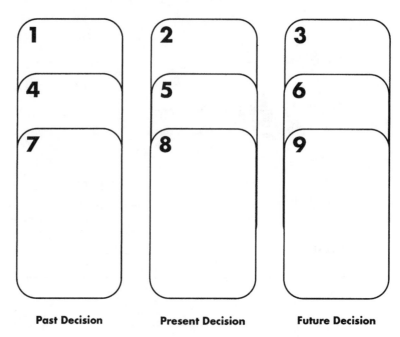

| Past Decision | Present Decision | Future Decision |

Next, interpret the cards, based on what they show for the past, present, and future of your decision. We've provided room for you to do that below.

Your Decision Spread

Your question: _____

The Past

1st card: _____

Interpretation: _____

4th card: _____

Interpretation: _____

7th card: _____

Interpretation: _____

The Present

2nd card: _____

Interpretation: _____

5th card: _____

Interpretation: _____

8th card: _____

Interpretation: _____

The Future

3rd card: _____

Interpretation: _____

6th card: _____

Interpretation: _____

9th card: _____

Interpretation: _____

Spinning the Wheel of Fortune

Life doesn't have to be like spinning the Wheel of Fortune if you've got a Tarot deck to guide you. The Tarot spreads we've shown you in these chapters can help you understand not only your own life, but the direction of the world as we move into the new millennium.

We've all got questions, but with a Tarot deck, we can find the answers as well. May all your cards be Wish Cards!

Out of Time

It's important when you're doing a Decision Spread to look at everything surrounding the question, and to be honest about what each card represents. You may not like what a particular card shows or says, but it's an important aspect of your decision, and you should use its information to its best purpose.

The Least You Need to Know

➤ You can take a look at your year 2000 with a Horoscope Spread.

➤ A look at Hillary Rodham Clinton's political future using a Horoscope Spread.

➤ Worksheets for spreads of your own.

➤ If you use the Tarot, you won't just be spinning the Wheel of Fortune.

Part 5

Know It All:
Psychic Intuition

We all possess intuition, but some of us use it more effectively than others. Before we take a look at some of our intuitive feelings about the new millennium, we're going to show you how you can improve your own intuitive power, and use the potential of mind/body medicine for your own peace of mind.

Chapter 18

Intuitive Tools for the New Millennium

In This Chapter

➤ What is intuition?

➤ Why is intuition important for the new millennium?

➤ How intuitive are *you*?

➤ Building your intuitive power

Astrology, numerology, and the Tarot are all tools you can use to improve your intuition. But what *is* intuition? Can you learn to develop it if you haven't got it? And what's it got to do with the new millennium?

In Part 5, we'll be exploring the role of intuition in both the new millennium and in your own life. Our expert for these chapters is Lynn A. Robinson, M.Ed., intuitive consultant and co-author of *The Complete Idiot's Guide to Being Psychic* (Alpha Books, 1999).

What Is Intuition?

"Follow your heart."

"Listen to your inner voice."

"Trust your guidance."

It all sounds so easy. But what do you do when your inner voice sounds like your inner critic, or worse, your inner child runs amok? How can you learn to distinguish between your own inner knowing and your deepest inner fears?

Speaking Y2K

Intuition is a way of acquiring knowledge without conscious thought processes.

Webster's Dictionary defines *intuition* as "the act or process of coming to direct knowledge without reasoning or inferring" and as "quick and ready insight." Derived from the Latin word *intueri,* which means "to see within," intuition is a way of knowing, of sensing the truth without explanations. Our favorite definition, though, comes from a 15-year-old girl: "Intuition is like when you know something, but, like, where did it come from?"

Intuition is a resource that provides an additional level of information that doesn't come from the analytical, logical, rational side of the brain, and can be a reliable and valuable tool when its language is understood and developed. Accurate intuition enables you to gain vital and valuable insight into yourself, as well as your children, friends, business associates—and the world around you.

The New Millennium Is a Time of Change

We all know our lives have become ever more complicated, high-pressured, and fast-paced, and we can see this in everything from high divorce rates to large companies' frequent down-sizing. In addition, we're all trying to keep up with the latest in high-speed technology and information processing. No wonder we're stressed!

All this is good reason why, as we enter the 21st century, our intuition will become even more important to understand, trust, and follow. We can use our intuition to help us sort through the myriad opportunities, directions, and decisions our life presents to us—and maybe we can use it to figure out how to program our VCRs as well!

We're also faced with constantly changing values. After all, the cultural, social, and religious beliefs we were born and raised with have been torn apart. Many of us feel we grew up in a world where there were simple decisions about right and wrong or good and bad; where our religious and community leaders as well as our families informed us of the "right way" to live our lives. If we obeyed and did the right thing, we were rewarded with a good job, a happy marriage, money to buy a home, an education for our kids, and a good pension on which to retire.

Was it really all so simple then? It's certainly gotten more complicated than that and is likely to get more complex still. All the more reason we need to develop the tools available to us—like intuition—to help us meet the 21st century.

Tools for the New Century

As we enter the 21st century, the ability to make decisions based on our own inner knowing will become more and more important. That's because we'll be less reliant on specific leaders, teachers, and institutions to inform and direct our lives. As mentioned in Parts 2, 3, and 4, one of the first tools we must learn to use in order to make our own decisions is that of intuition.

You can think of your intuition as that part of you that's connected to a Higher Knowing. Not only does it inform you of your life's work—the service you've come here to do or the wisdom you're here to impart—it gives you direction, shows you the path to knowing how to love, forgive, work together, resolve differences, use compassion, live with authenticity, *and* to have a reverence for life. Intuition does all that? Indeed it can—and these are all skills and qualities we'll need as we move into the new millennium.

Why Is Listening to Intuition Important?

When you listen to your intuition, it connects you with a greater knowledge. Whether you call that knowledge God/Goddess, Oversoul, All That Is, Divine Intelligence, or any other name/concept that works for you, what's important is that this part of you has an overview of your life and has your best interests at heart. Your intuition helps guide you to inner peace, brings you to harmony, helps you release judgments, and gives you confidence to take action and prepare for change in your life.

How can you use your intuition? Here's one example: A man in one of Lynn's intuition classes used his newly developed abilities to "tune into" his wife, with whom he was having communication problems. "I saw myself from her perspective. It's not like I'm right and she's wrong anymore. I received specific information that would help resolve our conflict."

Ask Spaceship Earth

Psychologist Carl Jung calls intuition one of the four basic psychological functions (along with thinking, feeling, and sensation). Intuition, according to Jung, is the function that "explores the unknown and senses possibilities and implications which may not be readily apparent."

Are You Intuitive? A Quiz

Before we talk about how you can build your intuitive power, let's see how intuitive you already are. You may be surprised at what you already "know."

1. Do you ever know who is on the phone when it rings? (Note: This is not intuition if you have caller I.D.!)

2. Have you ever had a flash of insight that helped you solve a problem?

3. Have you ever had a physical sensation that let you know you were about to make a bad (or good) decision?

4. Do you ever have strong feelings about someone you just met that prove to be true?

5. Do the right words pop into your head when you're faced with a difficult conversation?

6. Have you ever felt nudged or encouraged to an action that didn't "make sense" but proved to be successful after acting on it?

7. Can you make "snap" decisions and know you're right?

8. Do you know what someone will say before they say it?

9. Do you have a knack for finding lost objects?

10. Do creative ideas often pop into your head unbidden?

11. Have you ever had a dream that proved to be true?

If you answered "yes" to any of the above questions, you're already on the road to using your intuitive powers—but if you answered "yes," you already know that. If you answered "yes" to more than one of these questions, your intuition is even more well developed. Either way, here are some ways you can build your intuition still more.

Building Your Intuitive Power

It's long been thought that intuition was a phenomenon of the gifted few, but more recent research is showing that, contrary to popular belief, intuition is a skill that can be developed and used effectively by all of us—even you!

The truth is, developing your intuition is like learning to develop any skill, whether mastering a new computer software program or becoming proficient at a musical instrument. In fact, the more you use your intuition, the better you get at it!

Practice Your Intuition

The more you practice using your intuition, the more it will become "second nature." In fact, if you use intuition regularly, you'll actually develop what we like to call an "instant knowing." This "second sense," "hunch," or "gut feeling" becomes a sure thing the more you use it, and soon you'll not only be trusting it but you'll be relying on it when you make decisions.

Intuition can take on many forms, including:

➤ Images

➤ Symbolic pictures

➤ Vivid dreams

➤ Feelings

➤ Aural sensations

One example is a designer who receives visual impressions. She might "*see*" the solution to a product design problem as a series of images relating to the product. Or, a mathematician might "dream up" a solution to an especially complex problem while he's fast asleep.

Feeling the "Vibes"

Intuitive impressions may also be experienced *kinesthetically.* This means that you "feel" the impression rather than visualize it, and these impressions might be felt as emotions, a sense of direct knowing, a hot or cold sensation in the body, or what we call a gut feeling. For example, an intuitive counselor like Lynn might receive impressions by "*feeling*" the direction she needs to take with her client.

Another way of receiving information is verbal. You might, for example, hear words in your mind, or find that your intuitive answers will be formed as metaphors or symbols. You "*hear*" the words telling you a new direction to take.

Speaking Y2K

Kinesthetic impressions are those that are felt rather than visualized. Some examples of kinesthetic intuition are an emotional sense, a sense of direct knowing, a hot or cold sensation, or what we call a gut feeling.

Take the Steps: Developing Your Own Intuition

There's no *right* way to experience intuitive information, and how *you* develop and perceive your own intuition will be entirely a matter of what works best for *you.* Here are some tips for developing this faculty of insight:

➤ Open-ended questions are helpful in eliciting intuitive information. Examples of this are:

"What should I do in this situation?"

"What do I need to know about this?"

➤ A meditation practice is useful in learning to still the mind and relax the body, both of which are important skills that assist in the development of intuition, as intuition appears to flourish during quiet times.

➤ Accurate intuition makes you feel relieved or at peace. You'll know when you're "right," in other words.

Out of Time

Intuitive answers may not pop into your mind immediately; in fact, the literature is full of stories about answers to complex problems coming to mind while someone's walking the dog or taking a shower. Why is that? Because those are the times when your "thinking" side's taking a break—and your intuitive side can kick in.

➤ Act on the information that's received. If using intuition is a new experience for you, of course, it may be best to use it for relatively low-risk situations at first.

➤ Keep a journal of intuitive information, writing it down as it's received. This might include a log of synchronicities or coincidences, for example, or just a note about something you "felt" that hasn't yet come to fruition. It's also helpful to look back at this journal from time to time, to see how accurate the intuitive information is. You may find an emerging pattern that differentiates intuitive hunches from those that turn out to be purely imaginary.

Using Your Head

You can develop your intuition into a powerful and highly reliable tool. After all, it's an increasingly needed resource in this complex world. Your intuition can assist you in understanding your purpose and direction in life as well as bring you closer to the peace and harmony you deserve.

A "safe" way to view intuition is as your soul's "instructions," guiding you to make correct decisions for yourself, according to your higher purpose in life. The messages we all receive can give us information about how to proceed in our lives, or they may provide insight into what lessons we should be learning from certain experiences, even painful ones. They may even offer suggestions for taking the next steps, large or small, along our path.

In addition to growth in our personal and spiritual lives, our relationships with others also benefit when we use our intuition. Intuitive insight can grant us greater understanding, empathy, and compassion for others, as well as inform us about our world in new ways, giving us a fresh perspective.

Time Capsule

Lynn used to joke with her clients that it would be helpful if we were all born with an instruction manual that contained information about our life purpose, tools to use to create a life we enjoyed, and how to bring more joy, love, hope, and honor into our world. Then it slowly dawned on her that we have all of that in the gift of intuition.

The challenge in the new millennium is to learn to listen to its whispers and act on its wisdom. That's why we like to call intuitive information "an instruction package for planet Earth."

"If Only": An Intuitive Exercise

Our intuition is constantly informing us of new directions we could take in order to experience more joy, peace, and happiness. As we approach the new millennium, it's to our benefit to pay attention to these intuitive cues for change in our personal lives. Many times we push aside the intuitive messages we receive, and like Scarlett O'Hara in *Gone With the Wind* decide that "Tomorrow is another day."

With that in mind, ask yourself this question. It may help you access some of your own hopes and dreams for your future:

> If you didn't have to worry about making money, what would you spend your time doing?

This question usually stops people in their tracks. Yes, that's a great big "if." And in fact, Lynn has noticed that when she asks people what they want to do for a living, they usually respond with some variation on the theme, "I'd love to do _____. But there's no money in it." That's usually the end of the subject, and they continue doing what they've always done until they retire.

You Can Do What You Want!

But what if it didn't have to work that way? There's a saying that goes, "If you always do what you've always done, you'll always get what you've always gotten." Remember that your intuition doesn't necessarily require you to make a huge change in your life. It suggests through gentle nudges that you pay attention to its wisdom and begin to take small steps toward creating a life you love.

Time Capsule

Lynn has example after example of clients, friends, and students who've taken the small steps that their intuition suggested to them. They went from jobs they hated to work that was fun, meaningful, and financially rewarding. Patience is important here. These changes don't usually happen overnight, after all. Books such as Marsha Sinetar's *Do What You Love and the Money Will Follow* (Dell, 1987) or Barbara Sher's *Wishcraft* (Ballantine, 1986) can be extraordinarily helpful when you're struggling with the concept of finding your passion—and being paid for it.

Experts predict that by the year 2000, 70 percent of all Americans will be engaged in some form of self-employment. If you're having trouble trying to figure out your true passion in life, you might read *Doing Work You Love: Discovering Your Purpose and Realizing Your Dreams* (Contemporary Books, 1997) by career coach Cheryl Gilman. Gilman's written an action-packed, insightful book, full of exercises that respect *your* intuitive messages.

Your New Millennium Doesn't Have to Be a Game of Chance

As we move into the 21st century, here are some things *you* can do to create a life you love.

1. Listen to What You Tell Yourself About Your Life

Pay attention to your thoughts and beliefs. Do you believe you have a right to be happy? Do you trust yourself to make good decisions for your future? Do you believe that other people wish you well? Do you believe there's a loving universe that will support you in your decisions for change?

Your thoughts, beliefs, and emotions have a huge impact on what you create around you in your life. If your thoughts tend to the negative or pessimistic, ask yourself, "What's another way of thinking about this?" or "What do I want to create in my life?" Apply "turnarounds" as needed. Remember: Would you rather be right or would you rather be happy? Do your beliefs and dominant thoughts express the true expectations you have for your life?

2. Practice Positive Statements and Envision Success

Philosopher Søren Kierkegaard once said, "Our life always expresses the result of our dominant thoughts." Many successful people confess to us that they spend time daydreaming about their futures. That's because they, like all of us, enjoy seeing positive outcomes.

What successful people are doing that you may not be is visualizing what are commonly called *affirmations*. This means that they tell themselves positive statements about their lives and their ability to achieve their goals. You can do this, too: It's as simple as imagining your own success!

The truth is, the power of your mind to imagine success is a key to creating a life you love. Some ways you can practice affirmations include the following:

Speaking Y2K

Affirmations are a way of telling yourself what's good about you and your life to help you to achieve your goals.

➤ Write down your affirmation statements, and then tape them around your home or office.

➤ Listen to uplifting motivational tapes as you drive to work.

➤ Practice turning your negative thoughts into positive ones. For example, instead of "I'm always broke," try "Money comes to me easily. I always have enough."

3. Pay Attention to What Excites You

Continue to think about what you'd like to create in your life. Pay special attention to the interests in your life that bring you joy or make you feel excited. These are the ways that your intuition brings information to you through your emotions. Simply put, if it feels exciting and enjoyable, take some steps toward it and test it out. If you feel upset or drained by something, figure out a way to change the situation or let it go entirely.

4. Ask Your Intuition Questions and Then Listen for the Answer

This involves paying attention to how your intuition communicates with you. Do you typically get answers in words, emotions, images, physical sensations, or as a simple knowing? Learn to seek out the wisdom of your intuition. Ask it questions throughout the day:

➤ "How should I handle this situation?"

➤ "Should I take this action or that action?"

➤ "Is this the best time for me to move ahead on this project?"

These are all questions for which your intuition will have a ready answer. Try it and see for yourself.

5. Pray and Meditate

This one used to be easy—and there's no reason it can't be again: Ask for guidance from God, or whatever you choose to call your Higher Power. State your intentions and ask for help if you're having difficulties. Spend time each day listening for guidance, meditating, or simply imagining yourself in the flow of Spirit and Divine Wisdom.

6. Take Action

Act on at least three things each week that will move you closer to your goals, visions, and dreams. Sure, making any change in your life often feels uncomfortable at first.

But small steps count here. Put the energy to create new things in your life out into the world. Your intuition will guide you as to what actions to take.

Here are some examples:

➤ Call a career counselor and make an appointment to discuss your interests. Work with him or her to create an action plan to bring your dreams into reality.

➤ Talk to someone who made a successful career change about how they got there.

➤ Interview someone who has your dream job.

➤ Sign up for a class in something that is either pure fun or a subject you may want to explore for a new career.

➤ Make an appointment with a financial planner to evaluate how you could make a career switch and maintain your financial security.

➤ Research your interests on the Internet or at the library. Remember: Small steps count. You're building a bridge to create the life you want.

7. Be Aware of Life's Natural Ebbs and Flows

It's important to view all obstacles as lessons and challenges rather than as indications of failure. Sometimes, in fact, the biggest challenge is to practice patience and detachment from the outcome you want, and, as you'll learn in Chapter 27, these lessons will become still more important in the new millennium.

When something appears to be an obstacle, don't simply assume you've done something wrong. Everything that shows up in your life is supposed to, and life doesn't always go in a straight line even when we're doing everything "right." Just as nature has seasons, cycles, ebbs, and flows, so do our lives.

Our task as spiritual human beings is to learn how to love, forgive, experience peace in ourselves, be of service, and have compassion for others. As we move into the 21st century, the universe has many ways to help us learn those lessons in our schoolroom called "Earth."

The Least You Need to Know

➤ Intuition is a way of knowing without conscience thought.

➤ Intuition will become even more important in the new millennium.

➤ You can build your intuitive power through exercises and practice.

➤ Part of intuition is trust in yourself.

➤ Your intuition can help you develop a more positive outlook on life.

Chapter 19

Mind/Body Medicine and Beyond: Using the Power of the Mind and Spirit to Heal

> ### In This Chapter
>
> ➤ Thinking about healing
>
> ➤ Mind over matter?
>
> ➤ Tapping into your own healing power
>
> ➤ Creating a balance for the new millennium

Now that you've learned how to increase your powers of intuition, it's time to take the next step and explore the connection between mind and body. Is your health really a matter of "mind over matter"? Can you tap into your own healing power and make yourself get better?

Even more important to the new millennium is the potential for all of us to use our intuition to heal our Earth. In this chapter, we'll look at the power of the mind to heal the self—and the world.

Thinking About Healing

In the past 150 years, humankind has gone through major shifts in thinking about health and healing. The first of these occurred in the mid 1800s, when physicians and lay people began to view the body scientifically. This involved the idea that we got sick because we were at the mercy of outside forces. So, when something made you sick, you would identify what that something was and then fix it.

The second era, which began in the early 20th century, brought in the connection between mind and body. People, and later, physicians, began to understand that there was a connection between the mind and the body, and that we could use the power of our minds to heal ourselves.

The third era introduces the idea of spirituality and intuition into the mind/body healing equation—and this era is just now dawning, along with the new millennium, in the late 20th and early 21st centuries.

The problem is, most U.S.-trained physicians are still back in the old model. This means that when you go to the doctor, you're usually asked about your symptoms. In fact, much of the medical model being used today is based on illness and disease, and a massive amount of research money continues to go to studying illness and finding out what causes a certain disease. We spend very little money in comparison studying people who are well and happy and what makes them that way.

In the 21st century, the Western medical model of the spine and nervous system will blend seamlessly with yoga's Eastern tradition of the chakras, centers of psychospiritual energy in the body. Illustration by Wendy Frost.

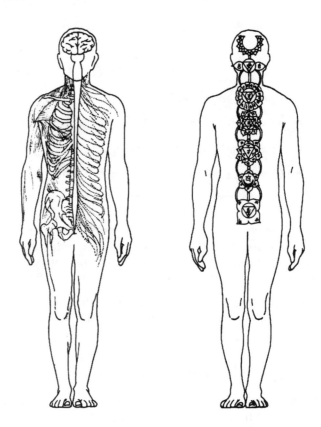

We're not saying researchers shouldn't search for the causes of certain diseases, but that there *are* some diseases that can be disarmed before they ever occur. This is what 21st-century medicine is all about.

21st-Century Medicine

When we visit our physicians of the future, we'll be seen by a variety of health professionals. Not only will they look at the physical manifestation of our illnesses, but they'll help us look at where we may be out of balance in our lives.

The physicians of the future (and we ourselves) will come to understand that our physical symptoms are indicating something out of balance in our lives, and so, rather than just asking where it hurts, those physicians of the future will be asking questions that cover the gamut of our mind, body, and spirit. For example:

Out of Time

Bringing prevention (Eastern medicine) and cure (Western medicine) into parity will return a balance to the treatment of patients that Western medicine's emphasis on allopathic cure has heretofore thrown out of balance. This integrative approach, advocated by physician Andrew Weil, may be the way of the future, and is embraced by a growing number of medical professionals and their patients.

➤ Are you eating properly?

➤ Do you get enough rest?

➤ Do you have enough fun?

➤ Do you have a community of friends and family that bring emotional support and sustain you through difficult times?

➤ Is your spiritual life in order?

➤ Are you experiencing joy and peace on a regular basis?

➤ Is your work fulfilling?

➤ Do you find a deeper meaning in your life?

These, and questions like them, are the starting points toward a direction for us to get back into balance.

Prayer as a Healing Force

We're beginning to accept that there's something to the notion that the power of the mind can affect bodily processes. In fact, there's an ever-increasing body of research that indicates that our consciousness, through prayer, can have an effect on other people and events, and that the power of our minds *and* spirit can affect not only our own health but those of our family and friends.

Most of us believe that our mind is localized in our brains. In reality, you can't find anything in the body that defines this consciousness, and many physicists now call "consciousness" *the non-local mind.*

Speaking Y2K

The non-local mind is a term physicists use to describe the lack of location of human consciousness in any specific place within the body.

When it comes to rational science, it's hard to find anything that can be pinpointed as "the mind." Non-local medicine says that our minds may not be localized to our brains and bodies—or even to the present moment. Further, what we're coming to understand is that, through prayer, we can "send" this non-local mind to affect healing.

Today, at the dawn of the new millennium, more and more scientists and doctors are beginning to acknowledge the capacity of the unseen world to affect the material one. Although the scientific community isn't quite sure what to call this ability, the spiritual community calls it God, or universal energy, or *chi*. Many religions call the effort to direct this force "prayer." And more scientists and medical professionals are looking at this force as a form of *distant healing*.

QiGong, *also called* chi kung, *is an ancient Chinese practice that facilitates the flow of "chi," the life force energy, through the body for maximum wellness. When we pray, we restore and nurture that life force. Illustration by Wendy Frost.*

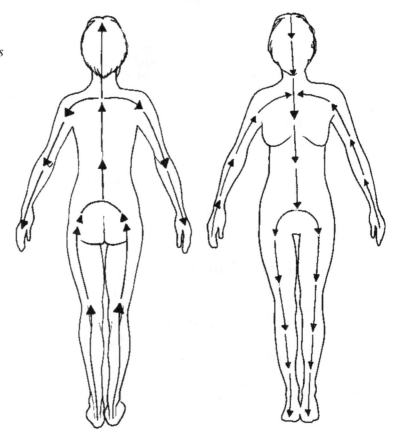

Tapping into Your Own Healing Power

Everyone—you, us, even our editors—can each tap into this same openness to the love, acceptance, and support that comes from the universe—or God, or a Higher Power, or whatever one wants to call it—to heal ourselves and others. It's important to remember, after all, that healing applies to various aspects of our lives, which often go beyond just the physical healing. Tapping into this all-powerful source of spiritual healing can have many names, but most people in Western society call it *prayer*.

Many people get upset with this kind of broad definition. A prevailing belief in this culture is to understand prayer as talking aloud or in silence to an all-powerful God who may or may not answer our requests based on some whim we don't—or can't—understand.

Despite these people's doubts, most cultures and religions continue to have prayer practices. Perhaps what we need is a broader definition of what "prayer" is. Interestingly, the research on prayer shows no correlation between religious affiliation and the effects of prayer in the laboratory. Rather, the factors that seem to work are love, compassion, empathy, and deep caring.

> **Speaking Y2K**
>
> **Distant healing** involves acknowledging and accepting a greater force than the self to help heal.

Webster's Dictionary defines prayer as "a solemn and humble approach to Divinity in word or thought," and this certainly expresses the importance of a person's mental intention to connect with a force beyond themselves. *Healing Words: The Power of Prayer and the Practice of Medicine* (HarperCollins, 1993) by Larry Dossey, M.D., provides a wealth of information on the ability of the mind and spirit to heal.

If you'd like to explore still more about how the mind works to enable spiritual healing, check out *Miracles of Mind* (New World Library, 1998) by physicist Russell Targ and spiritual healer Jane Katra, Ph.D.

Miracles of the Mind

A frequently cited study of the effects of prayer and healing was done by Randolph Byrd, M.D., in 1988. Over 10 months, he studied 393 patients with heart disease at San Francisco General Hospital. All of the subjects received appropriate high-tech coronary care, but some of them were also receiving help of another kind: Half of the patients were assigned to people who were to pray for them faithfully; the other half got no assigned prayer helpers.

The results were astonishing if looked at from a "rational" standpoint. The patients who had people praying for them showed improvement rates that were 5 to 7 percent higher than their not-prayed-for counterparts. They had less need for antibiotics and diuretics, fewer cases of pneumonia, and no deaths. Of course, this type of experiment contains many factors that are hard to control or measure, but this one certainly got people thinking!

A Prescription for the New Millennium

While you probably won't find many doctors writing prescriptions that read, "Healing prayers, three times a day," physicians *are* becoming increasingly willing to admit the importance of the mind and spirit in healing the body. Evidence for this can be seen in the increasing use of visualization as a treatment technique for patients with chronic pain and terminal disease—and the frequency of how often they improve. On the other hand, patients who express little hope of recovery or faith in healing have more of a challenge—both physically and mentally—in staging a comeback.

Time Capsule

There's a tendency among some folks who take the mind/body/spirit connection seriously to believe that if you are truly spiritual you don't get sick, or that if you live your life right you won't ever die. To dispute this theory, note that the Buddha was said to have died from food poisoning. The fact is that none of us ever make it out of this alive—whether we're perfect in all ways or not!

Ask Spaceship Earth

To try to deny death its due is to throw life itself out of balance. Death is a very real part of life, and coming to grips with its inevitability (for our loved ones as well as ourselves) is part of achieving balance in your life.

While it's important to understand that prayer does have an impact on healing, it can't save us from death or guarantee we won't become ill. At present, the mortality rate for the condition called "Life" is 100 percent. No research has been completed that indicates that this will change in the new millennium no matter how perfect we become.

When Your Life Is Out of Balance

Your symptoms of illness and disease are part of your body's intuitive feedback system, which is part of your body's way of letting you know that something is out of balance in your life.

It's very important that we not blame ourselves for getting ill: There are very few of us who would consciously want to be sick. Still, by understanding that illnesses are often created by behavioral patterns that no longer support us or by bitter and angry attitudes we hold, we can begin to feel empowered to change, and, in so doing, we can greatly improve our health as well.

We need to begin by becoming more sensitive to body signals such as stiff necks. That's the one that gets Lynn every time. When she gets one of those, it's usually a sure sign that she's feeling overwhelmed by too much to do.

Lynn's learned that when this symptom rears its little head, she takes it as a sign to step back, take some time for herself, and re-prioritize. Lynn knows that if she chose to not pay attention, her symptoms would get worse, and even turn into migraines and/ or painful muscle spasms.

So now, at the first sign of tension, Lynn gets out her appointment book and starts eliminating things from her schedule. Once she's cleared some space, she schedules a massage, meditates more than usual, takes long walks in natural settings, *slows down,* and breathes.

Learning to Listen to Your Body

Instead of taking annoying or painful symptoms for granted, you can, like Lynn, take the attitude that they're trying to get your attention about something, and trust that they hold a meaning for you. The next time your "early warning system" gives you a "You're under stress" message, take a moment for quiet reflection to listen to its message. Instead of trying to figure out what it means from an intellectual point of view, get into a dialogue with it.

Ask yourself, "If I knew that anything I chose to do right now would be successful, what would I decide to do right now?" Or, you might ask yourself, "What are my options here?"

When we ask open-ended questions like these, they can make our world open up. At the same time, when we listen for the answers by tapping into our intuitive knowing, we get in touch with the movement of our soul deep within us. Everyone's soul has a voice, and that voice can send us messages.

Ask Spaceship Earth

Just as a baby has a similar cry whether she's hungry, tired, wet, or hurting, our bodies have similar cries to tell us something's not right. And just as a mother instantly knows whether her baby's hungry, tired, wet, or hurting, you can learn to differentiate among your body's various cries.

Our souls guide us throughout our lives. The good news is that more people are turning within to their intuition and acting on its guidance. So next time you feel trapped, angry, depressed, tired, or fearful, take it as an indication that you're stuck in some part of your life, because those feelings are a cry for help. They can indicate something is out of balance, and there's a need to look to inner guidance for help in your healing.

Why We Get Sick

You may have figured out that your life is out of balance, but what do you do now? How do you go about resolving the problem, now that you know what it is? In the next millennium, we'll be using the theories of *guided imagery* to help us understand the purpose of the symptoms we experience, as well as what it will take to allow healing to proceed.

Speaking Y2K

Guided imagery is a form of day-dreaming. Specific images are used to visualize the body healing and staying strong. Examples of this are conjuring up images of a tumor shrinking or of high blood pressure decreasing.

Accept for now the idea that physical and emotional symptoms are indicators of something out of balance. While your physical and emotional symptoms are usually uncomfortable, they're not the "enemy." They are, in fact, part of an intuitive warning system that can help keep you healthy. Symptoms should be viewed as early warning systems. Ignore them at your peril!

In the next millennium, we'll come to understand that our bodies are intelligent and can communicate with us through our intuition, and we'll learn to value the feedback our bodies give us. Imagine what it would be like if we were able to understand our symptoms and use the wisdom of our bodies, our feelings, and our intuition, and you've got a very good picture of the 21st century's potential for healing.

When Getting Sick Has a Payoff

In many intuitive readings that Lynn's done for clients, she's noticed that there are often positive outcomes to being ill. As we've said, most of us don't consciously want to become sick. But there are often some obvious payoffs:

1. We may allow ourselves to be loved, attended to, and nurtured by others when we're ill.

2. Being sick may give us a way out of having to deal with a difficult situation that seems to have no positive resolution.

3. Having an illness may be the only way we can give ourselves permission to take time to regroup emotionally and spiritually. It may allow us the time and peace to acquire a new perspective.

4. Many people find that when they're ill they can make a change for the better both personally and spiritually. There's a sense that they have "nothing left to lose" and might as well make the change they had previously feared.

5. In this culture, we have incredibly high expectations for success. Illness is often the only excuse for letting go of the unrealistic expectations we have for ourselves or others.

At worst, if you recognize any benefits that come with being ill, you can make the best use of them. If your symptom solves a problem for you, focus on ways to enjoy the benefits—without having to be sick.

Using Imagery to Explore Your Symptoms

A simpler, more direct way to understand your symptoms is through your intuition. We all have an area in our bodies that works as our own "intuitive early warning system." It's that nagging physical symptom that tells us something is out of balance in our lives or in our bodies. It's usually something relatively minor: a mild stomachache, a pulled muscle, a slight headache—even a tendency to cut your fingers can be a sign. No matter how it manifests, though, it's your body's way of telling you, "Warning! You're on overload! Caution ahead!"

Rather than being your enemy, a disease can be an incredible gift of wisdom that leads you on a new path. It may be a messenger from your intuitive guidance system trying to get your attention. And, if you pay attention, you can reap the benefits as well. Here's an exercise to help you learn how to pay attention.

Out of Time

Our society is so focused on popping pills to make illnesses go away that we've adopted a passive response to illness whereby we rely almost solely on medication. We lose sight of the need to actively bring our lives into balance to keep our illnesses to a minimum, as well as to focus our energy on getting well when we are sick.

Your Inner Physician: An Exercise

How can you use your intuitive guidance system to heal yourself? This exercise can help you practice "listening" to what your body's trying to tell you.

You can tape-record this exercise, have a friend read it to you, or simply read it through several times yourself and do it on your own. You may want to have some meditative music playing quietly beside you, although that's certainly not a requirement. Some of us need silence to meditate, after all.

When the time comes in the exercise to write down what you receive about your symptoms, write down *everything*. We all have many different ways we receive intuitive impressions. You may get a voice, an emotion, an image, a kinesthetic impression, or even a scent, and these are all ways your intuition communicates with you. Don't discount anything: Like the images of dreams, the messages of your intuition may come in unexpected ways.

Don't try to analyze it while it's happening. Consider everything as data. You can try to figure it out later. You may feel at first as if you're just making this up. Stay with it and write everything that occurs to you. Don't judge it. You can write as you do the exercise or remember the impressions and write them later. Lastly, pay attention to the pauses. They will help you focus and relax as you work through this exercise.

1. First, what physical symptom do you have that concerns you?
   Describe it here:

   _____

2. Now, sit or lie in a comfortable position and close your eyes. Take a few deep, relaxing breaths. Exhale slowly each time. Count slowly from 10 down to 1 and feel yourself become more deeply relaxed with each breath. If it helps you to relax, you may want to imagine that you're in a peaceful nature scene as you do this exercise.

3. Begin to gently focus on the area of your body that concerns you. Allow your attention to float there. Allow any images or sensations to come into your awareness. You may want to imagine that your symptom has a voice. Ask it, "What is it you're trying to tell me?" or "What can I do to help you?" Write any information here:

   _____

   pause

4. Do any feelings or emotions arise when you do this exercise?
   If so, write them here:

   _____

   pause

5. What sensations arise in your body or the area of the symptom? Write them here:

   _____

   pause

6. Is there anything else your symptom would like to reveal to you? Write it here:

   _____

7. When you're ready, open your eyes and return to normal consciousness. What have you learned? Describe several ways you could react differently if your symptoms arise.

By using imagery this way, you're inviting your intuition to tell you what's going on with you. You need to cultivate an attitude that allows you to look at what your intuition is telling you and explore its meaning. When it becomes clearer how your physical and emotional symptoms may relate to something out of balance in your life, you can then take remedial action.

A Healthy Balance for the 21st Century

We all sometimes believe that things outside ourselves—such as a new job, a wonderful relationship, or more money—are just what we need to make us happy. But being at peace is an inside job, and we must choose to be at peace first, before anything else will make any difference.

The 1990s have been characterized as a time when we wanted to do all the things we didn't have time to do. As we leave this rush-rush decade, we'll begin to understand that our lives are about balance on all levels—body, mind, and spirit. Once we begin to choose being at peace in our individual lives, we can begin to create it around us on Planet Earth.

When we're content and at peace, we also begin to hear our inner voices more clearly. Within each of us, there's a voice or feeling that guides us as we make our way through our lives. But usually, we must slow down, be content, and listen inside before our own voice can be heard.

Your inner voice informs both your direction and your purpose. In the next chapter, we'll explore how we can all listen to our inner voices—and then get them to sing together in harmony.

The Least You Need to Know

➤ Thinking about healing can actually help the healing process.

➤ Your symptoms are messages from your body about being out of balance.

➤ Tapping into your own healing power is a powerful intuitive tool.

➤ Creating a balance for the new millennium takes individual healing power to the next level.

Chapter 20

Psychic Awareness for the New Millennium's Global Community

In This Chapter

➤ Learning to use the energy of hope

➤ Paying attention to intuitive nudges

➤ Some visionaries look at the future

➤ Connecting spiritual traditions

➤ Envisioning a world community

The coming millennium represents significant new opportunities, and, as we've said in Chapters 18 and 19, what we each hold in our thoughts, beliefs, and emotions has a huge impact on what happens in our individual lives. It can also affect our larger outer world in ways we can only guess.

Our best chance at a positive future is to hold a vision of the world we want. When each of us very consciously and prayerfully imagines a world of peace, kindness, and love, it creates a space for those qualities to flourish. Are you ready to connect to the global community?

Consciousness Tools for the 21st Century

As the countdown toward the next millennium continues, two distinct camps seem to be emerging: the optimists and the pessimists. Count us among the optimists. We see the coming years fraught with some lessons to learn, yes. But we also see it full of potential for rediscovering our spiritual side and for getting in touch with our humanity. This will be a new era in which we can develop our expanding spiritual wisdom in practical endeavors.

While the pessimists may view the proliferation of technology as evidence of their doom-and-gloom philosophy, we see the proliferation of the Internet and other newer wide-scale telecommunications as moving toward a "one world" view. Never before have we been able to communicate so easily with others on opposite ends of the globe and in radically different cultures. We really are in this together—so we'd better learn to cooperate.

We Don't All Think Alike... and That's Good!

We can put forth the energy of hope and use our higher wisdom and intuition to more efficiently help solve the world's problems. We believe there's a vast wisdom in our universe that's guiding our human journey as individuals, as a nation, and as humanity. In the new millennium, we'll make a shift to begin to think more globally. As we have said, we're all in this together.

We don't all think alike, however, and that's actually a good thing. Some of us approach things mathematically, while others start with a picture in our head. Understanding that we don't think alike, and then using our differences to strengthen what we have in common, is one of the first steps toward interconnectedness.

A loving intelligence, working through all of us, is behind the transformation that's coming about in the next decade. When we open up to our inner guidance, we can tap into the vast rivers of this intelligence to further understand our purpose in the unfolding, discover our own path of growth in life, and our own particular spiritual mission—the personal way we can contribute to the world.

Meditation Techniques Tap Psychic Intuition

Many of us struggle with the concept of our life purpose, and perhaps just as many of us wish that a vision would appear to us stating, "JOHN SMITH. YOUR PURPOSE IS TO SECURE WORLD PEACE." Unfortunately, our life purpose doesn't usually come to us in quite that way.

Time Capsule

Our intuition constantly gives us messages through our feelings, an inner voice, a nudge, a body sensation, and myriad other ways. Often, we discount these impressions as we rush about in our daily lives, so it's important to remember that it takes just a moment to slow down and check in with this valuable resource called intuition, so we can hear the messages of our soul encouraging us to move toward what brings us joy and excitement.

To practice tapping into your psychic intuition, we're going to provide a meditation technique to help you hone your skills. Before beginning this exercise, think of a question you'd like to ask your intuition. The question should be phrased to evoke more than a yes or no answer. Here are a couple of examples:

➤ What is my life purpose?

➤ What new path should I take that will help me be more successful in the coming years?

Write your question here:

_____

Intuitive Insight Exercise

Keep a pen and paper handy while you do this exercise, in case you want to jot down some "intuitive notes." Or you may want to do this exercise with a partner, or use a tape recorder to record it.

1. Close your eyes and take in a deep breath and then exhale. As you do, say to yourself the word "relax."

2. Visualize a sun over your head, glowing radiant and warm.

3. Imagine the light from the sun flowing through your body, filling your head, down through your neck, across your shoulders, down your arms, through your hands and into your fingers. The light fills your chest, back, belly, and hips, and flows down into your legs, feet, and toes.

4. Imagine the light is bathing every cell of your body with healing and calming energy. The light also brings knowledge and wisdom.

5. Now visualize the light flowing down through your physical body and out around your body (into your *aura*). Feel it soothing and relaxing you.

6. In this calm and relaxed state of mind, ask your intuition your question. Then pause for a moment and pay attention to any thoughts, feelings, words, or body sensations that you may experience.

Speaking Y2K

Each of us has an **aura**, a field of electromagnetic energy that permeates and surrounds all living things.

Write down your impressions here:

_____

_____

_____

_____

_____

Pay attention to any cues from your intuition. Is there an image that leaps to mind, or an inner voice encouraging a shift in perception? Perhaps you feel a surge of pleasure about a change that you're considering. All of these impressions are ways that your intuition gives you messages.

What information did you receive? Consider these ideas to be intuitive advice that offers you options for the future.

Are you willing to act on the information? If so, what steps can you take starting today? Sometimes intuitive answers don't come immediately. You may find that an answer will pop into your mind when you awaken in the morning or later in the day.

You may also experience what we call an *intuitive nudge*. As you begin to take action on the intuitive information you've received, you'll find that "coincidences" will begin to occur all around you. Here's how the highly acclaimed Deepak Chopra, M.D. puts it: "Seekers are offered clues all the time from the world of the spirit. Ordinary people call these clues coincidences."

Speaking Y2K

You'll find that as you take small steps in the right direction you'll experience an **intuitive nudge**. This may come in the form of a coincidence or synchronicity. Things will begin falling into place. It's your intuition telling you you're on the right path.

Deepak Chopra, M.D., born in New Delhi, India, is a highly acclaimed medical doctor, who has brought the connection of the body, mind, and spirit to the attention of mainstream American audiences through his books and workshops.

You might, for example, receive some information about a job opening that would be perfect as a next step in your career. Or a friend may call with the perfect resource for a new course of study you've decided on.

Pay close attention to the coincidences and synchronicities that occur in your life. Notice when something happens that makes your life easier, when something you need magically appears. As you begin to trust this intuitive wisdom, you'll come to believe in the universal wisdom that guides us all. It's part of our salvation in the coming years.

Getting Along in the New Millennium

As you gain confidence in your intuition, a universal source of wisdom begins to support your every need. Intuition always leads you to what is the highest and best for you in your life. When you begin to trust it and act on its wisdom, you'll set in motion a higher order for your life.

Each of us comes here with an assignment. Sometimes, it's something as seemingly simple as learning to allow yourself to be loved. It may be to learn to love by forgiving someone who has hurt you. Perhaps the lesson is standing up for yourself and claiming your power.

No matter what the lesson, as you tap into your intuitive wisdom, you'll start to "remember" a fuller vision of what you wanted to accomplish with your life. We believe that many of us came into this life at a particular time to bring a common vision of peace and harmony to our world.

When we take the actions suggested by our intuition, we're being guided by our souls—and by a higher spiritual purpose that imbues our lives. In

> **Ask Spaceship Earth**
>
> Understanding your life purpose and taking action on it tends to increase the flow of synchronicities or coincidences as you're guided toward your destiny. First, you have a question; then your dreams, daydreams, and intuition lead you toward the answer.

this decade before the millennium, millions of people are very quietly doing just that. They're praying, tapping in to their inner guidance, meditating, exploring new ways of living in harmony, and pursuing countless other ways that lead to a reconnection with God. What's happening now is that we're going through a new mass experience of our spiritual nature, which is changing the way we'll experience life in the new millennium.

Economic, Social, and Personal Challenges

One of the best sources of information about the economic, social, and personal challenges we'll be facing in the new millennium is, not surprisingly, the World Wide Web. When we went online and poked around ourselves, we discovered an ongoing forum called *21st Century Online Magazine* (**www.21net.com**), which has asked each of its interviewees to spontaneously explore their vision of the 21st century. For more new millennium resources, see Appendix B.

On the social front, for example, Douglas Adams, author of *The Hitchhiker's Guide to the Galaxy* (Ballantine, 1995) and other books, believes that "in the 21st century, biology will be the queen of sciences." Adams suggests that the computer has had an amazing effect on our understanding of evolutionary science and that its "high technology... will allow us to live on the earth much more lightly" in the new millennium.

Another interviewee, entrepreneur Charles Whitlock, commented on how the social and economic arenas will become ever more interwoven. "Millions of Americans," Whitlock says, "are going to find themselves with a computer, modem, fax machine, a copy machine and a telephone, working out of their homes." This in turn, he says, will be closely tied to the "synergistic relationships" that will develop "to meet the needs of the world market."

Another who explores the new global economy is Dr. James Canton, the editor-in-chief of *21st Century Online*. Canton suggests that the winning entrepreneurs of the 21st century will be those who provide "smart knowledge packaged for specific business, recreation, entertainment, educational needs that enhance the quality of life and work." The "key competitive edge," according to Canton, "will be how smart your products and services are."

On the personal front, Jack Canfield, co-author of the best-selling *Chicken Soup for the Soul* series, sees more and more people learning to trust themselves, and, in turn, learning to trust each other. Paulette Ensign, the president of the National Association of Profession Organizers, agrees: "I believe people will find there are many more choices in every aspect of life and will make choices that are much more a match to their true spirit and who they are." And world-renowned futurist Peter Russell believes that our society's current "deep and widespread questioning of our value systems" will lead to an "inner development" that will allow us to "manage ourselves better."

You can ask yourself this question, too. What is your vision for the 21st century? Do you see major economic, social, and personal challenges? Where do you think you—and the world—will be in 10 years' time? A hundred? A thousand? Do you agree with the experts, or does your intuition provide you with some insight of your own?

Our Human Intuition Could Be Our Salvation

Futurist Peter Russell believes that our future is very bright, "because as soon as we begin to seriously explore the human mind and begin to understand that as well as we now understand subatomic physics and molecular biology, then. . .we will all stand on the threshold of collectivity." This, Russell goes on, will be "our collective awakening to our true spiritual potential."

Another person who's given the future of our collective intuition some thought is Jaime Snyder, the grandson of innovative architect Buckminster Fuller and Senior Vice President of the Buckminster Fuller Institute. Snyder is certain that "our consciousness is very much larger than humans," and that "the key to the 21st century is our own individual union and realization of that larger whole system consciousness which is running the whole show."

We, too, believe in the interconnectedness of not just all humans, but all life. As a first step toward making a world community more than a futuristic vision, it's time to recognize our shared humanity.

Recognizing Our Shared Humanity

Let's begin with an affirmation that author Marianne Williamson has posted on her Web site (**www.marianne.com**):

> I see this country bathed in love.
>
> I see this love as a corrective, healing force. I pray for my mind to be a source of peace and love.
>
> May good cast out all fear in myself and in the world.
>
> Amen.

Also on her Web site, Williamson discusses a concept called the Peace Group Movement, which works from the basic premise that love is stronger than fear, that the positive is stronger than the negative. "Good is not a negative; it is not the absence of evil," Williamson points out. "Rather, evil is the absence of good."

Williamson suggests beginning with the prayer above (or something like it), first individually. Then ask someone to join you. Perhaps each of you will then ask someone else, or you may choose to keep your group to the two of you. You may do this meditation once, or frequently for the rest of your life. The important thing is taking the message to heart, which is one first step in recognizing our shared humanity.

Existential theory would have us believe that we are each lonely and adrift, but spiritual traditions have always known otherwise. You don't have to start a peace group to connect with others—there are traditions throughout the world that recognize our commonalties. And it's within the power of our minds to create the world.

Connecting Spiritual Traditions

Mythologist/author Joseph Campbell (1904–1987) devoted his life to finding the connections among various spiritual traditions, and the common themes he discovered can offer us keys to "what's missing" in our lives as we enter the new millennium.

One of Campbell's most accessible contributions was the concept of the *Hero's Journey*. This archetypal motif shows the pattern that's common not only to all heroic adventures, but to things we face in our everyday lives as well.

Here are several of the crucial steps of the *Hero's Journey* as outlined by Campbell in *The Hero With a Thousand Faces* (Princeton University Press, 1949):

1. The call to adventure
2. Refusal of the call

Speaking Y2K

The **Hero's Journey** is the name mythologist Joseph Campbell gave to the pattern of adventures—both heroes' and your own.

3. Crossing to the "other world"

4. Trials and tribulations

5. Meeting the enemy

6. Defeating the enemy

7. Returning to one's world with the "prize"

Let's use a contemporary film as an example of how the Hero's Journey works. In *Good Will Hunting,* Will is called to adventure by the equation on the blackboard. At first, he ignores it, but soon he can't help but solve it, and he crosses to the "other world," in this case, academia.

Once he's crossed the threshold, there are all sorts of trials and tribulations he must face. In Will's case, the enemy is within himself—his image of academia—and he must face this enemy before he can return to his world with the "prize" that it's okay to be smart.

Now that you have that example, see if you can apply this formula to something that happened in your own life. Maybe you decided to apply for a job in a new field. Or perhaps your call to adventure was more literal—you had an opportunity to fly to Paris. See if you can identify each step of the Hero's Journey in your own story.

Next, think of some problem that you're facing now. What's standing in your way? Can you use the previous steps to help you approach your problem? Whether it's a difficult child or an illness, the Hero's Journey can help you chart your course.

Ask Spaceship Earth

What's important about the Hero's Journey is that it's a formula that humans have been using as long as they've been telling stories. Whether ancient Africans or equally ancient Persians or Native Americans, people everywhere have told stories that used this formula to help them understand things they could not have understood otherwise.

The Power of Our Minds to Create the World

Joseph Campbell's work is but one example of how we use our minds to create the world. People of various religions use their minds to create their worlds, too, and with the advent of the new millennium, some groups have taken on decidedly negative tones.

As Marianne Williamson suggests, it's better to think of evil as an absence of good than good as an absence of evil. Do you see the glass as half-full or half-empty? It's within your power to turn what seems to be negative into something positive.

Instead of viewing possible Y2K computer glitches as problems, for example, why not view them as opportunities for people to work together in new and different ways to solve problems? Instead of viewing people who are different from us as "wrong," why not think of them as people just like us, developing unique ways of answering life's questions?

Just as our individual minds create our own worlds through our imaginations, our collective minds can create the larger world through our universal imagination.

Princeton scientist Dr. Roger Nelson has measured the statistically significant effect that focused meditations and events have upon the earth's energy field. His studies show that the greatest effects occur when groups synchronize their focus. The evidence is there: We do have the power within us to change the world.

Many peace groups have requested that their members meditate upon specific affirmations in unison to achieve the power of a singular group focus. In his book, *Emissary of Light: A Vision of Peace* (Little Brown & Company, 1998), "Peace Troubadour" James Twyman recounts the incredible series of coincidences which led him through war-torn Bosnia to a secluded mountainous area. It was there he met the Emissaries of Light, a secret society said to have existed for thousands of years.

The first outsider to witness their extraordinary meditations and experience their powerful effects, he discovered that peace is a powerful reality that already exists within all our souls. Peace is, in fact, our destiny.

Twyman has since traveled around the world, often risking his life, to sing prayers of peace. At each event he called for the participants to join him in focused meditation sharing their vision of "a world transformed by love."

Here's the format of his meditation:

> We are asking everyone to follow this simple format during the meditation. As scientific studies at Princeton University show, the more focused a group meditation or event is, the stronger the effect.

1. Opening:

   Begin with this affirmation, said with great power and commitment:

   I am an Emissary of Light.

   I extend this Light to all beings, in compassion and love, knowing that they are one within me.

   This moment the world is healed, and I along with it.

   I will it, and it is so.

2. Then spend five minutes creating a sound (such as "Aum") to carry the spiritual energy and vibration. This can be done with a single tone or by singing a song such as "Amazing Grace."

3. Spend five minutes in silence allowing your spirit to receive the light and love which you yourself extended to the world.

4. End with this prayer:

"It is done!

I am one with all, and all is healed.

Let love reign where fear once was.

I accept this for myself and for the world.

I am an Emissary of Light now and always. Amen"

Then, with reverence, bow your head and thank God for this grand opportunity. The universe gives thanks to you for being part of this great experiment!

Star Trek Isn't Just Science Fiction

If you're not a "Trekkie," you're at a disadvantage—because all of the authors and experts here are! Why? Because *Star Trek* isn't just science fiction, it's a global vision of a world community. Further, the community that *Star Trek* is exploring isn't "strange new worlds" at all—it's our own!

Now, wait a second. How can a series (and films) that takes place in the 23rd and 24th centuries be about the 20th and 21st? Simple. *Star Trek* uses *myth* and *parable* to show us how to solve the problems of today.

Envisioning a World Community

Using *Star Trek* as an example, it becomes easier to envision a world community. Let's look at several *Star Trek* episodes to see how this works.

One example is an episode from the original *Star Trek* TV show, entitled "Let That Be Your Final Battlefield." Two humanoids, each the last of his kind, are battling to the death, because one is black on the left side and white on the right side, while the other is the opposite. Yes, it's a silly story, but that's the point: racial differences are silly, too.

A better example is the classic film *Star Trek IV: The Final Frontier*. That's the one where Captain Kirk and company must travel back in time to save the whales—because their mother species is getting ready to destroy the earth for destroying the humpbacks. The allegory here is clear as well: Be kind to your sea-living friends/'Cause a whale may have a stronger mother.

Reaching for the Stars in the New Millennium

The United Federation of Planets can serve as a model for our future, especially if we view that organization as a myth and parable for the possibilities of our own time. The "Federation," after all, isn't without its in-fighting, any more than today's United Nations or NATO is.

What's standing in the way of the UN becoming a global community like the Federation? Why can't we reach for the stars in the new millennium?

The answer is that we can. The only thing standing between people and a global community is people themselves. It begins with you and us. And then, who knows? Perhaps by the end of the new millennium, we'll have moved to embrace a universal community that includes species we haven't even dreamed of!

Speaking Y2K

Parables are stories that represent other stories. By using examples that seem to be different from one's own society, stories can make points that might not otherwise be made. George Orwell's *Animal Farm*, for example, uses barnyard animals to show how humans can abuse power.

We Are the World: Embracing Hope and Optimism

As we've discussed in this chapter, we have enormous power within us to create a world that is based on mutual cooperation and peace. What does your intuition inform you about your role? You may feel drawn to join a group that works for peace. Or you may want to study issues of multiculturalism or work on an issue requiring your negotiation and mediation skills at your office.

There's a saying that "peace begins with you." What commitment are you willing to take toward a positive new millennium? Your first step can be one of many that creates a future world that embraces hope and optimism.

The Least You Need to Know

➤ You can learn to use the energy of hope instead of the energy of despair.

➤ Paying attention to intuitive nudges can help you tap your own psychic power.

➤ Many of today's visionaries forecast a bright future.

➤ Spiritual traditions throughout the world share common themes.

➤ We can tap into our common humanity to envision a world community.

Chapter 21

Psychic Prophecies and Predictions for the New Millennium

In This Chapter

➤ A quick course in Bible study: Is the Y2K the end of the world?

➤ Taking a closer look at the prophecies of Nostradamus, Edgar Cayce, and Robert Ghost Wolf

➤ The ancient voices of the Hopi and the Mayan

➤ How psychic intuition can help us make the millennium shift

---

According to a recent Associated Press survey, almost 25 percent of American Christian adults believe that Jesus will arrive in their lifetimes, and a majority of that 25 percent are so positive, they're devoting their lives to spreading the word.

Predictions and prophecies about the new millennium abound, from the return of Jesus to the end of the world in a hail of fire and brimstone (just what *is* brimstone, anyway?). In this chapter, we'll look at what a variety of prophets predict for the new millennium, and see just how their prophecies stack up against what we know. Is it all doom and gloom? Or is there a proverbial light at the end of the tunnel?

Is the Y2K the End of the World?

There are those who truly believe that signs point to the "end of the world as we know it." In fact, in true new millennial fashion, this phrase has become a well-known acronym: *TEOTWAWKI*. Any Internet search for Y2K information uncovers a variety of sites dealing with TEOTWAWKI, from discussions of the Y2K computer bug to apocalyptic predictions.

So just what are the signs that some of these prophets point to? Some that Christians and Messianic Jews believe are alluded to in the Bible include the following:

➤ Earthquakes

➤ El Niño

➤ AIDS

➤ Germ warfare

➤ Saddam Hussein

➤ Environmental problems

Speaking Y2K

TEOTWAWKI is an acronym for "the end of the world as we know it." It's become a popular phrase on Internet sites discussing everything from the Y2K computer bug to apocalyptic predictions.

Out of Time

In Chapter 20 of the Book of Revelation, Satan leaves his prison and proceeds to wreak havoc on Earth with his lies, which leads to an apocalyptic end-of-the-world battle. Is Saddam Hussein Satan? There are those who believe he is.

In addition, some of those who believe that these signs herald the end of the earth point to Matthew 24:14, which says, "And this good news of the kingdom will be proclaimed throughout the world, as a testimony to all nations; and then the end will come." They devote their lives to spreading the gospel.

Exactly when TEOTWAWKI will occur, however, seems a point of contention even among believers. While there are doomsday cults whose members believe that the end of the world will occur precisely at the stroke of midnight on December 31, 1999, other Messianic groups have different ideas. In fact, many Christians point out that even Jesus said, "No one knows the hour." William Miller, 19th-century Adventist founder, predicted the end of the world would occur by cleansing fire between March 21, 1843, and March 21, 1844. Oops.

The Catholic Church, however, takes a different stance. According to Pope John Paul II, Y2K is a good time for spiritual reflection on the symbolic teachings of the Bible. The concept of symbolism is key here. In fact, it may be the most important lesson about Y2K doomsday predictions.

Prophecies and Predictions

The Bible's not the only source of new millennium prophecies and predictions. Many who believe that Y2K will be TEOTWAWKI use sources such as the 16th-century seer Nostradamus, the 20th-century psychic Edgar Cayce, and current prophets like Robert Ghost Wolf, to support their cases.

Others look to more ancient sources, such as Hopi prophecies of the Fifth World and the Mayan calendar's dating of the apocalypse. Did these ancients have a better way of knowing, similar to psychic intuition, and, if so, should we be paying closer attention?

Let's take a look at some of these prophecies and predictions and see what keys they hold for us today.

What Exactly Did Nostradamus Predict?

The thing about the predictions of Nostradamus (1503–1566) is that they're so, well, obscure. Written in four-line verse forms called quatrains in the mid-16th century, Nostradamus's prophecies are almost Sphinx-like in their mystery. Let's look, by way of illustration, at one such quatrain, and what some interpreters have to say about it.

> Rain, famine, war, in Persia not stopped
> Faith too grand will betray the Monarch
> By the end, in France it starts
> Secret Omen for he who is of the Three Fates

What do Nostradamus's interpreters say about these lines? They believe they point to the Shah of Iran and the revolution that occurred in Iran in 1978 that overthrew him.

This section, in fact, is one of three that together are referred to as predicting "the Three Antichrists." According to Nostradamus's interpreters, the first Antichrist is Napoleon, the second is Hitler, and the third could be construed possibly to be Saddam Hussein.

If so, does Nostradamus predict TEOTWAWKI after these three Antichrists have appeared? Here's a quatrain that some believe supports that idea:

> 20 years of the reign of the Moon pass
> 7000 years another holds his monarchy
> When sun resumes his days pass
> When accomplished and finishes my Prophecy

This verse, however, and the following, point to TEOTWAWKI in 2005, if the interpreters have got their math right:

> Antichrist 3 very soon annihilated
> 20 & 7 years shall last his war
> The heretics dead, captured, exiled
> Human body Red Sea, gray drizzled earth

If Saddam's war lasted "20 & 7 years," it would end in 2005.

Nostradamus did predict that after his own death, his own tomb would be ransacked, and that one of the participants would die by gunshot the next day. Nostradamus even seems to be discussing the Holocaust in portions of his predictive quatrains.

329

Still, as we said when we began, these verses are by their nature hard to pin down. While it's easy to attach meaning to them after the fact, we're not saying that the interpreters are wrong about the meanings they've attached. But no one gets it right 100 percent of the time. For an example, let's look at 20th-century psychic Edgar Cayce.

Edgar Cayce and the New Millennium

Edgar Cayce (1877–1945), also known as the "sleeping prophet," was a Christian mystic and the founder of the Association for Research and Enlightenment (A.R.E.) in Virginia Beach. Cayce's nickname came about because he would lie down on his couch, close his eyes, and then dictate what he was discovering on the "other side." Cayce and his disciples kept scrupulous and detailed accounts of all of his sessions, and he was approached by people all over the world to answer questions both personal and cosmic.

Many of Cayce's predictions for the 20th century, however, failed to come to pass, especially those of massive geographical shifts, including the Great Lakes emptying into the Gulf of Mexico, Japan sliding into the sea, and much of Europe and both coasts of America dropping into the ocean.

Time Capsule

Among the many areas of knowledge he explored, Edgar Cayce discussed a text called the *Akashic Records*, a sort of symbolic Book of Life into which the past, present, and future of all souls is written. In his trances, he would pass through a tunnel until he came to a sort of librarian, from whom he would request information on his current client. He would then pass the information on to the client. Like all his sessions, these were recorded, and are available through the Association for Research and Enlightenment (A.R.E.).

Now that some of his predictions have failed to live up to their expectations, Cayce's followers at the A.R.E. have taken a closer look at his other ones as well. His predictions about the new millennium, for example, included one that the period from 1958 to 1998 would be one of great global transformation, including the geographical cataclysms just mentioned.

Cayce's followers assert that global transformation is indeed occurring. In fact they say, the error is in waiting for some "'Big One' as evidence of 'changing times.'" Instead, they suggest, "It's time for us to wake up and realize that the changing times are happening *right now*. Our world, our civilization, and our individual lives are all undergoing dramatic personal and collective change. Yet, this is sometimes hard for us to recognize because the changes have not been a single event. They have been a process. Cayce's predictions for the future are not really about earthquakes; instead, they are about the fact that a new world is being born."

Sound intriguing? You can learn more about current interpretations of Edgar Cayce's predictions at the Web site **www.are-cayce.com/millen.htm**. For more new millennium Web sites, see Appendix B.

We agree that the world is in the process of change. Did Cayce predict just that? You be the judge.

Contemporary Voices: The Predictions of Robert Ghost Wolf

The prophecies of Native American Robert Ghost Wolf are so dire, we hope they're not true. Ghost Wolf says that he uses both metaphor and "left-brain logic" to arrive at his predictions, and he's worked with Hopi Elders to incorporate Hopi myth (which we'll be exploring in more detail in a few pages) into his theories. According to Ghost Wolf, the year 2000 is the latest the series of "earth changes" he outlines will occur.

Ghost Wolf predicts ocean storms and flooding, especially in the North Sea, which will in turn churn up long-buried toxic wastes and send them to Canada and Alaska, destroying what fisheries are left there.

In addition, he suggests, outbreaks of new forms of tuberculosis may reach epidemic proportions. The Ebola virus may cause widespread death, Ghost Wolf asserts, and life in "synthetic environmental conditions" will continue to take its toll. (See Chapter 24 for another take on these predictions.)

Ghost Wolf also believes that we'll be merging with the Photon Belt, giving rise to internal "Emotional Storms." "That which we have called the earth changes begin within ourselves as we are reflections of the earth," Ghost Wolf concludes.

These are but three of a long series of dire predictions that Ghost Wolf outlines in his books *Last Cry (Wolf Lodge Cultural Foundation, 1997)* and *Winds of Changes (Wolf Lodge Cultural Foundation, 1998)*. How good are Ghost Wolf's predictions? His prophecy that "1998 will be particularly devastating for Japan, England, and Central America," is at least partially true if we look at the collapse of the yen in Japan and the destructive hurricane Mitchin Central America. Note, however, that it wasn't a particularly bad year for the U.K. So here's another outcome to debate: "Sometime between 1998 and 1999, the U.S. government as we now know it will collapse and no longer be." Certainly, the impact of the impeachment proceedings against President Clinton will be debated far into the 21st century.

Let's hope Ghost Wolf's wrong. And let's look at the source of some of his wisdom: the ancient Hopi predictions.

Ancient Voices: Hopi and Mayan Predictions

Despite their relative geographic proximity, the Hopi and the Mayan have delivered their new millennium predictions to us in two very different ways. The Hopi predictions are based on word of mouth, while the Mayan predictions come to us from the Mayan calendar, a sophisticated system of analyzing time cycles.

What these two ancient prophecies do have in common, however, is their apocalyptic vision. Are the Hopi and the Mayan predicting TEOTWAWKI? Once again, you be the judge.

Emergence to the Fifth World: Hopi Prophecies

The Hopi people, who continue to flourish in northwestern Arizona, are the holders of an ancient oral tradition, passed down from elder to elder throughout the generations.

The Hopi are widely believed to be among the descendants of the Ancient Ones (you may know them by their Navajo misnomer "Anasazi") who prospered in the Four Corners area many hundreds of years ago.

Frank Waters' *The Book of the Hopi* (Viking, 1985) was the first book to record the Hopi prophecy. Note that, unlike the quatrains of Nostradamus, there's nothing mysterious about what's written here. In fact, the Hopi predictions are notable for their specificity and clarity.

According to Hopi prophecy, nine signs will herald the end of the Fourth World and the beginning of the Fifth World. Further, if we take Hopi prophecy at its word, all nine signs have now occurred. Here are the nine signs. See if you can identify them. We'll give you the most common interpretations after this list. The quotations come from Martin Gasheseoma's "White Feather, Bear Clan," which we've taken from the website, http://www.dreamscape.com/morgana/pan.htm.

➤ First Sign: The coming of "white-skinned men . . . who took the land that was not theirs and who struck their enemies with thunder."

➤ Second Sign: "The coming of spinning wheels filled with voices."

➤ Third Sign: "A strange beast like a buffalo but with great long horns will overrun the land in large numbers."

➤ Fourth Sign: "The land will be crossed by snakes of iron."

➤ Fifth Sign: "The land shall be crisscrossed by a giant spider's web."

➤ Sixth Sign: "The land shall be crisscrossed with rivers of stone that make pictures in the sun."

➤ Seventh Sign: "The sea (will turn) black, and many living things (will die) because of it."

➤ Eighth Sign: "Many youth (will) wear their hair long like our people, (and will) come and join the tribal nations, to learn our ways and wisdom."

➤ Ninth sign: "You will hear of a dwelling-place in the heavens, above the earth, that shall fall with a great crash. It will appear as a blue star. Very soon after this, the ceremonies of the Hopi people will cease."

Any ideas? Here are some common interpretations for these signs. Compare them with your own and see if you agree or disagree.

➤ First Sign: Self-explanatory, except perhaps for the guns ("thunder").

➤ Second Sign: Covered wagons

➤ Third Sign: Longhorn cattle

➤ Fourth Sign: Railroad tracks

➤ Fifth Sign: Power and phone lines

➤ Sixth Sign: Roads (and, in the West, the mirages that appear on them)

➤ Seventh Sign: Oil spills

➤ Eighth Sign: Hippies

➤ Ninth Sign: The comet Hale-Bopp? Or . . . ?

Hopi prophecy goes on to say that after all nine signs have occurred, the Blue Kachina, a representative of a blue star that will soon appear, will remove his mask as he dances in the plaza. The white man will go to war, causing great destruction and fire, but the Hopi will be safe. After all the destruction, the Hopi will begin to rebuild, and then Pahana (the "White Brother") will return, bringing the dawn of the Fifth World and planting his seeds of wisdom into Hopi hearts.

Ask Spaceship Earth

No one is certain who "Pahana" might be. While he's called the "White Brother," no white man or group yet has passed the traditional Hopi test that will reveal Pahana. According to prophecy, however, Pahana will "return from the east." The Hopi are waiting.

The Mayan Calendar: Does It Pinpoint the End of the World?

Oh, those amazing Mayans. Thousands of years ago, they created complex calendars based on their astronomical observations. But that wasn't all. Using these calendars as a basis of time, they designated a period called a *Great Cycle*, but until recently, Mayan scholars were at a loss as to exactly what a great cycle represented.

Speaking Y2K

The **Great Cycle** is one of the basic concepts of the ancient Mayan calendar. It represents 5125.36 years according to the Gregorian calendar we use now.

We won't give you all the math, but a man named J. Eric S. Thompson eventually concluded that the current cycle will end December 21st, 2012. So, is *that* TEOTWAWKI?

Actually, not at all. John Major Jenkins, writing in the December 1994–January 1995 issue of *Mountain Astrologer,* discovered that what's most striking about this moment astronomically is that the darkest part of the Milky Way will appear, from Earth's vantage point, to be a dark pathway. Further, this conjunction happens only once every 5125.36 years.

Symbolically, such a conjunction would have had enormous meaning for an astronomy-based society like the Mayans. The "opening of the dark path" could mean people might be swayed to the Mayan equivalent of the dark side. In a larger symbolic sense, it could even mean TEOTWAWKI—and the beginning of a new world.

What's truly amazing is that Mayan astronomers, using their mathematical calendar system, could pinpoint this event with such accuracy. But, while the winter solstice of 2012 heralds an unusual astronomical event—and astonishing forecasting prowess by an ancient society—it's not TEOTWAWKI.

Earth Changes: Our Magnetic Shifts

You probably don't give it much thought, but the earth's current magnetic configuration is called a dipole; that is, a pair of poles. Why do we bring this up at all? Because recent discoveries have found that this may not have always the case—and it may not be again in the near future.

If, for example, millions of years ago four or even eight polar magnetic fields existed, the continents would all have been naturally grouped around the equator. (Don't ask us why. This is complicated stuff.) It therefore follows that if a magnetic shift occurred again, the land masses would shift as well.

Some suggest that magnetic shifts are already wreaking havoc with the earth, and point to increases in both earthquake and volcanic activity over the past few years. While some predict an apocalypse of the scale predicted by Robert Ghost Wolf, others feel a polar shift may instead provide the opportunity for humans to work together to meet the crisis.

What all of these visions have in common is a forecast of change. The question is whether the change is the unfolding drama suggested by Edgar Cayce's A.R.E. followers, or the unexpected cataclysm predicted by others. If we all tap into our psychic intuition, perhaps we can come up with some answers of our own.

Is the New Millennium a Renaissance of Intuition?

In past generations, only a few mystics were thought to have the gift of intuition, or "second sight," as it was often called. As we approach the 21st century, more and more people are going to be guiding their lives by spiritual principles. We don't mean a dogmatic religion per se, although it can include that. Rather, we're talking about people who feel guided by a "Higher Knowledge," "Divine Wisdom," "God/Goddess," or whatever they choose to call it.

No matter what they call it, what these people share is a purpose in their lives that has to do with a greater good. You, too can experience this; this guidance will come from your own inner voice or intuition.

How Psychic Intuition Helps Us Make the Millennium Shift

The Chinese symbol for crisis consists of a symbol that is a combination of danger and opportunity. The danger is what the crisis has brought up; the opportunity is to use the crisis to move in a new direction.

It should come as no surprise that you feel "stuck" when you're in place A and you want to be in place Z, yet many people feel terribly frustrated when this happens. That's because the leap between A and Z seems too wide, or the path from one to the other seems covered or unclear.

When this happens to you, it may be helpful to consider what *small* step you can take to at least get on the path. Pay attention to what brings you joy, happiness, or even a ray of hope. This is often your intuition's way of leading you to the path that's going in the right direction. When your feeling is inviting, open, and positive, you'll know it's time to take action.

Trusting your intuition is listening to the voice of the Spirit within you, which is precisely what all the people in the earlier examples were doing. Just as listening to their inner voices helped them define the future, listening to your inner voice can assist you in finding your path and restoring balance in your life.

Crossing the Border

No one would disagree with the statement that we're living in a time of rapid change. Only a few generations ago, very few questioned the status quo, our religious and political leaders defined our values, and we got married, had children, stayed married, and remained in the same job for most of our lives until we retired. Today, the belief systems we grew up with are being constantly questioned.

The years leading up to the new millennium have been fraught with change, so it should come as no surprise that as we cross the border into the year 2000, we'll experience even more.

Still, this constant change makes us full of anxiety. We question our decisions. Are they good or bad, right or wrong? Because most of us don't rely on our minister or rabbi (or heaven forbid, our president!) to define our moral values any more, whenever we face a transition we question ourselves. *Is this (job, relationship, move, religion, school) right for me? How do I make these decisions?*

Whenever you make any decision, you have to get information. If you were trying to make a decision about a job change, for example, you would find out things like:

➤ What's the salary?

➤ Who's my boss?

➤ What's the job description?

These questions are easy to answer. But how do you answer those trickier ones that you can't ask anyone, such as:

➤ Will I like my job?

➤ Is this the right career move for me?

➤ Will I get along with my boss and co-workers?

This is where intuition can help. We often ignore its clues, so we'd like to provide you with some ways to use it. The following questions can help you approach the seemingly unanswerable questions about decisions armed with answers.

When you think about your career move, how do you feel? Do you feel "up" and happy, excited about the new opportunity, or do you feel mildly depressed and lethargic? Those are intuitive clues! Do you experience any body sensations associated with this decision? Is there a current of excitement that runs through your body as you anticipate accepting the job, or do you have that awful "pit in the bottom of your stomach" feeling? These are also ways your psychic intuition system can guide you. Each of you will find the special way your own particular intuition speaks.

We often ignore and push aside these clues, signs, and messages from our intuition because we've been taught to view them as "not logical" or "making no sense." But as we approach the new millennium, we'll have to rely more and more on this sixth sense to assist us with our decision-making if we're to successfully "cross the border."

No Looking Back

As you move into the 21st century, you'll find you have many lessons to learn. Your task as a spiritual being is to become a student of love. In *Hands of Light (Bantam Doubleday: 1993),* Barbara Ann Brennan writes, "Love is the face and body of the

Universe, the stuff of which we are made. Love is the experience of being whole and connected to Universal Divinity."

Similarly, the Dalai Lama, who is considered the 14th incarnation of the Buddha of Love, says that love is the natural state of the universe. Because we've caused wars and massive destruction on our planet through hate and misunderstanding, we now have a role to play in order to co-create a world where the dire predictions of more bloodshed and environmental devastation do not occur.

It's important to remember that we all have free will, and that the roles that we play as individuals *do* matter. We need to understand that we're all in this together. Our ability to love, forgive, empathize, and have compassion for others is a starting place for finally experiencing peace on our planet.

A Thousand Years from Now

Web sites exploring life a thousand years from now suggest such things as not just a global political entity, but a universal one—not unlike *Star Trek*'s United Federation of Planets—as well as people literally living in the clouds and hybrid races co-existing peacefully side by side.

Why not tap into your own psychic power and imagine what the world may be like a thousand years from now? It's as simple as the following exercise:

1. Quiet your mind. Take a few deep breaths. Let go of any worries for the time being.

2. Focus your attention on your breathing. Concentrate.

3. Ask your intuition the question, "What will the world be like in a thousand years?"

4. Allow information to come into your mind. Receive it. Don't push it. You may receive this information in words, images, symbols, dialogue, physical sensations, feelings, and/or ideas. However you receive it is right for you.

5. You may want to write down the information you receive. If you're not clear, you may ask your intuition for more information. Pay attention to all of your impressions.

What do you think? Will we have a peaceful planet where we all live in harmony? Will we have destroyed our planet through ecological neglect? Perhaps a new spiritual renaissance will have occurred. Maybe we will have been taken over by an alien species by then!

The information you're seeking is more than a thousand years away, so of course there's no way you can prove your accuracy at this time. Maybe you'll want to add your insights to the growing number of prognosticators. Who knows? You may be the next Nostradamus!

When you tap into your psychic intuition, you're getting in touch with your greater self—as well as the psychic power all around you. You can use this power to explore both your own future and the future that awaits us all in the new millennium.

The Least You Need to Know

➤ A number of different religions and societies include end-of-the-world predictions—but none specifically for Y2K.

➤ Nostradamus's quatrain predictions are notoriously hard to interpret.

➤ Edgar Cayce's predictions of geographical shifts in this century have gone largely unproved.

➤ Robert Ghost Wolf's apocalyptic predictions are already being proven wrong.

➤ The ancient voices of the Hopi and the Mayan may tell us more than more modern voices when it comes to new millennium predictions.

➤ Developing your psychic intuition can help you make the millennium shift.

Part 6

In Your Hands: Palmistry

Palm readers do far more than read individual palms—they can look at the palms of generations of people and note common events and challenges in their hands. After an introduction to palm reading, we'll explore what we think some of those events and challenges may be for the new millennium.

Chapter 22

A Hand-y Map to the Future

In This Chapter

➤ There's a lot more to palmistry than lines

➤ Your fingers are characters

➤ Your lines are plots

➤ Your mounts are where the action is

➤ Putting together the map of your hand

You've probably heard of your life, head, and heart lines. You may even know where on your hand these lines are. But you may not know that there's a lot more to palmistry than these lines: Your fingers and your thumb, as well as every area of your palm, called *mounts,* have a hand in the story of you.

More than that, the hands of a generation provide a key to that generation's particular story. In this part, we'll be introducing you to the ancient science of palmistry. Our expert is Robin Gile, who's been a professional palm reader for over 20 years and is the co-author of *The Complete Idiot's Guide to Palmistry* (Alpha Books, 1999). The wonderful palmistry instructional drawings in chapters 22 through 24 were made by Kathleen Edwards.

What Is Palmistry?

Palmistry, or *chiromancy*, is a way of studying the macrocosm of the self through the microcosm of the hand. It may be helpful if you think of your hand as a mirror, reflecting everything about you. And, like you, your hand changes to reflect what's going on in your life.

You can think of palmistry as a way to help you understand yourself and others. Because your hand is unique, it paints a clear picture of who you are and the way you do things. Even your doctor will tell you that your hand reveals a great deal about you—but a palm reader can tell you still more.

The Hand as a Map

Learning to read the map of the hand takes years and years of practice, but with a key to guide you, you'll have a good start. We recommend *The Complete Idiot's Guide to Palmistry*, of course, as an in-depth guide to reading this map, but we can give you an overview here.

Like any map, the map of your hand has a key for understanding what each area represents.

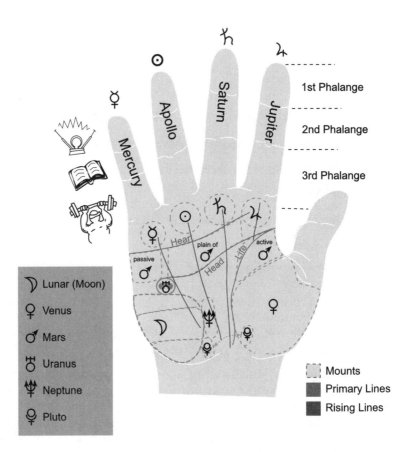

The first thing you'll probably notice is that everything in the hand is named for a planet. That's because the planets are in turn named for Roman gods. Classically trained young men (this was before young women were allowed to go to school) immediately understood what each god represented.

The next thing you'll see is that there's not anything in the hand that's not taken into account when it comes to reading palms. That's no accident: The entire microcosm of the hand represents the entire macrocosm of the self. Just as one strand of your DNA is a key to your larger self, your palm holds a key as well.

Now that you've got your map, are you ready to learn what each area of the hand represents? Let's take at look at the story of you that's in your hands.

The Strength of the Thumb

Nothing, repeat nothing, is more important to your character than your thumb. That's because this most revealing digit reflects:

➤ Your willpower

➤ Your generosity

➤ Your flexibility (or stubbornness)

➤ Your ability to hold onto a goal

➤ Your subtlety

➤ Your quality of thought

➤ Your self-doubt

Ask Spaceship Earth

Here are two important things to remember about reading palms:

1. It takes two hands. That's right. Palm readers look at both your hands to tell the story of you.

2. Your hands change as you do. Lines come and go, mounts rise and fall. Watch your hands for a while, and you'll see what we mean.

Wow! Palm readers look at everything from the length of the thumb, to the shape of the thumb's tip, to the thumb's *set,* to the relative length of the thumb's *phalanges* to discover your potentials in these areas. We can't give you more than an overview here, but here goes:

➤ The *set* of the thumb (or any finger) is a term for where on the hand the finger literally sits. In the case of the thumb, for example, it may begin at the wrist, or it may appear to start higher up on the side of the hand. A thumb that starts closer to the wrist is called *low-set.* One that starts higher up is called *high-set.*

➤ The *phalanges* of the thumb (or any finger) refer to the three sections separated by the finger's joints. In the case of the thumb, the third phalange is also the *mount of Venus*, an area that shows how much love you've got to give. The first phalange of the thumb, the one with the nail, is an indication of your will; the second, middle phalange, is the location of your logic; and the third, the lowest one, which is also the mount of Venus, reveals your capacity for love. The following illustration shows you which phalange is which.

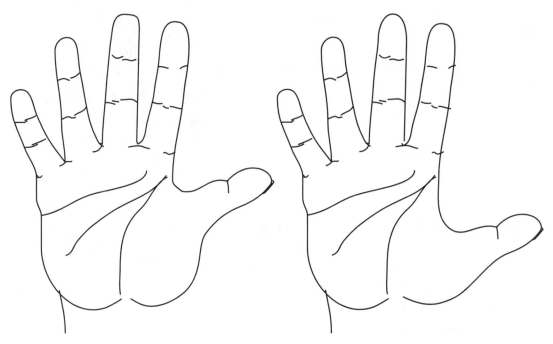

Left to right: a high-set thumb, a low-set thumb.

The first phalange of the thumb reveals your will; the second, your logic; and the third, your capacity for love.

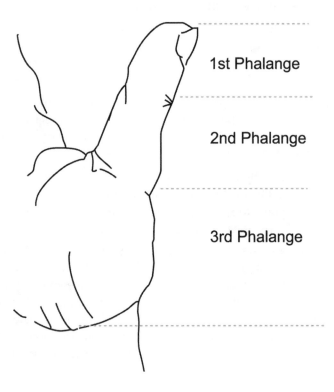

1st Phalange

2nd Phalange

3rd Phalange

When you look at your thumb, you'll want to determine what's dominant. Is your thumb long or short? Which phalange is longest? Does its tip have any flexibility when you try to push it back? Here's a list of key words for some of those possibilities:

Thumb Aspect	Key Word
Long	Independent
Short	Easy-going
Average	Well-adjusted
Longest first phalange	Willful
Longest second phalange	Thinker
Longest third phalange	Sentimental
Bends back easily	Flexible
Doesn't bend back	Stubborn

Then there's the shape of the thumb tip itself. The following illustration can help you determine the shape of your thumb tip, and the table will help you see just what that shape says about you.

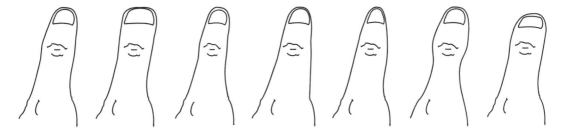

The many variations of thumb shapes.

Shape of Thumb Tip	Characteristics
Square	Practical, down-to-earth, routinized
Spatulate	Hands-on, can-do, everyday person
Conic	Quick-thinking, sensitive, artistic
Pointed	Intuitive, dreamy, introspective

The last aspect of the thumb we're going to look at here is what's called the *angle of generosity*. This space between your thumb and Jupiter (pointer) finger, measured when your hand is lying at rest, reveals how you relate to others.

The angle of generosity is a reflection of your giving nature. The ideal angle of generosity (top) is practical and giving, but won't be taken advantage of. A narrow angle (middle) can indicate a tendency to hang on to things, while a wider angle (bottom) can indicate too much generosity.

Speaking Y2K

The **angle of generosity**, measured between the thumb and the Jupiter (pointer) finger, shows how generous you are.

The wider the angle of generosity, the more giving you are. You should measure this angle when your thumb's in a natural position—don't try to stretch it or hug it close to the hand. If your thumb naturally hugs the finger next to it, you probably prefer to hang on to things rather than share them, while if it naturally forms a wide angle—90° or more—you may be too giving for your own good.

A Tour of the Fingers

Each of your other four fingers is a character, too, and palm readers look at everything from which finger is *dominant* to the length of each finger's phalanges, as well as the individual finger's set and angle, to tell the story of you. Just which finger is which, though? To find out, take a look at the following illustration.

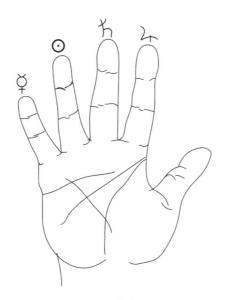

A who's who of the fingers. Mercury ☿ is the little finger; Apollo ☉ is the ring finger; Saturn ♄ is the middle finger; Jupiter ♃ is the index finger.

Just as your thumb is divided into phalanges that relate to specific areas, your fingers' phalanges also cover certain territories. The first phalange of each finger (the one with the nail) relates to that finger's intuitive sense. The second phalange (the middle one) is concerned with its mental capacities. And the third phalange (the one closest to the palm) is the area of that finger's materiality and groundedness.

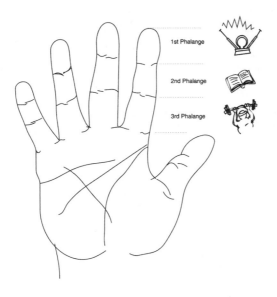

The phalanges of the fingers.

347

Next, there's the matter of the fingers' tips. Use the following illustration to determine your fingertip shape, and then check the table to find out just what that says about you.

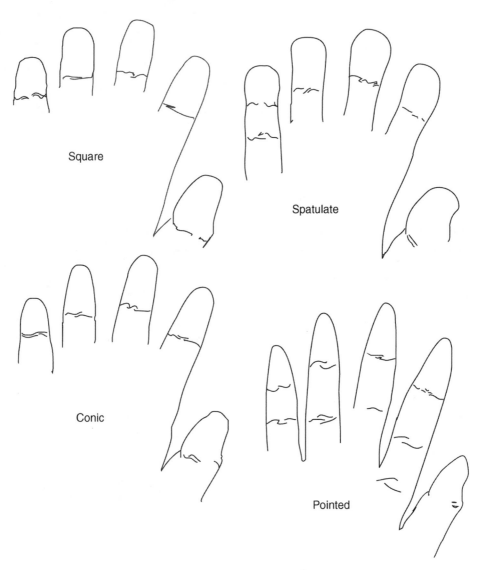

Fingertip shapes: square tips, spatulate tips, conic tips, pointed tips.

Fingertip Shape	Indications
Square	Practical, routinized, down-to-earth
Spatulate	Hands-on, can-do, fixer
Conic	Quick-thinking, intuitive, artistic
Pointed	Dreamer, sensitive, psychic
Mixed (different types together)	Changeable

The last thing we'll look at is how the fingers stand up to each other. The average hand's fingers will look like the ones in the next illustration—but very few fingers actually do stack up this way. As we look at each finger individually, we'll discuss what it means if it's relatively longer or shorter than the "average" example.

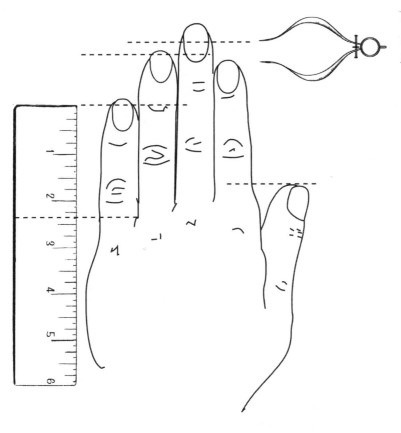

The fingers of an "average" hand. Your fingers will probably not be like this.

The Mercury Finger: The Communicator

Your Mercury, or little, finger is the area of communication and commerce. If it's longer than average, it can indicate someone who's "too clever by far," and if it's shorter than average, the person may prefer to stay close to home and those with whom he's familiar. An average-length Mercury finger is a good communicator, and adequate in the business world.

Another thing palm readers look at is the set of the fingers, especially the set of the Mercury finger, which is quite often found set lower on the hand. The following illustration shows you a low-set Mercury, which can indicate that one's childhood was economically or socially deprived in some way.

Evenly set fingers, plus a low-set Mercury and a high-set Saturn.

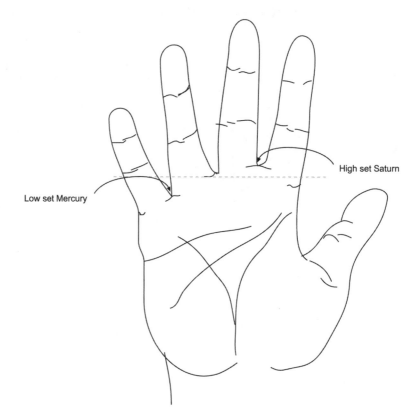

High set Saturn

Low set Mercury

Sometimes the Mercury finger sits farther away from the other fingers. This is called the *angle of eccentricity*, and indicates whether your behavior departs from what your society considers the norm.

You may also want to look at whether your Mercury finger's straight or leaning one way or the other, as listed in the following table.

Narrow space between Mercury and Apollo, balanced angles between fingers, wide angle of eccentricity.

Lean of Mercury	Indication
Straight	Honest, square, and true
Lean toward Apollo	Shrewd observer, tactful
Lean away from Apollo	Gentle eccentric
Extreme lean away from Apollo	Antisocial eccentric

The last thing to look at is which Mercury phalange is longest. Use the following table to find out what this says about you.

Longest Mercury Phalange	Indication
First (the one with the nail)	Intuitive, perceptive, sensitive to people
Second (the middle one)	Mentally active, the philosopher
Third (the bottom one)	Attention to appearance, works with material world

The Apollo Finger: The Creator

Your Apollo, or ring, finger is your artistic side. It's here you'll find your capacity for performance and your creativity. If your Apollo finger is long, you've got strong artistic tendencies and are probably a risk-taker as well, while if it's short, your interests lie in other areas. The average-length Apollo finger indicates someone who appreciates beauty but probably won't be artistically inclined himself.

Next, see if your Apollo is straight, or leans toward Mercury or Saturn. This angle indicates your taste in art or the things you collect. Then use the following table to find out what that says about you.

Lean of Apollo	Indication
Straight	Definite opinions about the arts
Lean toward Mercury	Collector of obscure things
Lean toward Saturn	Tastes that "go with the flow," follows popular opinions

Another aspect of the Apollo finger that palm readers look at is whether it's fleshy or thin. If your Apollo finger is full, you may be attracted to many areas of the arts, while if it's narrower, your scope may be narrower as well.

Now, let's look at the Apollo finger's phalanges. Which one is the longest? The following table indicates just what this says about your relationship with art and beauty.

Longest Apollo Phalange	Indication
First	Sensitive to art and beauty
Second	Love of detail and nuance
Third	Down-to-earth tastes

The Saturn Finger: The Lawmaker

Your Saturn, or middle, finger represents your structure, boundaries, and approach to law and order. If it's long, you may have a deliberate and serious nature, while if it's short, you may not have a great respect for the law. The average-length Saturn finger indicates someone whose relationship with authority is healthy without being extreme.

Next, look to see if your Saturn finger is straight or leans one way or the other. This shows how you feel about law and order, and you can use the following table to determine what your Saturn's lean says about your relationship to authority.

Lean of Saturn	Indication
Straight	Good relationship with authority
Lean toward Jupiter	Good personal discipline
Lean toward Apollo	The philosophical outlaw

Another thing to look for is whether your Saturn finger "stands alone," so to speak. Is the angle between your Saturn finger and Jupiter or Apollo more pronounced than the angles between the other fingers? If so, you may have a more pronounced need for privacy than other people.

Now, let's look at the Saturn phalanges. Which one is longest? This is an indication of how you see your relationship with authority. Use the following table to determine what your dominant Saturn phalange says about your Saturnian expression.

Longest Saturn Phalange	Indication
First	Appreciation for nuances of law and history
Second	A slow but steady and strong thinker
Third	Conservative dress and expression, acquisition of land or property

The Jupiter Finger: The Leader

Your Jupiter, or pointer, finger is the area of your leadership, sociability, and charisma. If your Jupiter finger is long, chances are you're a born leader, someone who just naturally goes to the head of the class. A shorter Jupiter finger indicates someone who is more cautious about attracting attention to herself, while the average-length Jupiter finger (and that's most of us) can either lead or follow, depending on the situation.

Another thing to explore is whether the angle of your Jupiter finger indicates sociability or a need for solitude. The greater the space (angle) between your Jupiter and your Saturn, the greater your need for isolation.

Next, look to see if your Jupiter finger is straight or leans in one direction or the other. Then use the following table to see what this says about your relationship to society.

Lean of Jupiter	Indication
Straight	Society's mainstream
Lean toward Saturn	Pragmatic, sticks with the status quo for self-protection
Lean away from Saturn	The revolutionary, traveling to the beat of a different drum

Last, take a look at your Jupiter finger's phalanges. Which one is longest? Use the following table to see what this says about your self-image.

Longest Jupiter Phalange	Indication
First	Headstrong, impulsive, sensitive
Second	Self-conscious, sometimes self-obsessive
Third	Appreciates the good things in life, has a unique sense of style and expression

Getting a Line on the Future

Now that you've learned a little bit about your fingers, it's time to move on to the lines in your hand. You've probably noticed that there are more than just life, heart, and head lines, and we'll take a look at the other lines on your hand, too, some of which are *rising lines* and others which can point to specific career capabilities.

Speaking Y2K

Rising lines start in the palm of the hand and point to a specific finger. They indicate added strength in that particular area.

We like to think of lines as the plots in your hand—the particular way your stories are unfolding. When palm readers look at lines, they explore just how deep and clear each line is, which is called a line's *quality*, as well as its curve and where it begins and ends.

Use the following illustration to find each of the lines of your hand. We'll discuss each line individually in the next sections.

Speaking Y2K

The **quality** of a line is an indication of the level of strength and vitality in that particular area of life. The deeper and more well-cut a line, the stronger its quality.

The Heart Line: The Story of Love

Your heart line, the uppermost of the three main lines on your hand, is an indication of the story of your love. Whom do you love? How do you love? And how do you show your love? All of these can be determined by various aspects of your heart line.

Heart lines begin on the edge of the percussion of the hand, under the Mercury finger. Heart lines end in a number of different places, from under the Jupiter finger to somewhere beneath the Saturn finger. Where the heart line ends is an indication of how you love.

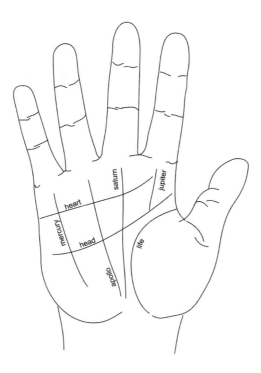

The lines of your hand.

Heart Line End	Indication of How You Love
Under Saturn	Materialistic
Between Saturn and Jupiter	Idealistic
Under Jupiter	Supportive
Connects to head line	Emotional need for "best friend" of same sex
Under without reaching finger	Direct emotional approach

The deeper the heart line, the more emotional a person is likely to be, while if a heart line is chained, broken, or shallow, a person's love may change with the weather.

The curve of the heart line is an indication of how directly (or indirectly) you approach matters of the heart: The straighter the heart line, the more direct and matter-of-fact the approach.

The Head Line: It's All in Your Head

Your head line crosses your hand at about the center of the palm (though it seldom goes all the way across). It's an indication of the nature of your thinking.

355

Palm readers look first at where your head line begins, as this shows how long your thinking was influenced by your family. Most head lines (as does the head line in the following illustration) naturally begin connected to the life line at the start, and some chaining between these two lines will often continue until you left home.

The head line.

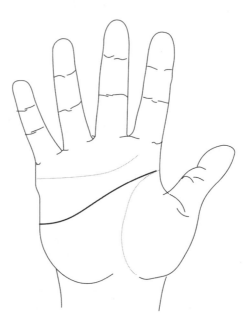

Out of Time

Head lines that start under the Jupiter finger indicate those who are very independent. In fact, these people may even be foolhardy, insisting on making every decision themselves. They simply can't accept others' input—no matter how good that input may be.

The length of the head line has nothing to do with intelligence. Rather, where the head line ends is a good indication of how quickly you process information and how you feel about dealing with details. A head line that goes all the way across the hand may be too detail-oriented, for example, while one that ends under the Saturn finger will have a more material focus. Sometimes the head line curves down toward the lunar mount (which we'll be discussing in a few pages). This indicates a vivid imagination.

Just as the quality of the heart line shows the depth of your emotions, the quality of the head line shows the intensity of your thought, and the deeper and more gently curved the head line, the more you're going to think things through. In addition, lines that branch from the head line are common. In fact, a forked head line end is an indication of balance.

The Life Line: Quality of Life

Your life line is the line that curves gently around your thumb. Let's make clear right now that the length of your life line has nothing to do with the length of your life. If this were the case, we would have lost Robin years and years ago, but he's still very much with us, writing this section.

What your life line does show is your strength, the quality of your life—and how much travel you've done and may do in your lifetime. The deeper and more clearly cut the life line, the stronger your energy and quality of life.

Ask Spaceship Earth

Most people assume that their life line is about the length of their life, but this is not necessarily the case. Other subtleties—and a large number of exceptions—void this assumption.

Time Capsule

The life line may arc out widely as it encircles the thumb, or it may stay closer to the base of the thumb. This is an indication of your sense of adventure, or, to put it another way, whether you'll ever move far from the home where you began. An extremely tight-hugging life line, in fact, can indicate someone who not only never leaves the old homestead, but inherits the family business as well.

Little lines around the life line are travel lines, though if you travel for a living, they may not be as noticeable as on someone who doesn't travel very often. Actual relocation lines are usually stronger, and appear as branchings off the life line.

Of course, there's much more to these three main lines than we can give you here. For more detail, we once again refer you to *The Complete Idiot's Guide to Palmistry*.

Rising Lines: Highlighting Your Strong Points

Rising lines begin in the palm and rise (point) toward specific fingers. In fact, these lines share those fingers' names, and their presence can help point to your strengths and weaknesses, and even to career possibilities.

Most people don't have rising lines to all of the fingers. Saturn lines are common, for example, while Jupiter lines are not. What does each rising line indicate? Use the following table to see where your strengths may lie.

Rising Line	Indication
Mercury	A talent for communication and commerce
Apollo	An interest in the arts
Saturn	Your opportunities for authority
Jupiter	A taste for the spiritual

Special Lines: Is Your Career in Your Hands?

A few other lines can show special talents or interests. Use the following illustration to see if you have any of these markings, and then check the table to find out just what these markings have to say about you.

Mark	Indication
The Camera's Eye	A knack for the visual
The Girdle of Venus	Patron of the arts
Via Lascivia	Love of carnality
Mark of the Teacher	A gift for teaching
Medical stigmata	A gift for the healing professions

Other markings on your hands include everything from dots to fingerprints. For more about these markings, see *The Complete Idiot's Guide to Palmistry.*

Your Mounts: Where the Action Is

Just as fingers are like characters and lines are like plots, *mounts* are like settings—the places where the action of your life unfolds. There is a mount under each finger, which shares that finger's name and energy, and the rest of your palm is divided into mounts as well. The next illustration shows you just where on your palm you can find each mount. You may want to tab this page for easy reference as your read about each mount.

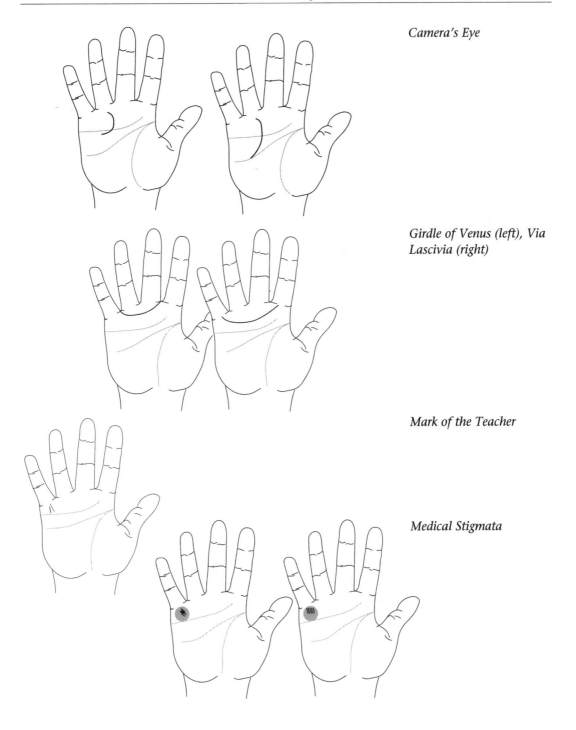

Camera's Eye

Girdle of Venus (left), Via Lascivia (right)

Mark of the Teacher

Medical Stigmata

Special marks on the hand.

Finger Mounts

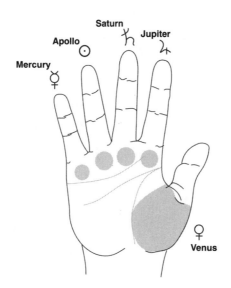

Palm Mounts

Lunar Mount

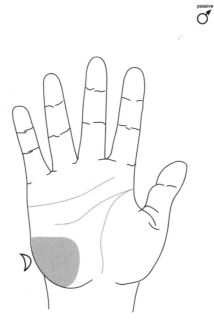

The mounts of the palm.

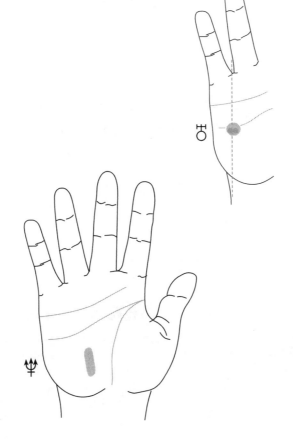

Mount of Uranus

Mount of Neptune

Mount of Pluto

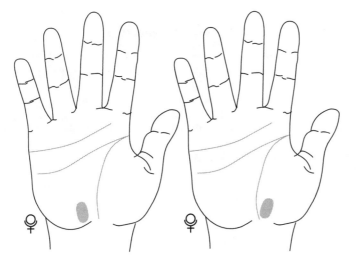

Mounts are measured by their inflation or deflation, as well as by markings that may appear on them. Which of your mounts seems to be the strongest—that is, the most prominent or clearly marked? That's the area of your life where you concentrate your energies.

The Mount of Mercury: Healer, Teacher, Cameraperson, Spy

The mount of Mercury, beneath the Mercury finger, is the area of your communication, teaching, healing, intelligence, relationships, and children. An inflated Mercury mount means you're a good communicator as well as a good businessperson. A less-emphasized Mercury often indicates a much quieter person, some-one who's less drawn to people.

Markings on Mercury include some of those we discussed earlier when we talked about special lines.

The Mount of Apollo: Where Your Talents Lie

The mount of Apollo, beneath the Apollo finger, is the area of your creativity and self-expression. An inflated Apollo mount indicates someone who's definitely creative in some way, but most of us have Apollo mounts that are neither inflated nor deflated—because most of us keep our creativity on the back burner much of the time. If the Apollo mount is diminished, in other words, it doesn't necessarily indicate a lack of talent. A rising line on the mount of Apollo, however, does indicate a strong specific creative discipline—and it's very desirable.

The Mount of Saturn: Dad, Grandpa—and Your Boss, Too

The mount of Saturn, beneath the Saturn finger, is usually not inflated, and in fact on most people is diminished. This is actually good news, as an inflated Saturn mount can indicate an obsessive nature. This is the area of your duties and diligence, and you probably know some party pooper who's got a little too much Saturn.

Among the marks you may find on your Saturn mount can be a cross that indicates your father, husband, or even your boss, or a square that shows that you work with land or property in some way. Marks on the Saturn mount can also appear when you're dealing with a bureaucracy or similar large organization.

The Mount of Jupiter: Spirituality, Strength— and Your Pets

The mount of Jupiter, beneath the Jupiter finger, is the area of your character and charisma. It's here you'll find your self-confidence and ambition—as well as your pets. If your mount of Jupiter is inflated, you're probably already leading something— whether it's your church or your company. A weaker Jupiter mount doesn't necessarily indicate a lack of physical strength, but decisiveness isn't always the person's strong point.

Among the marks you'll find on the Jupiter mount, the more interesting ones have to do with pets. Your animals are found on your hand as small lines on the side of the hand beneath the Jupiter finger, and you can use the following illustration to discover everyone from your earthworm farm to your horses.

Animals on the hand.

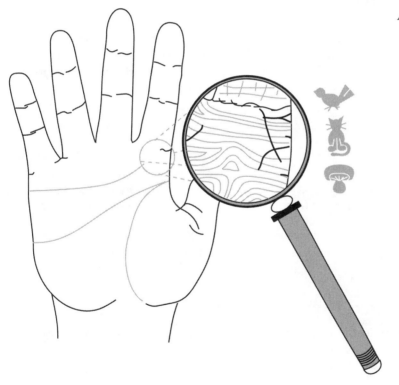

A particularly long animal marking can indicate that you are—or will be—a breeder of animals or involved with them to a great degree. If there are also medical stigmata, you may well be a veterinarian.

The Mounts of Mars: Anger and Passivity in the Hand

Mars, the planet of anger and aggression, represents three areas of the palm: active Mars, passive Mars, and the plain of Mars. You can locate each of these areas on the illustration you tabbed a few pages back.

➤ *Active Mars*, located between your thumb and your head line, is the mount where you'll find your anger, and in fact, this mount rises and falls (that is, inflates and deflates) on a regular basis. When you're getting angry, your active Mars will rise with your anger.

➤ *Passive Mars*, located on the opposite side of the palm underneath the heart line, under the mount of Mercury, is the area where you hold your own against the world. Most of us have a rather deflated passive Mars, and that's too bad, as this is the area where you meet everyone else and stand up for what you believe in. It *is*, however, possible to increase your passive Mars, because this area, like everything about your hand, can change.

➤ You can think of *the plain of Mars*, between active Mars and passive Mars and the head line and the heart line, as your private proving ground. This is the area where you deal with the world on a daily basis, from insult to injury, and from conviction to the light of day. If you've got a streak of vengeance, you'll find it here in the form of a dot or short independent line.

Ask Spaceship Earth

If you're a naturally high-tempered sort, indicated by an active Mars that's somewhat inflated in its natural state, you can keep an eye on your active Mars and avoid unnecessary outbursts you may later regret.

Other lines come into the plain of Mars and meet the world, so if your rising lines change, it's often here that they will. A rising line to Mercury may suddenly turn and branch off to Apollo, for example, meaning that the communication's going off in a creative direction. Or, a rising line to Saturn may end here, suggesting you're not afraid to challenge authority when necessary.

The Mount of Venus: How Much Love You've Got to Give

The Mount of Venus probably sounds familiar, and it should, because, as you may recall, this is also the third phalange of the thumb. This is the area of your own particular love, and if you've got a lot of love to give, your mount of Venus will be strong and full.

When you're feeling blue, in fact, your mount of Venus will appear a little "blue," too, while if it's red, you may be feeling particularly passionate. You can even look at your new lover's mount of Venus to see if it's more than mere lust: If it's true love, white dots will appear there, promising long-lasting love and happiness. Of course, you should both sport these white dots!

The Lunar Mount: The Ability to Receive, Your Mother, and Your Creativity

Opposite Venus on the lower part of the hand is the mount of the Moon. This area of your deepest psyche is where you'll find everything concerning your feminine side (just as Mars is your masculine side)—from your imagination to your mother and sisters, your subconscious to your ability to receive and nurture.

When the mount of the Moon is inflated, and, in addition, the head line drifts toward the lunar mount, you may have an over-active imagination. If you have this configuration, you already know the scenarios you conjure up when someone doesn't call when he said he would. Less lunar mount can indicate someone calm and realistic, though she won't be terribly imaginative.

Latecomers: The Mounts of Uranus, Neptune, and Pluto

Not all palm readers discuss the mounts of Uranus, Neptune, and Pluto. These mounts are harder to find, and may not even appear on all hands. But they're all very much a part of modern life, so we'd like to take a moment to discuss each at least a little.

The mount of Uranus is located at the conjunction of the passive Mars, the lunar mount, and the plain of Mars. It's here you'll find your idealism and inventiveness, including how you use the media. We like to think of Uranus as the mount of modern styles.

The mount of Neptune can be found where the lunar mount approaches the lower center of the palm, and it's the area of psychic foundations and dreams. A strong mount of Neptune can indicate someone who's learned how to be practical about what may seem impractical to others—the innovative architect or engineer, for example.

Out of Time

If the head line heads toward the lunar mount, it can indicate an imaginative mind. There is a danger, if the line descends all the way into the lunar mount, that dreams may take precedence over reality. But this can be tempered by strong Saturn or Jupiter mounts and fingers, as well as by another branch of the head line that continues in a straighter direction.

The mount of Pluto is a shifting area of healing and transformation, as well as your karmic lessons and relationship with your siblings. Pluto is so karmic, you never know where in its area in the lower of the center palm it may show up, and it may be equally hard to determine why your Pluto mount appears as well. That's because we aren't always aware of our karmic lessons. But, if you pay attention to your Pluto mount when it shows up, you'll at least be aware that something karmic is going on.

Putting It All Together

Armed with this very brief overview of the hand, you're now equipped to take a good look at your own hand. For this purpose, we'd suggest a plain sheet of paper and something to draw with.

First, trace your hand onto the sheet of paper. You don't have to be a master artist to do this. After you've got a reasonable facsimile of your hand, draw in the major lines, which mounts seem inflated or deflated, and note where each finger's (including the thumb's) phalanges begin and end.

You can also put your hand onto your photocopier and use that image. Photocopiers actually do a rather good job of reproducing what a hand looks like, albeit in negative form.

Whether you have a drawing or a photocopy, you're now ready to go back through this chapter and find out what your hand reveals about you. You may be surprised by what you learn! Then get ready to find out in Chapters 23 and 24 how you and your extended family have got a hand in the transition to the new millennium.

The Least You Need to Know

➤ Most people know about the life, heart, and head lines, but there's much more to palmistry than lines.

➤ You can think of your fingers as characters, each representing an aspect of yourself.

➤ The lines on your hand are like story plots, sometimes just what you expect, sometimes turning unexpectedly.

➤ The mounts on your palm are the places where the action of your life unfolds.

➤ When you put together the map of your hand, you have a picture of yourself.

Chapter 23

The Imprint of Each Generation

−1940 −1960 − 1980 − 2000

In This Chapter

➤ A generation's future is in its hands

➤ 1921–1940: The conservative pragmatists

➤ 1941–1960: The revolutionaries

➤ 1961–1980: The conservative backlash

➤ 1981–2000: The cheerful eccentrics

➤ How to find a generation in its hands

We're all unique, and yet we all share certain things in common with our peers. Robin has looked at thousands and thousands of American hands, and one of the things he's been most struck by is just how similarly people of particular generations view and deal with the world around them.

In this chapter, we'll examine the hands of four generations of the century that's drawing to a close, and take a closer look at what these sets of 20th-century Americans have in common. But we won't stop there—we'll show you how you can learn to find a generation in its hands as well.

Every Generation's Hands Are Unique

The first thing to understand about the hands of any generation is that there are no hard and fast rules about where to look for the subtle differences that define a generation. For example, the Depression/World War II generation's acceptance of rules and boundaries can be found on their accentuated Saturn mounts, while the idealism of the current generation's children is an aspect of their strong Jupiter mounts.

Those same children share the Baby Boomer generation's full lunar and Venus mounts—but this characteristic skipped the generation born between 1961 and 1980.

Time Capsule

How is the 1961–1980 generation's lack of Moon manifesting itself? We Baby Boomers humbly propose that you listen to a generation's music. While we have a love of romance, lyrics, and harmony, our children seem to prefer cacophony and dissonance. Do our children's children's full lunar mounts suggest that they'll once again love "our" music? We hope so!

While it takes years of practice and hundreds of hands before you can start to correlate a particular generation's specialness, the fact remains that each generation's hands are unique. At the end of the chapter, we'll give you some tools to do some scientific studies of your own. But first, let's explore a thousand years of hands.

From Leonardo to the Borg

Leonardo da Vinci was a man centuries ahead of his time, and yet his hands still bore the characteristics of his generation: They were sensitive, idealistic, detail-oriented, spiritual, very intellectual, and pragmatic. It's possible Leonardo would have felt quite at home at the beginning of the 21st century because he shares both the Baby Boomer's idealism and today's children's pragmatism.

It's also possible you've never heard of the Borg, though we Trekkies find that hard to believe. A vast, universe-trotting collective consciousness in humanoid bodies that lives in "hives" and "assimilates" any new species it encounters, the Borg have been the scourge of starship captains from Picard to Janeway.

Time Capsule

Some of those living today will see the development of a cybernetic species that combines human physical attributes with the mind of a machine, à la Borg. We bring this up because the hands of a Borg-like species would be as different from Leonardo's as your hands from Cro-Magnon Man's. Borg hands would be all Saturn—and no Moon or Venus. Where Leonardo's fingers were long and nearly pointed, Borg fingers would be square and tool-oriented for getting the job at hand done. Still, it's interesting to speculate about how the Borg might show aspects of loyalty and family in their hands.

While we can only imagine Borg hands (although they won't have long or pointed Jupiter fingers!), we can see the real hands of a generation—and then use those hands to predict some things about that generation's future. But where do you begin? What do you look for? Read on.

Finding a Generation's Future in Its Hands

The two most important questions to ask when you begin looking at hands are:

➤ What's dominant about a hand?

➤ What's dominant about a generation's hands?

The more hands you look at, the more you'll begin to see certain commonalties among a generation's hands. But this won't happen overnight.

Let's begin by showing you the generations we'll be discussing in this chapter. We'll even give each group a name so that you can differentiate among them. After all, when we say "our" generation (as we've mentioned, we're Baby Boomers), we may not be referring to "your" generation.

Out of Time

Don't try to define the future by looking at the hands of your children or grandchildren. What you see in their hands will be affected by your natural prejudices toward these precocious beings—and you may miss important aspects in the process.

369

A Who's Who of the 20th Century

Born 1921–1940	The Depression/World War II Generation
Born 1941–1960	The Baby Boomers
Born 1961–1980	The New Conservatives
Born 1981–2000	Today's Children

Born 1921–1940: Conservative Pragmatism

Were those of the Depression/World War II generation conservative and pragmatic because they went through these world-changing events, or did they survive those world-changing events because they were conservative and pragmatic? We'd suggest that both of these statements are true, because a generation and its history are interwoven.

So what does a typical Depression/WWII hand look like? Take a look at the following photograph before you continue on and note what you think is dominant in that hand.

The hand of a person born in the WWII generation.

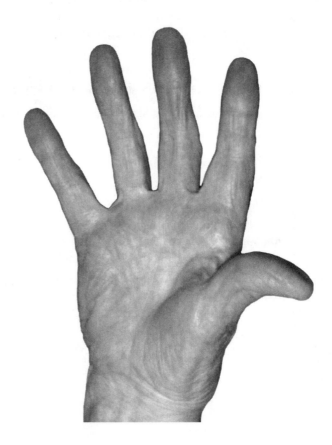

A Depression and a World War Leave Their Marks

What happens when history forbids a generation to be idealistic, optimistic, or to have many expectations? The mount of Apollo, the area of idealism, is diminished. Think about it, though: Apollonian risk-takers and gamblers couldn't have survived these life-changing, years-long events.

Another important aspect of these peoples' hands is their conservative, thumb-hugging life lines and solid heart lines. This was a generation of Tess Truehearts and Tom Tenaciouses. They trusted each other. They married for life, and they stayed married. And, unlike their children, they didn't move as often or as far.

Ask Spaceship Earth

The Depression/WWII folks had their Martian energy sucked right out of them, resulting in all their Mars mounts being diminished. A Bill Mauldin WWII cartoon, in fact, depicts two soldiers, one just aching for a fight. "He must not be in combat," the other observes.

Time Capsule

There's a clear appreciation for authority in this generation's hands. Even those who didn't go off to war accepted rationing and respected the president of the United States (the same man, Franklin Delano Roosevelt, for 14 years, it should be noted). This aspect is evidenced by clearly defined Saturn mounts and long, strong rising lines to Saturn, which you can see in the previous photo as well.

These people knew the importance of suffering in silence and keeping up a good front, no matter what the reality was, both of which can be found in the tactful lean of their Mercury fingers and less Mercury line influence. They also felt it was important to keep their personal business to themselves. Feelings weren't accentuated—and so neither was the lunar mount.

"Think of the Poor Starving Children in China . . . "

The Depression left an entire generation with a critical view of any kind of waste and inefficiency, especially wasting food. The phrase, "Think of the poor starving children in China . . . " can probably be attributed to the novels of Pearl Buck, such as *The Good Earth,* which this generation read with fascination.

They believed what they were told because they believed in authority—that Saturn influence again. In addition, there was less Uranian or Neptunian influence for this generation. What building was done, in other words, was done for more practical, Saturnian reasons—bridges, superhighways—rather than for the sake of invention or innovation.

What marks this generation above all, however, is its sober-mindedness and tendency to judge other, more radical generations. You'll find this, once again, in its straight Saturn fingers, clear Saturn lines, and strong Saturn mounts.

Born 1941–1960: You Say You Want a Revolution?

Talk about night and day! The children of the Depression/WWII folks couldn't be more different from their parents. Out of a generation of hard-working conformists came a generation of rule breakers. The Baby Boomers questioned everything, from authority to boundaries—to themselves.

Let's take a look at a typical Baby Boomer hand. Take a moment to study the following photograph and see if you can discover some of the dominant traits of this generation.

The hand of a Baby Boomer.

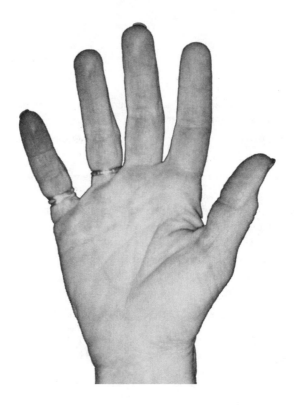

What's happened to Saturn? Compare this hand with the hand of the Depression/WWII person. See how this person's rising line to Saturn is broken, compared to the other's strong Saturn line? In addition, the Saturn finger's no longer straight—and so the person's no longer straight-forward when it comes to authority.

What's Uranus Got to Do with It?

Where the Depression/WWII folks had practically no Uranus mounts at all, the Baby Boomers have accentuated mounts of Uranus. What this amounts to is a revolutionary approach to everything—whether it's inventing the laser or taking LSD.

There are several other factors to add to this Uranian energy to create the unique Baby Boomer outlook. First, there's the adept communication abilities of their accentuated Mercury fingers, mentioned previously. They've also got almost too much Moon, which means not only do they wear their hearts on their sleeves, their emotions change as quickly as the Moon phases. Add this to broken or chained heart lines with more than one branch, and you've got a generation of people who, unlike their parents, just can't stay married to the same person "till death do us part." Or, for that matter, to the same career, place, religion, car . . .

Ask Spaceship Earth

Another thing to notice is that the mount of Saturn actually leans toward the mount of Apollo, a configuration that says, in capital letters, PHILOSOPHICAL RULE-BREAKER. Add in the bent or crooked Mercury finger and eccentric Mercury angle, and you've got someone who can't help but question everything.

Time Capsule

Baby Boomers are more idealistic than their parents. Witness their heart lines, flat under Jupiter, and pointing toward the Jupiter/Saturn split, as well as their emphasized lunar and Venus mounts. In addition, they're much more materialistic. You can find this in that heart line branch toward Saturn, and again, in that emphasized mount of Venus.

The Baby Boomers are a generation who lost the faith that their parents had. Baby Boomer head lines branch in many directions, rather than being straightforward like their parents'. Baby Boomers question everything—but especially themselves. Witness their Apollo energies.

Struck by the Sun: Apollonian Talents and Risk-Taking

Apollo is about appearances, and when it comes to Baby Boomers, pointed and conical Apollo fingers point to a self-conscious concern with outward appearances. From salons that specialize in nothing but fingernails to sweating it out at the corner gym, all kinds of businesses have sprouted up to meet Baby Boomers' need to look good—whatever the cost.

But Apollo is also about the critic, and Baby Boomers are often very good at self-evaluation. Post-modernism, in fact, which, in a nutshell, is a style of ironically self-evaluating everything, is a product of a generation of conic and pointed Apollo fingertips.

In addition, Apollo is the risk-taker, and Baby Boomers took (and continue to take) chances on everything from drugs to careers to the stock market. In fact, when it comes to Baby Boomers' tendency to completely change their lives at 40, there's a name for it: the Quantum Leap.

The Quantum Leap: What's All This About a Mid-Life Crisis?

Speaking Y2K

The **Quantum Leap** is the name given to a life line that changes radically at mid-life to reflect a major career or life change at that time.

More Baby Boomers' life lines change at mid-life than any other generation's. Where Depression/WWII generation folks would stick with any decent job that paid the mortgage or any decent wife that kept the house looking good, Baby Boomers will chuck it all and jump off into an entirely new direction. This is seen in the radically shifting life line we call the *Quantum Leap.*

Look around you. There are several people you know who have made dramatic changes in their lives—maybe even you. Here are some of the life line-changing changes that Baby Boomers we know personally have made:

➤ A man who quit his job as a construction manager and went back to school—to become a poet

➤ A woman who left her husband, children, and paid-for suburban house to join a Zen monastery

➤ A man who didn't know how to drive who became a long-distance truck driver

➤ A woman who left a convent to start a massage parlor—and marry another woman

➤ Millions who became parents after the age of 40

One other thing to note about the Baby Boomer generation's changeability is how many people have conic fingertips. Conic fingertips not only say, "What can we do?" They add, "What *can't* we do?" This translates to a tendency to try this and then try that, because, "Why not?"

Too Much Moon: From Moods to Indulgences

What happens when an entire generation has strong lunar mounts? You have a generation of confessional, heart-on-the-sleeve, carriers and traders of emotional baggage. No generation has been so prone to "tell all" or seek outside help for what's "inside"—namely, the emotional chaos of too much Moon.

The mount of the Moon, remember, is the area of the imagination and emotions. When emphasized, it's also an area of moodiness—and of self-indulgence—which, when coupled with the Apollo tendencies we've already discussed, translates to a generation that indulges its every "need"—whether that need is a new hair color, a new designer drug, an art therapist, or a cat therapist.

What's interesting about Baby Boomers is that despite all this self-indulgence and attention to what's seemingly superficial, they're also survivors. Let's examine why.

We Are Survivors

Perhaps more than anything else, Baby Boomers are flexible and adaptable (those conic fingertips again)—which means they're also risk-takers. What they're not is inclined to plod along, never changing anything—their eccentric Mercury angles mean they thrive on change and far less structure than their parents.

In addition, their strong Mercury fingers make them hungry for stimulation—changeable stimulation: the new, the different, the never tried. In fact, Andy Warhol summed up this generation beautifully when he said, "In the future everyone will be world-famous for 15 minutes." He was right.

Born 1961–1980: The Conservative Backlash

And then they had children. You may recall the sitcom *Family Ties* that propelled Michael J. Fox to stardom in the '80s. The latter-day hippie Baby Boomer parents were nonplussed by their conservative children. But that's exactly what the generation of the New Conservatives is all about.

The following photo is of one New Conservative's hand. Take a moment to study this hand and note what you think are its dominant characteristics.

The hand of a New Conservative.

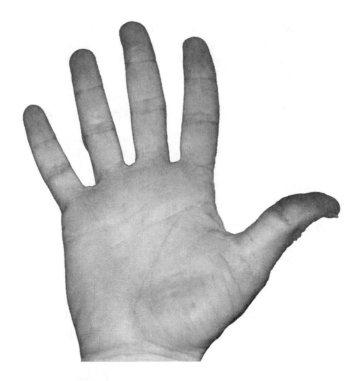

Life Without a Strong Moon

Baby Boomers may have too much Moon, but their children have practically no Moon at all. "Punks 'R' Us," the New Conservatives say. Actually, they say far worse, which we'll translate loosely into "Screw you." You get our drift. They're not impressed with their parents' emotional baggage. Far too many New Conservatives bore messages back and forth between their divorced parents, after all, and tried their best to adjust to new and different stepparents as well.

The New Conservatives aren't the pair-bonders their parents were, either. We'd like to say they're more pragmatic, but this too, boils down to a lack of emotional connection—or emotional baggage. While they're more materialistic (more heart lines branching toward Saturn), they're less idealistic (fewer heart lines branching toward Jupiter).

They're also less likely to have the communal mentality of their parents. This me-first spirit can be found in the New Conservatives' more highly set thumbs and much narrower angles of generosity between their thumbs and Jupiter fingers. What's theirs is theirs, the New Conservatives believe.

Defining One's Own World

It may surprise you to learn that the New Conservatives' central issues go back to the issues of the Depression/WWII generation. What's strong here is passive

376

Mars—self-insulation against what others may say, so they're more cynical than the generations before them. There's also a diminished active Mars, so they're less likely to get angry about "stuff we can't change anyway."

In addition, New Conservatives have little Jupiter or Apollo mount activity. They prefer to live in a world of their own defining, something illustrated beautifully several years ago as one of our authors drove her daughter and three friends to a weekend camping trip. Each of the four teens wore her own individual headphones and bopped her head to her own beat for the entire two-hour drive.

"I Vant to Be Alone!"

Those individual headphones are also an aspect of this generation's desire for solitude. Interestingly, this tendency is found, once again, on the New Conservatives' thumbs' lack of generosity. What this means is that they're less likely to give or share, and more likely to hold onto what they have for themselves.

New Conservatives also have relatively inflexible thumbs (remember the test of a thumb's flexibility is whether you can push back the tip when you press on it). Not only are they less generous than their parents, they're less flexible as well, and far less likely to compromise—no matter what the issue.

This generation has its own criteria for attachments, and it's a much more business-like approach than their parents'. This, once again, is because of a lack of lunar influence—and a much more straightforward Mercury finger.

"I'll Never Have Kids!"

This is in quotes because the daughter of one of our authors says it fairly regularly, and, born in 1979, she's at the heart of this generation. But she's not the only one—this generation doesn't have the same commitment to child-bearing of previous generations. Let's examine why.

First of all, New Conservative women's lack of lunar activity points to a lack of reproductive energy—they're just not as fertile as women of previous generations. New Conservative lunar mounts, in fact, often appear withered and flat. This same lack of Moon suggests that, unlike their mothers, they won't suddenly hear their biological clocks ticking as they get older.

New Conservatives also have diminished Venus mounts. Venus, remember, shows how much love you've got to give, and New Conservatives are much more selective in whom they give their love to. They haven't got as much to go around, after all, nor are they as emotionally motivated as their parents.

Lastly (and we haven't really discussed this before), the lowest fourth of this generation Jupiter mounts are often quite deflated. Robin tells us that this means they don't like messes—and that includes dirty diapers and projectile vomiting—as well as finger-painting. In fact, they're often fastidious to a fault.

Politicians Aren't Special

One of the more positive things to come out of President Clinton's impeachment trial will be new expectations for politicians, and the New Conservatives will be the generation that insists that politicians be workers, not performers. In addition, they'll expect their politicians to be real people, not demigods of perfection.

New Conservative politicians, like their peers, will have far less emphasized Jupiter mounts than today's politicians. They'll also have less Apollo and more Saturn. We welcome the change. As a contemporary politician might say, "It's time for the country to get down to business."

Born 1981–2000: Cheerful Pragmatists

The last generation we're going to look at in this chapter has an idealism that's tempered by more realistic expectations of others. We call them Today's Children because they've been born between 1981 and 2000.

Let's take a look at the hand of one of Today's Children. What do you notice about it? Make a few notes and then see how you do when we discuss the hands of this generation.

The hand of one of Today's Children.

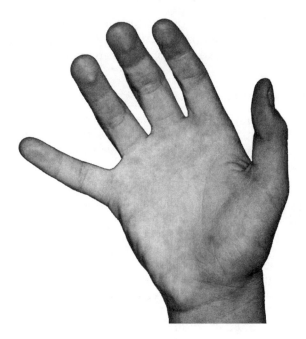

What's Eccentricity, Anyway?

Look at those Mercury aspects—the Mercury finger's long, the Mercury mount's strong, the Mercury line is clear and long, and the angle of eccentricity is clear and pronounced.

What this translates to is a new approach to "weird" that could mean everything from living in treehouses to an acceptance of even the fringes of society. To Today's Children, "eccentric" is just a word.

These cheerful pragmatists also have strong and more pointed Jupiter fingers than prior generations, which means that they're idealistic without having their heads in the clouds. They also have less Mars—they don't get mad as quickly, or hold a grudge, for that matter, and their flexible thumbs show that they'll be far more compromising than some of the earlier generations of the 20th century.

In addition, their balanced heart lines, and good but not over-emphasized lunar and Venus mounts, mean they understand the difference between relationships and Relationships. And, with their straightforward Mercury fingers, they can tell each other exactly what they mean.

The Multi-Talented Synthesist

Today's Children have thumbs that are both high-set and wide-angled, and this means they'll be skilled at a wide variety of things. In addition, you'll find more spatulate fingers (good tool users) and conic fingers (a variety of skills)—both of which indicate people who are multi-talented.

Another notable aspect of the hands of Today's Children is a nicely diminished Saturn mount. This, coupled with their particularly widely arcing life lines, translates to an eagerness to try everything—without worrying too much about the consequences. If the business venture fails, in other words, "Oh, well."

Staying Close to Home

You won't find many travel or relocation lines on the palms of today's children because, unlike their parents or grandparents—but far more like their great-grandparents—they'll maintain strong geographic bases near their families.

Time Capsule

It's interesting to note that Today's Children *do* have the widely arcing life lines that indicate people who want to explore and see new things. The difference is that this generation will operate from a more definitive "home base" than any generation since the Depression/ WWII, because of their strong lunar and Venus mounts.

No Mid-Life Crisis for Us, Thanks

Remember the Quantum Leap of the Baby Boomers? By the time we get to Today's Children, it's gone, gone, gone. Today's Children will focus their careers on broader areas; rather than shift wildly from career to career, they'll simply shift focus within their career area. The TV camerawoman may become a producer, for example; or the insurance salesman may become a stockbroker. But you won't see so many lawyers-turned-priests, or nuns-turned-saleswomen. No mid-life crisis for Today's Children, thanks!

Bad Tempers Wane

With less mount of Mars emphasis and a more clearly defined mount of Saturn, Today's Children will (at last) be less litigious than previous generations. In addition, their more compromising thumbs means they'll be less likely to try to assign blame, and more likely to shrug their shoulders and go on to the next thing.

Remember, Today's Children also have more generous thumbs, which means they're far more likely to "forgive and forget" than the two generations before them (and far more like their great-grandparents).

The three areas of Mars are also where we find our temper (active Mars), ability to hold our own (passive Mars), and need for vengeance (plain of Mars). Today's Children won't have much active Martian influence, and bad tempers, for whatever reason, will be a thing of the past. As we'll discuss next, however, their passive Mars will be stronger.

Celebrating Diversity

As we've just mentioned, there will be far less assigning blame. Factors that reveal this in this generation's hands include:

➤ Good, clean, and uncrowded Saturn mounts

➤ Strong, inflated passive Mars

➤ Straight and long Mercury fingers

➤ Good, full and not too lined Venus mount compassion

➤ Strong, healthy, not too lined lunar receptivity

All of these factors combined mean that Today's Children will be willing to accept difference. In fact, they won't even describe things like race or sexual orientation as "separators," hard as it is for us to imagine today. The combination of Venus and Moon compassion (with the Venus giving equaling the lunar taking, in other words), points to a simple acceptance of "All people being created equal."

Life, Health, and the Pursuit of Happiness

As many hands as Robin's seen, he's noticed certain broad tendencies that change from generation to generation. Whether it's life, health, or the pursuit of happiness, in fact, you can learn a lot about a generation's future from its hands.

Finding a Generation's Longevity in Its Hands

When Robin looks at a generation's potential for longevity, he looks at far more than the lengths of its life lines. More important, in fact, is the *quality* of those lines, as well as the quality of the head and heart lines and the lunar and Venus mounts.

It will take you thousands of hands, as Robin's seen, before you can accurately discover a generation's longevity in its hands. But you don't have to take the time to look at all those hands—Robin already has, and he's going to share his findings here.

Generation	Potential Life Span
Depression/WWII	70+
Baby Boomers	83+
New Conservatives	90+
Today's Children	100+
The Next Generation	120+ ??

Medical statisticians are proving Robin's predictions to be an accurate trend. Indeed, while the average human life span in 1900 was about 45 years, at the start of our new millennium it has stretched to about 75 in the United States, and even longer for many American women. Some geriatricians (doctors who study the affects of aging) are now asserting that the maximum human life span is 120 years—if diseases or compromising accidents are absent.

With the tremendous advances in medical science occurring now, including biomedical discoveries and genetic research, humankind may be able to affect its own evolution in the third millennium. The fountain of youth? Well, maybe that's still elusive. But a long, vital life by the year 3000, beyond even our 21st-century imagination? Anything is possible!

Finding a Generation's Health in Its Hands

One of the most important reasons for the ever-increasing life span to be found in succeeding generations' hands is what's happening when it comes to the medical field. Not only are there daily Mercurian (remember, Mercury's the area of healing) advancements, but people are more willing to be true to themselves and their needs (lunar and Venus mounts)—and to communicate their needs to those who can help them.

A generation's health can be found quite specifically in the quality of its lines. The generations of the 20th century have had ever deeper and more well-cut life lines, and in the 21st century, life lines will be deeper still. There are many reasons for this: Everything from seat belts to vitamin supplements has helped succeeding generations stay healthier.

Another aspect to look at is preventative medicine as opposed to disease-oriented medicine. This can be found in the number of people outside the medical profession who now sport medical stigmata (see the illustration of special marks on the hand in Chapter 22), a good sign of awareness about health issues and prevention.

Vaccinations, while there are religious groups that oppose them, are doing their part to create succeeding generations of healthier children. And medical technology takes three giant steps forward for every step back—a good sign for future generations.

Finding What Matters to a Generation in Its Hands

Look at your thumb. Look at your spouse's thumb. This is the beginning of finding what matters to your generation in your hands.

But the set of the thumb is quite literally the beginning. Look at your mounts. Which are strong? Which are diminished? Now look at the fingers. Which are longer? What are the shapes of the fingertips? What about angles between fingers?

Now, look at the lines. Which are stronger? Are there lines that are broken or frayed? Using your own hands as a start, you can begin to discover what matters to your generation. And the more hands of different generations you look at, the more you'll discover about other generations as well.

How Many Hands Does It Take to Make a Generation?

The ideal way of exploring a generation would be to look at the hands of everyone, but of course that's not possible. Looking at just your children's or grandchildren's hands won't do it—partly because you're going to be looking through rose-colored glasses.

You'll *begin* to see certain similarities in a generation's hands after a dozen or so, but you won't truly be convinced until you've looked at over a hundred. Chances are, most of what you noticed in the dozen will hold true for 60 to 70 percent of that hundred.

So how many hands does it take to make a generation? Let's take a cue from the pollsters: a representative sample of at least a hundred. Happy hunting!

The Least You Need to Know

➤ You can discover a generation's future by looking at the hands of its children.

➤ The generation born from 1921 to 1940 were conservative pragmatists.

➤ The generation born from 1941 to 1960 were revolutionaries.

➤ The generation born from 1961 to 1980 are the new conservatives.

➤ The generation born from 1981 to 2000 are cheerful eccentrics.

➤ You can find what matters to a generation in its hands.

Chapter 24

A Hand in the New Millennium

In This Chapter

➤ What to expect in the hands of the future

➤ Animals are people, too

➤ Race becomes a non-issue

➤ From tattoos to six-million-dollar bodies

➤ Our future's in all of our hands

Now that you've learned about the areas of the palms and taken a look at the palms of the generations of the 20th century, it's time to explore the hands of the future. Are there possibilities for the future that already exist in our own hands? How can we use what we've learned about palmistry to take a look at the new millennium?

Once you've looked at enough hands, you'll begin to see how the patterns of lives are reflected in the patterns of people. In this chapter, we're going to do just that to find out what the hands of the future may say.

What We Can Learn About Tomorrow from the Hands of Today

Just as your own hands can help you explore your past, present, and future, the hands of present generations can help palm readers look at future generations.

For example, the generations of the 20th century have been dealing with their Jupiterian idealism in a variety of ways, but at the same time, each generation has, in its way, been progressively more idealistic than the one before it. This means that if we use palms as our guide, idealism will continue to grow, and further, it will expand into still more areas of life.

Using the hands of today, Robin's got some definite ideas about the hands of the future. Let's begin by taking a look at where and how we'll live.

Not Lost in Space

While Hollywood's got us not only living in space but exploring other galaxies in the not-too-distant future, the truth, at least for the next hundred years or so, is that space colonies just aren't in our hands. More specifically, future generations are unlikely to have the Neptune and Uranus mount emphases or the expanded life lines that would indicate a spaceward Diaspora.

Time Capsule

Interestingly, of the 20th-century generations, Baby Boomers, with their strong Neptune and Uranus mounts, probably could have pulled off colonizing space. Unfortunately, they also share a certain amount of lunar instability that prevented them from doing so—except on TV and in film.

This is not to say that space exploration will cease. Quite the contrary. Our Mercurian curiosity won't go away, nor will our Uranian desire to engage the unknown and "boldly go where no one's gone before." It's just that there won't be many people with the eccentric Mercury angle required to take that bold leap to actually *live* in space. But who knows? Another hundred years could change our hands radically.

Life on Earth

Meanwhile, here on Earth, the trend for more natural living will take its next logical step, and some people will begin to live in earth berm houses that are partially underground. The desire to live in a home that's in harmony with its environment arises directly out of a clearer understanding that humans are neither omnipotent nor "in charge of" the environment.

In the hand, this trend will be clear in 21st-century generations' simpler Saturn mounts, as well as Saturn fingers that are decidedly more pointed. You may recall from the previous chapters that pointed Saturn fingers are quite unusual in the hands of today, so it's hard for some of us less-pointed Saturns to imagine what people like this might be like.

But let's do the math. Pointed fingertips indicate sensitivity. The Saturn finger is the area of rules and responsibility. Pointed Saturn fingertips point to a more sensitive approach to rules and responsibility, and so, in turn, a greater intuitive understanding of living in harmony with everything on Earth.

Animal Rights

Over on the Jupiter mount, animal lines are going to assert themselves, forking, attaching to the heart line, even ending in unexpected stars or protective squares. What this means is that while someone of the Depression/WWII generation's Jupiter mount animal activity might have indicated someone who trained dogs, a similar marking will now indicate someone who might train wolves to live in the wild, or train whales to return to the ocean.

But there's far more to animal rights than simply how we relate to other species. Many people eat animals, after all. How does that fit in with this increasing awareness of species interconnection?

A World of Vegetarians?

Vegetarianism can be found in a small rising line on the mount of Jupiter, and, if this line is coupled with a similar marking on the lunar mount, you've got the truly committed vegetarian. More and more people bear this mark today, and this trend will continue.

In fact, vegans (people who eat no animal products whatsoever) versus ovo-lacto vegetarians (those who do eat eggs and use dairy products) versus meat eaters will become the smoker/non-smoker issue of the 21st century. Vegans will wrinkle their noses at those who drink milk and eat eggs; vegetarians will picket those who continue to order steak, or even the fish fillet special at the drive-thru.

The possibility of the world being entirely vegetarian by the end of the 21st century isn't entirely a pipe dream, either. If, as Robin suspects will occur, the majority of future generations' hands reflect more and more of this Jupiter activity, the future may well be more and more meat-free. However, when it comes to humans, we can always expect that 10% backlash of eccentrics.

Mushrooms: The Meat of Tomorrow

So what do we eat if we don't eat cows and chickens, or even fish? Allow us to introduce mushrooms, the meat of tomorrow.

Mushrooms, as a fungi, appear on the hand in the same area as other animals: in the horizontal lines coming from the side of the hand into the Jupiter mount (there's an illustration of this in Chapter 21). They're already showing in some people's hands, in fact, because more and more people are discovering the pleasures of a portabello mushroom "burger."

Now wait. How do we know people aren't *training* mushrooms, if the fungi marking is similar to the other extensions of animal lines that will become apparent? The answer is that these Jupiter animal configurations have to do with husbandry, just as gardening shows in the hand with a low cross or double bar on the Jupiter mount. Mushroom cultivation is very low on Jupiter, and somewhat indistinguishable from worm farming and the like.

Mushrooms as a new staple of the diet are just one more example of how we'll be striving to live in harmony with our environment, rather than trying to master it. It's an important advancement from the environmental battles of today. This means that big business will accept this, too. We say: It's about time!

Ask Spaceship Earth

Our 21st-century counterparts will discover that mushrooms are good for them. There will be big money in discovering the secrets of mushrooms, in fact. Invest now and reap the rewards tomorrow. As Robin points out, "A mushroom's a 'fun-gi' to be around."

Animals Are People, Too

Another aspect of living in harmony with our environment will be more and more people accepting that animals have rights, too. This will evidence itself in a number of different ways, from a continued growth in all aspects of the pet industry, from snakes to horses; to animal rights groups becoming strong enough to wield political influence.

Interestingly, even as more and more people own pets, the issue of businesses owning animals will become more divisive. Circuses, in fact, may well become a thing of the past.

All this animal activity will naturally be evidenced in Jupiter mount activity, as we've discussed earlier, as well as pointed Jupiter fingers and idealistic, Jupiter-branching heart lines.

What's in It for the Animals?

With the passage of at least two generations, the "Free Willy" syndrome, as well as the work of PETA (People for Ethical Treatment of Animals), will strongly support the idea that some species are *so* domesticated that they can't live without humans. At the same time, the "watch dog" people of animal rights will be increasingly strident—and popularly supported.

Race Is Less of an Issue

We're pleased to say that as the 21st century progresses, race will be less and less of an issue. Rather than viewing racial differences as dividers of people, in fact, future generations will celebrate diversity and express their racial differences as aspects of their characters, which are appreciated in the same way as specific talents and skills.

This homogenization without loss of identity will be found in emphases on two areas of the hand: Jupiter, the idealist, and Uranus, the innovator. Let's look at each of these areas and how they'll be changing in the hands of the 21st century—and just what that portends.

Jupiter Is an Idealist

Not only will future generations' hands have inflated and well-marked Jupiter mounts, their Jupiter fingers will be more pointed than ours are today. This means that more people will be willing to make self-sacrifices to further their ideals. In addition, the idealism of the Baby Boomer generation will return—without the deep intensity of other issues that made it difficult for that generation to follow through on their ideaistic ideas. Future generations, unlike the Baby Boomers, will put their principles before their comforts.

Another Jupiter finger shape that will appear more often is the spatulate—which we hardly ever see today. People with spatulate Jupiter fingers are political pragmatists, and believe that change is possible against the odds. A good example might be found in the film *Mr. Smith Goes to Washington,* where small-town boy Jimmy Stewart saves the day—because he thinks he can. Spatulate + Jupiter = someone who can improve politics.

Uranus Is the Innovator

Why is it so hard to explain *Uranus*? This mount represents the innovator, but it's the innovator with a twist. Think of Uranian emphasis as the screwdriver of a particular age, whether it's Einstein's theory of relativity or virtual reality. An important aspect of this metaphor is that the screwdriver must be held—it can't work without assistance, and neither can Uranus. The Uranian *may* design the first working model, but she's unlikely to built a physical prototype alone.

One way to explore Uranus's emphasis is to look at its possible combinations with other mount emphases, because Uranus hardly ever dominates. Instead, it rather lends itself to other profound and powerful strengths and potentials in the hand to create its potential for new directions.

➤ *Uranus-Mars* and *Uranus-Saturn.* Here's the 20th century influence that created the military-industrial complex, as well as our ever-more confusing legal technocracy. We're pleased to say that this emphasis will be declining in the new millennium.

➤ *Uranus-Mercury.* Here's the "God of the Pocket Protector," a powerful combination that's just now coming to the forefront in the hands of today. This communicating innovator combination will become so prevalent in the new millennium that we're going to discuss it in more detail in the next section, "When Nerds Rule the World."

Speaking Y2K

The mount of **Uranus** is notable for working with other mounts to achieve its innovation and invention. Because its adaptive energy is passive, other influences are required for the Uranian energy to complete its task.

Out of Time

To have a dominant Uranus–Moon configuration is almost a contradiction in terms, as its literal meaning is "dominant passive energies." But it's also a configuration with wonderful potential—although not very specific.

➤ *Uranus-Moon.* When a strong Uranus-Moon configuration begins to withstand the test of time, we'll start to see a stronger emphasis on feminine "technology," such as child-birthing, psychology, and the spiritual aspects of nurturing. While Robin does see this combination in the hands of the future, he uses the phrase "to withstand the test of time" because neither of these mounts is often a dominant one, preferring another stronger mount to take the lead, so to speak. Needless to say, a generation with a Uranus-Moon dominance will be a very unusual one.

➤ *Uranus-Jupiter.* When this combination begins to be the dominant one, there will be great hope among all. Not only do these two mounts together herald political and sociological breakthroughs, but there's also the possibility of a spiritual leader who will appeal to a broad array of people, a secular Dalai Lama, so to speak, who will help change the face of global spiritual understanding. This Uranus-Jupiter person would be someone who thinks big, and doesn't accept standard boundaries.

➤ *Uranus-Venus.* When both Uranus and Venus are strong mounts, there's the potential for profound universal love and understanding, and we're pleased to say that more and more people of future generations will evidence just such a combination.

With all these Uranian possibilities, it's easy to see that there's great hope for the new millennium. Even nerds will have their day, in fact.

When Nerds Rule the World

Imagine a Uranus mount that's dominant without any other mount to influence it. This configuration means Uranus's invention goes forward without, say, Jupiter's *chutzpah* or Saturn's pragmatism. When the head line also enters the mount of Uranus, thought without decision, and invention without any thought of its practical application, are both givens. In other words, nerds will, at least for a short time (say, 15 minutes?), rule the world.

The problem with a Uranian dominance without any other mount to temper it is that people with this Uranus dominance will think that they "get" everything—from love to people—when, in reality, those with just Uranus can't "get" anything: Their comprehension doesn't approach their intellect. For Uranus to succeed, in fact, it's got to be combined with another mount's emphasis. It takes synthesis for Uranus's innovation to have a lasting effect. Let's take a look at two such possibilities.

Pocket-Protector Spirituality

When a strong Uranus mount is coupled with a rising line on the Jupiter mount, the potential for pocket-protector spirituality becomes a distinct possibility. If this combination appears on a great number of hands (and that could happen in the new millennium), there may well be a statue of Bill Gates burning his pocket protector in downtown Seattle to celebrate the ascendancy of the nerd mythology. Another way that pocket-protector spirituality can assert itself is via a Uranus-Mercury mount emphasis. When the invention of Uranus is combined with the communication ability of Mercury (that's so abstract, we should add, in Uranus itself), the possibility exists of nerds who can communicate their message (imagine, if you will, software manuals that make sense!).

What's important to note here is that nerd power can't remain a force without another mount to complement the Uranian energy. Sometimes, in fact, the energy might result in a less positive spirituality while they're trying to fix other things.

Gods and Monsters

Another combination that could well appear in the new millennium are those charismatic few who mislead many because of their Jupiter charisma rather than because they have any true Uranian adaptability skills. While their strength lies in their ability to inspire, they won't create much of their own. And the real spiritual leaders will be known by the work they do—not the words they preach.

From Tattoos to Six-Million-Dollar Bodies

Today's tattoos are nothing compared to the "six-million-dollar bodies" we'll be seeing in the new millennium. The Apollo + Mercury + Jupiter activity that today is seen as adornment will tomorrow evidence itself as embedded chips that will allow people to alter themselves at will.

Whether it's an internal hearing aid or breast or penile implants that inflate and deflate on a whim (horrors!), body enhancement may well become as prevalent as pierced ears and painted nails.

As today, radial keratotomy to correct vision defects will be an option, but by the end of the 21st century, both eyeglasses and contact lenses could be a thing of the past as more and more people have this simple laser surgery. In addition, surgeries such this one will be available to correct other "defects."

From Adornment to Enhancement

How will the hands of the future evidence the increasing use of everything from ear implants to clothing that changes temperature as you do to jewelry that also increases memory function? Let's take a look at the hands of the new millennium—which may well, we should note, be enhanced themselves.

First, the Apollo mounts are going to be stronger, as people seek to enhance the physical attributes they were born with. Add to this fuller Saturn third phalanges, which indicate a desire to control one's physical environment, and you've got a formula as simple as 1 + 1 = 2. In addition, tradition won't be as strong a concern in the future, because square Saturn fingers won't be as common.

There will also be greater angles of eccentricity found between the Mercury and Apollo fingers, as well as the wider Jupiter angles that demand individual expression. The third phalange of Apollo will be fuller, too, because personal enhancement is an aspect of the physical taste that's found there.

Mr. Data, I Presume?

As we write this chapter, the news has just broken that the first human hand transplant has been completed in New Jersey. The potential that this surgery (and other transplant surgeries) poses is a question: What, as a *Star Trek: The Next Generation* episode once asked, is "The Measure of a Man"?

The idea that a new limb, eye, or kidney can surpass its original isn't unreasonable, and what we might be squeamish about today won't be judged so harshly in the future. We propose that if one acquires a new hand, that hand will soon become a map of its new holder, because that's what a palm does.

Spiritual Breakthroughs

The generations of the new millennium will be fortunate in their ever-increasing lack of judgmental behavior and acceptance of others. With their less rigid Saturn influences and their more pronounced Jupiterian idealism, the people of the future will become more and more capable of transcending what appear today to be unbreakable laws of science.

Spirituality comes in many guises, from belief in a greater "force" to sanctification of rites such as birth, marriage, and death. In the new millennium, spiritual breakthroughs of all kinds will lead to a less chaotic life for all.

Children of a Greater "God"

Even today, there are physicists, such as Will Keepin, who are taking another look at esoteric sciences like palmistry. Keepin, for example, believes that the microcosm/macrocosm relationship palmistry portrays may well be connected to the inner/outer reality that physicists are now exploring and defining.

More and more people in the new millennium will have pronounced Jupiter mount idealism as well as the flat heart line under Jupiter that indicates a lack of attachment to formal relationships. Some will also have a secondary life line that adds spirituality to the mix, and all this, combined with either strong Apollo or Jupiter influences, plus support from Uranus and Mercury, will lead to a revived spirituality not seen since Martin Luther and the Protestant reformation.

Global spirituality requires a number of other aspects to become a reality, including:

➤ The acceptance found in multi-faceted (e.g., branched) heart lines

➤ A few flat heart lines under Jupiter to carry the ideas

➤ A more pragmatic, less marked Saturn mount

➤ Less lunar and Venusian sentimentality

In short, the people of the future will be more dedicated to their spiritual beliefs, as well as more accepting of others' spirituality—because they'll recognize the similarities rather than the differences. Many will practice a spirituality that works for them, rather than a prescribed set of rites and rituals.

In Order to Create a More Practical Union...

Robin believes that the generations of the new millennium will have a very different idea of what marriage is about. In fact, he suggests that marriage contracts will be circumstantial; that is, connected to various life obligations. People might get married to go through college, for example, or in order to travel overseas for work reasons for several years. In addition, the bond to raise children may be more for the child's benefit than for the relationship itself.

Robin's already seeing this possibility in more and more straight (and hence, straightforward) Mercury fingers, as well as a lack of defined relationship lines on the Mercury mount. In addition, heart lines are becoming shorter and more Saturn-bound, a configuration that says, "We're not here for the laws—the laws are here for us."

The other variable in this interesting equation will be, as we've mentioned, less lunar and Venusian sentimentality. In order to create more perfect unions, love won't have a lot to do with it anymore—hard as it is for us heart-on-the-sleeve types to imagine. Our expectations may be far more realistic.

A Lack of Cataclysm

The future of a generation is in all of its hands. For example, before World War I, the hands of young British males foretold a massive catastrophe for them. So it's good news that the hands of today don't show any cataclysms on the horizon. How do we know? There are no concurrent stars, bars, dots or other markings appearing on anywhere near enough life lines that Robin's seen.

In order for a catastrophe to show up on the hands of a generation, it's got to be major—and the possible cataclysms we all worry about—asteroids, AIDS, and accidental bombs, for example—are just that. Where does a palm reader like Robin look to see if there are potential catastrophes in the future? Let's take a look.

Time Capsule

When asked if the bombing of the federal building in Oklahoma City appeared in Oklahoma City hands before it occurred, Robin said no (he'd read quite a few Oklahoma City palms before that catastrophe). He went on to explain that in order for a cataclysm to appear in a generation's hands, it's got to be on the order of the Holocaust, the bombing of Hiroshima and Nagasaki in August 1945, or an earthquake that would wipe out the California coast. And, Robin adds, *he's never seen this.* We're very relieved.

Asteroids, AIDS, and Accidental Bombs

Just for fun (because now we know they're not going to happen!), we're going to explore our greatest fears in the hand. If asteroids, AIDS, or accidental bombs were going to wipe out future generations, where would these events appear in their (and our) hands?

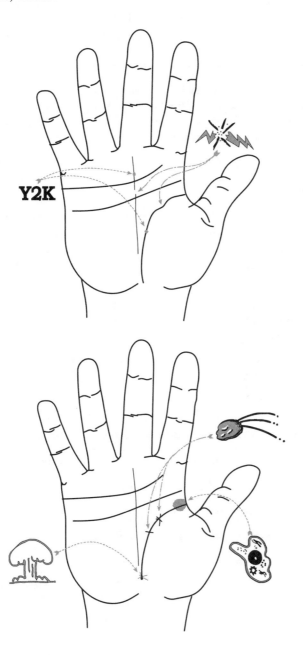

These aren't in our future, but here's where they'd appear in the hand: the Y2K computer crisis, the breakdown of technology, an asteroid, a viral epidemic, nuclear destruction.

Catastrophe	What Would Show in Everyone's Hands
Y2K computer crisis/ breakdown of technology	blue dot on life line or Saturn line. concave dip on life line, break on Saturn line
Asteroid	bar or star on life line
Viral epidemic	blue or black area where life line crosses on percussion of hand in passive Mars
Nuclear destruction/ third World War	star, bar, or black dot on life line with no continuing of line

The main thing to note about each of these markings is that none of them appears in a generation of hands. In order for a marking to indicate a catastrophe of global proportions, it's got to appear on the hands of *everyone* in that population or geographic area. What's notable about the hands of today—and tomorrow—is how different each person's hands are.

The Survivor Instinct

One last thing to note about the hands of the future is a legacy that will continue from the hands of today: We are survivors. Life lines are by and large clear and deeply cut; head and heart lines aren't running off in foolish directions. Truly mixed fingertips are seldom seen these days, and each generation successfully meets its particular Saturnian lessons.

Further, the Quantum Leap (see Chapter 23) that's seen so often in the hands of Baby Boomers isn't concurrent from hand to hand, which means no global catastrophe is in the forecast any time in the near future.

In fact, if one thing's clear about the human race, it's that we *are* survivors. It's in more than our hands—it's in our hearts and souls.

The Least You Need to Know

➤ The hands of the future will reflect the idealism of the new millennium.

➤ Animal rights will become as important as human rights.

➤ Six-million-dollar bodies will become the norm.

➤ Spiritual breakthroughs will be possible because of Jupiterian idealism.

➤ The future of the new millennium is in all of our hands.

Part 7

Living in the New Millennium

What do scientists, medical researchers, and economists have to say about the new millennium? Will it be a Brave New World or 2001? Perhaps most importantly, are we ready for a new millennium? We'll see what the Tarot cards—and all of the New Age Collective—have to say about that!

Chapter 25

Science and Medicine

In This Chapter

➤ Living in a wired world

➤ "How does an aspirin know where to go?"

➤ Six-million-dollar men—and women

➤ Harnessing nuclear power

➤ Saving Spaceship Earth

As we discussed early in Part 1 of this book, the borders between New Age ideas and scientific discoveries are blurring more and more. Just as Aldous Huxley's early 20th-century fantasy of genetically engineered babies is a 21st-century reality, Einstein's theory of relativity laid the groundwork for everything from fusion to nuclear-powered space travel.

But what will our everyday lives *really* be like in the 21st century? Let's take a peek at the science of today to see what the science of tomorrow will bring.

A World Without Borders

According to Harold Varmus, the director of National Institutes of Health, "There are three great themes in science in the twentieth century—the atom, the computer, and the gene." In fact, human knowledge now doubles every 10 years, and computer knowledge doubles every 18 months!

These days, the world is quite literally at our fingertips—but computer futurists predict that very soon the world will be *in* our fingertips, as well as everywhere in our homes, cars, and even our jewelry. The future of computer technology, suggests Mark Weiser, former head of Xerox's Palo Alto Research Center's Computer Science Laboratory, is in "ubiquitous computing."

The Internet Century: A Wired World

PCs may be the technology of today, but remember, they replaced the word processors and Apple IIs of yesterday, which in turn replaced IBM Selectrics, which replaced Royal Standards. Anyone who's not up to speed on the Information Highway risks being dubbed "Gutenberg." Not since German printer Johannes Gutenberg became the first to print with movable type in the mid-15th century—basically the invention of the book for the masses (or at least the gentry)—has an invention been introduced with the potential to revolutionize the way we receive and understand information.

Ask Spaceship Earth

We're already taking microchip technology for granted: There are, for example, microchips all over your car—one running the tape deck, another for the power mirrors, still another telling you to check your washer fluid level.

Unlike earlier technologies, computer technology is based on the microchip, which has become so small, so powerful, and so inexpensive that it can be placed anywhere and everywhere.

In the near future, living in a wired world will mean that you'll no longer go to your computer, your computer will be with you—no matter where you are! For example, when you wake up in the morning, a microchip sensor will alert your thermostat and your coffee maker. As you walk through the hallway, lights will turn on before you and dim behind you as microchips sense your location.

Rather than walk to your desk to check your e-mail, a microchip sensor in your pinkie ring will let you know that you've got mail, which you can then access by asking whom it's from. You'll also be able to wake the rest of your family by speaking to this pinkie ring (think of the com badges *Star Trek* officers wear—or an even earlier example, Dick Tracy talking into his watch!), as well as locate your secretary and talk to him, notify the door that the dog wants to come in, and check the front door to see if the paper's on the other side of it. Of course, the paper will be in the form of microchip technology, too!

The Information Collective: Our Thoughts Are One?

With everyone in the world wearing a pinkie ring com badge, will our thoughts be one? Many computer scientists believe that by 2020, *artificial intelligence* will take over from microchip technology, with reasoning machines unobtrusively taking care of the mundane so that we can tend to the exciting—including instantaneous communication with anyone, anywhere.

It's interesting to note that, as we discussed in Chapter 18, we already have the potential to connect with each other using our latent psychic abilities. Does that mean that using ever-advancing computer technology is the easy way out? Will instant access mean that we won't try to enhance our psychic abilities because machines will do it for us?

Speaking Y2K

Artificial intelligence refers to a machine's capability to think for itself and emulate the human mind. True artificial intelligence would actually think, feel, and sense as a human does. This technology is far, far in the future.

We believe that the opposite is true. As we become more and more accustomed to instant communication with each other via our pinkie ring com badges, we'll become more and more tuned in with each other, and will naturally learn to tap into our psychic abilities. And all this will be happening by the year 2020!

Smart Stuff

Microchip technology will be so prevalent very soon that, as Michio Kaku points out in *Visions: How Science Will Revolutionize the 21st Century* (Anchor, 1997), "Companies that don't include a few computer chips in their products will be at a severe competitive disadvantage." The hugely popular Furby toy, for example, which mimics its "owner" to learn to "communicate," has more computer power than the computers that existed before 1950.

Now, let's add genetic advances into the equation. Coupled with microchip technology, exponential progress in genetic engineering will revolutionize everything from medicine to clothing to the houses we live in. Let's look at a few examples.

Smart Medicines

In one of his more well-known routines, comedian Jeff Foxworthy asks, "How does an aspirin know where to go?" The real answer isn't as funny as Foxworthy's: Aspirin actually heads for the brain and dulls the nerve sensors that "feel" the pain, rather than actually stopping the pain itself.

Smart medicines of the near future, though, *will* know where to go. W. French Anderson, head of his own institute at the University of Southern California, suggests that medicine is entering the third of three stages:

➤ First Stage (through the early 20th century): Plants used by shamans and medicine men

➤ Second Stage (post-World War II): Vaccines and antibiotics

➤ Third Stage (21st century): *Molecular medicine*

Not since American bacteriologist Jonas Salk isolated a vaccine for polio in the 1950s has medicine taken such large strides toward enhancing human health and wellness. Treatments and medications, as we know them today, may well be thought quaint and primitive several generations into the new millennium.

In the last decade of the 20th century, the U.S. Department of Energy and the National Institutes of Health teamed up to begin the Human Genome Program. Scientists and researchers have worked diligently to identify the 80,000 genes present in human DNA, deoxyribonucleic acid, which is thought to be the building block of life. They are also attempting to plot out the sequences of the three billion chemical bases that make up human DNA.

Speaking Y2K

Molecular medicine uses genomes, or all the DNA in an organism, including its genes, to identify its molecular weaknesses.

Decoding genetic information gives researchers clues to the causation of disease processes, and perhaps also clues as to how to repair and restore damaged genes and DNA. The surgeon's scalpel may become obsolete in the new millennium as researchers find micro-treatments and cures that operate on a cellular level, as humankind learns more about the body's physiological processes and mechanisms of function. Cures for AIDS, cancer, and heart disease, among others, may well lie in an understanding of genes, enzymes, proteins, and hormones.

Smart Clothing

While some of us like the idea of a sweater that would materialize when we asked Scotty to "beam it up," smart clothing is really an entirely different concept. Smart clothing of the future may include everything from glasses that are also computer monitors, shoes that contain our biographies, to lapel pins that contain our medical histories.

In fact, that same lapel pin could be programmed to call 911 if you had a heart attack, or to call your pharmacist when you needed a refill for your medication.

At a conference in early 1999, Sun Microsystems provided each participant with a ring whose "stone" was actually a microchip encoded with everything from which breakout sessions the participant would be attending to how she preferred her coffee. In the case of the latter, the participant could walk up to a "replicator," scan her ring, and get her coffee just as she wanted it.

What else might smart clothing do?

➤ Fabrics might sense your body temperature and adapt so that your temperature is kept at an ideal of your choosing.

➤ Shoes would know when the going got tough, and be equipped with retractable grips for walks in icy conditions.

➤ Pants would adapt to daily weight fluctuations. (If only they could help us lose weight, too!)

➤ Clothing could actually be altered with a command to go from office to dinner date. Corsages optional, of course.

Who knows? Perhaps we will be able to have our sweaters appear when we need them!

Bill Gates' Smart House

Our clothing won't be the only thing with smarts. Our homes will be smart too. It's not enough that Microsoft's chairman and CEO Bill Gates predicts that PCs will be in 60 percent of American households by 2001 ("The PC and the Internet will become as fundamental tomorrow as the automobile is today."), but not much farther down the new millennium road, our houses will be electronic marvels as well.

Bill Gates's own 60-million-dollar, 40,000-square-foot house on the east bank of Lake Washington near Seattle is his model "home of the future." The house features dozens of video screens and monitors displaying paintings, photographs, and artwork programmed to the taste of each room's occupant. Gates writes about his house in the best-seller, *The Road Ahead* (revised edition plus CD ROM, Penguin USA, 1996).

It's not hard to imagine microchip-controlled heat and air-conditioning, even the temperature of tap water in the faucets. Phone, TV, VCR, stereo, and computer will merge into one seamless stream of data services into and out of our homes—and may even include electricity and other energy sources as well. Who knows, by 2800 maybe even electricity will be an outmoded and discarded technology—just a memory of the 20th century!

Human-Engineered Evolution

Remember the Human Genome Project mentioned earlier in the chapter? It's not only ahead of schedule, it's under budget! Francis Collins, the head of the project, predicts that 99 percent of the gene mapping will be done by 2002.

Time Capsule

The medical potentials of the Human Genome Project are truly mind-boggling. By 2000 alone, according to Harvard Nobel Laureate Walter Gilbert, scientists will have discovered the genetic codes for up to 50 hereditary diseases such as cystic fibrosis and hemophilia. By 2010, as many as 5,000 diseases may have been decoded. And by 2030, we may all wear our personal DNA codes on our sleeves!

Of course, there are other aspects of decoding our genetic key, such as cloning plants and animals, and possibly finding an aging gene and learning to extend our life span. Let's look at each of these individually.

Attack of the 300-Pound Tomato?: Feeding the Earth

As we discussed in Chapter 3, human population continues to expand exponentially. After water and land, the most important thing to all these people is food. Genetic engineering is addressing this very issue.

Since the 1980s, scientists have been using a .22 "DNA pellet gun" to shoot DNA into plants. Agriculturists believe that by early in the new millennium, as much as half the acreage of major crops in the U.S. will be genetically engineered in some way, for example:

➤ Plants that create their own pesticides

➤ Plants that are more resistant to disease

➤ Plants that are resistant to weed killers

➤ Plants that can produce drugs

In addition, plants have been engineered to grow much larger than their normal size, as well as to produce more fruit and less foliage. But think about it—none of this should be a surprise. Mendel's cross-breeding of peas in the 19th century was a natural precursor to this—and you probably remember that from high-school biology class!

Cloning: Copies vs. Originals

Of course, there's another kind of cloning that's a bit more controversial—the cloning of animals, and of humans. Dolly, the cloned sheep, created quite a sensation when she was born in Scotland in 1997. Her creators, scientist Ian Wilmut and his team at the Roslin Institute, discovered the "missing link" for cell reproduction by "starving" the cells for a week before mixing them together.

One of the problems that Wilmut and his team have discovered is that, because Dolly was cloned from a six-year-old sheep, she began as a six-year-old, too, and may be aging prematurely. Still, some predict that we may see a human clone as soon as 2005.

The likelihood of a scenario like Ira Levin's *The Boys from Brazil,* where hundreds of little Hitlers were cloned from one of his hairs, is extremely unlikely. Still, it does give pause about where cloning may lead us in the new millennium.

The Human Life Span: The 120-Year-Old Teenager

Some scientists are convinced that the discovery of an "age gene" could be the key to the fountain of youth, but others believe that the question of why we age is not so simple. Here, for example, are some of the things that happen as one ages:

➤ Hormone levels decrease

➤ Cells deteriorate

➤ Free radicals destroy cell chemistry

These scientists believe that until we find a "unified theory of aging" to take into account physics, information theory, and genetics, advances beyond 120 years aren't likely. Yet according to the MacArthur Foundation Study of Aging in America, by 2050 there will be over 600,000 people over the age of 100 in the United States, 80% of whom will be women. In 1900, centenarians were rare and the average human life span was about 45 years. Increases in the life span in just the last decades of the 20th century have been astounding. In fact, MacArthur researchers estimate that "of all the human beings who have ever lived to be sixty-five years or older, half are currently alive."

Scientists have isolated a gene that seems to be hereditary in those who live unusually long lives. If this "age gene" is isolated, the human life span could well be extended to 150 years. And if this becomes a reality, we'd better get moving on developing ways to

Out of Time

One potential side effect of genetic engineering is that people with allergies to certain foods might not be aware that they've been added to others. Someone with a peanut allergy, for example, might unknowingly eat a peanut-enhanced strawberry and have a severe reaction. Clearly, plant engineering's going to require some big warning labels.

Out of Time

The ethical questions about cloning are staggering. Will people seek out "designer children"? The world community is already demanding that human cloning be banned before it begins—but that probably won't stop it from happening.

Ask Spaceship Earth

One thing scientists researching aging agree on is that life can be prolonged by eating right. Research has shown that a lower calorie intake decreases the metabolic rate, which in turn leads to longer life. Popeye was right: Eat your spinach!

make earth's moon sustain human communities! The U.S. Census Bureau reports that the earth's population, currently about 6 billion people, will climb to 8 billion by the year 2026 and 9.3 billion by 2050. In developed nations, however, deaths will exceed births as the population mushrooms in age. The number of over-65ers will more than double while those under age 15 will grow by only 6 percent.

One other area that could change how we age is the field of growing new organs. Even today, researchers are experimentally growing human organs in pigs, and some predict that by 2020, we'll be routinely harvesting such organs to replace worn-out ones in humans. Some of the parts of the body that can be replaced include:

➤ Eyes

➤ Skin

➤ Ears

➤ Kidneys

➤ Bones

The January 1999 issue of *Popular Mechanics*, in fact, suggests that the bionic man has arrived. One thing's for certain, he'll be here in the 21st century!

Back to the Future: Will Mr. Fusion Be a Reality?

Do you remember the film *Back to the Future*? At the end of the movie, crazy scientist Doc Brown "arrives" on Michael J. Fox's driveway in a hovercraft, rushes to the trash can, and digs out a banana peel to toss into his gas tank, "Mr. Fusion."

Like everything in well-researched science fiction, "Mr. Fusion" is as much science as it is fiction. Today's physicists can affirm the possibility of everything in *Star Trek,* from the nanoprobes that unite the Borg to the warp engines that energize the starships.

Fusion and Fission

As we exhaust more and more of our fossil fuels like coal and oil, we'll have to turn to other sources of power. Some of the possibilities that today's scientists are exploring include fusion power, breeder reactors, and solar energy.

Fusion power, which uses the natural repulsion of hydrogen nuclei to create energy, has been harnessed via inertial confinement to create hydrogen bombs, and this same energy could theoretically be used to power not only spaceships but the power plants of Earth itself. In fact, some predict that by 2050, the majority of power plants on Earth will be fusion plants.

Fusion power is a safe alternative to more controversial fission power, especially in light of the disasters at Three Mile Island and Chernobyl. In addition, the unchecked Cold War build-up of fission weapons has resulted in nuclear dumps that estimates say could cost as much as $500 billion to clean up.

Unlike fission power, fusion power doesn't create radioactive waste. Nor can its reactors melt down, or its explosions create mass destruction, although they could potentially blow up their containers. Because of these various problems, breeder reactors, which use fission power, have fallen out of favor.

Speaking Y2K

Fusion power is a way of using hydrogen atoms to create energy, and is the method behind hydrogen bombs.

The other alternative for energy seems the most promising for the future: solar energy. It's unlimited, it's free, and it's there. Up until now, it hasn't been cost-effective, but this will change in the new millennium, as advances in solar technology become more mainstream.

Nuclear-Powered Space Travel

The future of space travel may well lie in a combination of rockets—one type to power the take-off, and another to power the spacecraft while in space. Potentially dangerous nuclear-powered booster engines probably won't be the choice when other options include chemical rockets similar to those used today, or rail guns that "shoot" space ships into space. Solar-electric ion engines could then power them without waste once they've cleared Earth's atmosphere.

Beyond 2100, the antimatter engines of *Star Trek* may become reality. Physicists know that antimatter exists, but they haven't yet isolated large enough quantities to use for propulsion. Some believe that it may be possible to "harvest" antimatter in space. It's an ideal propellant: There's no waste, and it creates massive thrust.

Even warp drives are consistent with the laws of physics. In the film *Star Trek: First Contact*, humanity "discovers" warp drive in the 21st century. Will this film prove prescient? Time will tell.

Will the Earth Survive Global Warming?

Global warming was first detected in 1896 by a Swedish chemist, Svante Arrhenius. Arrhenius noted that the industrial revolution had led to increased carbon dioxide releases. Because carbon dioxide has a role in the heating of the earth, Arrhenius predicted that the earth would warm.

While Arrhenius's predictions were ignored a hundred years ago, they've become common knowledge as the new millennium approaches. Scientists have discovered that 80 percent of global warming has occurred since 1750, when the burning of fossil fuels began.

Global warming is responsible for everything from a slow melting of the polar ice caps, which in turn leads to a sea-level rise (predicted to be over 17 inches by 2080) to dying coral, diseased shellfish, and an increase in human viruses off coastal waters.

Other effects of global warming include changing weather patterns and reduced evaporation rates as a result of a change in plant carbon exchange rates. Perhaps it's time to pay attention to Gaia Theory.

Speaking Y2K

The **Gaia Hypothesis** is based on the concept that the earth is a "super-organism" that encompasses all planetary processes. "Gaia" is another term for "Mother Earth."

Earth as a Living System: James Lovelock and Gaia Theory

The *Gaia Hypothesis* is the brainchild of atmospheric scientist Dr. James Lovelock and microbiologist Dr. Lynn Margulis. Basically, it's the idea that all planetary processes are part of a living "super-organism."

According to Gaia Theory, the earth, like any organism, is "sick" whenever any of its systems isn't working properly. Gaia theory encompasses all other scientific disciplines, as well as traditional stories and spiritual concepts from throughout the world.

Lovelock and Margulis propose that "Mother Earth lives," and further, that it's our responsibility to see that she remains healthy. Whether it's recycling aluminum cans or using organic pesticides, this responsibility begins with each one of us.

Planetary Collapse or Global Salvation?

There's nothing like the prospect of planetary collapse to bring the world together, and the 1995 UN Intergovernmental Panel on Climate Change (IPCC) predicted the potential of global collapse in the next century if carbon dioxide levels keep going up.

According to this report, the following potential disasters could occur:

➤ As many as half the world's glaciers could melt.

➤ Sea levels could rise, threatening 92 million people in coastal areas.

➤ Tropical diseases could spread.

➤ Agricultural areas could become dust bowls, leading to widespread starvation.

➤ More erratic weather patterns, with hurricanes and tornadoes more common, and more fierce.

There is hope, however. Global warming is directly related to fossil fuel consumption. As more and more nations begin to feel the effects of global warming, international cooperation can save the day—and the world.

As we become more and more interconnected via microchip technology and human engineering advances, we'll also hold the future of the world in all of our hands. It's our hope that saving Spaceship Earth will become a common goal; it's one that's still within our grasp.

The Least You Need to Know

➤ In the near future, we'll all be wearing our computers.

➤ The new millennium will bring smart aspirin—and other smart medicines.

➤ Six-million-dollar men—and women—will be commonplace in the 21st century.

➤ *Star Trek* starships and space travel may become reality.

➤ Saving Spaceship Earth will become the goal of all of us.

Chapter 26

Economics and Finances

In This Chapter

➤ Taking stock of the future

➤ What about Social Security?

➤ A question of cash

➤ Looking toward a global new millennium economy

"Money, money, money, money, mo-ney," sang the O'Jays in the 1970s. What will their counterpart be singing in 2070? Chances are, it won't be "Diamonds Are a Girl's Best Friend." As we discussed in the previous chapter, we'll be moving away from the use of dead by-products of our planet (which includes diamonds!) and looking to the stars.

So what will the economy of the future look like? Will there be recognizable leftovers from the 20th century, or will there be a whole new way of approaching economics? It's time to peer into our crystal ball for a glimpse into the future of economics and finance.

Mr. Greenspan, Are We at the Dawn of the New Economy?

Alan Greenspan's been head of the U.S. Federal Reserve Board since 1987. While he began his career as a private economic consultant, he's been involved in government fiscal policy in one way or another since the Ford administration in 1974.

Greenspan's emphasis as chairman of the Federal Reserve Board has been on fighting inflation, which he's controlled by raising and lowering interest rates to keep inflation in check. Whenever Greenspan's about to make an announcement, the stock market holds its collective breath in anticipation, and the market will often rise or fall dramatically based on what Greenspan does announce.

Greenspan would be the last person to predict that we're at the dawn of a "new economy." That's because he believes in the free-market economy we've got, with its ups and downs. Still, some important changes are taking place in the economy as we begin the new millennium. For example:

➤ Asia will remain a key component of our global economy.

➤ The gap between rich and poor will widen.

➤ The "underground economy" (that is, the "Black Market") will continue to grow.

➤ Leading-edge technology companies will dominate the "new" economy of the future.

Clearly, there's "good news and bad news." Let's take a look at the tech world of our future, and see what's what.

Tech World

Here's a startling statistic from the U.S. Department of Labor: Ninety percent of today's kindergartners will grow up to work at jobs that don't yet exist! We'd bet that a good many of those jobs will have to do with computer technology that's not yet in common use, such as voice-recognition software, temperature-sensitive sensors, and nanotechnology.

Future forecasters believe that the Internet will drastically change people's approach to thinking and behavior, and in fact, it's already done so in ways we're not even aware of.

Time Capsule

Not only was this book researched largely online, much of it was written via e-mail. When we finished the book, our editors reviewed our work and then sent it back to us via e-mail for author review. In addition, the book's producer arranged for all the artwork online as well. Remember when we wrote letters to do such things?

Futurists point out that the Internet is the "ultimate democracy," where all people truly are created equal. Rich, poor, or middle class; black, white, or purple; American or Indonesian; glasses on, glasses off: On the Internet, you're simply human. How refreshing!

Even when you've only been online a few months, you can't imagine how you ever did without your e-mail. As for online research, take a look at the sidebar to assess our take on that.

Taking Stock

As we write this, the stock market continues to flirt with a 10,000 Dow—been there, done that. The question is, how high can the stock market go? Are stocks over-valued already? Will there be a backslide as speculators decide to take their money out of the stock market? And what about foreign stock markets and their effect as we look forward to increasingly interdependent national economies?

With the advent of the Internet, there's a whole new breed of investor out there. These people are online all day, following the market and buying and selling as the spirit moves them. These day traders, along with the enormous amount of control wielded by managers of huge money market funds, are partially responsible for the rapid ups and downs of today's stock market.

The truth is, the stock market could rise forever—provided there are investors to invest, companies to invest in, and ideas that are promising. At the same time, however, merger fever will continue, so that ultimately there will be a very few large corporations in each sector, such as banking, manufacturing, energy, technology (hard and soft), media, and consumer products.

Out of Time

Never before have investors poured so much money into so many start-ups. One online bookseller, for example, probably won't begin earning money for its investors for another few years, yet its stock was highly valued right from its Initial Public Offering (IPO). Speculative investing may well be driving stocks well beyond their values—and there could be a backlash in the future.

Speaking Y2K

The **Dow** refers to the Dow-Jones Industrial Average, which is a measure of all the stocks listed on the New York Stock Exchange. (Check it out online at **www.nyse. com**.) There are other measures, too; for example, the NASDAQ, which measures technology stocks; and the Standard & Poor (S&P) 500, which measures mutual funds.

At the same time, by the year 2000, 80 percent of the equities on the New York Stock Exchange will be owned, not by individual investors, but by financial institutions such as investment companies, foundations, mutual funds, and pension funds. This means that the ups and downs of the *Dow* will be influenced by the actions of large-fund managers moving potentially huge blocks of stocks in response to market stimuli.

One last aspect of global investment to consider is that the United States is by far the largest investor in the world. In 1993, for example, the U.S. invested $20 billion in emerging Asian markets, as opposed to the $9.5 billion invested by Great Britain and $6.8 billion invested by Japan. The continued success of world markets at the start of the 21st century hinges, to a significant degree, on the United States' continued solvency.

During the Asian and Russian currency crisis of 1998, Alan Greenspan, speaking for the Federal Reserve Board, kept U.S. interest rates low—considering that the foreign drag would be sufficient to slow the American economy's growth enough to avoid inflation dangers. So, even in the last years of the 20th century, the United States has begun a debate over its duty to keep America strong, and its potential responsibility to protect global markets and the world economy at large. We guarantee this debate will intensify in the 21st century!

What About Social Security?

Guess who was in charge of the National Commission on Social Security Reform from 1981 to 1983? Alan Greenspan. This commission was responsible for revamping the entire Social Security system, supposedly to assure its solvency. If that's the case, why is the question of Social Security's solvency once again in the news?

Time Capsule

For information about Social Security itself, you could go straight to the source at **www.ssa.gov**. There you'll find the history of the Social Security system (it was begun during the Depression), a form you can fill out to find out how much you've contributed thus far, as well as how much you'd earn if you retired right now. There's also information about where your Social Security money goes—if you really want to know!

Some forecasts indicate that unless the current Social Security system is reformed, it will begin to run at a deficit around 2018—and become insolvent by 2031. That's because Baby Boomers will begin to retire in 2018, while at the same time the number of workers contributing to Social Security will decline.

Among the plans being put forward to keep this from happening is one that would allow workers to invest part of their Social Security accounts in IRAs. Another would permit the Social Security Administration itself to invest in the private sector, a prospect that suggests all kinds of conflicts of interest. Other proposals include raising the withholding for Social Security, decreasing benefits, or both.

The mandatory retirement age has already been set for incremental increases, but forecasters aren't sure that alone will be enough to save the program. Interestingly, many government employees opt out of Social Security entirely. Perhaps those in the private sector should have the same option.

Keeping Current

If you've ever used a credit card in another country, you know that your credit card company conveniently (and perhaps to its advantage) converts your expenditures into dollars. What those dollars—whether U.S., Canadian, or Euro,—are worth is determined daily by an *exchange rate*.

Interestingly, the true value of currency is based on—nothing! This transpired in the early 1970s, when Richard Nixon and other world leaders decided to do away with the gold standard. "Money," as Barry Howard Minkin points out in *Future in Sight* (Macmillan, 1995), "is just there on faith."

While a global economy is just around the corner, the world's currencies are as diverse as its cultures. The following table lists some of our world's many forms of money.

Speaking Y2K

The **exchange rate** between two currencies is determined by their relative values and is recalculated daily.

Currencies of the World

Country	Currency	Symbol
Algeria	Dinar	DA
Angola	Kwanza	Kw
Australia	Dollar	A$
Bangladesh	Taka	Tk
Bhutan	Ngultrum	N
Brunei	Ringgit	Br$

continues

Currencies of the World   *(continued)*

Country	Currency	Symbol
Cambodia	New riel	CR
Canada	Dollar	C$
China	Yuan	Y
Cuba	Peso	Cub$
Czech Republic	Koruna	Kcs
European Union	Euro	
Finland	Markka	FMk
France	Franc	Fr
Germany	Deutsche mark	DM
Greece	Drachma	Dr
Hong Kong	Dollar	HK$
Hungary	Forint	Ft
India	Rupee	IR
Iran	Rial	Rl
Iraq	Dinar	ID
Israel	New shekel	NIS
Italy	Lire	L
Japan	Yen	¥
Kuwait	Dinar	KD
Mauritania	Ouguiya	U
Mexico	Peso	Mex$
Morrocco	Dirham	Dh
Myanmar	Kyat	K
Norway	Krone	NKr
Portugal	Escudo	Esc
Saudi Arabia	Riyal	SAR
South Africa	Rand	R
Spain	Peseta	Pa
Thailand	Baht	Bt
United Kingdom	Pound	£
United States	Dollar	$
Vietnam	New dong	D
Yugoslavia	Dinar	YuD
Zambia	Kwacha	K

In the future, though, none of this may matter at all. Will we move to a global unit of money, or even to a cashless society? Let's take a closer look at the economy of the new millennium.

Euros vs. Dollars vs. Yen (and Don't Forget the Renminbi...)

In January 1999, Europe became united in a very 21st-century way: For the first time ever, every country in Europe uses the same currency, the Euro. No more Deutsche mark, no more pound, no more lira or lire. Early reports indicate that the Euro will eventually be as strong as the U.S. dollar.

Meanwhile, the Japanese yen isn't faring so well. Japan's seemingly endless economic boom came to grinding halt in mid-1998, and recovery has been very slow since then. At the same time, remember, Asia will be the largest segment of the world market in the very near future. It's possible that the dollar or the Euro could become the currency of choice there as well. And don't forget about billions of Chinese citizens who use the renminbi—and that the Chinese currency is, with the yen, the stabilizing currency of the Asian countries. Will we all be using renminbis someday? Only future generations will know the answer...

When Credit Is King: The Cashless Society

As we move into the 21st century, more and more of us are buying everything online, from books to computers. From initial discomfort with giving our credit card numbers online, we've come to take it as much for granted as giving a credit card to a waitress who then takes it somewhere we can't see to run it through.

If, as some futurists suggest, we'll be purchasing everything online in the not-too-distant future, will the need for money disappear? A number of new Internet start-ups would suggest that this may already be happening.

Some futurists predict that someday we'll have online "wealth accounts," which will include valuations of all of our assets, including things like our homes, cars, and insurance policies. These accounts would be accessed via "wealth cards," which would supply instant credit based on available assets.

These same futurists believe that buyers and sellers will use global electronic bulletin boards, bypassing banks and other middlemen and instead going straight to the source. Online auction sites are already operating in this way, and the possibilities are endless.

Ask Spaceship Earth

Sites like InterCoin, CyberCoin, and ValueCoin allow you to set up an account that you can then access for online purchases. This is not the same as giving your credit card number online, but rather is a password account you set up and control.

One Earth, One Economy

The next logical step after the Euro and online "wealth accounts" could be one currency for all the world's countries. Would that it were that simple. Many countries can't seem to stop arguing with their neighbors about borders—imagine what would ensue if they had to share money, too!

English is quickly becoming the global language (it's the accepted language, for example, of air traffic controllers), and more and more people are hooked up to the World Wide Web every day. The world truly is getting smaller, and a global economy offers one more way of connecting us. Could it happen in our lifetimes? Read on.

Is a Global Economy in Our Future?

Many economic forecasters feel a global economy is indeed in our future—in the new millennium. They cite examples such as the "wealth cards" we just mentioned, or the use of credit and debit cards instead of cash, to support their claims.

Remember, as we've stated, money isn't based on anything, so it follows that cash could go the way of the dinosaur and the dodo. So could plastic, for that matter, because, as we mentioned in Chapter 25, we'll all soon be wearing (in a microchip) what we need for any transaction.

In our brave new world of instant communication, a global economy makes sense for a number of reasons, including:

➤ Accessibility to a diverse array of products worldwide

➤ Ease of transactions between remote buyers and sellers

➤ Shared accountability for the financial stability of the world's communities

➤ A united interest in environmental concerns and in using *sustainable* and responsible technologies in both developed and developing nations

Speaking Y2K

A **sustainable** technology is one that does not harm the environment in the manufacturing process and that utilizes natural resources and recycling techniques to gain production efficiencies without hurting the planet or depleting valuable resources.

Why Diversity Is a Good Thing

The smaller the world, the greater the diversity. Imagine a place where everyone looked the same, dressed the same, and liked the same food, wine, and furniture (not to mention pets). Even on a less-than-global scale, that would make for a terribly dull and monotonous place. Our world, though, is anything but monotonous, because of our diversity.

In the same way, the more global the economy, the more specialized various countries become. Whether it's technology, natural resources, or labor, every country has something different to contribute to the greater whole. Diversity is a good thing!

The *Star Trek* Generation

One of our favorite movies, *Star Trek IV* (that's the one with the whales), contains a scene where Captain Kirk and the woman he's just met in 1990s San Francisco go out for pizza. "I suppose you don't have money in the 23rd century either," she says when the cash register rings. The answer is, of course not.

Out of Time

It took nearly 50 years for Europe to agree on, and then implement, a common currency. So, while the reasons for having a global economy are compelling, getting everyone to agree on just how it should work may take another 50 years—or more!

According to various *Star Trek* Web sites, money hasn't been used for centuries by the time Captain Kirk orders that pizza. Replicators can provide for one's every need, the Web sites note, so there's no need for currency.

Time Capsule

Despite its lack of money, there seems to be some lively trading going on out in deep space in *Star Trek's* "current" 24th century. Witness the Ferengi and their relentless pursuit of a profit. Witness *Voyager*, trading dilithium crystals, antimatter technology, warp engines, and whatever else those bad-hair guys need as *Voyager* makes its way across the Delta Quadrant.

Unfortunately, as Lawrence M. Krauss points out in *The Physics of Star Trek* (Harper Perennial, 1996), replicator technology is simply not feasible. This means that, while there may be no money in the 24th century, there will most likely be something. The question is, what?

Will Humankind Outgrow the Need for Money?

It's possible that money represents an inclination that we won't outgrow—because we don't want to. Let's examine just what money means to us. It's a measure of:

1. Net worth

2. Self-confidence

3. Social status

4. National wealth

We've ordered these aspects of money in this way for a reason. That's because more than anything else, money is a measure of how much we're "worth"—in more ways than one. In order to do away with money, we would need to find new ways of measuring value.

As we've discussed throughout this book, the new millennium may see the replacement of "old ways" of doing things with entirely new systems, which will arise out of dynamic shifts in thinking, including:

➤ A shift from consulting "experts" to trusting our own inner voices

➤ A shift in how we view cause and effect from external to internal

➤ A shift from viewing things as separate to viewing everything holistically

In economic terms, this could mean that we'll no longer be dominated by financial institutions, but instead will choose how to conduct transactions ourselves, for the good of all concerned.

One Universe, One Economy?

If we truly do go universal in the new millennium, we'll need to move beyond our limited ways of thinking in more ways than one. We'll have to stop fighting with each other, for one thing, and, for another, we'll need to start thinking globally instead of nationally.

We do have the potential for a more synergistic, holistic economy in our future, one that encompasses not just the world, but the universe. Like everything about our future, it's up to all of us.

What We Value

As we've discussed, we value money for what it says about our own worth in a number of ways. If we're measured by what we value, however, perhaps it's time to examine what it is we do value, and see if our *return on investment* is the best we can get.

Throughout this book, we've examined a variety of ways of learning about yourself, from the metaphor of your

Out of Time

Economic futurists suggest that before we arrive at a universal economy, we'll have to move away from the "gambling casino" that our current global economy represents. From state lotteries to the stock market, it seems that everyone wants "a piece of the action."

birth chart to the microcosm of your palm. We believe that the value of a person has nothing to do with her fiscal wealth (or lack of wealth). Rather, it has to do with her *psychic* wealth—her interconnectedness with everyone and with all things.

The economy of the future could well learn to value compassion and cooperation, but it will begin with each of us. Remember, we reap what we sow. We can realize a return on our investment that benefits not just us, but the entire universe.

Speaking Y2K

Return on investment is a financial term for how much one's principal earns.

The Least You Need to Know

➤ The economy is now more technologically based.

➤ The stock market also rises—and falls.

➤ We're moving toward a cashless future.

➤ We need to examine what we value.

Chapter 27

Are We Ready for the New Millennium?

In This Chapter

➤ An interview with the experts

➤ We ask the Tarot cards if we're ready

➤ The experts take a look at the cards

➤ *You* take a look at the cards!

➤ Humanity's future on Spaceship Earth

What better way to wrap up our exploration of the new millennium than a return to the New Age Collective for their final thoughts on the subject?

In this chapter, Tarot expert Arlene Tognetti did a reading on the question, "Are we ready for the new millennium?" We then shared the cards that came up with our other experts, for their unique takes on what the cards had to say.

What the Cards Have to Say: Are We Ready?

Here are the cards that came up when Arlene asked the question, "Are we ready for the new millennium?" on February 23, 1999.

Are we ready for the new millennium?

1) Temperance R
2) The Lovers
3) Knight of Pentacles R
4) The Hierophant
5) 6 of Swords R
6) Knight of Cups R
7) The Tower
8) Ace of Pentacles
9) 6 of Cups
10) Knight of Swords

1st card: Temperance R. Ready or not, patience is not our forte! This card, which represents the question, shows a society that wants everything and wants it NOW!

2nd card: The Lovers. Covering the question is the matter of choices. Are there choices we must make in order to be ready for the new millennium? Or will the choices of the new millennium force us to come to terms with ourselves? Time will tell.

3rd card: Knight of Pentacles R. This card represents a lack of focus, slow motion, and an overall lack of progress. It's possible this is directly related to the lack of patience evidenced by Temperance R in the 1st position: Maybe we're rushing so quickly toward tomorrow that we're not making any progress today.

4th card: The Hierophant. Here, in the passing away position, is the very concept of tradition. In order to meet the new millennium, we may have to do away with our outmoded ways of thinking.

5th card: 6 of Swords R. This possible future energy already exists, and the 6 of Swords R suggests that we may feel stuck in a negative situation for a while longer. We may have to shelve some of our plans (could this be the Y2K computer bug?), or we may have to shift our mindsets in order to get going again.

6th card: Knight of Cups R. We'll definitely have our hands full, with the Knight of Cups reversed. People don't relate well when this card is upside-down, and there's both a fear of commitment and a lack of trust of others.

7th card: The Tower. We don't like surprises, and the Tower in the 7th position of fears reminds us that we may need to expect the unexpected if we're to be prepared for what the new millennium brings.

8th card: Ace of Pentacles. Fortunately, there's the promise of new beginnings as the millennium unfolds. This card brings the promise of prosperity, wealth, and new directions, and here in the 8th position of others, it's certainly good news. Could it be another nation will step into the fray to save us from ourselves? Or, maybe, visitors from another planet?

9th card: 6 of Cups. As we move toward the future, it's important to remember the lessons of the past—and to learn from them. The 6 of Cups in the 9th position reminds us that the past and present are our most reliable guides for the future—and we would do well to pay attention to them.

10th card: Knight of Swords. Onward! The Knight of Swords is a card of forward momentum, and a message to pay attention to what's coming. This card always brings the truth—even if it hurts. "Be alert! Be ready!" says the Knight of Swords. "The new millennium is coming!"

The cards seem to be saying that we need to be patient—and to be ready for anything—when the new millennium comes. If we're not ready, the Tower may have some surprises in store, so it's best to stay alert, and to pay attention to the message the Knight of Swords is bringing. If we work together, we can be ready for anything the new millennium has to offer.

An Interview with the Experts

We thought it would be fun to ask our other New Age Collective experts what they made of this reading, based on their particular areas of expertise. We asked each expert to study the cards in the Tarot spread Arlene did for the question, "Are we ready for the new millennium?" and then to respond, based on their discipline. Here's what each of the experts had to say.

Astrological Insights

Astrologer Sheila Belanger wrote:

I find the grouping of four Major Arcana cards and three royal cards (all Knights) in the 10-card spread to be compelling and intriguing. This reading feels connected to expansive spiritual and karmic energies (four Major Arcana cards) and the challenge to master important millennium challenges from the highest and best part of ourselves (three royal cards).

1st card: Temperance R. This card is often linked to Sagittarius, the zodiac sign of questing for personal and philosophical truths. Temperance in the position of the Tarot question says we each need to quest to find out our own answers as we enter the new millennium. We are called to balance the duality of mind and body, technology and the earth. Temperance is about the creative blending of seemingly opposite aspects of life. The reversed position of the card indicates the need to seek understanding of, and balance of, dualities within ourselves so that we don't express a dualistic stance in our outer world.

2nd card: The Lovers. What is crossing Temperance is the card associated with Gemini, the zodiac sign of diversity, exploration, and communication. We enter the next millennium in the midst of an Internet communication revolution and the deep challenge posed by the Y2K dilemma. The Lovers invites us to get intimate with our data streams. Create a true relationship between all the diverse Gemini ways that we manage and engage with data. The Sagittarius card Temperance is crossed by the Gemini card Lovers. The balance between Sagittarius and Gemini is the ability to deeply synthesize and make meaning out of the potential random and fragmenting data we are constantly living with in our modern lives.

3rd card: Knight of Pentacles R. The developed nations of the West come from a place of prosperity and a level of mastery of the material plane. The reversed Knight of Pentacles challenges us to deepen our mastery of the material plane by being good stewards of physical resources. The key challenge of Y2K for the modern world is, do we remember how to truly live off the land without technological support? The new millennium asks us to consider the impact of our modern world on the earth and all its creatures.

4th card: The Hierophant. What is passing away is the card associated with Taurus, the zodiac sign of physical security and sensuality. The challenge of Taurus is not to fall into greedy self-serving ways where we hoard material resources. Taurus is also about survivorship, especially on a material level, which is a motivating question emerging from Y2K issues: how to survive the possible upcoming changes? The Hierophant is a card of an inner spiritual teacher who manifests wisdom on the material plane. Can we make the technological Internet a true manifestation of spiritual interconnectedness on a physical level with the earth?

5th card: 6 of Swords R. The card for possible future energy links to a strong analytical ability. To be ready for the new millennium, the reversed position suggests that we need to access our inner logic about how to navigate through the many changes to come. It also challenges us not to make the mind the only possible guide through the gateway of the next millennium.

6th card: Knight of Cups R. This card speaks to the challenge to master our emotions. We need to blend our mind and emotions in a healthy, mutually respectful way. The danger is a position of emotional reactivity based on ego that our way is the right way. The millennium shift evokes drama and extremism. The reversed card asks us to release close-heartedness that comes from fear and activate the generous and mutually supportive stance emerging from a healthy balance between mind and heart.

7th card: The Tower. In the position of hopes and fears sits the card connected to the planet Mars, the archetype of the Warrior. Our challenge is to face our fears bravely and courageously. Yes, upcoming millennium changes may shift our outer technological world. This card says: More to the point, what parts of your inner self must come tumbling down to prepare the way for the new aspects of self to emerge in the new millennium? Mars challenges us to take action on cleansing the old, to restructure our lives so that emotional reactivity no longer dominates our personality.

8th card: Ace of Pentacles. In the position of others, this card invites us to start anew (the Ace of beginnings) with how we connect physical resources with our relationship. In 1999, some people are initiating new relationships with neighbors and local community members based on the mutual need to be prepared for possible Y2K challenges. Our shared technological, physical, and emotional challenges are forcing us to rethink and restructure our relationship dynamics. What does the concept of "others" mean in the 21st century of Internet connections?

9th card: 6 of Cups. This card is connected to a full and loving nature. To access this state of mind, we need to release emotional attachment to old ways of life. The suit of cups links with the water element, the place of deep emotions within us. Let's not dwell on disappointments from the past (i.e., what is changing as we enter the new millennium). Rather, let's celebrate our capacity to feel deeply and express honestly to one another.

10th card: Knight of Swords. The outcome of the Tarot question is a card of mental consciousness and mastery. It's all in our heads, so to speak. This is a card of activism and moving forward toward a goal. We're ready for the new millennium if we bring our minds to that goal in a positive way. We must bring personal will and a passionate mind to the challenges of the transition times.

Doing the Numbers

Before numerologist Kay Lagerquist reviewed the Tarot spread numerologically, she graciously took the time to give us some numerological information about the United States. These numbers are based on the name of the country and its date of birth: 7/4/1776.

> **UNITED STATES OF AMERICA**
>
> **Birthday** = 7/4/1776 = 5 (Change!)
>
> **Soul Number** = 9 (generous, wants to help all mankind)
>
> **Destiny** = 3 (we are destined to be creative, inspirational, friendly, happy)
>
> **Personality** = 3 (friendly, happy, lighthearted, energetic persona)
>
> **Ultimate Goal** (also True Self number) = 8 (the authority, leader, organizer, powerful, successful, and has got the money)
>
> **Life Path** = 14/5 (karmic path of patience, cooperation, self-discipline, and adaptation; resonates to the Temperance card in Tarot deck)
>
> **Birth Day** = 4 (has to set boundaries, be disciplined, do the hard work, manages things well, but can get stuck in a rut, become rigid)

Armed with this information, Kay was numerologically prepared to look at the cards' answer to the question, "Are we ready for new millennium?" She felt that the overall message was learning to cooperate with existing conditions. "Hold hands and stick together," she wrote in her response to the cards.

1st card: Temperance R (Key 14). This number 14 says that at the core of the issue is the need for resourcefulness, adaptation, and change (the reduced number 5) around facing readiness. The 1 and 4 of this card say that the message we are getting is that it will be necessary to do the hard work—cooperate, have patience, go with the flow, and learn to stick together—and that harmony will then prevail. This card says the root of the issue is cooperating with existing conditions, being resourceful, and adapting to change.

2nd card: The Lovers (Key 6). This card carries the number 6. It suggests a choice that needs to be made is the opposing force. What is this choice? Do we have an unwritten commitment to care for all of life and care for the earth we live on? Now we will have a choice about honoring that commitment. This card suggests we will have a new direction for the heart, that there will be a desire to join with others, to learn the value of loving each other, and to create harmony around us. Are we going to love our way through this next millennium?

3rd card: Knight of Pentacles R. Remember, Minor Arcana cards also show timing. The timing of this card is 12 months. The question this card raises is, "Do we have it in us to adjust to this change?" Progress is impeded but we're not surprised. The very nature of the 2, as in 2000, is delays, a slowdown, going more gently. If we look at the year 2000, January is a 3 month in a 2 universal year. This means there will be delays in communications, and that we will find it necessary to join together and create. In addition, it suggests that we'll have to be patient with our emotional responses. We have the option of abandoning the "loner" position and joyfully joining with others.

4th card: The Hierophant (Key 5). This card is a number 5. Something changes. It suggests unconventional ways of doing things are what is at hand, because the conventional ways are passing away. There can be a fear of rocking the boat—but not to worry, the boat is actually full of water and a little rocking won't hurt. The tune changes from the long-held tradition of "Merrily, merrily, merrily/Life is but a dream," to "We will, we will, rock you!"

5th card: 6 of Swords R. Note that in its reversed position, the boat is not afloat. Here we see a 6 again, reminiscent of the 6 of the Lovers card. There is once again a choice. The question becomes, "Do I have the inner reserves to look for solutions, be patient, and change my thinking?" or the alternative choice, to be engulfed by fear, and take from everyone who will give. This is the golden opportunity to have a change of heart, to find the way to be in service, and to nurture others in order to have harmony or balance. These are the positive aspects of the number 6. This card suggests that we must recognize that our thoughts, attitude, and beliefs will either sink the boat or save it. It is our choice.

6th card: Knight of Cups R. Twelve months is the timing suggested by this card. But 12 months of what? Fear, turbulent times, not relating well with others? And when does this 12-month period begin? Remember, this is the energy already at work. So it is now, or it began in 1999, when this reading was done. If we're going to have a change of heart, as promised by the earlier cards, we have to wrestle with our fears and emotions; after all, we're human. If fear is what will happen, then we might want to remember FDR's famous words as he led people through the Great Depression: "We have nothing to fear but fear itself."

It looks as if this card says what will happen, or, that the outcome of facing down the new millennium will be each of us having to face our fears head-on. We will come to know that at the root of our worst moments is a very human fear—fear of the unknown. We can change that fear into hope.

Time Capsule

Four ways to deal with fear:

1. Identify what it is you're afraid of. Get clear. Be specific.
2. Write a positive affirmation for changing this fear energy from the negative to the positive. "I am safe and everything is working out for the best."
3. Breathe. Breathe in—draw in positive, hopeful thoughts. Breathe out—release fear and negative thinking. Do this three times.
4. Remember: You have a choice. You can choose to care for and nurture others and yourself, or you can isolate yourself and foster fearful thinking.

7th card: The Tower (Key 16). This card calls on us to expect the unexpected. The wake-up call is found in the reduced number 7 of this card (1 + 6 = 7). This is a chance to change our perceptions. It can be a rude wake-up call, not one that coddles us. But the Tower says it's time to reevaluate our values, for the old way has come to an end.

Now what is the fear? Fear of letting go of our cushy, convenience-programmed way of life? We all know we're too smart, too clever, and that we've come too far to go back to the Stone Age. But what if we gave up a little convenience? This card says we have great fear of losing it all, being lost from our "Tower" of protection.

But this card actually says, look again. Here is a time to challenge our fears and move beyond them. It is the 7 that says reevaluate, draw from inner wisdom. Make a commitment to live in a loving way. Examine the things we have long kept hidden: our values, emotions, priorities, and motivation. The New Age Collective might argue that the great "awakening" is a wake-up call to place spirituality at the forefront of our value system.

8th card: Ace of Pentacles. A new time, a new direction. A time of abundance, health, new regard for the earth, a time to demonstrate caring in more real and tangible ways. This is the energy of the number 1: new beginnings. This card comes after the big fear card, the Tower. So is that to say that after we get past our fears, we have a lovely new beginning, a time of abundance and good new energy? Yes, we think so. It is the long-promised "heart" of the new millennium—2,000 years of peace and harmony. It is the dawn of the Age of Light, the golden age.

9th card: 6 of Cups. Happiness comes from past—Are we wishing for the past?

10th card: Knight of Swords. "Caution! Stay alert!" says this card. Pay attention to coming events. Something important is being told to us. This is urgent! It's time to get at the truth; if we want to be ready for the new millennium, we will need to be truthful and ask: Even if things look good, is it really working? What is the truth about how our lives and our economy are structured? Can we afford to ignore the rest of the globe? Can we continue to have a two-bedroom house cost $250,000? Can we really work 10 to 16-hour days? Can we do it all for money? Can our bodies tolerate this much stress? Our bodies, as symbols for the earth's body, call us to ask: Can the earth stand this much stress?

We have a choice, and the time is now. We can't put it off any longer: We have come to the new millennium. As Robert Fulghum humorously says in his book, *All I Ever Really Need to Know I Learned in Kindergarten* (Fawcett, 1993), "When you go out into the world, it is best to hold hands and stick together!"

Using Psychic Intuition

When intuitive psychic Lynn A. Robinson, M.Ed. meditated on the cards in our Tarot spread, she wrote the following response.

1st card: Temperance R. The U.S. has often shown a weakness in the area of planning for long-term goals. We have a tendency to take actions that result in short-term effectiveness and long-term problems. This is seen in the 1st card, Temperance R, a lack of patience or an unwillingness to listen. I see this as continuing to be a serious problem in the U.S. for the next decade. As we progress into the new millennium I see us relying more and more on consensus among many nations, with patience becoming a virtue and a willingness to plan for future generations replacing the desire for immediate gain.

2nd card: The Lovers. This card intrigues me, as it has to do with making choices. A predominant theme of the latter part of the current century has been to see ourselves as victims: Someone has done something to us, we weren't at fault, or we didn't have a choice. I see the issue of free will and conscious choice becoming a major theme in the near future. There will be renewed emphasis on self-reliance and individual responsibility. "What can I/we do to change this situation for the better?" will be the question we ask in the new millennium.

3rd card: Knight of Pentacles R. In the 1990s we have experienced an alarming lack of cohesiveness in our political system: The impeachment of a president and the divisiveness of the two major political parties are two examples. We can see this in the Knight of Pentacles R, which is frequently defined as a lack of focus or scattered attention. There will not be a significant healing for this situation as we approach the year 2000, but I do see a third political party emerging in the next decade. While it may seem trite to call it "the Unity Party," the focus of this party appears to be consensus-building. There will be a profound shift toward working together toward a common vision, while accepting that there may be many different paths to reach the same goal.

4th card: The Hierophant. In the next decade we will find ourselves questioning tradition much more. We may re-visit a scenario similar to what we experienced in the 1960s. While the transition from "the way we've always done it" to "this doesn't work any longer" may be awkward and painful, the Hierophant in this 4th position represents to me a healthy change as it symbolizes the passing away of outmoded traditions. It's often seen as following the rules or staying within conventional bounds. New systems will be replacing outworn ones in politics, health care, religion/spirituality, and education.

5th card: 6 of Swords R. This card is often interpreted as getting over a tough time, picking up the pieces, heading toward a more positive place, and feeling hope once more. Again, I think this speaks to the divisiveness we have experienced as a country. We'll feel hopeful, regain our strength and compassion as a people, and begin to work together again.

6th card: Knight of Cups R. My sense of this card is that it represents our country's fear of the truth or of seeing the other side of an issue. We often reward leaders who say the right things, are charismatic, or just plain look good. We seem to place value on the superficial rather than the deeper, spiritual aspects of our lives. We want a solution and we want it now. We don't like to make commitments to long-term goals or to spend much time thinking about the values we act upon. Unfortunately, I see this as being slow to change in the next century.

7th card: The Tower. This card usually indicates sudden change, upheaval, or undergoing a crisis of some kind. In my intuitive readings for individual clients, I find that when someone doesn't choose to take action on an issue despite repeated warnings, a crisis usually erupts. For an individual, this may mean a job loss or a divorce. My reading for this card as it represents the country is that we will continue to experience the political scandals that we've experienced in the 1990s. Quite often the whole structure of something needs to be knocked down and destroyed before it can be rebuilt on a stronger foundation. The positive outcome is that when the crisis is over we'll be on our way to having many of the systems in this country—such as politics, health care, Social Security, and education—based on honesty and integrity.

8th card: Ace of Pentacles. This card is a symbol of possibility in the area of prosperity and abundance. Many of us appear to be experiencing this now with a booming economy and healthy investment market. However, there are presently many Americans who are not the recipients of wealth and good fortune. We have developed what I call an "us and them" mentality: "We have it and you don't." This is seen in our current approach that forces people off of welfare. We have go to extremes in order to ultimately bring about balance. I feel that in the next decade we will bring better reforms to this system so that it's based on rewards rather than punishment and failure.

9th card: 6 of Cups. Despite a lot of anger, violence, and mean-spiritedness, we will also experience good will and hope in this next decade. This is represented by the 9th card, the 6 of Cups. When I focus on this card I think about Rodney King saying, "Why can't we all just get along?" I see a growing spiritual movement that's not so much focused on religious dogma as it is on lending a hand, helping a neighbor, and resolving differences. The 6 of Cups is a card of simple goodness. It encourages you to be kind, generous, and forgiving. That's what we're all here to learn, and I feel hopeful that in this next decade we can begin the path of healing.

10th card: Knight of Swords. When I focus on this card I see a leader emerging in the presidential elections of 2004. I feel this person is likely to be a woman who will have a keen intellect and express ideas succinctly. She seems to speak very clearly with direction, purpose, and a great deal of charisma. There will be a sense of relief in this country when she's elected by a huge popular vote. There will be an end in sight to the divisiveness that has been occurring in politics up to this point. This woman will be seen as a true reformer! (See our reading about a woman president in Chapter 15!)

Lending a Hand

Palmist Robin Gile is also a Tarot reader, so he couldn't really separate the cards from their meanings. Here's what he wrote:

1st card: Temperance R. An intemperate, perhaps immoral and unwise use of self and resources lies at the basis of the question.

2nd card: The Lovers. The necessity of choices, perhaps with a degree of divine protection, asks that we choose between what appears safe and known, and what is idealistic and of the spirit.

3rd card: Knight of Pentacles R. Underneath this process is misapplication—a misuse of land, property, contracts (lawyers), and education.

4th card: The Hierophant. Passing out of influence are the standard teachings of religion and spiritual truths as new styles of teaching and paths to truth are manifested.

5th card: 6 of Swords R. A possible future is expressed in a headstrong attempt to maintain the status quo and not "roll with the punches" or learn from others' hardships to avoid learning the lesson manifested.

6th card: Knight of Cups R. A more probable future is seen in a rejection of wishful thinking and a pragmatic willingness to see the facts, to

Out of Time

The answer to "Are we ready for the new millennium?" is clearly a "No!", especially in light of the 1st card, Temperance reversed. However, the changes are more in keeping with a mental and philosophical set of values rather than a breakdown of supplies and service.

read the evidence as it lies, and to allow ourselves to believe what *is* rather than what we wish was.

7th card: The Tower. This card is in a rather curious place. We expect dramatic change thrust upon us; however, the other cards may indicate that this change is in values and thinking, rather than environment.

8th card: Ace of Pentacles. Again, this is a very potent card. New ideas, concepts, and practices in the material world will be expressed outside the country for our approval. There could be quite different types of social and material organization processes for a different style of culture.

9th card: 6 of Cups. A benign card, which probably says it is the next generation who will grow and grasp this dynamic of change. A card of innocence and living in the present moment, it doesn't portray a difficult transition or journey. It speaks well for the children.

10th card: Knight of Swords. Here speaks of dramatic new mental energy, communications that are different and abrupt—and a very rapid pace of change—but again, this is a mental side, not a material one.

How About It: Are *You* Ready?

You don't have to take our word for it. If you've got a deck of Tarot cards, you can find out if *you're* ready for the new millennium. In the following sections, we've created a workbook for you to use each of the disciplines in this book to examine your own Tarot spread about the new millennium. Are you ready?

Your Tarot Spread

Before you begin, select a card to represent yourself in your spread. Many people select a Minor Arcana King or Queen, but you can choose any card you want. This card will be placed in the 1st position of your Celtic Cross Spread.

Ask Spaceship Earth

Many Tarot readers suggest cutting the deck with your left hand to tap into your intuitive energy more fully. It can't hurt!

Now, shuffle your deck of Tarot cards as you meditate on the question. Remember, as we told you in Chapter 12, that each time you shuffle, you should turn one part of the deck in the opposite direction, so that some cards will be reversed.

Shuffle the cards until you feel they're ready, then, if you wish, cut the deck as well. Then, continuing to think about the question (you can say it out loud, if you want), lay the cards out in the rest of the Celtic Cross Spread.

You can use the spaces we've provided below to write your cards. Or, if you'd like to make copies of this form so you can use it for all your Celtic Cross Spreads, that's fine, too.

Now, using either the quick card meanings in Chapters 12, 13, and 14 of this book, or the more detailed card meanings you'll find in *The Complete Idiot's Guide to Tarot and Fortune-Telling*, write down your interpretations of the cards below.

1st card (you) _____

2nd card (cover) _____

3rd card (basis) _____

4th card (past) _____

5th card (could happen) _____

6th card (will happen) _____

7th card (attitudes) _____

8th card (others) _____

9th card (go through) _____

10th card (outcome) _____

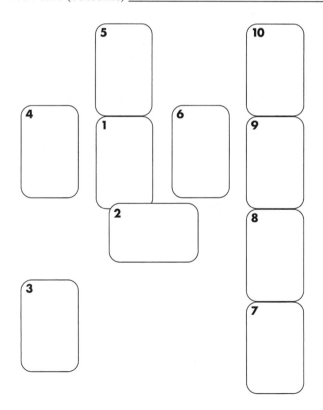

Your Celtic Cross Spread.

What did you discover? Do your Tarot interpretations say that you're ready for the new millennium? Or are there areas where you need to do some more preparation?

But don't stop with just the Tarot interpretation of the cards. Here are some ways for you to use the cards to gain some other insights as well.

Other Insights

Just as Sheila did above, you can use astrology to interpret your Tarot reading. Chapters 4 and 5 (as well as the "Astrology and Tarot" chapter in *The Complete Idiot's Guide to Astrology*) will give you the background you need to do just that. Take your time—the connection between the Tarot and astrology is a subtle one.

Next, using the numerological insights you gained in Chapter 9, you can, like Kay, explore the numerological aspects of your Tarot reading. In this case, you'll be looking at the numbers on the cards, whether it's the key numbers of the Major Arcana, or the face numbers of the Minor Arcana. The "Tarot and Numerology" chapters in *The Complete Idiot's Guide to Tarot and Fortune-Telling* and *The Complete Idiot's Guide to Numerology* will also be quite helpful to you.

Ask Spaceship Earth

Don't forget—the numbers on the cards can also tell you something about possible timing for the question.

Next, it's time to return to Chapter 19 of this book and see what your psychic intuition can tell you about your Tarot reading, as Lynn did earlier. Looking at your Tarot spread, meditate on the pictures themselves to explore what your intuition can tell you about the cards and what they're telling you.

In Chapter 23, we explored the basics of palmistry. If you'd like, you can use that chapter to explore the connections between your Tarot reading and palmistry. Can you make any connections between the microcosm of your palm, the macrocosm of your self, and what your reading has to say?

Humanity's Future on Spaceship Earth

One thing's clear from this book—humanity's here to stay—or at least for a long, long time. There's no *apocalypse* in the cards, there's no asteroid racing toward a collision with Earth, and there's no AIDS-like virus waiting to wipe us all out.

Rather, what's clear is that the future of our planet—and our universe—is in all of our hands. It's *synergy* that we need to focus upon. When we look to the stars, we can see not only our future but our past and present, and we can count on our future to be everything we can make it.

Perhaps, over the next thousand years, future gen-erations will live in tune with the ancient Music of the Spheres—the ethereal music that Pythagoreans believed set the heavens in motion. Perhaps new millennium physics will understand these musical metaphysical theo-rems. Perhaps humankind will grow beyond the orb of the earth. Only time will tell!

With this book, you've got the tools for a better tomorrow. Now, it's up to you! Welcome to the new millennium.

Speaking Y2K

An **apocalypse** is any world-ending event. Obviously, such an event would be of massive proportions, such as nuclear holocaust, an asteroid, or a killer virus. The New Age Collective foresees no apocalypses in our future! **Synergy**, the notion that teamwork creates more than individuals can on their own, could be the lesson of surviving and thriving in the new millennium.

The Least You Need to Know

➤ The experts examine if we're ready for the new millennium.

➤ The cards say we need to be patient and ready for anything in the new millennium.

➤ The experts take a look at the cards.

➤ You can use the Tarot to find out if *you're* ready.

➤ Humanity's future on Spaceship Earth is up to all of us.

Glossary

In numerology, the **1 millennium** governs years 1000–1999 (it's what we're leaving behind). The **2 millennium** governs years 2000–2999. We're raising the vibration with this move.

Affirmations are a way of telling yourself what's good about you and your life to help you to achieve your goals.

You can think of the **Akashic Records** as a "cosmic memory bank," containing information about everything that has occurred in the universe, including details of every soul and every life ever lived.

In palmistry, the **angle of generosity**, measured between the thumb and the Jupiter (pointer) finger, reveals how you relate to others.

Your **Apollo finger**, or ring finger, is where you'll find your creativity and taste.

Archetype is a term used by psychoanalyst Carl Jung to represent patterns of the psyche, such as characters that have universal meaning. The Hero is an archetype, for example, and so is the Villain.

Artificial intelligence refers to a machine's capability to think for itself and emulate the human mind. True artificial intelligence would actually think, feel, and sense as a human does. This technology is far, far in the future.

In astrology, an **aspect** between two planets in your birth chart is a measurement of the spatial relationship between the two planets in the sky for the moment you were born. Astrologers also track the spatial relationship between different planets as they move in their orbit around the Sun, and how they aspect one another at any given moment in time.

Astrology is the study of planetary cycles and their connection to events and people on Earth.

Each of us has an **aura**, a field of electromagnetic energy that permeates and surrounds all living things.

In numerology, the **balance number**, found by adding together the numbers for the initials of your name, tells how you might deal with the challenges of the new millennium.

In astrology, your **birth chart** uses the date, time, and place of your birth to show the positions of the planets in their signs and houses at the moment of your birth. It creates a unique symbolic map of who you are.

In the Tarot, **Cups** explore your emotional life and creativity.

Days are based on the length of time from sunset to sunset.

Distant healing involves acknowledging and accepting a greater force than the self to help heal.

A **dystopia**, the opposite of a utopia, is a society where the conditions of life are dreadful.

In astrology, the four **elements**—fire, earth, air, and water—are the four basic components of life on the earth.

In astrology, the two **energies**—*yin* and *yang*—describe the universal balancing act between the active and passive components of life.

In astrology, an **event chart** uses the time, date, and place of an event to calculate its potentials and possibilities.

Fusion power is a way of using hydrogen atoms to create energy, and is the method behind hydrogen bombs.

The **Gaia Hypothesis** is based on the concept that the earth is a "super-organism" that encompasses all planetary processes.

In astrology, a **grand earth trine** occurs when all three earth element planets are in trine, an astrological aspect of 120°, which is considered quite favorable.

The **Great Cycle** is one of the basic concepts of the ancient Mayan calendar. It represents 5125.36 years according to the Gregorian calendar we use now.

Guided imagery is a form of daydreaming. Specific images are used to visualize the body healing and staying strong. Examples of this are conjuring up images of a tumor shrinking or of high blood pressure decreasing.

In astrology, **hard aspects**, the conjunction, squares, and opposition, are so-called because they symbolically invite deep change and adjustment processes.

The **Hero's Journey** is the name mythologist Joseph Campbell gave to the pattern of adventures—both heroes' and your own.

In the Tarot, a **horoscope spread** is a yearly overview for your life, using the format of an astrological chart as its basis.

The **houses**, the *where* of astrology, are symbolic territories in your life in which the planetary characters hang out. Like rooms in your home, they're places where different activities take place: You sleep in the bedroom; eat in the dining room; socialize in the living room, and so on. Each of the 12 houses encompasses a specific arena of life and is the stage where the drama of the planets unfolds.

439

Intuition is a way of acquiring knowledge without conscious thought processes.

The **intuitive arts** include astrology, numerology, palmistry, psychic and intuitive abilities, and the Tarot. Because they can't be "proven" in the strict sense demanded by "rational" science, there are those who feel these aren't legitimate sciences.

You'll find that as you take small steps in the right direction you'll experience an **intuitive nudge**. This may come in the form of a coincidence or synchronicity. Things will begin falling into place. It's your intuition telling you you're on the right path.

In palmistry, your **Jupiter finger**, or pointer finger, is where you'll find your wisdom, leadership qualities, and optimism, as well as your self-esteem and charisma.

Kinesthetic impressions are those that are felt rather than visualized. Some examples of kinesthetic intuition are an emotional sense, a sense of direct knowing, a hot or cold sensation, or what we call a gut feeling.

A **light year** is the distance that light travels in one year, moving at its speed of 186,000 miles per second. One light year equals six million million miles.

In numerology, **master numbers** are thought to be stronger and more charged with energy than numbers 1–9. Master numbers are 11, 22, and 33.

In palmistry, your **Mercury finger**, or little finger, is the area of communication, commerce, and healing.

Molecular medicine uses each germ's genome to identify its molecular weaknesses.

Months are based on the lunar cycle (month = moon).

In palmistry, your palm is divided into **mounts**, each of which is an area where specific action unfolds.

Myths are stories that are told to explain what's difficult to understand. Myths are not lies, but ways of understanding. You can think of *The Wizard of Oz* as a myth that helps us understand that "our heart's desire is in our own backyards."

New Age is a collective term for practitioners and followers of the intuitive arts. Its derivation comes from the concept of the "new age" of Aquarius, which, based on the precession of the equinoxes, will be occurring at about the same time as the new millennium.

In astrology, the **Nodes**, North and South, are a paired set of points that relates to the Moon's orbit around the earth. Their energies show what behaviors you've inherited and where your potential for growth lies.

The **non-local mind** is a term physicists use to describe the lack of location of human consciousness in any specific place within the body.

Numerology is a system of relating names and numbers to gain insight into the human condition.

Palmistry, or **chiromancy**, is an ancient method of studying the macrocosm of the self through the microcosm of the hand.

Parables are stories that represent other stories. By using examples that seem different from one's own society, stories can make points that might not otherwise be made.

George Orwell's *Animal Farm*, for example, uses barnyard animals to show how humans can abuse power.

In the Tarot, **Pentacles** are the cards of your material and financial world.

In numerology, a **personal year number** tells the theme of a particular year for you personally.

In palmistry, the **phalanges** of the thumb (or any finger) refer to the three sections separated by the finger's joints.

In astrology, **planetary pairs** are two planets that have a unique timeline for completing their cycles with each other.

The **planets** are the *what* of astrology. They symbolize key characters that live within your personality and the culture at large as archetypes, or universal patterns. The planets are those heavenly bodies that, from our perspective on Earth, appear to rotate around us. The planets are the Sun, the Moon, Mercury, Venus, Mars, Jupiter, Saturn, Uranus, Neptune, and Pluto. In this book, we'll also include the comet Chiron and the North and South Nodes (which aren't actual planets).

The **precession of the equinoxes** is the term given to describe the Sun's apparent motion into different zodiac signs through the ages.

In astrology, the three **qualities**—cardinal, fixed, and mutable—describe a three-fold developmental process that shows a sign's mode of operation.

In palmistry, the **quality** of a line is an indication of the level of strength and vitality in that particular area of life. The deeper and more well-cut a line, the stronger its quality.

In palmistry, the **Quantum Leap** is the name given to a life line that changes radically at mid-life to reflect a major career or life change at that time.

A **rectification** of your birth chart is done when you don't know the exact time of your birth. An astrologer will use important events in your life and how you behave in certain situations to determine the time you were born.

In astrology, when planets are **retrograde**, their motion from our perspective on Earth appears to be backward. Planets do not actually move backwards, though. **Transiting retrogrades**, which occur in our day-to-day lives, occur according to the movements of the planets, and affect us all. A **personal retrograde** is a fancy way of saying that a planet was retrograde at the moment you were born.

In palmistry, **rising lines** start in the palm of the hand and point to a specific finger. They indicate added strength in that particular area.

In palmistry, your **Saturn finger**, or middle finger, is in charge of rules, regulations, and discipline.

In palmistry, the **set** of the thumb (or any finger) is a term for where on the hand the finger literally sits. In the case of the thumb, for example, it may begin at the wrist, or it may appear to start higher up on the side of the hand. A thumb that starts closer to the wrist is called **low-set**. One that starts higher up is called **high-set**.

The **signs** are the *how* of astrology. They are descriptions of how the planetary characters express their energies. The 12 zodiac signs are Aries, Taurus, Gemini, Cancer, Leo, Virgo, Libra, Scorpio, Sagittarius, Capricorn, Aquarius, and Pisces.

The 12 astrological **Sun signs**—Aries, Taurus, Gemini, Cancer, Leo, Virgo, Libra, Scorpio, Sagittarius, Capricorn, Aquarius, and Pisces—describe how planetary characters express their energies.

In the Tarot, **Swords** are the cards of conflict, obstacles, and aggression.

Synchronicity is the concept, first discussed by psychoanalyst Carl Jung, that everything in the universe is interrelated. "As above, so below" is a synchronous concept.

The **Tarot** is an ancient method of fortune-telling, which uses the 78 cards of the Tarot deck to create a story of you—past, present, and future.

A **Tarot deck** contains 22 **Major Arcana** and 56 **Minor Arcana** cards. The Major Arcana depict an archetypal journey through life, while the Minor Arcana show everyday events.

Tarot spreads are different methods of laying out the cards during a Tarot reading. **Tarot readings** occur when the cards are laid out to reveal a particular story, often in answer to a question.

TEOTWAWKI is an acronym for "the end of the world as we know it." It's become a popular phrase on Internet sites discussing everything from the Y2K computer bug to apocalyptic predictions.

Every year, the entire planet earth is under the same calendar year. This is called the **universal year** in numerology. For example, 1999 ($1 + 9 + 9 + 9 = 8 + 2 = 1$), is a 1 universal year.

In numerology, a number's **vibration** is its intensity of energy, or the emotional response associated with the number.

In the Tarot, **Wands** are the suit of enterprise, growth, and development.

Years are the time from spring equinox to spring equinox.

The **zodiac** is the name of the circular path through the stars against which the earth travels in its annual orbit of the Sun. The zodiac is divided into 12 equal segments called the **zodiac signs**. From our perspective on Earth, it looks like the planets are circling around us as they move against the backdrop of the zodiac.

Y2K Hotline and Web Sites: Be Prepared!

The transition to the new century presents a challenge to our high-tech computer technology. Are you ready? Y2K computer bug or no, people are questioning the efficacy of high-tech gadgets and advances: Are high-tech advancements *really* enhancing our lives? Where is the balance between the old way of doing things (before PCs, VCRs, TVs, even cars or light bulbs) and the new way.

The wonderfully amazing technological innovations introduced in the 20th century will have a lasting impact on life in the 21st century and into the new millennium. How humanity will use this new knowledge and integrate it into the daily lives of human beings around the globe... well, we feel that's one of the major challenges and priorities we all face today.

Performing an Internet search on "Y2K" or "Year 2000" will no doubt produce hundreds of links to Web sites and resources on issues related to coping with the millennium transition. We've listed several places to get you started. Remember that the democratic nature of the Internet means that everyone can air an opinion or create a site. Use sound judgment in assessing the information you access on the Internet. As always, assembling your own personal community network of professionals is a good way to prepare for any life event.

Ready or not, here's to a safe journey to the new millennium!

Y2K Hotlines

You don't have to go online to get up-to-the-millennium information about the Y2K computer bug. The Federal Information Center of the U.S. government has set up a hotline to answer your questions! Here's the number:

> 1-888-USA-4-Y2K (1-888-872-4925)

In its first month of operation, this number logged more than 50,000 calls. Mostly, says one of its operators, "People want reassurance... about what's going to happen."

Some of the information available from the government Y2K hotline includes:

➤ Information from various government agencies about Y2K compliance

➤ Updates on whether people with special medical needs should plan ahead

➤ Answers to questions about how the millennium bug could affect everything from your microwave to your car

Operators on the government hotline can tap into a 1.75-million-item database to answer your questions. And, if you call after hours, pre-recorded information is available that addresses most FAQs (that's WWW-ese for "Frequently Asked Questions").

Web Sites to Access

The following Web sites cover a broad spectrum of approaches to the Y2K transition. Inclusion of a source in this list does not mean that the New Age Collective endorses the viewpoints, advice, services, or opinions expressed therein. Our goal is simply to present a selection of Web sites as a starting point for individual exploration. As ever, the future belongs to *you*. We leave it to you to evaluate and assess the information you access about Y2K.

In the words of Utah Republican Senator Robert Bennett, chairman of the Senate's special committee on Y2K, "When we get to New Year's Eve, everybody, no matter how informed we think we are, is going to be holding his breath."

8 Myths About the Millennium Bug
www.cnet.com/Content/Features/Dlife/Millbut/index.html

What's true and what's hype? Check it out.

Cassandra Project
www.cassandraproject.org/cassabout.html

This grassroots non-profit organization exists to "raise public awareness and alert Public Sector organizations of potential Y2K related health and safety risks, and interruption of basic and essential services." The site advocates preparedness and community action.

Dr. Ed Yardeni's Economics Network
www.yardeni.com

The Chief Economist and Global Investment Strategist of Deutsche Bank Securities in New York gives his take on the Y2K conundrum.

duh-2000
www.duh-2000.com

This site hosts a monthly contest to award the stupidest thing said about the Y2K problem. You'll see everyone who's anyone listed here—from politicians to business leaders to the average Joe or Jane on the street.

Human Services Outreach Center
U.S. Department of Health and Human Services (DHHS)
Y2K Resources Homepage
http://y2k.acf.dhhs.gov

This Web site is a collaboration of several U.S. agencies, supplemented with funding from Congress. The site has two areas: Y2K 101 and Y2K Solution Center. Y2K 101 is aimed at nontechnical users, answering questions and providing information. The Y2K Solution Center is a resource for experienced visitors who are looking for solutions to technical problems. The site includes links to state, federal, and vendor sites, as well as a document library and glossary.

Information Technology Association of America
www.itaa.org

This association of IT professionals gives extensive information on the Y2K computer bug and how it will affect business systems and operations. The site is a good source for legislation and legal ramifications of the Y2K bug too.

IT2000: The National Bulletin Board for Year 2000
www.it2000.com

This site is a comprehensive clearinghouse for Y2K issues and information.

Prepare Today
www.y2kfoodsource.com

This site is an independent food broker. If you're inclined to store foods, you'll want to investigate sites such as this one.

U.S. Federal Government Gateway for Year 2000 Information Directories
www.itpolicy.gsa.gov/mks/yr2000/yekhome.htm

This site is a clearinghouse for Y2K information, "from best practices for the Y2K project team to advice for the consumer and citizen." Links include "Community Web Guide to Y2K," "President's Council on Year 2000 Conversion," "International Y2K Conference," and "Y2K for Kids."

Y2K Citizen's Action Guide
www.utne.com/Y2K/index.html

The *Utne Reader* staff has a wonderful Web site, which includes this citizen's primer to Y2K.

Y2K Today
www.y2ktoday.com/modules/home/new_body.asp

Here's an all-purpose forum for Y2K issues around the world and in major industries from aerospace to media to transportation and utilities. Y2K Today features a comprehensive library of links to other interesting sites from the Federal Reserve Board to the American Booksellers Association, to find out what other organizations have to say about life in the year 2000.

Further Reading About the New Millennium

New Millennium, General

Appel, Allan. *A Portable Apocalypse*. New York, NY: Riverhead, 1998.

Braden, Greg. *Awakening to Zero Point*. Bellevue, WA: Radio Bookstore Press, 1997.

Kaku, Michio. *Visions: How Science Will Revolutionize the 21st Century*. New York, NY: Anchor, 1997.

Minkin, Barry Howard. *Future In Sight*. New York, NY: Macmillan, 1995.

Tyl, Noel. *Predictions for a New Millennium*. St. Paul: Llewellyn Publications, 1996.

Yourdon, Edward and Jennifer Yourdon. *Time Bomb 2000*. Upper Saddle River, NJ: Prentice-Hall, 1998.

Astrology

Gerwick-Brodeur, Madeline and Lisa Lenard. *The Complete Idiot's Guide to Astrology*. New York, NY: Alpha Books, 1997.

Gimbutas, Marija. *The Language of the Goddess*. New York, NY: HarperCollins, 1989.

Matthews, Caitlin. *The Elements of the Goddess*. Longmead, England: Element Books Limited, 1989.

Meece, E. Alan. *Horoscope for the New Millennium*. St. Paul, MN: Llewellyn Publications, 1997.

Sjoo, Monica and Barbara Mor. *The Great Cosmic Mother: Rediscovering the Religion of the Earth*. San Francisco, CA: Harper and Row, 1987.

Tarriktar, Tem. "Millennium Alignments: 1999–2000." *The Mountain Astrologer*, June/July 1998, pp. 67–71; 129.

Tyl, Noel. *Astrology Looks at History*. St. Paul, MN: Llewellyn Publications, 1995.

_____. "Jupiter-Saturn Synthesis: 20-Year Cycles of History in the Making." *The Mountain Astrologer*, July 1995, pp. 39–49.

Numerology

Decoz, Hans. *Numerology, Key To Your Inner Self*. Garden City Park, NY: Avery Publishing Group, 1994.

Goodwin, Matthew. *Numerology, The Complete Guide* vols. 1 and 2. North Hollywood, CA: Newcastle Publishing, 1981.

Jeanne. *Numerology, Spiritual Light Vibrations*. Salem, OR: Your Center for Truth Press, 1987.

Jordan, Juno. *Numerology, The Romance in Your Name*. Marina del Rey, CA: DeVorss & Co., 1966.

Lagerquist, Kay and Lisa Lenard. *The Complete Idiot's Guide to Numerology*. New York, NY: Alpha Books, 1999.

Palmistry

Benham, William G. *The Benham Book of Palmistry*. North Hollywood, CA: Newcastle Publishing, 1988.

Campbell, Ed. *The Encyclopedia of Palmistry*. New York, NY: Berkley, 1966.

Cheiro. *Cheiro's Language of the Hand*. New York, NY: Prentice Hall, 1987.

Costaville, Maria. *How to Read Palms*. New York, NY: Crescent, 1988.

Gile, Robin and Lisa Lenard. *The Complete Idiot's Guide to Palmistry*. New York, NY: Alpha Books, 1999.

Psychic Intuition

Manning, James. *Prophecies for the New Millennium*. New York, NY: HarperCollins, 1997.

Robinson, Lynn A. and LaVonne Carlson-Finnerty. *The Complete Idiot's Guide to Being Psychic*. New York, NY: Alpha Books, 1999.

Seale, Alan. *On Becoming a 21st Century Mystic: Pathways to Intuitive Living*. New York, NY: Skytop Publishing, 1997.

Sinetar, Marsha. *Developing a 21st Century Mind*. New York, NY: Ballantine, 1991.

Timms, Moira. *Beyond Prophecies and Predictions: Everyone's Guide to the Coming Changes*. New York, NY: Ballantine, 1994.

The Tarot

Arrien, Angeles. *The Tarot Handbook*. Sonoma, CA: Arcus Publishing Co., 1987.

Carlson, Laura. *Tarot Unveiled: The Method to Its Magic*. Stanford, CT: U.S. Games Systems, Inc., 1988.

Connolly, Eileen. *Tarot: A New Handbook for the Apprentice*. North Hollywood, CA: Newcastle Publishing, 1979.

Fairfield, Gail. *Choice Centered Tarot*. Smithville, IN: Ramp Creek Publishing, 1984.

Garen, Nancy. *Tarot Made Easy*. New York, NY: Fireside, 1989.

Gray, Eden. *The Complete Guide to the Tarot*. New York, NY: Bantam, 1972.

_____, *Mastering the Tarot*. New York, NY: Penguin, 1988.

Greer, Mary. *Tarot for Your Self*. North Hollywood, CA: Newcastle Publishing, 1984.

Louis, Anthony. *Tarot, Plain and Simple*. St. Paul, MN: Llewellyn Publishing, 1997.

Martello, Leo Louis. *Reading the Tarot*. Garden City Park, NY: Avery Publishing Group, 1990.

Tognetti, Arlene and Lisa Lenard. *The Complete Idiot's Guide to Tarot and Fortune-Telling*. New York, NY: Alpha Books, 1998.

Index

Symbols

1 millennium, 135
1984, 16
2 millennium, 135
2001: A Space Odyssey, 17
21st century, growth
  assignments, 117-121
21st Century Online Magazine,
  319-320
8 Myths About the Millennium
  Bug Web site, 446

A

A.R.E. (Association for Research
  and Enlightenment), 330
Ace of Cups (Minor Arcana
  card), 201
Ace of Pentacles (Minor Arcana
  card), 218
Ace of Swords (Minor Arcana
  card), 210
Ace of Wands (Minor Arcana
  card), 194
Active Mars, 364
adapters, 44-45
affirmations, 300
African-Americans, statistics,
  28
age statistics, 29-31
Age of Aquarius, 118-119, 124
Age of Aries, 124
Age of Gaia, 145-146
Age of Pisces, 119
Age of Taurus, 124
agricultural engineering,
  predictions, 404
AIDS, predictions, 262-265, 395
air signs, 46
All That Is, 295
Alpha Centauri, 34
Anderson, W. French, 401
angle of eccentricity, Mercury
  finger, 350
angle of generosity,
  thumbs, 345

animal rights, predictions,
  387-389
anno domini, 19
Antichrists, Nostradamus
  prophesy, 329
apocalypses, 437
Apollo moon missions, 7
Apollo finger (ring finger), 352,
  362
Appel, Allan, 449
Aprilus, 20
Aquarius, 42-45, 54-55
archetypes, planets, 41
Aries, 42, 50
Armstrong, Neil, 5
Arrhenius, Svante, 407
Arrien, Angelis, 451
art predictions, 16-19, 270-273
artificial intelligence, 400
aspects
  hard aspects, 71-74
  measuring, Sun and Moon,
    71
  planets, 62-64
Association for Research and
  Enlightenment, *see* A.R.E.
asteroids, predictions, 395
astrologers, locating, 88
astrology, 20, 39-44, 127,
  449-450
  archetypes, 41
  Belanger, Shelia, 426-428
  birth charts, 47-48, 81-101,
    111-116
  event charts, 48-49, 81-85,
    91-93
  houses, 42, 57-59
  Nodes, 60
  planets, 41-43, 59, 59-71
  signs, 42-46, 50-55
  synchronicity, 41
  zodiac, 42, 50-55, 59-61
aura, 317
aural sensations, intuition, 296

B

Baby Boomers
  birth charts, 112
  palm features, 372-375
Back to the Future, 406
balance, 145, 308-313
balance numbers, 165-167
Belanger, Shelia, 3, 8, 426-428
Benham, William G., 450
Biblical prophesies, 327-328
birth charts, 47-48, 57-59,
  81-101, 111-116
body enhancements,
  predictions, 392
bookstores, metaphysical,
  locating, 88
Borg, *Star Trek*, 368
Bosch, Hieronymus, 5
Boys from Brazil, The, 405
Braden, Gregg, 145, 449
Braque, Georges, 17
Breathnach, Sarah Ban, 148
Brennan, Barbara Ann, 336
Buck, Pearl, 372
bulls, 51
Byrd, Randolph, 307

C

Caesar, Julius, 20
calendars, 19-22, 159-161
Campbell, Ed, 450
Campbell, Joseph, 4, 321
Cancer, 42-45, 52
Canfield, Jack, 320
Canton, James, 320
Capricorn, 42-45, 54
Cardinal quality, signs, 44
cards, Tarot, *See* Tarot
Carlson, Laura, 451
cashless society, predictions,
  417
Cassandra Project Web site,
  446
cataclysms, predictions,
  394-396

Catholic Church, 21st Century view, 328
Cayce, Edgar, prophesies, 330-331
Celtic Cover spread, 239
Celtic Cross spreads, 234
centaurs, 65-66
centuries, challenges and achievements, 22-23
change agents, 64-68
Chariot card (Major Arcana card), 182
chi, 306
Chinese calendar, 21
Chinese numerology, 153
chiromancy, *see* palmistry
Chiron, 43, 63-66, 71, 78-79, 100
Chopra, Deepak, 318
Christianity
  Biblical prophesies, 327-328
  Judgement Day, Associated Press survey, 327
chronos time, 148-150
Clarke, Arthur C., 17, 24
Clinton, Hillary Rodham, 250
  balance number, 167
  birth chart, 89
  political future, prediction, 277-282
clock time, *see* chronos time
cloning, predictions, 404-405
clothing, predictions, 402-403
Collins, Francis, 403
conjunction aspect, 62
conjunctions
  Chiron-Pluto conjunction of December 30, 1999, 100
  Jupiter-Saturn conjunctions, 102-111
  Neptune-Pluto conjunction of 1982, 94-96
  New Moon of May 2000, 100-101
  New Moon solar eclipse of August 1999, 98-100
  planetary pairs, 72
  Uranus-Neptune conjunction of 1993, 97-98
  Uranus-Pluto conjunction of 1965–1966, 96
connectedness, two, 144
Connolly, Eileen, 451
Copernicus, 5
Costaville, Maria, 450

Council of Nicea, 19, 21
cubism, 17-19
cultural diversity, United States, statistics, 30
Cups (Minor Arcana cards), 176, 192, 201-208, 236-237, 285
  See also specific cards
currency predictions, 415-417
cusps, birth charts, 89
CyberCoin, 417
cycles
  numerology, 153
  planetary pairs, 70-71, 74-81

D

Dalai Lama, 337
dark moons, 82
days, 20
death, 308
Death card (Major Arcana card), 185
December, 20
Decision Spread, 287-289
Decoz, Hans, 450
demographics, United States, statistics, 28
Depression/World War II generation, palm features, 370-372
Devil card (Major Arcana card), 186
diameter, earth, 33
dipoles, 334
distant healing, 306-307
Divine Intelligence, 295
Dole, Elizabeth, 250
dollar, exchange rates, 417
dominant fingers, 346
Dossey, Larry, 307
Dow-Jones Industrial Average, 414
Dr. Ed Yardeni's Economics Network Web site, 446
dreams, intuition, 296
duh-2000 Web site, 446
Dylan, Bob, 153
Dyson, Freeman, 17
dystopia, 16

E

earth, 33-34, 46, 334
Easter, 21
eastern horizon point, 59
Ebola virus, 331
economy, global, predictions, 234-238, 418-419
Eden, Gary, 451
ego, dissolution and liberation, 67
Egyptian calendars, 20
eight, 133, 164-166
Eight of Cups (Minor Arcana card), 205, 237
Eight of Pentacles (Minor Arcana card), 221
Eight of Swords (Minor Arcana card), 214
Eight of Wands (Minor Arcana card), 197
Einstein, Albert, 6
elements (signs), 44-46, 76
Emperor card (Major Arcana card), 180
Empress card (Major Arcana card), 180
energies, 44
  numbers, 132-134
  yang and yin, 44
English (global language), 418
environment, predictions, 267-273
European Union currency exchange rates, 417
event charts, 48-49, 81-84, 91-93
exchange rates, 415-417
expressions, numbers, 139

F

fabrics, predictions, 403
Fairfield, Gail, 451
family values, predictions, 246-248
FAQs (Frequently Asked Questions), 446
February, 20
Federal Information Center of the U.S. government, 445
feelings, intuition, 296-297
female president, prediction, 248-251

feminism, rise of, 123-127, 145
Ferraro, Geraldine, 250
finance, predictions, 243
fingers, 346-354
    Apollo finger (ring finger),
        352, 362
    dominant finger, 347
    Jupiter finger (pointer
        finger), 353-354, 363
    Mercury finger (little
        finger), 350-351, 362
    mounts, 358-365
    phalanges, 347
    Saturn finger (middle
        finger), 352-353, 362
fire signs, 46
First Quarter phase (Moon), 70
First Quarter Saturn Square
    Neptune cycle, 71
First Quarter squares, 73
five, 133, 158, 163, 166
Five of Cups (Minor Arcana
    card), 203, 236
Five of Pentacles (Minor
    Arcana card), 220, 236
Five of Swords (Minor Arcana
    card), 212, 237
Five of Wands (Minor Arcana
    card), 196
Fixed quality, signs, 44
Fool card (Major Arcana card),
    172, 178
forms, intuition, 296
four, 133, 158, 163, 166
Four of Cups (Minor Arcana
    card), 203
Four of Pentacles (Minor
    Arcana card), 219
Four of Swords (Minor Arcana
    card), 174-175, 212
Four of Wands (Minor Arcana
    card), 195
Foxworthy, Jeff, 401
Full Moon phase (Moon), 70
fusion power, predictions,
    406-407

G

Gaia theory, 125, 408
Galileo, 6
Gandhi, Indira, 250
Garen, Nancy, 451
Gasheseoma, Martin, 332
Gates, Bill, 403

Gemini, 42-44, 51
Generation X, palm features,
    375-378
generational birth charts,
    111-116
generational differences in
    palms, 368-382, 385-387
genetic engineering, predic-
    tions, 403-406
Gerwick-Brodeur, Madeline, 12,
    449
Gilbert, Walter, 404
Gile, Robin, 3, 8, 9-10, 341,
    433-434, 450
Gilman, Cheryl, 300
Gimbutas, Marija, 124, 449
"Girl Before a Mirror," 18
global community, 337-338
global economy, predictions,
    234-238, 415-419
global warming, 267, 407-409
God/Goddess, 295
Goddesses, 123-127
gold standard, 415
Good Will Hunting, 322
Goodwin, Matthew, 450
grand earth trines, 126
Great Cycle (Mayan calendar),
    334
Greenspan, Alan, 412, 414
Greer, Mary, 451
Gregorian calendar, 21
Gregory XIII, Pope, 21
growth assignments, 21st
    century, 117-121
guided imagery, 310
Gutenberg, Johannes, 400
Gypsy Wish Spread, 284-287

H

hands
    aspects, 71-74
    fingers, 346-354, 362-365
    head lines, 355-356
    heart lines, 354-355
    life lines, 357
    line quality, 354, 381
    markings, 358
    mounts, 358-365
    planet names, 342-343
    rising lines, 354, 357-358
    thumbs, 343-346
Hanged Man card (Major
    Arcana card), 184

head lines (palmistry), 355-356
healing, 265, 303-311
health, 262-265, 381
hearing, intuition, 297
heart lines (palmistry), 354-355
heavenly bodies, *see* planets
Heisenberg, W.K., 18
Hermit card (Major Arcana
    card), 183
Hierophant card (Major Arcana
    card), 181, 228
High Priestess card (Major
    Arcana card), 179
high-sets, thumbs, 343
Hitler, Adolph, 329
homes, predictions, 403
Hopi people, prophesies,
    332-333
Horoscope Spreads, 276-282
houses, 57-59, 93-94
    astrology, 42
    cusps, 89
Human Genome Project,
    403-406
Human Services Outreach
    Center Web site, 447
Hussein, Saddam, 329
Huxley, Aldus, 16

I

IC&C (Intuitive Consulting &
    Communication), 11
illnesses, positive aspects of,
    310-311
imagery
    guided imagery and healing,
        310-311
    intuition, 296
immigration, United States,
    statistics, 28
impressions, 18
index fingers (Jupiter finger),
    353-354, 363
Information Technology
    Association of America Web
    site, 447
initiators, 44-45
InterCoin, 417
interconnectedness, 316
interdependence, 149-150
Internet, 413

intuition, 3-7, 39-43, 293-308,
319-320, 431-433
    balance, 308-313
    guided imagery, 310
    meditation, 316-319
Intuitive Consulting &
    Communication, *see* IC&C
IPCC (Intergovernmental Panel
    on Climate Change), 408
IPOs (Initial Public Offerings),
    413
IT2000: The National Bulletin
    Board for Year 2000 Web site,
    447

J

January, 20
Janus, the god of doorways, 20
Jeanne, 450
Jenkins, John Major, 334
Jesus, second coming of,
    Associated Press survey, 327
Jewish calendar, 21
JFK, 16
jobs, predictions, 412
Johnson, Lyndon B., Viet Nam,
    troop build-up, 80
Jordan, Juno, 450
Joseph, 15
journals
    intuitive information, 298
    Tarot, 173, 232-233
Judaism, Biblical prophesies,
    327-328
Judgement card (Major Arcana
    card), 189
Judgement Day, Associated
    Press survey, 327
Julian calendars, 20
Jung, Carl, 4
    archetypes, 41
    intuition, 295
    synchronicity, 41
Junius, 20
Jupiter, 60, 63-65, 450
    Jupiter-Saturn conjunctions,
        70, 75-76, 102-111
    Jupiter-Saturn cycles, 70,
        75-76
    symbol, 43, 60
Jupiter finger (pointer finger),
    353-354, 363
Justice card (Major Arcana
    card), 184

K

kairos time, 148-149
Kaku, Michio, 401, 449
kalendae, 19
Kardashev, Nikolai, 17
karma spreads, 226-229
Karmic Spread, 283-284
Katra, Jane, 307
Kierkegaard, Søren, 300
kinesthetic intuition, 297
King of Cups (Minor Arcana
    card), 208
King of Pentacles (Minor
    Arcana card), 224
King of Swords (Minor Arcana
    card), 217
King of Wands (Minor Arcana
    card), 200
Knight of Cups (Minor Arcana
    card), 207, 236
Knight of Pentacles (Minor
    Arcana card), 223
Knight of Swords (Minor
    Arcana card), 216
Knight of Wands (Minor
    Arcana card), 199
Kowal, Charles, 65
Krauss, Lawrence M., 419
Kubrick, Stanley, 17

L

labor, predictions, 412
Lagerquist, Kay, 3, 8-10,
    428-431, 450
Last Cry, 331
Last Quarter phase (Moon), 70
left handed cutting, Tarot deck,
    434
Leo, 42-45, 52
Leo X, Pope, 5
Leonardo da Vinci, 368-369
"Let That Be Your Final
    Battlefield," *Star Trek*, 324
letters, number designations,
    151, 165
Levin, Ira, 405
Libra, 42-45, 53
life expectancies, 381, 405-406
life lines, 357, 374-375
life paths, 155
light years, 34

line quality, palmistry, 354,
    381
little finger (Mercury finger),
    350-351, 362
Louis, Anthony, 451
Lovelock, James and Lynn
    Margulis, Gaia Theory, 408
Lovers card (Major Arcana
    card), 181, 228
low-sets, thumbs, 343

M

MacArthur Foundation Study
    of Aging in America, 405
Magician card (Major Arcana
    card), 179
magnetic shifts, 334
Maius, 20
Major Arcana Tarot cards, 172,
    177-187, 227-228, 236
Manning, James, 450
Margulis, Lynn and James
    Lovelock, Gaia Theory, 408
Mars, 40, 43, 60, 63
Martello, Leo Louis, 451
Martius, 20
master numbers, 151
Matthew 24:14, 328
Matthews, Caitlin, 125, 449
Maya
    calendar, 22
    prophesies, 333-334
measurements, earth, 33
medicine, predictions, 262-265,
    305, 401-402
meditation, 297, 316-319
Meece, E. Alan, 79, 95, 449
Meir, Golda, 250
Mercury, 43, 60, 63
Mercury finger (little finger),
    350-351, 362
metaphysical bookstores, 88
Mexico City, 30
Michelangelo, 19
middle finger (Saturn finger),
    352-353, 362
"Millennium Alignments:
    1999–2000," 449
Miller, William, 328
Minkin, Barry Howard, 415,
    449

Minor Arcana Tarot cards, 172, 191-208
  Cups, 201-208, 236-237, 285
  Pentacles, 209-221, 236
  Swords, 174, 209-217
  Wands, 193-200
months, designated numbers, 160
Moon, 60
  aspect, measuring, 71
  New Moon phase, 82
  Nodes, 60, 68
  phases, 70
  symbol, 43, 60
Moon card (Major Arcana card), 188
Mother Mary, 125
mounts of planets, 343, 358-365
movements, 18
mushrooms, predictions, 388
Muslim calendar, 21
Mutable quality, signs, 44
Myss, Carolyn, 147
myths, 321-325

N

Napoleon Bonepart, 329
NASDAQ, 414
National Commission on Social Security Reform, 414
negative expressions, 139-141
Nelson, Roger, 323
Neptune, 43, 60, 63-64, 67-68, 71, 80
Neptune-Pluto conjunction of 1982, 94-96
Neptune-Pluto cycle, 80
New Age, intuitive arts, 3-7
New Age Collective, 3, 7-12
New Conservatives, palm features, 375-378
New Moon phase, 70, 82
  May 2000, 100-101
  solar eclipse of August 1999, 98-100
New York Stock Exchange, 414
nine, 134, 158, 164, 167
Nine of Cups (Minor Arcana card), 205, 236, 285
Nine of Pentacles (Minor Arcana card), 222
Nine of Swords (Minor Arcana card), 214

Nine of Wands (Minor Arcana cars), 198
Nodes, 60, 63, 68
non-local mind, 305
North Node, 43, 60, 63, 68
Nostradamus, 329-330
November, 20
nuclear holocaust, predictions, 395
nuclear technology, prediction, 257-259
numerology, 132-135, 151, 158, 192
  Age of Gaia, 145-146
  balance, 145, 165-167
  Chinese numerology, 153
  chronos time, 148-150
  cycles, 153
  kairos time, 148-149
  Lagerquist, Kay, 428-431
  letters, designations, 151, 165
  life paths, 155
  master numbers, 151
  millennia, meaning, 136-138
  one, 139
  paradigm shifts, 146
  personal years, 158-164
  Pythagoras, 132
  recommended reading, 450
  two, 140-150, 153, 159
  vibrations, changing, 135
  western numerology, 153
  Y2K, explantaion of, 150-153
  zeros, 150

O

October, 20
Old Style calendars, 21
one, 158
  balance number, 165
  as dominating energy, 136
  energy, 132
  negative expressions of, 139
  personal years, theme, 163
  positive expression of, 139
open-ended questions, intuition development, 297
oppositions, planetary pairs, 62, 73
optimists, 315
orbits, 63, 66

Orwell, George, 16, 325
Oversoul, 295

P

Page of Cups card (Minor Arcana card), 176, 206, 237
Page of Pentacles (Minor Arcana card), 223
Page of Swords (Minor Arcana card), 215
Page of Wands (Minor Arcana card), 199
Pahana, 333
pairs, planetary, 63-64, 70-71
  Chiron-Pluto conjunction of December 30, 1999, 100
  conjunctions, 72, 102-111
  cycles, 70-71, 74-81
    Chiron, 78-79
    Jupiter-Saturn cycles, 75-76, 102-111
    Neptune, 80
    Pluto, 81
    Saturn, 76-78
    Uranus, 79-80
  First Quarter squares, 73
  hard aspects, 71-74
  Jupiter-Saturn conjunctions, 70, 75-76, 102-111
  Neptune-Pluto conjunction of 1982, 94-96
  New Moon of May 2000, 100-101
  New Moon solar eclipse of August 1999, 98-100
  oppositions, 73
  Third Quarter squares, 73-74
  Uranus-Neptune conjunction of 1993, 97-98
  Uranus-Pluto conjunction of 1965–1966, 96
palmistry, 341-343
  fingers, 346-354, 362-363
    mounts, 358-365
  generational differences, 368-382, 385-387
  Gile, Robin, 433-434
  hands, planet names, 342-343
  head lines, 355-356
  heart lines, 354-355

Leonardo da Vinci, 368-369
life lines, 357
line quality, 354, 381
markings, 358
mounts, 364-365
reading palms, 343
recommended reading, 450
rising lines, 354, 357-358
thumbs, 343-346
parables, 321-325
paradigm shifts,
  numerologically, 146
Passive Mars, 364
Past, Present, Future Spreads,
  260
Peace Group Movement, 321
Pentacles (Minor Arcana cards),
  192, 209-224, 236
  See also specific cards
perception fragments, 18
personal retrogrades, 61
personal years, 158-164
PETA (People for Ethical
  Treatment of Animals), 389
phalanges, 343, 347
phases, Moon, 70
Picasso, Pablo, 17
pills, 311
Pisces, 42-45, 55
plain of Mars, the, 364
planets, 59-60
  archetypes, 41
  aspects, 62-64
  astrology, 41
  centaurs, 65-66
  change agents, 64-68
  Chiron, 65-66
  conjunctions, 94-111
  Nodes, 60, 68
  orbits, 63
  pairs, 63-64, 70-81, 100-111
  retrogrades, 61
  social planets, 65
  symbols, 43, 60
  transit effect, 64
  transpersonal planets, 64,
    67-68
Pluto, 43, 60-64, 67-68, 71, 81
pointer fingers (Jupiter finger),
  353-354, 363
Pope, predictions, 251 328
positive expressions of
  numbers, 139-141
prayer, healing power, 307-308
precession of the
  equinoxes, 119

predictions
  astrology, 426-428
  Biblical, 327-328
  Cayce, Edgar, 330-331
  global economy, 415-417,
    418-419
  global warming, 407-409
  Hopi people, 332-333
  Human Genome Project,
    403-406
  intuition, 431-433
  Mayans, 333-334
  medicine, 401-402
  Nostradamus, 329-330
  palmistry, 387-396, 433-434
  stock market, 413-414
  Tarot, 423-425
Prepare Today Web site, 447
Princess Diana, personal year,
  161
prophesies
  Biblical, 327-328
  Cayce, Edgar, 330-331
  Hopi people, 332-333
  Mayans, 333-334
  Nostradamus, 329-330
  Wolf, Robert Ghost, 331-332
psychic intuition, *see* intuition
Pythagoras, numerology, 132

Q

qualities (signs), 44-45
quality, lines, palmistry, 354,
  381
Quantum Leap, 374-375
Queen of Cups (Minor Arcana
  card), 207
Queen of Pentacles (Minor
  Arcana card), 224
Queen of Swords (Minor
  Arcana card), 216
Queen of Wands (Minor Arcana
  card), 200
Quintillus, 20

R

readings, *see* Tarot and
  palmistry
rectifications, birth charts, 88
retrogrades, planets, 61
reversed cards, 176
Rilke, Rainer Maria, 12

ring finger (Apollo finger), 352,
  362
rising lines, 354, 357-358
Robinson, Lynn A., 3, 8, 11,
  293, 431-433, 450
Roman calendar, 20
Roosevelt, Franklin D., 371
Russell, Peter, 320

S

Sagan, Carl, 6, 24, 34
Sagittarius, 42-45, 54
Saturn, 60, 65
  cycles, 76-78
  First Quarter Saturn Square
    Neptune cycle, 71
  Jupiter-Saturn conjunction
    cycle, 70
  Jupiter-Saturn cycle, 75-76
  orbit, 63
  symbol, 43, 60
Saturn finger (middle finger),
  352-353, 362
Saturn-Chiron cycle, 76
Saturn-Neptune cycle, 77
Saturn-Pluto cycle, 77
Saturn-Uranus cycle, 77
SB Consulting, 8
Scorpio, 42-45, 53
Seale, Alan, 450
September, 20
sets, thumbs, 343
seven, 158
  balance number, 166
  energy, 133
  personal year, theme, 164
Seven of Cups (Minor Arcana
  card), 204
Seven of Pentacles (Minor
  Arcana card), 221
Seven of Swords (Minor Arcana
  card), 213
Seven of Wands (Minor Arcana
  card), 197
Seven-Card Spreads, 242
sextile aspect, 62
Sextilis, 20
shapeshifters, 66
shared humanity, intuition,
  321-324
Sher, Barbara, 299
shuffling Tarot cards, 176
sicknesses, positive aspects of,
  310-311

signs, 42, 43-46
  Aquarius, 54-55
  Aries, 50
  Cancer, 52
  Capricorn, 54
  elements, 44-46
  energies, 44
  Gemini, 51
  Leo, 52
  Libra, 53
  Pisces, 55
  qualities, 44-45
  Sagittarius, 54
  Scorpio, 53
  Sun signs, 44, 47-50
  symbols, 42
  Taurus, 51
  Virgo, 52-53
Sinetar, Marsha, 299, 450
Sistine Ceiling at the Vatican in
  Rome, 19
six, 133, 158, 164, 166
Six of Cups (Minor Arcana
  card), 204
Six of Pentacles (Minor Arcana
  card), 220
Six of Swords (Minor Arcana
  card), 213
Six of Wands (Minor Arcana
  card), 196
Sjoo, Monica and Barbara Mor,
  123, 449
Snyder, Jaime, 320
social planets, 65
Social Security, predictions,
  242-243, 414
solar eclipses, 90
soma, 16
Sosigenes, 20
South Node, 43, 60, 63, 68
spiritual traditions, 321-322
spreads (Tarot), 173, 225-229,
  283-284
  Celtic Cover spread, 239
  Celtic Cross spreads, 234
  Decision Spread, 287-289
  Gypsy Wish Spread,
    284-287
  Horoscope spread, 276-282
  karma spreads, 226-229
  Karmic Spread, 283-284
  Past, Present, Future Spread,
    260
  Seven-Card spread, 242
  Three-Card spread, 243

square aspects, 62
stabilizers, 44-45
Star card (Major Arcana card),
  187, 237
Star Trek, 324-325
  Borg, the, 368
  "Let That Be Your Final
    Battlefield," 324
  Star Trek: First Contact, 407
  *Star Trek IV: The Final
    Frontier*, 324
  United Federation of
    Planets, 325
Stone, Oliver, 16
Strength card (Major Arcana
  card), 182, 227
Sumerian calendar, 19
Sun, 34, 40, 60
  aspect, measuring, 71
  Moon, phases, 70
  symbol, 43
Sun card (Major Arcana card),
  174, 188
Sun signs, 44, 47-55
Swords (Minor Arcana cards),
  192, 209-217, 237
  See also specific cards
symbolic pictures, 296
symbolic shapeshifters, 66
symbols
  planets, 43, 60
  signs, 42
synchronicity, 41
synergy, 436, 437

T

Targ, Russell and Jane Katra,
  307
Tarot, 171-172
  cards, 173-176
    left handed cutting, 434
    Major Arcana cards, 172,
      177-187
    Minor Arcana cards, 172,
      191-208, 209-217
    readings, 225-229
    reversed cards, 176
    shuffling, 176
    spreads, 225-229
    Universal Waite decks,
      175
    upright cards, 176
  journals, 173, 232-233

predictions, 234-251,
  256-257, 262-273, 276-282,
  423-425
readings, 173, 252-254
recommended reading, 451
revelations, 233
spreads, 173, 283-284
  Celtic Cover spread, 239
  Celtic Cross spreads, 234
  Decision Spread, 287-289
  Gypsy Wish Spread,
    284-287
  Horoscope spread,
    276-282
  karma spreads, 226-229,
    283-284
  Past, Present, Future
    Spread, 260
  Seven-Card spread, 242
  Three-Card spread, 243
Tarriktar, Tem, 449
Taurus, 42, 51
technology
  predictions, 256-262, 395,
    399-403
  sustainable technologies,
    418
Temperance card (Major
  Arcana card), 177, 186
Ten of Cups (Minor Arcana
  card), 206
Ten of Pentacles (Minor Arcana
  card), 222
Ten of Swords (Minor Arcana
  card), 215
Ten of Wands (Minor Arcana
  card), 198
TEOTWAWKI (The End of the
  World As We Know It), 327
Thatcher, Margaret, 250
themes, personal years,
  162-164
Third Quarter Chiron Square
  Neptune cycle, 71
Third Quarter squares, 73-74
Thompson, J. Eric S., 334
three, 158
  balance number, 166
  energy, 133
  personal years, theme, 163
Three of Cups (Minor Arcana
  card), 202, 236
Three of Pentacles (Minor
  Arcana card), 219
Three of Swords (Minor Arcana
  card), 211

Three of Wands (Minor Arcana card), 195
Three-Card Spreads, 243
thumbs, 343-346, 364
time
    chronos time, 148-150
    fragments, 18
    kairos time, 148-149
Timms, Moira, 450
Today's Children generation, palm features, 378-380
Tognetti, Arlene, 3, 8, 11-12, 171, 423, 451
Tower card (Major Arcana card), 187
transcendent time, *see* kairos time
transit effect, planets, 64
transiting retrogrades, 61
transits, birth charts, 94-101
transpersonal planets, 64, 67-68
trine aspect, 62
tuberculosis, 331
TV-Free America's (TVFA) Web page, 29
two, 140-150, 158
    balance number, 165
    connectedness, 144
    energy, 132
    interdependent living, 149-150
    negative expressions of, 140-141
    personal years, theme, 163
    positive expressions of, 141
    relationships, 147-148
    universal years, 164
Two of Cups (Minor Arcana card), 202
Two of Pentacles (Minor Arcana card), 218
Two of Swords (Minor Arcana card), 211
Two of Wands (Minor Arcana card), 194
Twyman, James, 323
Tyl, Noel, 24, 75
    Astrology Looks at History, 450
    Predictions for a New Millennium, 449

U

U.S. Census Bureau Web site, 31
U.S. Federal Government Gateway for Year 2000 Information Directories Web site, 447
U.S. Stock Market, predictions, 239-242
United Federation of Planets, *Star Trek*, 325
Universal Waite decks, 175
universal years, 153, 159, 161, 164
upright cards, 176
Uranus, 60, 67-68
    conjunctions, 96-98
    cycles, 71, 79-80
    orbit, 63
    symbol, 43, 60
    transit effect, 64

V

Varmus, Harold, 399
Venus, 40, 43, 60, 63
Very Large Array, 24
vibrations, 132-135
viral epidemics, predictions, 395
Virgo, 42-45, 52-53
vivid dreams, intuition, 296

W-X

Wands (Minor Arcana cards), 192-200
    See also specific cards
waning phase, Moon, 70
Warhol, Andy, 19
Washington, George, 21
water signs, 46
Waters, Frank, 332
waxing phase, Moon, 70
Web sites, 446-447
    CyberCoin, 417
    InterCoin, 417
    New York Stock Exchange, 414
    TV-Free America's (TVFA) Web page, 29

U.S. Census Bureau, 31
    ValueCoin, 417
weight, earth, 33
Weil, Andrew, 305
western numerology, 153
Wheel of Fortune card (Major Arcana card), 183, 236
Williamson, Marianne, 321
Wizard of Oz, The, 324
Wolf, Robert Ghost, prophesies, 331-332
world, *see* earth
World card (Major Arcana card), 189, 227
World Wide Web
    21st Century resources, 319-320
    see also Web sites

Y-Z

Y2K, 24, 150-153
    crisis, prediction, 256-257
    hotlines, 445
    Y2K Citizen's Action Guide Web site, 447
    Y2K Today Web site, 447
yang, 44
Year 2000, numerological explanation of, 150-152
years, 20
yen, exchange rate, 417
yin, 44, 125-127
Yourdon, Edward and Jennifer, 449

zenith, 59
zeros, numerology, 150
zodiac, 42, 50-55, 59-61

SPECIAL OFFER FOR READERS OF THE COMPLETE IDIOT'S GUIDE TO
New Millennium Predictions!

Free: Call for Lynn Robinson's free psychic referral list: (800) 925-4002.

Free: Sign up for a free *e-mail* Intuition Newsletter. Order through Lynn's Web site: www.lynnrobinson.com.

AUDIO TAPES BY LYNN ROBINSON, M.Ed.

Prosperity! The Intuitive Path to Creating Abundance (ICC101) $10.00

Side 1 - *Prosperity Meditation*

Prosperity begins in your mind and imagination. Use this powerful guided meditation to attract the prosperity you desire.

Side 2 - *Affirmations for Prosperity*

Enlist the power of your subconscious mind to create prosperity by listening to affirmations of abundance and success.

Your Inner Sanctuary/Inner Guide* (ICC102) $10.00

Side 1 - *Your Inner Sanctuary Meditation*

Create a unique inner sanctuary in your mind where you can access wise intuitive guidance.

Side 2 - *Your Inner Guide Meditation*

Tap into your higher self to gain greater wisdom and spiritual growth. Learn to trust your intuition to enhance your decision-making.

Creating the Life You Want* (ICC103) $10.00

Side 1 - *Creating the Life You Want Meditation*

This tape will assist you in using your mind's ability to create reality from your hopes and dreams.

Side 2 - *Affirmations for Success*

Positive affirmations will fill you with confidence and enable you to create the life you want. Listen while driving to work!

How to Develop Your Intuition (ICC104) $5.00

You'll learn new skills to deepen your intuition in this lively half-hour interview with Lynn.

*These audio tapes contain the remarkable music of Thaddeus, created to assist you in expanding your consciousness and opening up to higher realms. Music by Thaddeus is available from LuminEssence Productions. Please call for details.

BOOKLET
Prosperity! The Intuitive Path to Creating Abundance (ICC105) $5.00

This 20-page booklet includes simple, effective methods for creating more abundance.

3 WAYS TO ORDER

By phone:

Call Intuitive Consulting & Communication (IC&C) at (800) 925-4002. We accept MasterCard and Visa.

Via Internet:

Order through Lynn's Web site: www.lynnrobinson.com

By Mail:

Please include your name, address, phone number, and the title and order number for the tape or booklet you are ordering. Massachusetts residents add 5% sales tax. Send your check or money order to:

Intuitive Consulting & Communication (IC&C)
P.O. Box 81218
Wellesley Hills, MA 02481

Please add $3.50 to all orders for shipping & handling.

Allow 4 to 6 weeks for delivery. All payment to be made in U.S. funds. Prices and availability are subject to change without notice.